Theory and Practice
In Interpersonal Attraction

Theory and Practice
In Interpersonal Attraction

edited by
STEVE DUCK
University of Lancaster,
Lancaster, England

1977

ACADEMIC PRESS
London · New York · San Francisco

A Subsidiary of Harcourt Brace Jovanovich, Publishers

ACADEMIC PRESS INC., LONDON, LTD.
24 — 28 Oval Road
London NW1

United States Edition published by
ACADEMIC PRESS INC.
111 Fifth Avenue
New York, New York 10003

Library of Congress Catalog Card Number: 76-016964
ISBN 0-12-222850-2

Printed in Great Britain by
The Lavenham Press Ltd., Lavenham, Suffolk

Contributors

ICEK AJZEN, *Department of Psychology, University of Massachusetts, Amherst, Mass., USA*

DONN BYRNE, *Purdue University, Lafayette, In., USA*

GERALD L. CLORE, *Department of Psychology, University of Illinois at Champaign-Urbana, Champaign, Ill., USA*

MARK COOK, *Department of Psychology, University College of Swansea, Swansea, Wales*

STEVE DUCK, *Department of Psychology, University of Lancaster, Lancaster, England* .

CHARLES R. ERVIN, *University of Texas*

ROM HARRÉ, *Subfaculty of Philosophy, University of Oxford, Oxford, England*

PETER KELVIN, *Department of Psychology, University College, London University, London, England*

JOHN J. LA GAIPA, *Department of Psychology, University of Windsor, Windsor, Ontario, Canada*

JOHN LAMBERTH, *Purdue University, Lafayette, In., USA*

BERNARD I. MURSTEIN, *Department of Psychology, Connecticut College, New London, Conn., USA*

BARBARA A. SEYFRIED, *Department of Psychology, State University of New York at Oswego, Oswego, NY, USA*

WOLFGANG STROEBE, *Fachbereich Psychologie der Philips Universitaet, Marburg/Lahn, W. Germany*

To J.C.S.

*with grateful thanks for many
instances of kindness and
generosity over the years*

Preface

This book has a somewhat unusual format which, I believe, reflects three questions that are relevant not only to workers in any given field but especially to students coming to study any topic at greater depth. These three questions are: (1) What theories do people use to explain the topics in this area? (2) What kinds of studies do people do in this area? (3) How does this area fit in theoretically with stuff I have read in other related areas?

Accordingly this book takes its model from Caesar's description of Gaul and is divided into three parts. For *Section 1* I approached authors who have made major contributions to our understanding of interpersonal attraction and invited them to examine the current status and the potential of their own standpoint. These authors have contributed original papers exploring and explaining the emphases of their characteristic perspective on the area of interpersonal attraction. On the other hand, *Section 2* contains previously published material (except in one case) which illustrates how these perspectives work out in practice. There are also papers illustrating methodological and conceptual points which have a more general application. The section as a whole is thus intended to give the reader a flavour of the variety of the empirical and practical approaches to the study of interpersonal attraction. *Section 3* presents further original papers — but these have a different scope and function from those in Section 1. Three eminent theorists who have previously been concerned primarily with other topics in social psychology were invited to consider the area of interpersonal attraction from their theoretical standpoint in order to show how they would encompass the phenomena of acquaintance in their framework. The style and origin of these papers is thus innovatory, speculative and exploratory — and the results are extremely challenging.

Since the purpose of this book is to allow authors to present their current theories and their own approach in their own way, I chose not to impose rigid guidelines. There are thus considerable differences of style which are both stimulating in themselves and also good vehicles for the enthusiasm of individual authors.

This enthusiasm was also reflected in other aspects of the work since any edited text like this depends for its completion on the goodwill and efficiency of the individual contributors—all of whom have, in this case, been very conscientious. I am especially grateful to Icek Ajzen for his perceptiveness and thoughtfulness on this score. George Levinger also offered valued help to some of the contributors, for which I am indebted to him.

I am also very grateful to some colleagues and friends at Lancaster who provided such a fertile atmosphere for the work, particularly Neil Johnson who offered his help and his time with equal generosity. I gained much from drawing upon his experience which was placed so unstintingly at my disposal. Barry McCarthy, Gordon Craig, Robin Gilmour and Charlie Lewis all helped by informal, though stimulating, discussion to clarify ideas for my own chapters; whilst Angela Westhead and Lynda Teale gave efficient and willing secretarial support. I am also grateful to the SSRC for the support of Grant HR2491/2. My thanks are also due to my wife Sandra, for her sensible insistence that I occasionally bicycled away from all the problems. Whilst this did sometimes merely enable me to replace mental anguish with physical torment, it more often helped me to get the difficulties into perspective.

STEVE DUCK
Halton-on-Lune, Lancaster

Contents

Section 3: The place of interpersonal attraction in psychological theories

1.

Tell Me Where Is Fancy Bred: Some thoughts on the study of interpersonal attraction

STEVE DUCK

University of Lancaster, England

I. Attraction to others

After millions of years of evolution (two or three thousand of them being relatively civilized and notable for the complex social structures which have been developed) we do not know what causes people to like each other, to choose their friends or to marry one person rather than another — despite the concern of many writers and thinkers of various sorts over this very issue. Some late arrivals on this scene are social psychologists who have given the problems of attraction and acquaintance thorough and systematic research for an extremely small number of years — indeed the last 20 years have seen the most vigorous growth of study into the area. The following chapters describe and illustrate the progress that has been made using the skills, theories and techniques that social psychology has to offer, not only in terms of short term relationships between strangers but also longer term friendships and marital choices. From simply scanning the contents page of this volume it is clear that the items covered here are diverse and the range of approaches large — illustrating not only the wealth of expertise which is available but also the many-faceted and complex nature of what appears to be a simple issue. It also illustrates the weight which psychology attaches to solving the problems of what causes attraction.

Whilst the function of an introductory chapter is to set the scene and introduce both the topic of the book and the book itself, this chapter is also the most suitable place for a review of several features of the attraction literature which otherwise may be ignored. Whilst looking at the wider aspects of attraction, I have therefore introduced into this chapter the consideration of some problems that surround conceptual and practical approaches to interpersonal attraction. I do this to give some food for thought to readers of individual chapters, and also as a source of afterthought when these have been read. Such thoughts concern problems like the relationship between commonsense and experimental approaches; use of terms; the focus of the current literature as a whole; and some suggestions for further lines of development — and why we study attraction at all.

A. WHY STUDY ATTRACTION?

There are indeed many practical applications for any developed understanding of interpersonal attraction, not least of which is clinical. Much aberrant or strange *social* behaviour causes rejection by other people or may be sufficient to induce clinical symptoms in the sufferer. In either case, disruption of normal acquaintance processes leads sometimes to these unpleasant consequences. In extreme cases of rejection or isolation it has been observed that hermits or prisoners deprived of human society will often hallucinate about people just as hungry individuals hallucinate about food (Schachter, 1959). Loneliness of less extreme forms can be unpleasant and aversive (hence the force of "sending people to Coventry") and much clinical depression is the result of rejection by other people (Sullivan, 1953). This is a challenging finding with theoretical and practical significance. It may be shown experimentally that rejection is due to some oddity in social behaviour and an inability to interact or acquaint in socially acceptable ways — or perhaps to some failure to tune in to the same cues as other people in the same circumstances. In these cases the symptoms would presumably diminish if the oddness of the social behaviour could be reduced by training or advice based on some clearer grasp of the social psychological processes involved (Duck, in press, a). Thus, if we conceive of acquaintance as some sort of skill, this has implications for clinicians. Other (more or less obvious) practical justifications for studying interpersonal attraction relate to other social problems like marital failure (if we can find out how it works, we can find out how it breaks down); or to commercial interests such as the requirement to select effective and socially coherent work teams; or to legal and human questions such as whether a fair trial depends on the attractiveness of the defendant; or to educational and developmental issues such as whether children learn how to acquaint, and whether this affects their psychological growth in other spheres.

Of course there is also the simple academic justification for studying attraction: the problems of acquaintance are theoretical issues in their own right and, as yet, there is no totally convincing answer to them. Resolution of these issues can have wider related effects also, although it is unlikely that research on acquaintance will ever produce household boons as spin-offs, like the non-stick frying pan. The implications are more likely to lie in relation to social structures or political issues in the wider human social context as well as to the narrower social problems listed above. Who knows what liberation movements are yet to be sparked off by work on attractiveness which finds that certain categories of individuals get rough deals or unfair and unjustifiable treatment (Ugly liberation?)?

The specific intentions of studying interpersonal attraction are, however, usually more down to earth. The basic aim is to identify by as many means and in as many circumstances as possible the rules, processes and empirical laws which operate on acquainting individuals. The purpose of interpersonal attraction research as a whole is not, therefore, simply to establish why people like each other or what makes someone attractive (although this is a major and significant part of the work). The ultimate aim is to acquire knowledge of the dynamics of *developing* relationships not just of static, once-for-all choices. Of course, in the process of doing this it is inevitable, necessary and desirable that some workers look at some topics and some at others so that the individual trees comprising the whole wood should be closely scrutinized: it *is* useful to know in detail why, how and in what circumstances relationships start and indeed most research on attraction presently tackles such issues (Byrne, 1971). Clearly, developing relationships have a point of origin and we need to understand thoroughly what it is.

However, even here there are at least three directions for study. It is important to assess the factors that start attraction where none existed before (e.g. when strangers meet, cf. chapters by Clore, Ajzen, Stroebe, Seyfried in Section 1). It is also necessary to know what factors and events affect or maintain attractiveness levels which are already established (e.g. why people change their minds about someone, or continue to feel attracted or start feeling more intense about someone they already like/dislike; cf. chapters by Murstein, La Gaipa in Section 1 and Kelvin, Duck in Section 3). It is also necessary to note how individuals indicate their attraction towards someone by ritual social behavioural means (cf. Harré chapter in Section 3) or by the subtleties of non-verbal communication (such as eye movements, gestures, seating positions; cf. Cook's chapter in Section 3). Studies and discussion of all these features of interpersonal attraction are equally important for a full grasp of the processes involved and have all received extensive examination through psychology's special methods.

B. PSYCHOLOGICAL STUDY OF INTERPERSONAL ATTRACTION

Once a specialist discipline has decided to claim a particular area for study, it applies two characteristic approaches (although the two basic categories can often be subdivided as here). These two things are a bank of *theoretical* thinking upon which to draw, and a fund of *practical* methods, devices, skills and techniques by which to operationalize the thinking and put it into practice. As the title of this book is intended to indicate, this is precisely true in the psychological study of interpersonal attraction. Social psychology has both a conceptual and a practical framework to apply to the topic of interpersonal attraction, although it is possible to subdivide this basic split into subcategories. On the one hand any psychologist would import certain broad frameworks, whether characterized by Freudian outlooks (cf. Murstein, 1971 Chapter 6); ethological approaches (Tiger and Fox, 1972); ethno-methodology (Garfinkel, 1962); an adherence to Exchange Theory (La Gaipa, Section 1) to Learning Theory in one of its forms (Clore, Section 1) or to Balance Theory (Newcomb, 1971). On the other hand, the last 20 years have produced a vast literature of more specific orientations (e.g. "matching" hypotheses about the extent to which individuals seek "the best" dates or settle for what they can get, and why — Stroebe, Section 1; theories about the place of and uses for information about others in interpersonal attraction — Ajzen, Section 1; or suggestions about complementarity and whether individuals choose friends who are similar to themselves or who can offer something they don't have — Seyfried, Section 1; or hypotheses about the way relationships develop, Murstein, Section 1).

On a practical level and as operationalizations of these theoretical viewpoints an equally interesting range and variety of phenomena is studied within the umbrella of "interpersonal attraction". Amongst other things work has looked at physical attractiveness (Berscheid and Walster, 1974a; Murstein, Section 2) the effects of status on attraction (reported in Argyle, 1969), importance of relative socio-economic position (Byrne, Clore and Worchel, 1966), effects of level of intelligence and a host of "sociological" cues (reviewed by Kerckhoff, 1974; Rosenblatt, 1974). Most work, however, looks specifically at the relationship between interpersonal attraction and cognitive or psycho-dynamic aspects of the individual: for example, Self Esteem (Stroebe, Section 1), Attitudes (Byrne, 1961a, 1969), Personality Needs (Rychlak, 1965); Personality otherwise conceived (Byrne, Griffitt and Stefaniak, 1967; Duck, in press, a); Actual Self/Ideal-Self discrepancies (Murstein, 1971; Griffitt, 1966) and many other concepts, usually examined in terms of the question: are individuals attracted to others who are psychologically similar? Some of these practical foci are illustrated and reported in detail as papers in Section 2 of this book.

II. Some conceptual issues in the study of interpersonal attraction

A. COMMONSENSE AND THE USE OF TERMS

Although, as outlined above, social psychological study of any topic implies its own characteristic conceptual and practical frameworks, social psychology suffers and benefits from its unique status relative to "common sense". No other discipline has the job of testing common sense to such an extent and no other discipline is so closely enmeshed with it. Ordinary individuals do not have a commonsense theory of nuclear fission; they do have commonsense theories of attraction: researchers on nuclear physics would be wise not to stand in particle accelerators in order to make their studies; but workers in interpersonal attraction do have friends and are part of the normal social world. Both of these facts colour research on interpersonal attraction wittingly and unwittingly. In some cases psychological hypotheses about facets of interpersonal attraction are generated by everyday observations (Aronson, 1973); in other cases the products of complex research can sound unsurprising and unfamiliar. However it would indeed be surprising if commonsense or novelists had not said *something* with a grain of truth in it, given the number of times that personal relationship have featured in their pronouncements. However the job of social psychology is important precisely because of this, for if commonsense and received wisdom were not only unequivocal but also right, then there would be no need — as there now is — for careful study and experiment to sort out the right from the wrong. And this is not as easy as it sounds!

Indeed commonsense on its own is a very inadequate explanation of interpersonal attraction. For example, there is nothing new in the observation that commonsense supports equally strongly the view that similarity is attractive ("Birds of a feather flock together") *and* that similarity is *not* attractive ("Opposites attract"). Like fortune tellers and oracles, commonsense covers its options carefully! The key point is that commonsense fails to specify either what it means (similarity of what? oppositeness in what respect?) or the circumstances under which either of these possibilities holds good; fails to show factors which limit their application (e.g. perhaps we seek, say, "similar" friends, "opposite" wives); fails to specify any operational rules of thumb (e.g. how to measure similarity or attraction). In short commonsense is neither precise enough nor empirical enough to be much use on its own in research here and although readers often cherish commonsense ideas, these do not stand up to any but the most superficial analysis as *explanations* of interpersonal attraction rather than observations or anecdotes about it. Commonsense is not sufficiently systematic to be reliable.

However, commonsense abounds with ideas which are useful *starting points* for the student of interpersonal attraction. For instance, there is the notion that positive relations with someone (attraction, dating, friendship, etc.) involve some form of liking or some sort of positive feeling about someone. Thus commonsense tells us that positive feelings and positive relations are connected, or, in more psychological terminology, that positive affect is correlated with certain forms of behaviour. This is a proposition for empirical study but it needs further refinement since it raises the practical questions of how to measure liking (e.g. one can look at actual choices made; or choices *expressed;* or ratings on a scale of liking); how to assess whether two individuals do have a positive relationship; what *types* of positive relationship are meant (friendship? casual acquaintance? marriage? liking? friendliness? see Lindzey and Byrne, 1968). It also raises the major theoretical issues about how liking should be conceived: is it a reflective attitude or an intuitive evaluation or a physiological or "gut" response? If it is an attitude, does it behave like other attitudes (e.g. can it be affected by the same techniques of persuasion?) and what influences it? Thus a simple statement (that positive relations involve liking) actually leads to a wealth of psychological research (e.g. Clore and Ajzen's contrasting approaches in terms of "affect" and "information", Section 1; or Stroebe's consideration of the influence of self-esteem on "liking behaviour", Section 1; or the study of important influences in *sequences* of behaviour, La Gaipa, Section 1). Analytic treatment of this issue is also given by Berscheid and Walster (1969), Byrne (1971), Huston (1974) and Duck (in press, c). However, it is intuitively clear that "liking" covers a great range of phenomena and that it does not in itself *explain* or predict behaviour. People do not like all those with whom they associate; nor (more significantly) can they associate with all those that they like; and occasionally individuals choose not to be *friends* with people they like but prefer to keep some as casual associates or acquaintances. One step forward is thus to agree on the differences between liking and related affective terms: and this presupposes a specialized vocabulary for use when examining the finer points of subjects' behaviour.

Some Terms for Types of "Liking"

Any area of specialist study generates its own use of existing terms and, in some cases, invents special terms of its own. The use of existing

terms has not yet been systematized in this field and I detect no
uniformity of use of these terms so far, but some general principles can
be observed. *Acquaintance* is usually used (e.g. Newcomb, 1961) to
describe the process of getting to know others, irrespective of whether
this results from or precipitates eventual liking; or whether it is caused
by circumstances. "An acquaintance" can thus be someone liked,
disliked or regarded neutrally. *Attraction* tends (after Byrne, 1969,
1971) to refer to initial responses to strangers rather than to long-term
relationships, but it is occasionally used as a synonym for "liking". In
one case it refers to a category of encounter; in the other to an affective
response. *Courting* is used (Murstein, 1971, and Section 1) to encompass
longer term dating relationships with a probability of marriage at the
end. *Dating* on the other hand is usually reserved for instances of single
dates, one-night stands (even experimentally induced assignations) or
for sequences of single dates where the relationship is not seen by the
participants to be "courting" (which implies paying attention to one
dating partner rather than several). Again, "date" can be used to refer
to a quality of relationship or a participant in it. *Friendship* is most
often used as a term to apply to established relationships (Izard,
1960a) that have developed over time. Friendships are thus acquaintances that have developed and which are definitely positive acquaintances associated with liking. The distinction between being *friends*
with someone and being *friendly with* them rests at the behavioural
level, i.e. "friends" is a state of relationship, "friendly" is a pattern of
behaviour. *Interpersonal attraction* seems, if any term is so used, to be
the usual blanket term which covers any instance of personal relationships with positive overtones ("friendship", "dating", "acquaintance",
"positive regard", etc. Berscheid and Walster, 1969; Huston, 1974).
Marital selection/choice speaks for itself, but is usually applied
(Murstein, 1971) in cases where the investigator is in a position at the
time of his research to know who married whom, as opposed to
"courting" where he may or may not know, since the process may or
may not have been completed and solemnized.

Clearly all of these terms amount to a frame of reference for a
multitude of phenomena and whilst individual researchers may use
different classification systems, one step towards greater clarity in
research is an agreed usage of terms. In the light of the above
considerations, how *does* one conceptualize liking and interpersonal
attraction theoretically (below) and how is it *measured* (see next
section)?

B. INTERPERSONAL ATTRACTION

In the light of the above comments it is clear that any theoretical conceptualization of interpersonal attraction is likely to be fairly general,
even if it is ultimately measured (see below) in terms of a score on a
rating scale from 1 (Do not like) to 10 (Like very much). However, one
thing is clear (Berscheid and Walster, 1969; Byrne, 1971; Huston,
1974; Lindzey and Byrne, 1968): it is safe at least to regard interpersonal attraction as a multifaceted activity. For example, if one
regards attraction or liking as an attitude about someone, then one
would expect to be able to measure the dynamics of the three
traditional components of attitudes: cognitive, affective and behavioural. That is, someone's liking for another person is a function of
what he knows about the person, how he feels about it and what he
does about it (Kelvin, 1970). However, one traditional finding of social
psychology is that these three parts are relatively independent and
what people *say* does not predict what they will *do,* so knowing about
one part does not predict the others! The emphasis of much research
on interpersonal attraction will thus always leave open the question of
whether people's *expressed* liking is actually a predictor of their choice
activity (i.e. whether people actually *do* behave as they say or think
they will, or as they would like to do). Now, psychology is quite fairly
concerned as much with relationships between some external stimulus
and what people think they will do, as it is between an external
phenomenon and what people actually do. However, in the context of
the aims outlined earlier (the specification of how relationships
develop) research on attraction will seek increasingly to predict actual
behaviour or real life choices and not simply *intentions* to behave in
certain ways (see Murstein, Section 1; Byrne, Ervin and Lamberth,
Section 2; Duck, Section 3).

C. SIMILARITY

Although there is variation in the way in which workers conceptualize
liking, there has been a considerable uniformity in the conceptualization of important features of interpersonal attraction. As will become
clear from attention to other chapters here, one major feature of much
research is its concern over the rewarding or positive aspects of
similarity between two people in the promotion of relationships —

whether similarity of beliefs, attitudes, personality or salary. The thrust of such work is directed to establishing the extent to which, and circumstances where, similarity is, *or is not,* attractive — and whilst this position is often referred to as "the similarity hypothesis" it is misleading to assume that this amounts to the view that similarity is always attractive (Byrne, 1971; Clore, Section 1). But what is meant by similarity in this context?

There are of course scores of ways in which two people can be similar. The question to which much research has been directed concerns the types and levels (in the sense of hierarchical layers) of such similarity which are significant influences on interpersonal attraction. The research can be conceived within a framework having three basic concerns at three different levels of analysis.

First, there is a wealth of research on the attractiveness of the non-cognitive stimulus properties of others (e.g. physical characteristics, Berscheid and Walster, 1974a; socio-economic status, Byrne, Clore and Worchel, 1966; proximity of dwelling place, Festinger, Schachter and Back, 1950). Is similarity of such characteristics likely to be attractive? Such has been claimed not only in terms of attraction (Festinger, Schachter and Back, 1950) or dating (Stroebe, Section 1) but also in terms of some stages of courting (Murstein, Sections 1 and 2). It could nevertheless be claimed (Duck, in press, a) that at least one component of the attractiveness of another individual, as seen in such non-cognitive stimulus terms, is the fact that any arrangement of stimuli inevitably and always leads observers to make assumptions about the underlying personality structure implied: e.g. from the fact that someone is red-headed we may infer he is quick tempered (cf. Ajzen, Section 1). Whilst such stimuli may therefore have an affective or evaluative loading in their own right, they may also derive some of their attractiveness from what they imply about the individual's cognition or personality (e.g. Dion, Berscheid and Walster, 1972 show that physically attractive individuals are assumed by subjects to have attractive personalities). Thus not only the stimuli themselves but also the implications could be evaluated — and both stimuli and implications could be assessed in terms of similarity to the observer himself.

Second, much research looks at the effects of judgements about the Other made by the subject or some third party — often in a disguised way (Duck, in press, a): for example, a person may be described by means of a list of traits ("extraverted, kind, intelligent, warm, industrious . . ."). It *feels* as if this list is really telling us about the person himself, i.e. as if we have information about him as a *stimulus,* but this is misleading. In these circumstances the subject is really being presented with someone else's *judgements* about the Other (the experimenter's judgements, for example) and is thus receiving *indirect* assessment of the Other's personality, cognition or character. Such information is thus of comparable but not identical status to the *inferences* a subject himself makes about stimulus Others; it is not the same as receiving the information from the Other himself directly.

Third, a common method in interpersonal attraction research is based on reactions made by subjects to Others' personality or attitude profiles (cf. Clore, Section 1). It should be noted that this presents subjects with *direct* access to Other's judgements about things and people, because it was "Other" who filled out the profile — so it reflects what he actually thinks. Since these things amount to self-ratings of his cognitive apparatus they are likely to be treated more significantly by subjects than is other information of different status. However, as yet, we do not know enough about the effects of *status* of information and its influence on interpersonal attraction (Duck, in press, a), let alone the effects of similarity within each status of information. Yet in real life an individual has at his disposal during acquaintance not only information about other people's stimulus characteristics (point 1 above) but also his own judgements or assessments of them (point 2 above) and occasional direct exposure to the Other's thinking in various ways (point 3 above). The ways in which these three things interact to influence attraction, and the value of each in terms of similarity, is not yet fully clear.

However, such things are important since attraction research in- evitably isolates certain features of the process for intensive study (e.g. it isolates responses to strangers). This can lead to the criticism of such research (cf. Sections 1 and 2 in this book) that it concentrates on evaluation of the influence of parts of the process or simple combina- tions of parts whereas, in real life, individuals are exposed to as many parts as they choose to observe and interpret. Furthermore, in real life, *they* (not an experimenter) make the selections of what is significant for them. But even this situation may be complex in real life, for simple exposure to single acts by Others are susceptible to a variety of explanations and inferences (was he kind? or did he just pretend to be?). Thus we are familiar with the fact that responses of different observers are also different as a function of their own personality and their experience of the Other or similar Others in the past. In other words, given the complexities of real life, real care needs to be taken in the selection of practical laboratory techniques employed for study and the uses or interpretations made of them.

III. Practical considerations in studying interpersonal attraction

The above discussion points up not only the theoretical questions about what is attractive but also the empirical problems and constraints which emerge when the attempt is made to measure the relevant features of the interpersonal attraction worker's equation. Equally it suggests some general problems of studying interpersonal attraction in the experimental laboratory. Can workers plausibly invite unacquainted individuals into the laboratory to form friendships with one another? Does study of interpersonal attraction depend on the selection of just a single paradigm or exemplar of the acquaintance which is susceptible to laboratory analysis? Are laboratory studies of interpersonal attraction informative or artificial? What can one study and what not because of this? Workers have solved these issues in various ingenious ways (all chapters here, and Byrne, 1971).

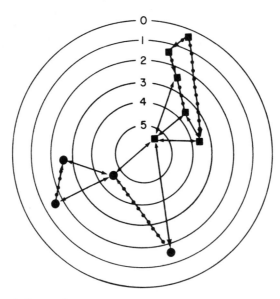

0–5 Number of times chosen   ●●●●►Unreciprocated choice

■   Males   ◄━━━► Mutual choice

●   Females

Choices made by individual

	A	B	C	D	E	F	G	H	J
A	●	X		/		/	X		
B	X	●	X		X	/			X
C		X	●			/			
D			/	●	/	/			
E		X			●	X		/	X
F					X	●		X	
G	X		/			/	●		
H						X	●	●	X
J		X			X			X	●

Individual making choice

X Mutual choice

/ Unreciprocated choice

FIG. 1. The first diagram indicates sociometric choices on a "target sociogram". Each individual is placed in the diagram in a position which indicates the number of times that he was chosen by others (the nearer the centre of the target, the more popular the individual). The diagram also indicates the subjects who chose a given individual (as indicated by the lines which join the circles and squares) and whether the choice was reciprocated (continuous line) or not (dotted line).

The second diagram indicates sociometric choices (not the same data as are included in the first figure) on a sociometric matrix. A given individual's choices are recorded in the row allotted to him and the number of times that he was chosen is indicated in the column allotted to him. Unreciprocated choices are indicated by a single stroke; reciprocated choices are shown by crosses.

A. PROBLEMS AND METHODS OF MEASUREMENT

It is clear from the vast range of manifestations of liking, acquaintance and attraction that no single example of them could hope to represent them all. Findings from experimental studies of marital selection may or may not be relevant to same-sex attractions or simple friendship and there is no intuitive means of deciding the question. It is therefore healthy rather than reprehensible that, as is clear from subsequent chapters, some workers study marital selection and some attraction, some acquaintance and some friendship. However, this is not to say that there need not be agreed measures through which to examine and compare these various phenomena; or that there is nothing to be gained from agreement on the tools to apply to the area.

As is shown in this book, different workers rely on different measures of attraction (see Ajzen, Stroebe, Section 1; Duck, Section 2, Berscheid and Walster, 1969; Byrne, 1971; Duck, 1973b; Lindzey and Byrne, 1968). The multitude of measures range from records of actual choices in real-life contexts (e.g. who marries whom: Murstein, Section 1, Section 3); through techniques of "sociometry" and graphical representation of choice patterns (e.g. diagrams indicating which members of a population chose which others, see Fig. 1); through a whole range of attitudinal measures based on social distance (i.e. techniques of assessing the degree to which individuals would accept others at different degrees of intimacy: e.g. to marry into the individual's own family; to move into the house next door). However, there is one technique used in much research. It is based on Byrne's Interpersonal Judgment Scale (IJS) where subjects rate Others on six 7-point rating scales, two of which assess how much they would like to work with the other and how much they like him (Byrne, 1971). The scores on these latter two subscales of the IJS can be computed into one overall score which is taken as the index of attraction. Each of the above and other methods (Lindzey and Byrne, 1968) is suitable for some purposes and not others and thus research on interpersonal attraction relies on several of them rather than just one. But there is a positive side to the uniformity of use of the IJS in that its frequent and general use by different workers in different circumstances facilitates comparison between results of different studies.

B. SOME CONCENTRATIONS OF THE LITERATURE

There is a negative side to uniformity and consistency, however. A surprising uniformity exists about the kinds of things that are studied as interpersonal attraction and hence a surprising consistency about the way in which certain facets of interpersonal attraction are under-researched. There is little demographic work comparing cultures and subcultures (Byrne *et al.*, 1971 being a noteworthy exception). Most work is done on subjects with English or American cultural antecedents;

most work is done on student subjects; most work is done on the age group between 16 and 25 years. Whether this limits the applicability of such work to different cultures and different age groups within a given culture is something requiring considerable research effort. For example, the concentration on the 16-25 age group naturally concentrates fortuitously on a group of individuals where pressures to acquaint are high, given that most people select both lifetime friends and marital partners at around that time (especially students). Their behaviour is therefore possibly not representative of what other people do, or how other people form friendships. The characteristically different Weltanschauung of old individuals (Burgess, 1961) could well influence their acquaintance processes in ways which are, as yet, unknown. Similar agruments apply to different class groups within a culture; and sex-differences in acquaintance have been studied serendipitously rather than systematically. Perhaps interpersonal attraction research concentrates too much on literate and articulate subjects whose behaviour does not reflect that of other individuals. If research is aimed at training (see above and Cook's chapter in Section 3 of this book) then the skills of individuals of different origins need scrutiny, as does the question of whether their order of priority among stimuli presented by others is the same order as that evidenced by the well-researched subjects. Again, perhaps some mentally-ill people do not just acquaint "worse" than normals, they do it in fundamentally different ways. Such questions await researchers' attention.

Equally remarkable are other omissions in the types of relationship upon which most work concentrates. In real life, certain beliefs that an individual holds about his relationships with others can influence his behaviour — but this is rarely manipulated in the laboratory study of interpersonal attraction. The relationship is important in several ways and in several senses. For one thing a relationship clearly occurs in a social context, not in the presence of the two participants only, and each individual is likely to be influenced by the knowledge that others at large either do or do not know about the existence of the relationship, *what* they know about it and how they view it. Presumably clandestine love affairs are psychologically different for the participants from affairs conducted without an illicit air. Similarly, the relationship has to be "presented" to the world (cf. Harré, Section 3) and the manner in which this is done contributes powerful evidence to each participant about his partner, himself and the relationship. Although a person may say that he likes another person in order to gain favour, his representation of this relationship to other people helps to clarify whether he is sincere. A person's interactions with others also offers his friends information about him: the friends may find him warm and loving but observe that he is cold, distant or shy in the presence of others and the friends are thus better able to grasp the finer shades of his cognitive structure from such observations. Whilst much research has been stimulated by the finding that A's comments about B will affect B's ratings of A (Aronson and Linder, 1965), it is curious that little work has examined A's comments about his *relationship* with B, nor given B the chance to see how A behaves to others. Always there is the assumption that A behaved towards B as he behaves to all others. However, if original selection is based in discovered similarities between A and B it follows that behaviour towards one another is a function of the similarity level and, to the extent that others cannot or do not provide a comparable level, A will behave differently towards B than he does to others, *ex hypothesi.*

Some agreement in this area has created considerable progress. Agreement on styles of approach has allowed workers to develop paradigms of research within whose bounds the limiting influences of certain factors upon others can be determined. The most heavily researched paradigm in this context is the attitudes-attraction relationship examined by Byrne (1961a, 1969 and 1971) and his coworkers (cf. Clore's chapter here). Not only has this work contributed to our understanding of attraction in its own right, but lively debate between proponents of the paradigm and those who object to it has often helped to foster research in the area and to clarify terms of reference (Byrne and Lamberth, 1971; Byrne *et al.,* 1973; Clore and Byrne, 1974; Kaplan and Anderson, 1973; Murstein, 1971). Most of this work makes use of a specific methodology which has often been borrowed by other workers or used in modified forms. Since it is so often used and referred to in other chapters of this book, it is elaborated here. Usually referred to as the "bogus stranger" or "hypothetical stranger" method, the essentials of the method are these: subjects complete an attitude profile (personality test, . . .) and hand it back to the experimenter whilst they perform some "filler" task (e.g. recording biographical details); the experimenter goes "to collect the profile from the subject in the next cubicle" (or similar excuse) but actually uses the time to construct another profile which resembles the subject's own to an extent required by experimental conditions (e.g. 80%, 60% or 20% similar to the subject). The "rigged" scale is then presented to the subject as if it had been completed by another subject (who, having no real existence is the "bogus stranger" who is immortalized in the title of the method) and obviously the success of this whole technique depends on ensuring that the subject actually believes that this "other subject" truly exists and has really filled out the scale. The subject's task is then to form an impression of this "other subject". By this means, precise manipulation of similarity levels between the subject and some hypothetical Other can be arranged and it is possible to gauge the extent to which attraction and the impression formed are dependent on or related to such similarity levels. As such, this basic design (the above is only a crude outline of the major components) has contributed greatly to work on attraction (Byrne, 1969, 1971; Duck, in press, c). The risk, however, is that subjects treat such information with increased significance since it appears to be provided by another individual as if it gave direct access to his cognition (see above and Duck, in press, a) whereas in real life such direct information would come to individuals only after much effort, experience and trips up blind alleys. However, other drawbacks of the method are well recognized (Byrne, 1971) and are not by any means as extensive as the advantages (Duck, in press, c).

C. THE PROBLEM OF ARTIFICIALITY

Not all research on interpersonal attraction is implausible, flawed or artificial, as the subsequent chapters indicate with clarity. Yet a frequent complaint levelled against much research in social psychology is that it is artificial—and this is an especial problem in work on interpersonal attraction which studies relationships between people and such volatile judgements as liking. Workers have naturally given considerable thought to this as a major practical constraint upon experiments, not least because of the ease with which the criticism can be made, the difficulty with which it is rebutted and the immediate and total blight which it hangs on any study where it applies. The charge is similar both in origin, status and effect to the mediaeval charge that someone was a witch; it evokes repugnance, disavowal and irremediable condemnation!

However, there are several types of artificiality and some are clearly less important in this context than others. An experiment may be artificial because it fails to convince subjects or fails to resemble real life; it may be artificial because it distorts normal behaviour or because it examines behaviour which, while normal, is irrelevant to the topic researched. Aronson and Carlsmith (1968) refer to realism in the former two categories as "experimental realism" and "mundane realism" respectively. The latter two categories are types of "mundane artificiality", so to speak. In the present context experiments clearly need to import both experimental and mundane realism before one would willingly grant that any findings had application to normal Acquaintance. In some other studies (e.g. longitudinal studies of acquaintance, Newcomb, 1961) there is no experimental situation to make real, although it is always a possibility that the simple presence of an investigator distorts normal behaviours.

Many studies of interpersonal attraction concentrate on single encounters and have been criticized (Wright, 1965) for acting as if subjects enter these encounters in a state of "affective neutrality": that is, in a state divorced from an historical perspective; without any background of emotional responses to certain types of information; as if they had never met any information about others before, and had no built-in reactions to it. Clearly this is a shaky assumption, especially in this context of evaluative judgements, where people have usually built up stereotypes of others or have their own theories about how other people "tick". Thus people are likely to bring to any encounter (or into any experiment on evaluation of others) a vast complex of individual cognitive processes which will ensure that no two subjects ever respond in exactly the same way to the same piece of information.

Another difference between two subjects is likely to lie in emotional or motivational states. Presumably it *does* matter whether a subject has just fallen out with his best friend or not — and this may influence his judgements about strangers (indeed one very early theory of attraction, Freud 1914, argued that we take instant "likes" or "dislikes" to people depending on whether they remind us of people that we already know). Equally there are occasions when individuals are "on the make" in encounters (e.g. "on the rebound" after collapse of close relationships; at college parties or dances) just as there are times when they could not be bothered (e.g. they would be less likely to be interested in a new female date after they had just become engaged to someone else). These internal states are thus often relevant to the acquaintance process in ways that such studies may not envisage or may not measure — although they usually assume that such differences are randomized during selection procedures. However, as La Gaipa notes, one man's "cognitive biasing effect" is another man's object of study — or to put it another way, whilst some workers want to eliminate individual differences in prior motivation (as above) these differences could form a legitimate area of study for someone else. Until they do, we cannot know the significance of such things for attraction and cannot therefore find out whether experiments are "artificial" if they fail to include special controls or procedures to exclude or mollify them.

One other possible "artificiality" of attraction research is that it tends to present subjects with simple bits of behaviour to evaluate. In real life however, examples of Others' behaviour occur in many categories and we are often strained to find the underlying consistency principle. Over time, and after many observations, it is possible to build up a more developed picture of the Other and to consider the layers and structure of his Self (Argyle and Little, 1972). In the context of real life developing acquaintance it is plausible that individuals at the early stages (e.g. encounter with a stranger) find the easiest explanations of Others' behaviour in terms of dispositional activity or "permanent" causes ("He did this because it is his nature"; "His personality is like that"). However, as a firmer understanding is built up over time, his behaviour can be explained *against this backcloth* and in terms of episodic activity or "temporary" causes (moods, variations within a framework, acts which are *not* representative of usual character). This leads to two thoughts: *first,* that research on interpersonal attraction has perhaps overstressed the static phenomena such as are visible and operative in short term encounters; and helps to make subjects assume (as a result of this) that all observed acts reflect "disposition" rather than "episodes". *Second,* it alerts one to the possibility that getting to understand interpersonal attraction and actually getting to know a person are similar processes — both built up by consideration of many different features! At present, explanations of the roots of attraction tend to be global, static and dispositional (e.g. "personality similarity causes friendship") and not sufficiently embedded in awareness of episodic fluctuations, differences of changes (e.g. "personality similarity causes friendship to deepen, but it doesn't start it off or finally cement it"). Subsequent work has the job increasingly now of identifying such limiting influences on the basically discovered antecedents.

Yet even where research looks at development (Murstein, Sections 1 and 2; La Gaipa, Sections 1 and 2; Duck, Sections 2 and 3 of this book) it makes one assumption that has remained untested because it seems intuitively plausible. It assumes that development of relationships is smooth, not jerky; that it takes place steadily, not by periods of activity followed by inactivity; that it is continuous, not discontinuous. Perhaps this is an error and acquaintance is really a process characterized by steps and plateaux rather than smooth curves of growth. If this latter suggestion (which has parallels in other forms of development, e.g. Fitts and Posner, 1967) is correct, then studies of development of acquaintance are "artificial" if they do not take it into account. The subsequent chapters put some flesh on these bones.

Several million years of evolution—plus a quarter of an hour or so—thus leave us looking at a picture whose gloomy side has received most attention! However, whilst there are some problems, there are also some ingenious answers to them as the next few chapters show. Interpersonal attraction is one all-pervading behaviour that goes to the root of, and influences most other forms of, social behaviour. The work done on interpersonal attraction is, as this selection shows, varied, interesting and extremely challenging. What's more it's very enjoyable!

Theoretical Approaches to Interpersonal Attraction

2.

Reinforcement and Affect in Attraction[1]

G. L. CLORE

University of Illinois at Urbana-Champaign, USA

A notable fact about the history of science is that investigators have tended to probe first those phenomena most distant from themselves. The behaviour of heavenly bodies attracted scientists' attention long before their own behaviour, and Galileo and Newton preceded Darwin and Freud by many years. Some recent psychological research on

1. Preparation of the chapter was facilitated by Research Grant MH-14510 from the National Institute of Mental Health, United States Public Health Service. Thanks are due to Judy S. DeLoache for helpful comments on the manuscript.

attribution suggests that such a tendency is not restricted to scientific thought. When asked to account for his own behaviour, the behaving person is more likely than an observer to find the explanation outside of himself, in situational factors (Jones and Nisbett, 1971). By contrast, observers are relatively more likely to see the causes of another's action in the personality or other characteristics of the actor.

The occurrence of this kind of actor-observer difference in attribution depends on a number of factors (Herzberger, 1975), but one critical variable appears to be visual perspective. In an experiment by Storms (1973), conversations were videotaped and later replayed for the participants. The videotapes focused either on the subject or on the partner as they engaged in dialogue. After watching themselves from the visual perspective of their partner, subjects tended to adopt the other's psychological perspective. Under these conditions the explanations subjects gave for their behaviour emphasized their own personality characteristics rather than situational factors. In other words, by reversing the visual perspective of the participants, Storms also reversed the kinds of explanations that seemed appropriate. The lesson would seem to be that we ordinarily overlook certain kinds of causal agents unless our attention is artificially focussed on them.

I shall argue in this chapter that the tendency to look outside ourselves for external causes is apparent not only in the distant history of science or in the responses of subjects asked to explain their behaviour, but also in the theories of psychologists interested in the general area of person perception. The kinds of explanations implied in most work in the area of impression formation, for example, stress factors external to the perceiver. Perhaps, as in Storms' (1973) experiment, the explanations considered are dependent on the perspective taken. A brief consideration of commonly used methods in the study of impression formation and attraction will illustrate the point.

I. Method and theory in impression formation and attraction

Adopted from Asch's (1946) classic work, the method still used in the area of impression formation is to present subjects with a list of trait adjectives and to ask them to form an impression of a person with those characteristics. The adjectives are typically scaled ahead of time to form a pool of stimuli with known values. Then, to create positive impressions, a list with primarily positive information about the stimulus person can be presented, and to create a negative impression, one simply presents negative information about the person. In other words, variation in impressions depends on variation in stimulus information. This is true in part because each trait adjective used in impression formation research has a more or less standard meaning. Everyone who speaks the language has basically the same reaction to each term. No one, for example, rates the adjective "rude" as more desirable than the adjective "helpful". It follows that the experimenter who relies on stimuli that elicit little perceiver variation is unlikely to develop a conception of attraction that emphasizes the affective responses of perceivers. Instead, such stimuli foster the view that the causes of attraction lie outside of the perceiver, in information about the stimulus person.

Work on attitude similarity and attraction (e.g. Byrne, 1961a) provides a somewhat different approach. In some studies (e.g. Byrne and Clore, 1966) a single set of responses to an attitude questionnaire can serve for all stimulus conditions. The subjects in the sample are likely to hold a wide range of positions on the issues, some in agreement with the stimulus person and some disagreeing. Thus, the variable under study becomes the position of the perceiver on these attitude items rather than that of the stimulus person. Investigators who use this method are more likely to see variation in attraction as related to variation in aspects of the perceiver, and the theoretical accounts they develop are also more likely to emphasize perceiver processes.

The two approaches also differ in the affective relevance of the stimuli typically used. Trait adjectives are abstract and general in their meaning. There are many ways to be "cautious" or "domineering". Without a more vivid description of the person, such abstract stimuli elicit little in the way of affective response. In contrast, the use of positive and negative personal evaluations as stimuli or the presentation of opinions that agree or disagree with the subjects' views have more affective potential. A person who displays similar or dissimilar opinions, for example, necessarily supports or opposes the subjects' own views. Byrne and Clore (1967) suggest that this consensual validation is often a rewarding experience and that disagreements are often experienced as punishing. A number of behavioural studies attest to the reinforcing effects of being agreed with (reviewed in Byrne, 1971). The psychophysiological experiment by Clore and Gormly (1974) reprinted in Section 2 of this book gives further evidence for links among the variables of attitude similarity, affect, and attraction. The point here, however, is simply to suggest that each kind of stimulus has its own particular characteristics, and therefore each encourages a particular way of conceptualizing the attraction process. Hence, theories developed to account for the results of experiments using affectively-relevant stimuli tend to see liking as a reflection of the perceiver's affective experience or anticipated experience with the stimulus person. Figure 1 depicts a continuum along which various approaches to research on person perception might be arrayed. At one end is research on impression formation; at the other, research on romantic love. It should be clear that one of the ways in which such diverse research efforts differ is that one involves little if any affective contribution by the subject or perceiver, and the other is defined by strong affective involvement.

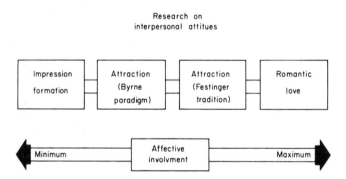

FIG. 1. Relative affective involvement generated in different kinds of attraction research. (From Clore, 1975, p. 7.)

In between the two extremes, two other common research paradigms are listed. The early studies of interpersonal attraction by Byrne and his associates using attitude similarity have been mentioned and will be discussed further later in the chapter.

The other approach, designated here as research on attraction from the Festinger tradition, often involves great emphasis on affective involvement. Studies in this tradition (e.g. Aronson and Linder, 1965; Kiesler and Baral, 1970) typically use elaborate deception to create life-like situations capable of eliciting substantial affective involvement.

The approaches depicted in Fig. 1 have somewhat different methods and different theoretical orientations. Research at the impression formation end of the continuum is more likely to assume an uninvolved subject whose primary role is simply to combine the stimuli presented to him. Little individual variation is expected and information about the stimulus person is the basic theoretical concept. Toward the other extreme, investigators are more likely to assume ego-involved individuals. Greater variation in the reactions of perceivers is expected, and greater theoretical emphasis is placed on affect. Each of these conceptions has some validity for the phenomena treated by it, and questions about *when* each fits reality are probably more appropriate than questions about which of them is "true".

It should be clear that one can begin an analysis of interpersonal attraction at any of several vantage points. This chapter will present data that show the importance of the affective processes of the perceiver as suggested by the reinforcement-affect model of attraction (Clore and Byrne, 1974). Reinforcement is, after all, something that changes the person who receives it. A reinforcement model of attraction is, therefore, one that explains attraction in terms of changes in the recipient. These include primarily changes in affective state and changes in expectations about future reinforcement contingencies.

I. Research on perceiver processes

A. INTERRODENT ATTRACTION

A variety of research projects illustrate the usefulness of extending one's analysis beyond the information about the stimulus person to include the affective processes of the perceiver. One is Latané's research on attraction among rats (Werner and Latané, 1974). In this research, rats were observed in a brightly lit, open area; a situation considered fear-producing for rats, who prefer dark, closed areas. When two animals are placed in the open, they respond by staying close together. To explain this interrodent attraction, Latané and his associates have altered various characteristics of the stimulus rat. They have shaved it to change its texture, perfumed it to alter the odour, anesthetized it to make it motionless, and replaced it with various substitute objects. All of these were efforts to change the characteristics of a stimulus rat to see what caused attraction in perceiver rats. According to Werner and Latané, none of these stimulus variables provides an adequate explanation for the observed attraction. Rather, the explanation lies in the fact that rats like to snuggle. Stimulus rats are apparently attractive in this situation, because they provide an opportunity to engage in this highly preferred behaviour. In other words, the stimulus variables are important only insofar as they provide an opportunity for the subject to make a highly preferred response.

B. ATTRACTION IN CONVERSATIONS

The rat work parallels in some respects a project with human subjects designed to change the attractiveness of stimulus persons (Clore and McGuire, 1974). We began with the view that attractiveness depends on characteristics of the stimulus person, but the results encouraged us to consider a different conception.

Forty women participated in the experiment. They came to the laboratory in groups of six and participated in a series of five-minute, get-acquainted conversations with each other. Each woman had six conversations and after each, she was questioned (in private) about how much she had enjoyed the conversation and how much she liked the other person. The resulting 240 conversations were later content-analysed from tape recordings to get an idea of what kinds of conversational behaviours made some women liked and others disliked.

In the preliminary analysis of the data, three kinds of questions were asked. The first was, 'what kinds of stimulus women were liked?' To answer that question, attraction and conversational enjoyment ratings were correlated with biographical information about the stimulus women. As a loose generalization, one might conclude that the women who received high ratings were tall, rich (high status father's occupation), sociable (drinks a lot), and oriented to other women (many older sisters, few dates).

The second question was, "how did stimulus women who were liked behave?" These behavioural data were obtained by asking independent observers to count the number of utterances that fit into each of 10 categories (e.g. questions, positive self-references, etc.). The observers also made global ratings on seven other dimensions (e.g. how interesting the stimulus person was). The results showed that the only stimulus person behaviour that consistently led to high attraction was that coded as "positive responses". Moreover, the only behaviours that consistently led to dislike were "negative responses" and "dissimilarity statements"

The third question was, "how did perceivers behave in conversations they enjoyed and with partners they liked?" In general, women who enjoyed themselves and who liked their partners were active and talked about themselves. They also made relatively many "affective statements", did not give "negative responses", and did not ask many "questions". Also, the judges rated their part of the conversation as more "interesting". One interpretation of these data from perceivers is that they were attracted to those with whom they enjoyed themselves, and that they enjoyed themselves in conversations in which they got to talk about themselves, and in which they found themselves being active and interesting.

The importance of reinforcement in these results is difficult to overlook. First, the only behaviours of stimulus persons related to attraction were positive and negative responses and disagreements, behaviours that are presumably rewarding and punishing for the perceiver. Second, the behaviours of the perceivers were at least as important as the behaviours of the stimulus persons in predicting attraction. Doubtless, more than one kind of process is at work in the results, but one possibility is that the perceiver enjoyed herself and liked her partner as much for what she herself got a chance to say as for what her partner (the stimulus person) said. These results remind one of the familiar situation in which a person who has talked about himself at length later comments on what a stimulating conversation it was and on what good company he enjoyed.

C. GAIN AND LOSS

Another experiment that allowed us to look separately at information about the stimulus person and affective responses of the perceiver concerned gain and loss effects in attraction (Clore, Wiggins and Itkin, 1975, a, b). In 1965, Aronson and Linder reported an experiment on a phenomenon they called the gain-loss effect. By an ingenious subterfuge, female subjects overheard what appeared to be candid remarks about them from another person. There were four different conditions. In one, they overheard comments that were consistently positive, and in a second, they heard comments that were negative at first but that later changed to positive (gain). The authors predicted that the subjects in this latter situation who experienced a gain in esteem, would like the evaluator more than those who received consistently positive comments. There were two additional groups. One heard consistently negative comments, and the other heard comments that changed from positive to negative (loss). The authors expected the loss subjects to dislike the evaluator more than those in the consistently negative condition. These predictions were somewhat counter-intuitive, since everyone likes warm, loving people and dislikes cold, hateful people. Nevertheless, the gain prediction was confirmed (the women liked positive evaluators who were initially negative), although the loss prediction was not statistically significant.

The gain-loss idea subsequently generated other experiments, many of which found no evidence of either effect (e.g. Mettee, 1971; Tognoli and Keisner, 1972). Some studies did find the effects, but it was never clear which of several explanations was most appropriate. For example, one explanation is the contrast hypothesis. Just as warm water seems warmer after cold water, the positive feedback in the gain condition may have seemed more positive simply because it was preceded by negative feedback. According to this hypothesis, the gain effect occurred because subjects perceived the positive feedback as more positive than it really was due to the contrast with negative feedback. An affect hypothesis, on the other hand, does not stress perceptions of the stimuli but rather the feelings of the perceiver. It argues that the gain effect occurred because the subject felt relieved when negative feedback changed to positive. A closely related possibility is that she felt competent at having won over an initially tough evaluator. The question becomes, then, was there something about the pattern of stimulus information that made the effects inevitable, or did they depend on the affective reaction of the person receiving the information?

The stimuli which influence attraction have two components — information and affect. Stimuli that are primarily informational often consist of aspects of the target person that are positive or negative but that do not have implications for the perceiver. Affective stimuli, on the other hand, are those that do reflect on the perceiver. Thus, for example, the observation that Mary is angry at John would convey information to any perceiver, but for John himself, such information engenders an affective reaction as well. Whether or not information has affective implications then, depends in part on one's point of view. The following experiment sought to apply this principle to the gain-loss problem. It assessed attraction in a gain-loss experiment from more than one point of view as a strategy for separating the effects of information and affect.

In a study designed to test these two explanations, Clore, Wiggins and Itkin (1975a) had subjects observe a videotaped conversation between a female and a male. As they watched the silent tape, the female performed a series of 42 nonverbal behaviours pre-calibrated for warmth and coldness. Some sample warm behaviours were: sitting directly facing him, smiling and nodding her head affirmatively; sample cold behaviours were: looking around the room, frowning, and playing with the ends of her hair. Each tape had two parts, in which the female was either warm or cold.

As in the Aronson and Linder study, the comparisons of interest were between Warm-Warm and Cold-Warm tapes (Gain) and between Cold-Cold and Warm-Cold tapes (Loss). However, in this experiment the subjects were observers who watched the scenarios and made ratings from three points of view: (1) how much the male in the tape liked the female, (2) how much the female liked the male, and (3) how much they themselves liked the female. The stimulus contrast hypothesis predicted gain-loss effects in all three sets of ratings (since all points of view shared the same stimuli). The affect hypothesis predicted gain-loss effects only in ratings from the male point of view and not in the other two. As the recipient of the female's warm and cold behaviour, the unique aspect of the male's point of view was his affective involvement. If only *his* ratings showed gain-loss effects, therefore, his affect must have been responsible.

Consistent with predictions from the affect hypothesis, gain and loss effects were found only in ratings of the male's attraction to the female, not in judgements of the female's or the subjects' own attraction (see Table 1). Thus, gain and loss were produced using nonverbal

TABLE 1. Means and orthogonal comparisons for subjects' judgements of attraction. (From Clore, Wiggins and Itkin, 1975a, p. 709.)

Dependent Variable	Treatment M			
	Warm-warm (n = 102)	Cold-warm (n = 89)	Cold-cold (n = 75)	Warm-cold (n = 72)
Male attraction to female	9.36	9.91	7.05	6.28
		$P < 0.04$		$p < 0.02$
Female attraction to male	9.10	9.58	6.80	6.74
		ns		ns
Subjects' attraction to female	8.21	6.61	5.18	5.77
		$p < 0.001$		ns

stimuli and, at least in this paradigm, they were not a necessary consequence of the stimulus pattern. The gain/loss effects depended on the affective reaction of the recipient (or in this case, the attribution of an affective reaction to the recipient). The idea that affect is the key to the phenomena is also consistent with Aronson and Linder's original explanation (1965).

D. WHEN "I LIKE YOU" INDICATES DISAGREEMENT

Perhaps the purest differentiation between information about the stimulus person and the affective reaction of the perceiver comes from a study done by Byrne, Rasche and Kelley (1974). Subjects first completed an attitude survey covering such issues as their opinion about political parties, the draft, school integration, and so on. They then were asked to communicate these opinions to a person in an adjoining room. Half of the subjects indicated their actual opinions, but the other half were instructed to lie. These subjects were told to state the opposite of their true opinions.

Following the communication, the subject saw on a television monitor an interview with the person he or she had been communicating with. In that televised interview, the person gave either positive or negative evaluations of the subject. In the positive condition, the subject heard himself described as: intelligent, well-informed, interesting, and fairly well adjusted. The interviewee indicated that, "We'd probably get along real well". Negatively evaluated subjects heard themselves described as: not particularly intelligent, well-informed, interesting or adjusted, and also heard the person state that the two probably would not get along very well.

People who agree usually like each other, and if required to do so will give positive evaluations of each other. In this experiment, subjects who lied about their views knew, therefore, that persons who gave them positive evaluations actually disagreed with their real opinions. Similarly, the subjects instructed to lie knew that negative evaluations about themselves actually indicated agreement with their true opinions. For the liars, the message "I like you" indicated disagreement; it was affectively pleasant but informationally negative. Conversely, "I don't like you" indicated agreement; it was unpleasant to hear but carried positive information.

Subsequent information from the subjects showed that they had clearly understood the reversed meaning of the evaluative comments.

However, they did not base their reactions to the evaluator solely on that informational meaning. Rather *both* affect *and* information had a significant effect on attraction. The mean attraction ratings are shown in Table 2; they suggest that compliments felt good and added some positive elements even when they conveyed the opposite meaning, and insults felt bad and added some negative elements even when they led to positive inferences about the person.

TABLE 2. Affective response: mean attraction responses as a function of affective meaning and informational content of Stranger's evaluative message. (From Byrne, Rasche and Kelley, 1974, p. 213.)

Informational content	Affective meaning		Total
	Negative	Positive	
Positive	9.45	11.30	10.38
Negative	5.25	6.35	5.80
Total	7.35	8.82	

The results remind one of related events in everyday interactions among friends. Although kidding may mean that the group likes the person, the barbed comments nevertheless carry a mild sting. Conversely, even obvious forms of flattery and ingratiation may be effective in producing some positive feelings. As Byrne *et al.* point out, "For this reason, ingratiation may seem obvious and odious to a bystander, but not to the recipient" (Byrne *et al.*, 1974, p. 210).

E. OTHER EVIDENCE

Byrne, Rasche and Kelley (1974) found that attraction is influenced by the affective experience associated with the stimulus person even when the experience should have been nullified by the information about the stimulus person. The same kind of effect appears to be present in unpublished data collected by Gergen (1962). In his experiment, coeds heard uniformly positive and reinforcing remarks about themselves from another coed under personal and impersonal conditions. In the personal condition, the girls had previously been introduced and had engaged in a pleasant and informative interaction. The stimulus person obviously had a lot of information on which to base her compliments. By contrast, women in the impersonal condition were told that the stimulus person had undergone extensive training to help her establish rapport in social interaction. This person had never seen the subject but only talked to her via an intercom.

Contrary to predictions, there was no difference between the two conditions in attraction to the stimulus person. The failure of Gergen's prediction has many possible explanations, but one possibility is that he simply underestimated the impact of hearing rewarding things about oneself. In their discussion of the study, Jones and Davis (1965) comment that subjects were reluctant to conclude that the compliments they had received were not really meant for them.

The reader may rightly feel that as evidence for a hypothesis, Gergen's null findings have about the same status as tea leaves and dreams. In response, I can only say that while tea leaves have not been informative, dreams do offer interesting possibilities. To wit, a friend recently reported an especially strong instance of a general phenomenon that many people experience from time to time. He spent the morning in a resentful mood towards his wife because the previous night he had dreamed that she was having an affair. Even after he had awakened and identified the event as a dream, he found himself spiteful and depressed. There are several plausible interpretations for this occurrence. The dream may have set in motion genuine fears of such an event or reminded him of past flirtations or other wifely slights. These are all distinct possibilities, but another interpretation stresses the emotional state produced by the dream. The intriguing feature of this instance is that the emotional events in the dream influenced his waking mood even though he knew he had only been dreaming. The realization that it was all a dream may have forestalled further logical thought on the matter, but it did not erase the fact of having felt powerful negative feelings toward the other person.

F. BELIEFS AND AFFECT

The results of each study discussed thus far have emphasized the role of affective consequences for the perceiver. The conversation experiment (Clore and McGuire, 1974) suggested two reinforcement-related conclusions; (1) Attraction is influenced by the direct rewards and punishments (positive and negative responses, disagreements) given by the stimulus person to the perceiver; and (2) one is attracted to those with whom one engages in enjoyable (reinforcing) behaviours. The behaviours included primarily talking about oneself (or snuggling in the case of Werner and Latané's rats). The gain-loss study (Clore, Wiggins and Itkin, 1975a) showed that the configurations of a stimulus person's behaviour produced gain and loss effects in attraction only when considered from the perspective of an affectively-involved perceiver. Finally, the study (Byrne, Rasche and Kelley, 1974) in which subjects knew that compliments and insults meant the opposite of what they appeared to mean, suggested that pleasant or unpleasant experience influences attraction independently of subjects' beliefs about the stimulus person.

However, the central assertion of Ajzen's position (discussed in the next chapter of this volume) is that attraction depends solely on the perceiver's beliefs about the stimulus-person, and that affective experience is irrelevant unless it eventuates in such positive beliefs. On the other hand, the position of the reinforcement-affect model (Clore and Byrne, 1974) is that attraction is an affective phenomenon, and that as long as the perceiver associates positive affective experience with the stimulus person, attraction will result.

It is, indeed, noteworthy that in most experiments beliefs and feelings are completely confounded; the same events may elicit both positive affect and positive beliefs about the other person. The same is true in naturally occurring situations; the two elements are intimately intertwined. Imagine, for example, a young man and woman about to go on an arranged date. Having heard positive things about each other, a positive impression based on these beliefs may be assumed. If the date is a rewarding experience, attraction develops between them. If successive experiences prove emotionally intense and enjoyable, romantic love may result. In one sense, these stages are defined by affect. Each is marked by a new level of affective involvement, without which such terms as "attraction" and "love" would lose their appropriateness.

In response to the idea that the stages are defined by affect, a proponent of the belief-oriented approach might rightly stress that each stage is also marked by a variety of relevant beliefs about the other person. As the experience with the person becomes more intimate, new and more positive traits may emerge or be inferred by the partner. Presumably, the belief that he or she has the traits of a good husband or wife is more highly valued than the belief that he or she has the traits of a good date.

With respect to beliefs, a reinforcement position would stress that the important beliefs are not those about the stimulus person and their traits but those about oneself (or the relationship). Only those that are self-relevant have the affective force required to be reinforcing or punishing. From this perspective, the beliefs that accompany our example might range from, "I shall have a diverting evening" to "I shall live happily ever after with this person".

G. CONSISTENCY

The central theme of our discussion thus far has been that there are two ways to acquire an attitude toward someone. One's attitude may depend on positive or negative beliefs (e.g. John is the best athlete in our class) or on positive or negative affective experience (e.g. John smiled at me today). Sometimes these components are consistent (e.g. both positive) and sometimes not. When they are not, however, we become uncomfortable. We find it stressful, for example, to discover negative facts about those toward whom we feel positive or to hear extolled the virtues and achievements of people we dislike.

The desire to maintain consistency between what we know and feel about a person has several important implications (Rosenberg and Abelson, 1960). When these components are inconsistent, there is a tendency to alter either beliefs or feelings to reestablish consistency. Acquiring a negative belief about someone we like makes us feel differently toward them. Conversely, a pleasant experience with persons previously disliked inevitably affects our beliefs about them.

The tendency toward consistency also has implications for attitude measurement. Attitudes may be based on either beliefs or affect, but since these two components tend to remain consistent, assessing either alone will provide a reasonably accurate measure of the attitude. To assess attitudes toward some public figure, for example, one could list a number of commonly held beliefs about the person (Fishbein, 1967). Subjects would be asked (1) to indicate the extent to which they held each belief and (2) to evaluate each belief as positive or negative. Thus, if one *believes* a particular politician to be dishonest and *evaluates* dishonesty as negative, we have one negative element in an attitude toward the politician. The final attitude would be accurately indicated by some combination of all of the relevant beliefs, each multiplied by the evaluation of that belief.

In everyday encounters, we use the same approach to attitude assessment. When asked about other persons, one typically indicates his attitude by mentioning an evaluative fact or belief about them.

One might respond, for example, by saying, "Sure I like John, he's a very bright fellow". In making such statements, we are careful to match the words with our feelings. To describe someone too positively or too negatively given our affect would be uncomfortably inconsistent. Belief-affect consistency thus enables attitudes to be assessed accurately from beliefs alone.

This approach to attitude measurement has one potential pitfall. Those who use it might mistake it for a complete theory of attitude formation rather than a handy procedure for measuring attitudes. That is, one might assume that the respondent in the example was attracted to John *because* he believed John to be a bright fellow. While the belief about John's intelligence is a good index of the speaker's attraction toward him, it does not necessarily explain the attraction. Theorists sometimes assume (by interpreting the beliefs used to communicate attitudes as causes) that beliefs are the sole basis of attraction. From that point of view, attraction and dislike seem to be more of a purely intellectual enterprise than is probably the case. It is possible, of course, that attraction is based solely on facts, beliefs, and inferences about the stimulus person, but the material presented thus far argues that affect is sometimes the critical element and hence that there is more than one way to acquire an attitude.

H. AFFECTIVE MEANING

Proponents of the informational approaches (Fishbein and Ajzen, 1975; Kaplan and Anderson, 1973; Wyer, 1974) maintain that one likes other persons whom one believes to have likeable characteristics. There is little doubt that such an assertion is true, but it appears to serve more as an invitation to a particular method of measuring attraction than as a basis for a conceptual understanding of the phenomenon. The problem with explaining the likeability of persons on the basis of beliefs about likeable traits is that one is still left with the problem of explaining the likeability of the traits.

Clore and Kerber (1975) were interested in looking at a sample of trait adjectives to study what kinds of words derived their likeability values from providing information relevant to the person described and what kinds were likeable because they provided information relevant to the perceiver. We selected 36 trait adjectives from Anderson's (1968) list (meaningfulness ratings from 100 subjects are provided in the list). The 200 were divided into four groups of 50 representing four quadrants of likeableness ratings (very positive, somewhat positive, somewhat negative, and very negative). Nine words were selected from each of these quadrants.

Eighty-six college students participated in the study, which involved rating each of the 36 adjectives on nine bipolar scales. Two of the nine scales dealt with the implications of having the trait for the person described and two others with the implications for the perceiver. In each case, one of the items asked about the pleasure-pain implications in a social situation and one asked about success-failure implications in a task situation. After appropriate examples and instructions, individual items appeared in the following abbreviated form:

Considering only his or her point of view in an
informal social situation, a person is reliable

| Likely to be pleasant for him/her | ___ ___ ___ ___ ___ ___ ___ | Likely to be unpleasant for him/her |

Considering your point of view in an
informal social situation, another person is reliable

| Likely to be pleasant for me | ___ ___ ___ ___ ___ ___ ___ | Likely to be unpleasant for me |

A person working on a task by him or herself is reliable

| His/Her success likely | ___ ___ ___ ___ ___ ___ ___ | His/Her failure likely |

Working with a person who is reliable

| My success likely | ___ ___ ___ ___ ___ ___ ___ | My failure likely |

Analyses of the ratings for each of the 36 adjectives were conducted to classify the words into those with more implications for the stimulus person (e.g. likely to be pleasant/unpleasant for him/her) and those that had greater implications for the subject (e.g. likely to be pleasant/unpleasant for me). Of the 36 words, 31 differed significantly ($p < 0.05$) in implications for own versus other's pleasure. Of particular interest was the distribution of the differences, as can be seen from Table 3. For example, in the social situation, there were significant differences between the two scales for all the 18 words at the two extremes (9 very positive and 9 very negative), and 17 of the 18 conveyed more information about consequences for the perceiver than about consequences for the stimulus person. This was significantly different from the distribution in the moderate quadrants ($p < 0.005$). In the moderate quadrants, composed of 9 somewhat positive and 9 somewhat negative words, 13 differed in their implications; but about as many were more relevant to the subject as to the stimulus person. Six conveyed more information about the subject, and 7 conveyed more about the stimulus person.

TABLE 3. Affective implications of trait adjectives for stimulus person and perceiver

Entries show the number of traits with significantly greater implications (either positive or negative) for stimulus person or for perceiver. There were nine traits in each quadrant. (After Clore and Kerber, 1975.)

Pleasant-unpleasant implications in social situation

		Quadrant of Anderson's List			
		+ +	+	−	− −
For stimulus person	Number	1	3	4	0
	% of Differences	(11%)	(50%)	(57%)	(0%)
For perceiver	Number	8	3	3	9
	% of Differences	(89%)	(50%)	(43%)	(100%)

Success-failure implications in task situation

		+ +	+	−	− −
For stimulus person	Number	2	3	2	1
	% of Differences	(25%)	(50%)	(22%)	(25%)
For perceiver	Number	6	3	7	3
	% of Differences	(75%)	(50%)	(78%)	(75%)

This first look at the data suggests strongly that extreme likeability scale values, or what is generally referred to as "information about the stimulus person", depend heavily on the affective implications for the perceiver. Extremely positive and negative traits derive their extremity of meaning from the fact that they imply extreme affective consequences for the perceiver. This conclusion is borne out, though not quite as strongly, by parallel analyses of the success-failure ratings ($p < 0.05$).

In some respects the results are not surprising. A functional theory of meaning would specify that words are retained in the language to the extent that they allow one to make useful distinctions. Presumably the sort of interpersonal information that would be useful to encode and store both for oneself and for communication to others are those that have to do with obtaining pleasure and avoiding pain. Osgood (1969) suggests that language serves a survival function in that it enables members of the species to communicate the good-bad, strong-weak, and active-passive features (but especially the good-bad feature) of persons, places, and things that the speaker has experienced. What is required is a perceiver-oriented account of these things, a functional account for the speaker himself and for others in his role.

These considerations suggest that the affective state of the perceiver is involved even in tasks at the impression formation end of the continuum. What is meant by this assertion is not that the subjects in such experiments are really more affectively-involved than they appear to be, but that the meaning of the words on which they make their judgements is based in part on expected perceiver affect (Osgood, 1969). The words are messages about the affective consequences to be expected in encounters with the person described.

III. Research on similarity

A. EARLY RESEARCH

The early research on attraction by Byrne, Griffitt, Nelson, Golightly, Clore and others was concerned with exploring and explaining the similarity-attraction effect. The role of similarity in attraction has long been of interest to psychologists. So reliable is the observation that similarity leads to attraction, that most attitude theorists have felt the need to account for it in one way or another. The frequent use of Byrne's (1961a) attitude similarity manipulation to study attraction phenomena left many investigators with the impression that similarity was a prime explanatory construct in the reinforcement-affect approach. In actual fact the main role of attitude similarity in this work was simply an operation to produce attraction. Its effect on attraction was often an object of study, but little if any weight was ever placed on similarity as a theoretical construct. Nevertheless, research on the role of similarity in attraction continues from many perspectives, and the ways in which different theories account for the similarity effect is of interest.

The procedure in the original attraction studies by Byrne was one in which subjects are asked to study another person's responses to an attitude or personality questionnaire after taking the test themselves. They are told that better than chance judgements can be made about another person on the basis of that person's answers to the test, and are instructed to try to form an impression of the stranger in order to rate him or her on an Interpersonal Judgment Scale (Byrne, 1961a). The scale is composed of six seven-point items requiring estimations of the stranger's intelligence, adjustment, and other qualities. Also included are two items concerning how much subjects believe they would like the stranger and how much they would enjoy working with him or her. Since these two items are typically correlated ($r = 0.69$, Ajzen, 1974; $r = 0.85$, Byrne and Nelson, 1965), they are usually summed to provide the measure of attraction.

In the usual procedure the responses of the other person are falsified by the experimenter, thus giving him the ability to program the stimulus properties of the supposed stranger. Typically the correlation between the proportion of similar attitudes and attraction is about 0.60.

B. EXPLAINING AWAY SIMILARITY

A variety of suggestions have been made concerning how similarity operates. The early work by Byrne and his associates, stressed that agreement provided consensual validation of one's opinions. Based on Festinger's (1954) concept of social reality and his work with social comparison processes, it was hypothesized that the perception of similar opinions in others increases one's confidence that one's own opinions are reasonable. In the process, it makes one feel more competent, satisfies one's effectance needs, and makes one feel good. Work on this hypothesis concentrated on varying the state of effectance motivation by exposing subjects to confusing movies (Byrne and Clore, 1967) or prior disagreements (Stapert and Clore, 1969) on the logic that similarity should be more valuable the more one needed it. This work met with moderate success. One of its virtues was the attempt to manipulate the variables believed to explain similarity effects independently of the information on which judgements about the stimulus person would be made. As we shall see, that has not been true of other attempts to explain the effect.

Aronson and Worchel (1966), for example, hypothesized that similarity influenced attraction only when subjects used it to infer that the stimulus person would be attracted to them in return. Hence, they gave subjects agreements and disagreements from another person but also indicated directly that the person either did or did not like the subject. The results of this 2 × 2 design revealed, as predicted, a main effect for like-dislike but not for similarity-dissimilarity. Aronson and Worchel concluded that the similarity effect had been explained.

In a subsequent study, Byrne and Griffitt (1966) reasoned that the previous failure to find an effect was due to the restricted range of the similarity variance. They used the same design except that instead of agreements or disagreements on only 5 of 7 attitudes, they increased the range so that subjects experienced agreements on either all or none of the 7 items. The result was a main effect for both like-dislike and similarity-dissimilarity. The means are shown in Table 4.

TABLE 4. Mean attraction responses toward confederate as a function of attitude similarity and expressed liking of the subject.
(From Byrne and Grifitt, 1966, p. 295.)

	Like	Dislike
Similar (7-0)	12.30	7.86
Dissimilar (0-7)	10.40	5.62

The Aronson-Worchel study is typical of a number of others done since then testing the same or a similar hypothesis (e.g. Insko *et al.*, 1973; Jones, Bell and Aronson, 1972). In each case, the logic is that one should manipulate the variable that is believed to control attraction and show that similarity has no effect. The conclusion drawn is, then, that the effect has been explained. The logic is in fact faulty. Such designs may show that the variable chosen has a more potent effect on attraction, but they are incapable of showing that the variable is more basic in the causal chain. As it happens, it is in fact easier to create attraction and dislike with compliments and insults than with agreements and disagreements. A direct personal evaluation has about three times the weight of an agreement in affecting attraction ratings

(Byrne and Rhamey, 1965), but that fact in no way explains the similarity-attraction effect.

An interesting experiment by Ajzen (1974; reprinted in Section 2 of this book) used this same basic strategy. He hypothesized that similarity was a relevant variable in attraction only when it led subjects to make positive inferences about the other person's traits. To test the hypothesis, he manipulated both similarity and the traits of the stimulus person.

Subjects completed a questionnaire containing 100 self-descriptive items selected at random from the Minnesota Multiphasic Personality Inventory. After leaving for a brief interval to score the test, the experimenter returned with feedback for the subject. This consisted of check marks on 12 bipolar adjective scales indicating his standing on each dimension. These evaluative dimensions included such traits as "selfishness", "friendliness", "politeness", "maturity", etc.

After inspecting their own alleged scores, subjects then saw the personality profile of another person on the same dimensions. These were arranged to give similar descriptions to the subjects on either 75% or 25% of the items. The result was a design in which two levels of similarity were crossed with two levels of positivity. In addition, control subjects saw either the positive or the negative description of the other person without information about themselves.

The results showed a significant effect for positive-negative information but none for similarity. Ajzen concluded that the similarity-attraction effect had been explained, and that similarity is usually effective merely because it is generally correlated with positive information about the stranger.

A closer look at this study, however, indicates that it cannot support such a case. The experiment is designed so that the scores of the stimulus person serve two purposes. They provide positive or negative information and similarity-dissimilarity information. We know from previous research (Byrne and Rhamey, 1965; Clore and Baldridge, 1970) that such highly evaluative trait adjectives are weighted about three times as much as similarity information. Given that fact, the information presented in Table 5 demonstrates that no similarity effect would have been predicted in the first place. The entries show predictions using Byrne and Rhamey's (1965) formula (expressed in percentage of positive elements) and also Ajzen's subjective probability formula. By either calculation one would expect a large evaluation effect and little if any similarity effect. From the Byrne-Rhamey

TABLE 5. Relative predicted and obtained similarity and positivity effects. (From Ajzen, 1974.)

	Predicted from Weighted Sum (Ajzen)				Predicted from Weighted Proportion (Byrne-Rhamey)				Obtained			
	+	−	Means	Difference	+	−	Means	Difference	+	−	Means	Difference
Similar	24	−12	6	12	75	37	56	13	10.6	7.2	8.9	1.6
Dissimilar	12	−24	−6		62	25	43		8.4	6.3	7.3	
Control	18	−18			75	25			9.2	3.7		
Means	18	−18			71	29			9.4	5.7		
Difference		36			42					3.7		

percentage entries (in which the possible range is by definition 100%), one can see what a small range (13%) was allowed for the difference between the similarity and dissimilarity means to emerge.

The only point of departure in the predictions from the two formulas is that the Byrne-Rhamey model predicts the obtained interaction between similarity and evaluative information, while the additive model proposed by Ajzen predicts only parallel results in the two evaluation conditions.

In summary, two points should be made about the Ajzen study with respect to its relevance to the similarity issue. The first is that only a relatively small similarity effect would have been predicted in the first place, and in a study with only four or five subjects per cell (108 *S*s in a 24 cell design), it was unlikely to be detected. The second and more important point concerns the impossibility of making causal arguments on the basis of the relative sizes of effects.

Fishbein and Ajzen (1975) have reviewed the results of studies comparing the effects of similarity and evaluative information. They found that a relationship was sometimes found for similarity even when evaluative information about the stimulus person was controlled, but they pointed out, "In contrast to these inconsistent findings concerning the effects of similarity, attribute evaluations were always found to have a strong effect on attraction" (p. 267). They conclude that "attribute evaluation" explains the effects of similarity. This is a tempting though unwarranted conclusion.

Whenever one adds additional information about a similar or dissimilar person, it necessarily alters the total pool of information. The weight of each element in the final judgement is relative to the amount of other information available. Once additional information of an evaluative nature is added, the initial information must of necessity become less important than when it stood alone. Therefore, it is faulty logic to conclude when that very predictable effect occurs that the additional information is more basic than the initial information or that it is what really makes the initial information have its effects.

C. SIMILARITY AND ANTICIPATED REWARDS

A slightly different approach to the previously discussed issue is evident in a study by Wyer (1975) in which similarity, evaluative beliefs about a stimulus person, and other relevant variables were all varied independently. Wyer selected trait terms from Peabody's (1967) list so that their descriptive and evaluative meanings could be varied separately. Examples included the traits "cautious" and "timid" which descriptively are equal but differ in evaluation ("cautious" being more positive than "timid"). The same is true of the words "bold" and "rash"; they refer to the same kind of behaviour but are evaluatively dissimilar. Conversely, the words "cautious" and "bold" have opposite descriptive meanings but are evaluatively equal. The same is true of the words "timid" and "rash"; they are descriptively dissimilar and evaluatively similar.

These and other sets of trait adjectives selected in the same manner were assigned in all possible pairs to two persons described simply as "A" and "B". Thus, the statements "A is cautious", "A is timid", "A is bold", and "A is rash" were crossed with "B is cautious", "B is timid", "B is bold", and "B is rash". Subjects rated the resulting 64 pairs once for the probability that "A" would like "B" and again indicating the probability that "A" would dislike "B".

The study was designed to meet the requirements of Gollob's (1974 a and b) "subject-verb-object" (S-V-O) model for analysing social inferences. The appeal of Gollob's model is that with the stimuli thus arranged, an analysis of variance yields the relative contribution of each of several independent variables. The results show that descriptive similarity was by far the most important variable for predicting liking. In contrast to Ajzen's (1974) conclusions, descriptive similarity was a potent variable even when evaluative beliefs about the stimulus person were held constant.

In addition to the effects of similarity, the design allowed a number of other effects to be assessed as shown in Table 6. One of the most interesting from a reinforcement perspective concerned variation in the descriptive aspects of the stimulus person. For example, subjects felt that "timid" stimulus persons would be more liked than "rash" ones and that "cautious" persons would be more liked than those described as "bold". These effects are noteworthy because they indicate a preference for some stimulus persons over others despite equally positive traits. The kind of finding represented by the preference of "cautious" over "bold" persons and "timid" over "rash" ones is interpreted by Wyer (1975, p. 1042) as consistent with the "suggestion that information about a person's attributes affects *P*'s attraction to him to the extent that these attributes imply that *P*'s approach responses will be positively reinforced".

TABLE 6. Examples of the effects found in Wyer (1975).

	Descriptive meaning	Evaluative meaning
Perceiver Variation	*Cautious* and *timid* perceivers like others more than do *bold* and *rash* ones	*Cautious* and *bold* perceivers like others more than do *timid* and *rash* ones*
Stimulus Person Variation	*Cautious* and *timid* persons are more liked than *bold* and *rash* ones	*Cautious* and *bold* persons are more liked than *timid* and *rash* ones
Similarity Variation	*Cautious* and *timid* persons like each other and *bold* and *rash* persons like each other	*Cautious* and *bold* persons like each other and *timid* and *rash* persons like each other*

Note: The two starred (*) effects were nonsignificant with the traits listed here but were significant with other comparable sets of traits.

D. DISSIMILARITY AND ATTRACTION

Attempts to explain the effects of similarity must take into account its functional role in the particular situation involved. Similarity can have a variety of positive consequences, some of which have recently been discussed by Clore and Byrne (in press). However, exceptions can be found. One can conjure up situations in which dissimilarity would have more functional value than similarity, but presumably the key to such exceptions is the functional or reinforcement value in the situation.

A study to test this hypothesis involved college students' attraction to their instructors (Grush, Clore and Costin, 1975). It was hypothesized that students would prefer teachers with different characteristics than their own. Specifically, we hypothesized that dissimilarity would lead to attraction on traits relevant to the teacher role but not on traits irrelevant to teaching.

To test the hypothesis, personality measures were obtained on students and teachers in 93 college classes. The 93 classes were divided into two groups and a different set of four personality scales were administered in each. From each set, one trait was chosen that was relevant to teaching (Ascendance and Personal Relations) and one that was irrelevant (Sociability and Cautiousness). A trait was considered relevant if scores on it were correlated with ratings of teacher skill, irrelevant if they were not. Teachers who were high, medium, and low on each of these dimensions were selected, and from their classes, equal numbers of students were chosen who were similar and dissimilar (one standard deviation or more below the teacher).

The results showed two effects. First, all the traits were desirable, and the more the teacher possessed each of them, the more attracted students were to him or her. Second, as predicted, dissimilarity effects were apparent for the instrumental but not the non-instrumental traits. In other words, regardless of a teacher's score on a given instrumental trait, those students who were most different from their teacher liked him or her most. The dissimilarity results did not reflect merely attraction toward good teachers nor did they reflect the tendency to attribute good traits to teachers that were already liked. The traits were equally desirable and similar, and dissimilar students attributed the same amount of the trait to the instructors. The difference in their attraction was due purely to how dissimilar he or she was from themselves. Those who were similar to their teachers on relevant traits were less attracted than those farther away on these dimensions. The students' reasoning seems to have been: "If teachers are to lead and direct me in the learning process, they ought to possess more of those traits instrumental for effective teaching than I do; if they possess only the same amount as I do, how can I learn anything from them?"

IV. Summary

Some conceptions of attraction focus on information about the stimulus person, and some stress the affective experience of the perceiver. This difference in conceptual orientation reflects comparable differences among theorists in the methods and stimuli typically used in their research. Therefore, questions about when each conception is appropriate are probably more reasonable to ask than questions about which of them is true.

Several recent experiments were reviewed that sought to look at information and affect separately. These studies suggest that: (1) attraction in quasi-naturalistic situations is influenced by reinforcements received by the perceiver, (2) that the behaviour of the perceiver is as important in predicting attraction as the behaviour of the stimulus person, (3) that gain and loss effects in attraction may depend on affective involvement in the perceiver, and (4) that the raw experience of rewards and punishments (in the form of compliments and insults) can influence attraction even when unsupported by consistent beliefs.

It was suggested that the affective and informational elements in one's attraction to another maintain a consistent relationship so that as one changes, the other changes. An important implication of this tendency toward belief-affect consistency is that attraction will generally be accompanied by positive beliefs about a stimulus person regardless of whether or not such beliefs play a causal role.

The essential explanation of attraction from the informational position is that we like those whom we believe to have likeable traits. Most research from the information perspective is oriented toward a formal characterization of how such inferences are made. But another direction that can be taken is to ask what makes a likeable trait likeable. A scaling study was discussed which suggested that the origin of likeability in trait adjectives parallels the origin of likeability for persons. Results showed that the most likeable and dislikeable traits were those that communicated the most extreme affective implications for the perceiver. Indeed the traits most extreme in evaluative meaning were not those that provided information about the stimulus person, but those that had implications for the perceiver.

Several recent studies of similarity and attraction were reviewed in the final section. It is sometimes assumed that similarity influences attraction either because it tells the perceiver that the stimulus person will like him or because it tells the perceiver that the stimulus person is likely to have positive traits. A common strategy in studies attempting to explain away the effect of similarity is to supply the subject directly with the information believed to be inferred from similarity. If this subsequent information reduces or eliminates the similarity effect, it is concluded that the basis of the similarity-attraction effect has been found. In fact, however, subjects make judgements of attraction on the total pool of stimuli available so that a reduction of the effect of similarity will always occur when new information is added, but this effect has no bearing on which kind of stimulus is more basic or causal. Finally, the point was made that either similarity or dissimilarity can lead to attraction depending on which was ultimately more rewarding for the perceiver. Although similarity is far more frequently associated with positive outcomes, an example of a situation in which dissimilarity was instrumental was discussed.

3.

Information Processing Approaches to Interpersonal Attraction[1]

ICEK AJZEN

University of Massachusetts, Amherst, USA

Interpersonal attraction is typically viewed as dealing with affective relations between individuals, with one person's feelings, sentiments, or emotions toward another. In unguarded moments, investigators of interpersonal attraction take credit for studying such fundamental facets of social life as friendship and enmity, love and hate, harmony and discord (see Berscheid and Walster, 1969; Byrne, 1971; Huston, 1974; Rubin, 1973). These aspirations are in marked contrast to the paucity of direct empirical evidence concerning affective reactions in interpersonal contexts. In most studies, investigators tend to rely on evaluative judgements or verbal expressions of liking to assess interpersonal attraction (cf. Lindzey and Byrne, 1968). Such deliberate, voluntary responses to another person do not appear to be adequate reflections of sentiments or emotions, reactions that are usually regarded as largely irrational and involuntary (Averill, 1974).

1. The author is grateful to George Levinger and to the editor, Steve Duck, for their comments on an earlier draft of this paper.

Consider, for example, Byrne's (1961a) interpersonal judgement scale which has come to be used with increasing frequency. Respondents indicate the degree to which they would like another person, and the degree to which they would like to work with that person in an experiment, on two seven-point items in multiple choice format. The sum over these two items serves as a measure of attraction. Other investigators (e.g. Ellsworth and Carlsmith, 1968; Schopler and Thompson, 1968) have used evaluative semantic differential scales, and some have constructed their own measures of liking for purposes of specific experiments (e.g. Aronson and Linder, 1965; Nemeth, 1970). All of these procedures elicit reflection and judgement rather than direct expressions of affect.

Interest in sentiments and emotions notwithstanding, the major thrust of research on attraction must thus be viewed as directed at discovering the determinants of favourable and unfavourable inter-personal evaluations. Although some may find the operational bias toward the cognitive aspects of interpersonal relationships discon-certing, this bias is quite consistent with recent conceptualizations of emotion and with the theoretical approach adopted in the present chapter. Averill (1976) defines emotions as "cognitive (information processing) systems or rules of behaviour". He views physiological factors as contributing to, and setting limits for, the social construction of emotional behaviour. The traditional distinction between emotion and cognition is rejected. "Standard emotions are as much a product of complex cognitive processes as are such other cultural products as religion, art, science, etc." Not unlike the work of Schachter (1964) and Bem (1972), Averill's analysis relies on notions of self-attribution to account for emotionality. Walster and Berscheid (1971) take a similar approach in their theory of "passionate love".

The above discussion suggests that cognitive judgements of evalua-tion and liking are more central and important for an understanding of interpersonal attraction than are direct measures of emotional arousal. The reliance on self-report measures thus appears quite justified, especially in light of the fact that it is very difficult to obtain adequate physiological measures of attraction. In any case, given the ubiquitous use of evaluative judgements, it is virtually impossible to understand research findings concerning attraction without a thorough analysis of the determinants of interpersonal evaluations. The purpose of the present chapter is to describe cognitive and information processing approaches to interpersonal attraction and to show how an information processing approach can provide a unifying theoretical framework for attraction research. Following a general discussion of information processing approaches, a model of interpersonal attraction is presented and compared to other models of its kind. The second part of the chapter analyses selected areas of research on attraction in light of the theoretical model.

I. Information and attraction

From an information processing perspective, the attraction of one person (P) toward another person (O) is determined by P's information about O. If the information is generally favourable, P will be attracted to O; if the information is unfavourable, P's evaluation of O will be negative. This is the basic principle underlying all cognitive, information processing approaches. It suggests that the only direct and immediate determinant of attraction is the information that is available to P. Any other factor can influence attraction only to the extent that it has an effect on this information.

A. MECHANISTIC VERSUS CONSTRUCTIVE APPROACHES

It is important at the outset to distinguish between two cognitive approaches whose underlying assumptions differ fundamentally. The first may be termed the *mechanistic* approach. It views individuals as rather passive receivers of information whose attraction toward another person is determined solely by the information to which they are exposed. The major question of theoretical interest concerns the way in which individuals combine or integrate the items of information to which they are exposed in order to arrive at an overall evaluation.

In contrast, the second cognitive approach views the information to which an individual is exposed as merely the first step toward the formation of interpersonal attraction. According to this *constructive* approach, a person actively processes the information which he receives; he makes use of some informational items but rejects others, and he may make inferences that go beyond the information given. The resulting evaluation of another person is based on all items of information available to the individual, not only on the information to which he was exposed. To understand the formation of interpersonal attraction from a constructive perspective it is therefore necessary to consider the factors that determine a person's acceptance or rejection of the information to which he is exposed as well as the inference processes whereby he goes beyond the information given.

The Mechanistic Approach

Most experimental investigations of interpersonal attraction can be viewed as relying on a mechanistic approach, although few attempts have been made to formalize this approach. One notable exception is the work of Anderson (1962, 1965, 1967) and his associates (Anderson and Barrios, 1961; Anderson and Jacobson, 1965) who have provided an extensive and systematic treatment of interpersonal attraction from a mechanistic perspective. This research has applied Anderson's (1970, 1971) general integration theory to judgements of liking or interpersonal attraction. The research paradigm employed in most of these studies can be described as follows: subjects receive a list of personality traits attributed to a hypothetical person. On the basis of normative data (see Anderson, 1968) traits differing in their desirability are selected. For example, the hypothetical person might be described as intelligent, good-natured, reserved, and obedient. The subjects are then asked to record their impressions of the person by rating his likeableness. They may be asked to assign a score of 50 to a person they would neither like nor dislike, lower numbers to persons they would dislike, and higher numbers to persons they would like (Anderson, 1965).

The mechanistic approach assumes that these evaluative judgements can be completely understood in terms of the information about the hypothetical stranger's personality traits given to the subjects. As noted above, the major question of interest is the combination rule used to integrate the discrete items of information. Anderson's (1970) integration theory advocates a weighted averaging model as descriptive of the combination process. According to this model, respondents assign a scale value to each item of information representing that item's location on the dimension under consideration (likeableness in the case of interpersonal attraction). In addition, each item of information is weighted according to its importance for the judgement. This model is shown in eqn 1, where A is attraction, s_i is the scale value of informational item i, w is the weight placed on item i, and n is the number of informational items to which the respondent is exposed.

Note that no direct measures of weights and scale values are obtained; instead, these variables must be estimated on the basis of the attraction scores. Clearly, it is possible to find many different sets of values for w and s that would produce any obtained attraction score. It follows that in this general form, the weighted averaging model makes no testable predictions and it thus has little explanatory power.

$$A = \frac{\sum_{i=1}^{n} w_i s_i}{\sum_{i=1}^{n} w_i} \tag{1}$$

Linear Weighted Averaging Model In most applications of the weighted averaging model, therefore, two assumptions are made (cf. Anderson, 1970). First, it is assumed that the scale value of any given informational item is not influenced by the remaining items of information used to describe the hypothetical person. The second assumption concerns the weights placed on different items of information. The total array of informational items is partitioned into different types or sets of information. For example, Set A may provide information about personality traits, Set B about demographic characteristics:

A = {intelligent, reserved}
B = {female, black}

One item from each set is used to describe the hypothetical person. It is assumed that although different sets of information may be given different weights, elements within sets are weighted equally; whatever item is selected from a given set, it receives that set's weight.

These two assumptions transform the general weighted averaging model into a linear model (see Fishbein and Ajzen, 1975). Certain predictions can now be derived and tested. Typically, all possible combinations in the Cartesian product of the sets of information are created and subjects are asked to rate the likeableness of each person thus described. For sets A and B above, this experimental paradigm would result in a 2×2 factorial design. The linear model predicts two possible main effects (on the assumption that scale values within sets differ significantly), and no interaction.

Note that evidence in support of these predictions could be interpreted as supporting any model that meets the two assumptions described above, not only the weighted averaging model. For example, main effects and no interaction would also be predicted by a linear summation model. The controversy surrounding averaging versus summation models will be considered below.

The linear model has found considerable support in a large number of investigations, although many studies have also demonstrated significant interactions. For example, Anderson (1962) partitioned a list of nine personality traits into three sub-sets, each containing one adjective of high desirability, one of medium desirability, and one of low desirability. By forming all possible combinations in a 3 × 3 × 3 factorial design, 27 hypothetical persons were described by means of three adjectives each. Twelve subjects rated the likeableness of each of the 27 stimulus persons on five different occasions, and a separate analysis of variance was computed for each subject. Most of the variance in each subject's attraction scores was accounted for. by the three main effects; the interactions were not significant for nine of the 12 subjects, but they did reach statistical significance for the remaining three subjects.

The significant interaction effects are usually of relatively low magnitude, and Anderson (1970) has argued that it is possible to remove the interaction by rescaling the response variable without violating the assumed scaling properties of the measuring instrument[2] (see also, Bogartz and Wackwitz, 1970). Anderson's treatment of rescaling has been criticized as inadequate since it provides no general method for testing whether appropriate transformations exist (Krantz and Tversky, 1971). More important, some of the research to be reviewed below has demonstrated strong interaction effects. No amount of rescaling would make the data of these studies conform to the linear weighted averaging model without violating the minimal assumption of an ordinal measurement scale (see also Birnbaum, 1974).

The Constructive Approach

In contrast to the mechanistic perspective with its emphasis on information integration, the constructive approach is concerned with the ways in which information is utilized to arrive at an evaluation of another person. According to the constructive approach, interpersonal attraction depends not so much on the information provided as on the beliefs about the other person formed on the basis of that information. A person's belief about an object may be defined as his subjective

2. The response measure is considered to be at least an ordinal scale which can be changed into an interval scale by applying a monotone transformation.

probability that the object has a given attribute (Fishbein and Ajzen, 1972, 1975). The terms "object" and "attribute" are used in the generic sense and they refer to any discriminable aspect of the individual's world. In dealing with interpersonal attraction, the object of interest is, of course, the other person. For example, an individual who believes another person to be reliable might indicate that there is an 80% chance that O is reliable. The belief object, "the other person," is linked to the attribute "reliable" with a subjective probability of 0.80.

According to Fishbein's (1963, 1967) theory of attitude, a person's evaluation of an object is a function of his salient beliefs about that object. Each belief links the object with a valued attribute. The attitude is determined by the person's evaluation of the attributes associated with the object and by the strength of these associations. Specifically, the evaluation of each salient attribute contributes to the attitude in proportion to the person's subjective probability that the object has the attribute in question. Theories of a similar nature, though narrower in scope, have been proposed by Edwards (1954), Rosenberg (1956), and others (see Feather, 1959; Fishbein and Ajzen, 1975).

Perceived Attributes Model of Attraction Fishbein's attitude theory can be applied directly to the area of interpersonal attraction. Equation 2 is a special case of Fishbein's (1963) summation theory in that it deals with interpersonal attitudes (i.e. attraction), rather than attitudes in general. In Equation 2, A is attraction, p_i is the individual's subjective probability that another person has attribute i, v_i is the subjective value of attribute i, and the sum is over the n salient attributes. Since attraction is here viewed as a function of the attributes the other person is perceived to possess, eqn 2 may be called the perceived attributes (PA) model of interpersonal attraction.

$$A = \sum_{i=1}^{n} p_i v_i \tag{2}$$

It is important to note again that according to the PA model, attraction is determined by the attributes the other person is *perceived* to have; these perceived attributes may correspond only in part to the information that was available. Consider, for example, a person who is described as hostile and withdrawing. Different individuals may utilize this information in different ways. Some may simply accept both items of information without modification. Their attraction toward the hypothetical person would be determined only by their beliefs that he is hostile and withdrawing, as predicted by a mechanistic approach. However, the constructive approach underlying the PA model of attraction leads us to expect that individuals will take a more active role. First, since it may appear inconsistent for a person to be both hostile and withdrawing, subjects may accept one of these attributes but not the other as descriptive of the stranger. They may now perceive the stranger as hostile, but not as withdrawing. Second, on the basis of the information provided, subjects may infer that the stranger has additional, unmentioned attributes. There is considerable evidence that subjects make far-ranging inferences about the attributes of another person on the basis of limited information about him (Asch, 1946; Wiggins, 1973; Fishbein and Ajzen, 1975). Such inferences are often said to rely on "implicit theories of personality" (Schneider, 1973). For example, if subjects accept the information that the stranger is hostile, they may come to believe that he is also aggressive, rash, and inconsiderate. Clearly, to gain a complete understanding of attraction to this person, it would be insufficient to consider only the information to which the subjects were exposed.

In contrast to the linear weighted averaging model described above, to test the PA model of attraction it is necessary to measure not only the attraction response itself but also the subjective probabilities and values associated with each of the salient attributes. An individual's salient beliefs about another person can be elicited in a free-response format by asking him to list the characteristics, qualities, and attributes of the person. The first few beliefs elicited may be viewed as most salient for the individual. Alternatively, it is possible to define a set of "modal salient beliefs" in terms of the 10 or 12 beliefs most frequently elicited by a sample of subjects from the population under investigation (see Fishbein and Ajzen, 1975; Kaplan and Fishbein, 1969).

To illustrate, Fishbein and Coombs (1974) elicited salient beliefs about Johnson and Goldwater, the two candidates in the 1964 presidential election. A total of 24 modal salient beliefs were obtained, involving such attributes as conservative, mentally healthy, political opportunist, in favour of medicare, and consistent in his views. An independent sample of subjects evaluated each attribute on a seven-point good-bad scale and, on a seven-point probable-improbable scale, they indicated the likelihood that a given candidate possessed the attribute in question. As specified by the perceived attributes model of attraction (eqn 2), the subjective probabilities and values were multiplied for each attribute, and the resulting products were summed across the 24 attributes.[3] In this fashion, estimates of attraction (or attitude) toward Johnson and toward Goldwater were obtained. In addition, subjects provided direct indications of their attitudes toward the two candidates by rating each candidate on a five-item evaluative semantic differential. The estimates of attraction were found to correlate significantly with the direct measures ($r = 0.69$ for Johnson and 0.87 for Goldwater).

The perceived attributes model has also been applied in the hypothetical stranger paradigm (Ajzen, 1974 and Section 2 of this book). Unfortunately, salient beliefs were not elicited in that study. Instead, subjects rated the stranger on a standard check list consisting of 100 adjectives selected from Anderson's (1968) list of 555 personality trait words. In addition, rather than asking the subjects to provide their own attribute evaluations, Anderson's normative values were used. In spite of these limitations, estimates of attraction toward the stranger based on the 100 attributes correlated significantly with two direct measures, the interpersonal judgement scale ($r = 0.68$) and an evaluative semantic differential ($r = 0.66$). A correlation of similar magnitude was reported by Anderson and Fishbein (1965). The results of these and other investigations (see Fishbein and Ajzen, 1975) provide support for the PA model of interpersonal attraction.

Comparison of Mechanistic and Constructive Approaches

In concluding the discussion of the relationship between information and attraction, it may be instructive to compare the mechanistic and constructive approaches. The first part of this comparative analysis concerns the controversy surrounding summation and averaging models of impression formation; the second part examines some advantages of the constructive approach.

---

3. As in most investigations of this kind, the two scales were scored in a bipolar fashion (from -3 to $+3$) before multiplication. Fishbein's summation model has been faulted on the grounds that procedures for quantifying subjective probabilities and values are not made clear (Wyer, 1974). For example, a linear transformation of either measure results in a nonlinear transformation of the sum (the estimate of attitude). In the case of a linear transformation on the subjective values, $A = \sum p_i (v_i + C) = \sum p_i v_i + C \sum p_i$. Fishbein and Ajzen (1975) have attempted to deal with some of these measurement problems.

Summation Versus Averaging Most recent reviews of attitude theory
or social judgements include a discussion of summation versus
averaging models (e.g. Anderson, 1971; Fishbein and Ajzen, 1975;
McGuire, 1969; Rosenberg, 1968; Wyer, 1974). The psychological
significance of this distinction can be seen in the following illustration.
Suppose a person is described first as honest (a highly desirable
attribute) and later as reserved (a mildly desirable trait). It is usually
argued that according to a summation model, attraction should
increase, whereas an averaging model would predict a decrease. This
can be seen most clearly by assigning numerical values to the two
attributes. For example, if honest had a subjective value of $+6$ and
reserved a subjective value of $+2$, taking the sum would lead to an
attraction score of $+8$ while computing the average results in a score
of $+4$. Numerous studies have been conducted in an attempt to test
the conflicting hypotheses, but no clear-cut conclusions have emerged.
Sometimes, findings appear to support a summation process and at
other times an averaging process (see, for example, Anderson, 1965).

A thorough analysis reveals the artificiality of this controversy. First,
Wyer (1974) has noted that the integration rule may vary for different
types of judgement. A respondent asked to estimate the material
wealth of a person who owns a house, a chain of supermarkets, and a
private jet, is likely to add up the total value of these assets. In
contrast, an individual asked to rate the social class of people living in
a given neighbourhood is unlikely to add up the incomes of all
residents; instead, he would probably base his judgement on the
average income in the neighbourhood. Although Wyer's point is well
taken, it is not clear which of the two integration rules, summation or
averaging, is appropriate for evaluative judgements of liking or
attraction.

A second, and more important, problem has to do with the research
paradigm employed in studies of the summation-averaging controversy.
Fishbein and Ajzen (1975) have noted that virtually all investigations
have tested the linear averaging model against a *linear* summation
model. We saw above that Anderson's weighted averaging model does
indeed take the form of a linear model in most of its applications.
However, Fishbein's summation theory of attitude is a nonlinear model
(as is the PA model of attraction). Unlike the linear averaging model
which assigns a constant weight to each set of informational items, the
nonlinear summation model allows subjective probabilities and values
to vary with respect to each belief. Most existing tests of summation

versus averaging are therefore irrelevant for a comparative test involving Fishbein's theory, although they may be of interest to investigators concerned only with *linear* summation and averaging models.

The most serious problem concerning research on the summation-averaging controversy, however, is neither the failure to consider the nature of the judgemental dimension nor the failure to distinguish between linear and nonlinear models. Rather, it is the failure to distinguish between mechanistic and constructive approaches to information processing. Tests of summation versus averaging models have, with only one exception (Fishbein and Hunter, 1964), been conducted within the framework of the mechanistic approach. Hypothetical stimulus persons are described in terms of different sets of traits, and attraction toward these persons is compared and interpreted as showing either summation or averaging characteristics. It is assumed that the information provided, and only that information, is responsible for the observed attraction. No attempt is made to measure the extent to which the information about the hypothetical person is accepted or to assess inferential beliefs that may have been formed. From the point of view of a constructive approach, this experimental paradigm does not permit a meaningful comparison between summation and averaging models. Although the empirical tests may be relevant for identifying rules of combining informational items such that accurate predictions of attraction can be made, they have little to say about the accuracy of models that rely on a constructive information processing approach. Such an approach requires measurement of subjective probabilities and values associated with the salient beliefs about the stimulus person. The probability × value products can be summed and averaged, and it then becomes possible to determine which of these two estimates (the sum or the average) affords better prediction of attraction. Although research to date has been inconclusive, it is conceivable that the average will prove to be the best rule for combining the informational items to which a subject is exposed. At the same time, it is possible that the summation rule has to be applied whenever subjective probabilities and values of salient beliefs are combined. (For some evidence in support of the latter argument, see Fishbein and Hunter, 1964.) The averaging model may thus be appropriate in the context of a mechanistic approach whereas the summation model may apply in the context of a constructive approach. In any case, the summation-averaging controversy is unlikely to be resolved unless more attention is paid to the distinction between mechanistic and constructive approaches.

Advantages of the Perceived Attributes Model As we have seen, the mechanistic approach considers only the items of information to which an individual is exposed, and it attempts to identify a rule for combining these items such that an accurate estimate of attraction is obtained. In contrast, the constructive approach assumes that information about another person may lead to the formation of beliefs about that person's attributes. Attraction is determined by the strength with which these beliefs are held and by the subjective values of the attributes associated with the other person. Again, it is necessary to specify a combination rule for the subjective probabilities and values which permits accurate prediction of attraction toward the other person. According to the perceived attributes model, attraction is a function of the summed products of probabilities and values (see eqn 2).

The mechanistic and constructive approaches are, of course, both legitimate information processing perspectives, each capable of making an important contribution to our understanding of interpersonal attraction. However, the constructive approach and, more specifically, the PA model of attraction, has a number of advantages worth noting. One advantage pertains to the information we obtain about the psychological processes underlying the formation of attraction. Consider, for example, two hypothetical persons — one described as a rapist and intelligent, the other as a rapist and inconsiderate. It appears reasonable to assume that both persons will be disliked, despite the difference in the second item of information.

Taking a mechanistic approach one could argue that the first item of information should be given greater weight because knowing that the person is a rapist is more "important" than knowing that he is intelligent or inconsiderate. However, this amounts to a restatement of the obvious. The interesting question is *why* one item of information is more important than another. The constructive approach directs our attention to the salient beliefs about the other person formed as a result of exposure to the information that he is a rapist and either intelligent or inconsiderate. Appropriate measurement procedures would in all likelihood reveal that many inferential beliefs are formed on the basis of the information that the person is a rapist. Most of these beliefs would, of course, be negative. Subjects might infer that if the person is a rapist, he must also be mentally disturbed, irresponsible, aggressive, mean, etc. The information that he is intelligent or inconsiderate, even if accepted, may produce comparatively few inferential beliefs. This would explain the greater importance attached to the information that a person is a rapist than to the information that he is intelligent or inconsiderate. The constructive approach is thus more likely to further our understanding of psychological processes underlying interpersonal attraction than is the mechanistic approach.

A second advantage of the constructive approach is its handling of complex informational settings. Suppose the following information about another person is made available to a subject: *O* is a male undergraduate applying for the post of student ombudsman at the University of Texas; he is a junior majoring in government with a 3.8 grade point average; he was president of the Pre-Law Association; a member of the National Government Honor Society; a Junior Fellow of the University; a member of the varsity swimming team; a past elected officer of the student government, etc. In addition, he is observed to spill a cup of coffee toward the end of an interview (see Helmreich, Aronson and LeFan, 1970). A mechanistic approach, such as Anderson's weighted averaging model, would have to assume that each and every item in this multidimensional array of data is integrated to arrive at an overall evaluation of the person in question. Such an assumption is clearly unrealistic, but there is nothing in the mechanistic approach to suggest which items of information need to be taken into consideration. The constructive approach avoids this problem by stipulating that attraction toward a person is a function of salient beliefs about that person; these salient beliefs may be based on a complex set of informational items, but attraction is not directly determined by the information itself. The application of the perceived attributes model in a complex situation is therefore no different from its application in a simple situation. Salient beliefs are elicited, and the subjective probabilities and values associated with these beliefs are used to predict interpersonal attraction.

Finally, Jaccard and Fishbein (1975) provided empirical evidence for the superiority of the constructive approach. A hypothetical stranger was described in terms of 12 personality traits. Six of the adjectives used were positive (e.g. loving, sincere) and six were negative (e.g. ugly, rude). Attraction to the stimulus person was measured on a seven-point like-dislike scale. In addition, each subject was asked to recall the adjectives used to describe the stimulus person, as well as to list any other adjectives (i.e. infer traits) that might characterize the person described. With respect to each adjective listed, the subject rated how certain he was that the person had the adjective in question (on a four-point not at all certain-extremely certain scale) and he evaluated each adjective on a seven-point good-bad scale. Finally, embedded within a longer list of traits, the 12 adjectives originally used to describe the stimulus person were each rated on the certainty and evaluation scales.

The mechanistic approach would rely on the measures of belief strength (p) and attribute evaluation (v) concerning the 12 traits used in the description of the hypothetical stranger. The sum (or average) of these 12 $p \times v$ products (A $= \sum_i p_i v_i$ — see eqn 2) had a correlation of 0.48 with the direct measure of attraction (the like-dislike scale). When the sum of products was based on the traits recalled and inferred, i.e. on all beliefs about the stranger — as required by the constructive approach — the correlation with attraction was 0.67, a significant increase in the accuracy of prediction.[4] A constructive approach, as represented by the perceived attributes model, thus appeared to describe more accurately the formation of interpersonal attraction than did a mechanistic approach.

In the following sections, the perceived attributes model will be applied to different areas of research on interpersonal attraction. An attempt will be made to show how the constructive information processing approach can provide a framework for the integration of diverse research traditions and findings.

B. ATTRACTION RESEARCH AND THE PERCEIVED ATTRIBUTES MODEL

Research on interpersonal attraction has a relatively long history. Since Moreno's (1934) pioneering work on the sociometric method, a large number of investigations have been conducted in attempts to identify the determinants of interpersonal attraction. Among other things it has been suggested that the attraction of one person to another is influenced by the degree to which O's beliefs, values, interests, and personality characteristics are similar to those of P; by the extent to which O's needs complement P's needs; by O's liking for P; by the extent to which O rewards or reinforces P; by O's eye contact

---

4. A sum of products based only on the adjectives correctly recalled correlated 0.47 with the direct attraction measure.

with *P*; by the intimacy of *O*'s self-disclosures to *P*; by *O*'s evaluations or appraisals of *P*; and by *O*'s behaviour in the presence of *P*, such as helping *P* or committing a blunder.

It is beyond the scope of this chapter to review in detail these various areas of investigation. Instead, selected studies will be described to illustrate the main lines of research. As we shall see, results of experiments have often been inconsistent. Although each of the variables mentioned has been shown to affect attraction in some situations, the same variables have also been found to have no appreciable effect on attraction or even in fact the obverse effect. In the reviews below, an attempt will be made to explain these conflicting findings in terms of the perceived attributes model of attraction. Unfortunately, only a few studies have been conducted within an information processing framework. Interpretation of most research findings must therefore by necessity be *post hoc*. Nevertheless, we shall see that the information processing approach can further our understanding of the factors underlying formation of interpersonal attraction.

Factorial Experiments on Attraction

Many studies on interpersonal attraction have examined the effects of two or more variables selected quite arbitrarily by the investigator without much concern for their theoretical significance. Frequently, the investigator's main purpose is to demonstrate that the effect of one variable is contingent upon the level of some other variable, i.e. that the two variables interact. In planning such an experiment, a premium is placed on the counterintuitive aspect of the reversal produced by the interaction (see Fishbein and Ajzen, 1975).

Consider, for example, a study by Mettee and Riskind (1974) concerning the effects of ability and performance on attraction. By means of an elaborate cover story and various deceptions, pairs of female subjects were led to believe that they were participating in an evaluation of a test measuring cognitive fluency and overall intelligence. In the course of taking the test, the other person appeared to perform much better or only slightly better than the subject. After completing the test, the subject was informed that her own ability level was average for the college population; the cognitive fluency of her partner was said to be about the same or much higher than her own level. Finally, subjects evaluated their partners on a 21-point liking scale.

The only significant effect in a 2 × 2 analysis of variance was the interaction between ability and performance. The person with superior ability was significantly more attractive than the person with average ability only if she also performed much better than the subject. When her performance was slightly better than the subject's, there was a nonsignificant tendency in favour of the average ability person.

Somewhat comparable results were reported by Aronson, Willerman and Floyd (1966). Subjects listened to a tape recording of an interview with a student who was purportedly a candidate for a university team. The candidate first provided general background information about himself and then responded to a series of knowledge questions. The emerging picture of the candidate was either that of a highly competent individual or that of an incompetent person. In addition, toward the end of the interview, he either sipped a cup of coffee or spilled the coffee over his new suit. As in the Mettee and Riskind study, a measure of liking revealed a significant interaction between the competence and blunder factors. Spilling the coffee had a significant adverse effect on liking for the incompetent candidate, while it produced a slight increase in attraction to the competent candidate. Although the increase was not significant, the authors concluded that a blunder enhances the approachability of an otherwise superior individual and that this "humanizing" effect leads to increased liking.

Unfortunately, later studies failed to replicate these findings. Kiesler and Goldberg (1968) found that a blunder had no effect on attraction toward a competent other. Helmreich, Aronson and LeFan (1970) reported that a blunder lowered atraction toward another person irrespective of his competence. Finally, Mettee and Wilkins (1972) obtained results that contradict the humanization hypothesis. In one of their conditions, a blunder lowered attraction toward a competent person and it had no effect on liking for an incompetent person.

Taken as a whole, the results of the studies reviewed above are conflicting and they do not permit us to reach any firm conclusions concerning the effects of inferior performance or a blunder on attraction (cf. Fishbein and Ajzen, 1975). Relatively minor procedural variations or differences in treatment combinations are found to influence the effect of a given independent variable. From an information-processing point of view such conflicting and inconclusive findings are to be expected. The studies under consideration have submitted subjects to experimental treatments designed to affect interpersonal attraction. On the basis of the information made available, the subjects are likely to have formed beliefs about the other person, but these beliefs were never assessed. Instead, attempts were made to demonstrate direct relations between experimental treatments and the measures of attraction.

The perceived attributes model of attraction suggests that in order to understand the effects of variations in some independent variable, it is necessary to examine how these variations influence beliefs about the other person. Once the effects on beliefs are known, the PA model can be used to predict attraction in the different experimental conditions. For example, in the Aronson, Willerman and Floyd (1966) experiment, subjects were exposed to various items of information about a candidate. Beliefs were probably formed about the candidate's intelligence, competence and ability, and perhaps about other attributes, such as his status, confidence, pleasantness, etc. Very different beliefs were probably formed in the high and low competence conditions. Introduction of a blunder toward the end of the interview may have led to the formation of new beliefs (O is clumsy, nervous), depending in part on the prior beliefs about O. In addition, the blunder may have changed some of the prior beliefs or it may have affected the subjective values of certain attributes associated with O. All these effects contribute to the final evaluation of O. Only when the subject's beliefs and attribute evaluations are assessed is it possible to understand the effects of a given independent variable on attraction.

Factorial experiments on attraction dealing with factors other than competence or quality of performance have also failed to produce conclusive results. For example, several studies have tested the "gain-loss" model proposed by Aronson and Linder (1965). The model deals with the effects of O's positive or negative appraisals of P on P's liking for O. Specifically, a negative-positive sequence is predicted to result in higher attraction than a positive-positive sequence (gain effect), and a positive-negative sequence is expected to lead to lower attraction than a negative-negative sequence (loss effect). Aronson and Linder reported a significant gain effect, but the loss effect was not significant. Later experiments have usually failed to replicate this study (e.g. Sigall and Aronson, 1967), and the results must, overall, be considered inconclusive (see Fishbein and Ajzen, 1972, 1975 and Clore, Wiggins and Itkin, 1975a for reviews of this research).

Eye Contact and Attraction

Recent interest in nonverbal communication has produced a number of studies dealing with the effects of various nonverbal cues on interpersonal attraction. Of particular interest in this context is the effect of eye contact on attraction. It has generally been assumed that attraction is positively related to the amount of eye contact (see Kleinke, 1972), but little empirical evidence was available until fairly recently.

One of the first studies to examine the effect of eye contact on attraction immediately revealed that the relationship is not as simple as originally assumed. Ellsworth and Carlsmith (1968) had an interviewer look at the female subject either very frequently or not at all. In addition, the content of the interview provided information that was either favourable or unfavourable to the subject. Liking of the interviewer was measured on a set of nine evaluative semantic differential scales. The effect of eye contact on attraction was found to interact with interview content. Liking increased with eye contact when the content was favourable, but frequent eye contact reduced attraction in the unfavourable content condition.

In a more recent study, however, Scherwitz and Helmreich (1973) reported exactly the opposite effects. In the first of three experiments using male subjects, three levels of amount of eye contact by a confederate were crossed with three levels of content favourability of the interview. In addition to a main effect of content favourability, the interaction was again significant. This time, however, liking (measured on a seven-point scale) increased with eye contact when the content was unfavourable and it decreased with eye contact under conditions of favourable content. In two additional experiments, Scherwitz and Helmreich found that the effect of eye contact on attraction was contingent upon the subject's self esteem and on whether positive content was personal or impersonal. The other's physical attractiveness had a main effect on attraction, but it did not interact significantly with eye contact.

In contrast, Kleinke, Staneski and Berger (1975) reported a significant interaction between eye contact and O's physical attractiveness. Under low eye contact, the unattractive interviewer was liked much more than the attractive interviewer. Under intermittent and high eye contact, there was a nonsignificant trend in the opposite direction. Other studies by Kleinke and his associates have revealed little effect of eye contact on interpersonal attraction (Kleinke, 1972).

From the point of view of an information processing approach to attraction, these conflicting findings are again not unexpected. Subjects in the studies reviewed were exposed to various items of information about another person, including his visual behaviour. Experimental manipulations in different studies may have produced very different beliefs about the person. His eye contact may have been interpreted differently, depending on the other information available. To understand why eye contact can have various effects on attraction, it is necessary to assess the beliefs subjects form about the person as a result of their interaction with him. Without such knowledge, results must appear inconsistent.

Interpretation of research findings in terms of the information processing approach has, up to this point, been entirely *post hoc.* None of the studies reviewed so far has made explicit use of an information processing strategy. In the following two sections (dealing with the effects of similarity and self-disclosure), some evidence will be reported which provides more direct support for the information processing approach to attraction.

Similarity and Attraction

In a considerable number of investigations, Byrne and his associates have demonstrated that the more similar *O*'s opinions, interests, or personality characteristics to those of *P*, the more *P* is attracted to *O*, (for reviews of this literature, see Byrne, 1971; Griffitt, 1974). In most of these studies, bogus strangers, described in terms of varying degrees of similarity, are evaluated on the interpersonal judgment scale mentioned earlier. Few investigators would question the conclusion that, under most circumstances, liking for the stranger increases with the degree to which his attributes are described as similar to those of the subject.

Byrne (1969, 1971; Clore and Byrne, 1974) has argued that similarity is related to attraction because it has reinforcement value. However, there is little direct evidence to support this view (see Fishbein and Ajzen, 1972). An alternative interpretation, relying on an information processing analysis, has been suggested by Ajzen (1974). According to this view, attraction is influenced not by the similarity of the information provided, but by the extent to which the similar or dissimilar information leads to the formation of positive or negative beliefs.[5] Since similar beliefs or personality traits tend to be

5. Based on Anderson's integration theory, Kaplan and Anderson (1973) have also provided an information processing explanation of the similarity-attraction relation. However, in contrast to Ajzen's constructive approach, Kaplan and Anderson adopt a mechanistic perspective.

evaluated more positively than dissimilar ones (e.g. Stalling, 1970), subjects will come to like a similar stranger more than a dissimilar stranger. In other words, similar items tend to convey positively valued information while dissimilar items tend to convey negatively valued information about the stranger. In the bogus stranger design, similarity and desirability of informational items are confounded, leading to potentially erroneous conclusions.

Several attempts have been made to separate the two confounded dimensions (e.g. McLaughlin, 1970, 1971; Stalling, 1970; Tesser, 1969). According to the information processing approach, if attribute similarity and attribute desirability are separated, similarity will be found to have little effect on attraction. The results of most studies support this expectation. For example, McLaughlin (1970) found that the effect of similarity was reduced to nonsignificance when attribute desirability was treated as a covariate. Similarly, Tesser (1969) reported a reduced correlation between similarity and attraction when attribute desirability was partialled out.

The most direct test of the information processing hypothesis was reported by Ajzen (1974) who devised an orthogonal manipulation of attribute similarity and attribute desirability. Since the study is reprinted in Section 2, it will be reviewed only briefly at this point. Hypothetical strangers were described in terms of 12 personality traits. These traits were either 75% similar or 75% dissimilar to those the subject attributed to himself; furthermore, 75% of the traits were either positive or negative. A semantic differential and the interpersonal judgment scale revealed only a significant main effect of attribute desirability; the similarity of the attributes had no significant effect on attraction.

The study also provided some evidence that these results were mediated by beliefs about the stranger formed on the basis of the 12 traits attributed to him. Subjects were asked to rate the desirability of each of the 12 traits. The subject's rating of each trait was multiplied by the strength with which that trait was attributed to the stranger in the personality description given to the subject. In accordance with the PA model of attraction, the resulting products were summed to provide an estimate of attraction. Correlations between this estimate and the direct measures of attraction were 0.59 for the semantic differential and 0.48 for the interpersonal judgment scale. Although significant, these correlations are only of moderate magnitude. However, it must be recalled that the estimate of attraction was based on the 12 attributes provided by the experimenter. Subjects may not have fully accepted some of these attributes, and they may have formed other (inferential) beliefs which also need to be taken into consideration.

Overall, then, research to date provides support for an information processing interpretation of the similarity-attraction relationship. Application of the perceived attributes model might also help account for the conflicting findings of several more recent investigations. For example, Kleck and Rubenstein (1975) manipulated another person's opinion similarity and physical attractiveness in a 2 × 2 design. Liking for the person was affected by her attractiveness but, in contrast to the findings of most studies, similarity had no significant effect on attraction. Novak and Lerner (1968) found that the effect of similarity on attraction interacted significantly with description of the stranger as normal or disturbed, but Bleda (1974) reported only a main effect of similarity and no significant interaction with adjustment. Since Byrne's interpersonal judgment scale was always one of the instruments used to measure attraction, the conflicting findings must be attributed to differences in treatments. In fact, close scrutiny of the studies reveals variations in treatments that are likely to have exposed subjects to different items of information in what should have been the same experimental conditions. For example, Novak and Lerner attempted to create the impression that the information about the other person's emotional adjustment had been provided inadvertently, whereas Bleda reported no attempt to create such an impression. As a result, subjects may have formed different beliefs about the other person. Had these beliefs been measured, it might have been possible to explain the apparently conflicting results of the two experiments.

Need Complementarity The same arguments can be made with respect to research on the theory of complementary needs (Winch, 1958; Winch, Ktsanes and Ktsanes, 1954). Tests of the theory have usually examined the need patterns of married or engaged couples, with contradictory results. Some studies have reported evidence for complementarity between the needs of married or engaged individuals while others have found no evidence for complementarity (for reviews see Berscheid and Walster (1969) and Seyfried in this book). Although measures of interpersonal attraction are usually not obtained in these studies, there is little reason to believe that such measures would exhibit more consistent effects of need complementarity.

One factor that may be in part responsible for the conflicting results is the difficulty of defining in advance whether or not one need complements another (Levinger, 1964). More important, from an information processing perspective there is no reason to expect that need complementarity will necessarily lead to attraction. Information concerning another person's needs will increase attraction if it leads to the formation of positive beliefs about that person, and — unlike the case of similarity — it cannot be assumed that complementary needs are evaluated more favourably than are noncomplementary needs. Again, to understand why information about O's needs, complementary or not, have a given effect on attraction, it is necessary to measure the information's impact on P's beliefs about O. Without such measures, results will appear to be inconsistent.

Self-Disclosure and Attraction

Research on the effects of self-disclosure provides an opportunity to further illustrate the importance of assessing the subject's beliefs about the stimulus person. It is often assumed that the disclosure of intimate information is a sign of a healthy, self-actualized individual (Jourard, 1971). Consequently, attraction toward a person is expected to increase with the degree of his self-disclosure.

Before turning to the empirical evidence, we can consider this issue from an information processing point of view. We saw above that similar items of information tend to be evaluated more favourably than dissimilar items, producing a rather consistent, albeit spurious, relation between similarity and attraction. However, there is little reason to assume that highly intimate information consistently associates the self-disclosing individual with more desirable attributes than does superficial information. The superficial information can easily produce more positive beliefs about the person than the intimate information, depending on the content of the information disclosed. It follows that no consistent relation can be expected between intimacy of self-disclosure and interpersonal attraction.

A review of the empirical literature supports this view (cf. Chaikin and Derlega, 1974). For example, Worthy, Gary and Kahn (1969) had female subjects exchange written information about each other, in response to questions that had previously been scaled for intimacy. A direct measure of liking showed that attraction increased significantly with intimacy of self-disclosure. A positive relationship was also reported by Jourard and Friedman (1970).

In contrast, Ehrlich and Graeven (1971) reported no effect of self-disclosure intimacy on attraction. Male subjects exchanged views with a confederate on a variety of issues. By using two different scripts, the confederate disclosed information of either high or low intimacy about himself. Two measures of attraction toward the confederate were found to be unaffected by this manipulation of intimacy. Other investigators have also reported no relation (Derlega, Walmer and Ferman, 1973), a curvilinear relation (Cozby, 1972), or interactions between intimacy of self-disclosure and other variables, such as the conventionality of the information disclosed (Derlega, Harris and Chaikin, 1973) and the timing of disclosure[6] (Jones and Gordon, 1972).

As might be expected on the basis of an information processing approach, intimacy of self-disclosure has not been found to have a systematic effect on attraction. Apparently, what is important is not whether the information disclosed is intimate or not, but rather whether it reflects positively or negatively on the person. Nevertheless, two potential effects of intimacy can be contemplated within an information processing framework. First, it might be argued that intimate information carries more implications (either favourable or unfavourable) than does superficial information. If so, the impact of self-disclosure on attraction would be greater for intimate than for superficial information. Second, it is conceivable that a person who reveals highly intimate information with undesirable implications will be viewed as honest, trusting, open, etc. That is, in addition to whatever negative beliefs are formed on the basis of the undesirable intimate information itself, the recipient of the information may also infer other more desirable attributes, an effect which would result in more liking than might otherwise be expected. Clearly, the occurrence of such indirect effects can be demonstrated only if P's beliefs about the self-disclosing other are assessed.

Some evidence for these arguments can be found in a preliminary investigation by Dalto, Ajzen and Kaplan (1975). The study's main purpose was to examine the extent to which attraction is affected by the intimacy of self-disclosed information, independent of the information's desirability. The investigators formulated a pool of 60 statements describing a female student. One sample of male and female subjects rated the extent to which each statement contained

6. Jones and Gordon (1972) actually manipulated information valence (positive versus negative) rather than intimacy. However, the negative information was also more intimate than the positive information.

intimate information (on a nine-point scale ranging from intimate to superficial) while a second sample rated the extent to which each statement contained desirable information (on a nine-point scale ranging from positive to negative). By selecting statements falling below or above the medians of the two distributions, four sets of statements were constructed, representing the four possible combinations of intimacy and desirability.

In the experiment itself, a new sample of male and female subjects were shown a set of 10 self-descriptive statements. They were told that a female student had been given a list of 28 statements and that she had selected the 10 statements as being most descriptive of herself. The subjects were also shown the list of 28 statements from which the 10 statements had presumably been selected. Actually, four standard sets of 10 statements were constructed. Each contained seven statements of a given intimacy-desirability combination, and one statement from each of the remaining three combinations. The following are examples from each of the four sets of self-descriptive statements:

Intimate-positive: I have a very warm and close relationship with my parents.

Intimate-negative: Sometimes I enjoy hurting people I love.

Superficial-positive: I enjoy reading good books.

Superficial-negative: I am always late for appointments.

Subjects were asked to evaluate the female student on Byrne's interpersonal judgment scale. Table 1 shows expressed liking for the stimulus person in the four experimental conditions; higher scores indicate greater attraction.[7] As might be expected on the basis of an information processing approach, the information's desirability had a strong and highly significant effect on liking ($F = 26.99$, $p < 0.001$), and the main effect of intimacy was not significant ($F < 1.0$). However, there was a significant interaction effect ($F = 4.18$, $p < 0.05$). Attraction was higher in the intimate-negative condition than in the superficial-negative condition, while there was virtually no effect of intimacy for positive information.

This finding would appear to support the previous argument that a person who discloses intimate, negative information about herself may be viewed as honest, sincere, open, etc. thereby increasing her attractiveness in comparison to a person who discloses superficial, negative information. Although beliefs about the stimulus person were

---

7. An evaluative semantic differential yielded identical results.

not elicited in a free-response format, subjects were asked to complete a check-list containing 100 of Anderson's (1968) personality traits. These data can be used to provide a tentative test for the information processing explanation of the significant interaction.

First, using Anderson's likeability norms, an estimate of attraction was computed on the basis of the perceived attributes model (see Ajzen, 1974 in Section 2 for a description of the procedure). This estimate was found to have a correlation of 0.73 with the direct measure of attraction. More important, examination of the check list revealed that, in comparison to the superficial-negative condition, the stimulus person in the intimate-negative condition was perceived as more serious, sincere, and modest. These findings can account for the differences in liking between the two conditions in question.

Table 1. Attraction as a function of intimacy and desirability of information

		Intimacy	
		Intimate	Superficial
Desirability	Positive	10.00	10.79
	Negative	8.07	6.63

II. Conclusion

Although necessarily brief, the above discussion of research on the determinants of interpersonal attraction has demonstrated how a constructive information processing approach can help clarify conflicting findings and can provide a conceptual framework for the integration of diverse lines of research. Subjects in experimental investigations of attraction are exposed to diverse items of information about another person. Sometimes, the information is provided in the form of discrete units, such as personality traits or opinion statements attributed to the other person. Alternatively, the information may become available as a result of the subject's interaction with the other person. The constructive approach assumes that subjects process the information to which they are exposed and that, in this fashion, they form a set of beliefs about the other person. Their attraction toward the other person is a function of these beliefs. Independent variables such as eye contact, similarity, complementarity, or intimacy of self-disclosure are likely to have an effect on attraction only to the extent that they influence the subjects' beliefs about the stimulus person. Given diverse histories and cognitive styles, different subjects will process the same information in different ways. It may therefore often be difficult to predict the beliefs that will be formed on the basis of a given set of information. To fully understand the effects of a given treatment, it is necessary to assess the beliefs in existence at the time that the measure of attraction is obtained. Measures of belief strength and of attribute evaluation can then be used to predict attraction in the different experimental conditions, as specified by the perceived attributes model (see eqn 2).

In contrast to this constructive approach, a mechanistic approach relies exclusively on the information provided in the experimental situation and, in most cases, it is assumed that different informational items combine additively. Our discussion of research on interpersonal attraction reveals the inadequacy of the linear model. Strong inter-actions are often obtained, in contradiction to such a model, and these interactions can usually be explained only with reference to formation of different inferential beliefs under different experimental conditions.

To be sure, investigators employing a mechanistic approach often make diverse assumptions about the ways in which subjects process the information available to them. Interactions between independent variables are typically predicted on the basis of such considerations. Similarly, *post hoc* explanations of unexpected interactions or lack of predicted effects also rely heavily on assumptions about unobserved cognitive processes. Unfortunately, independent evidence concerning these assumed intervening processes is usually not available since the subject's beliefs are not assessed. By way of contrast, the constructive information processing approach focuses explicitly on these cognitive processes. Instead of speculating about the possible effects of treatment combinations on belief formation, the PA model of attraction insists on the measurement of these beliefs and thus provides a means of testing the investigator's assumptions about the cognitive processes.

Note that the PA model does not specify the variables that influence beliefs about another person. Specification of such variables continues to be the province of the investigator's imagination. However, by emphasizing beliefs as the immediate determinants of attraction, the PA model permits a better understanding of the processes underlying formation of interpersonal attraction. Specifically, it helps understand why a given treatment had, or failed to have, an effect on attraction. In doing so, it may also provide a more appropriate theoretical account of observed relationships, as we saw with respect to the relations between similarity and attraction and between self-disclosure and attraction. According to a cognitive approach, attraction is determined not by similarity, self-disclosure, or eye contact but rather by the beliefs that are formed on the basis of the information that these variables provide.

4.

Self-Esteem and Interpersonal Attraction[1]

WOLFGANG STROEBE

Universitaet Marburg, Germany

Research on self-esteem and interpersonal attraction has concentrated on two seemingly unrelated topics: the choice of dating partners and attraction towards an evaluator. The choice of dating partners has been investigated assuming that one selects partners who are similar to oneself in those attributes (e.g. physical attractiveness, intelligence, socio-economic status) which determine a person's market value on the

1. I am indebted to Dr. Steve Duck, Prof. Alice Eagly, Prof. Gerold Mikula and Dr. Margaret Stroebe for their helpful comments on an earlier draft of this paper.

dating and marriage market. As we will see, there is only tentative support for the "matching hypothesis". Even more ambiguous are findings on the relationship between self-esteem and affective reactions to positive or negative appraisal from others. This question has become one of the major battlegrounds between consistency theory (we react positively to appraisals which are consistent with our self-evaluation and negatively to inconsistent appraisals) and esteem theory (we react positively to approval and negatively to disapproval; this reaction will be stronger, the more we are deprived in our need for approval). An attempt will be made to integrate the two areas and to provide a set of hypotheses about the consequences of high or low self-esteem for the initiation and development of interpersonal relations.

I. Self-concept, self-esteem and self-evaluation

Self-concept and self-esteem form together the attitude a person has toward his self (Secord and Backman, 1965). The *self-concept* can be understood as the cognitive component of the attitude, that is, the beliefs or cognitions a person holds about self (for example, that he is intelligent, fairly tall, etc.). *Self-esteem* refers to the affective component of the self-attitude, that is, the positive or negative evaluation of the beliefs about self. While most people will evaluate being intelligent rather positively, being tall may be evaluated positively by some people but negatively by others. Thus, the cognition that one is very tall may raise the self-esteem of a man, but lower the self-esteem of a woman.

   Self-evaluation as used here refers to both the person's evaluation of self on a given dimension and the process by which he arrives at that evaluation. In the former sense, self-evaluation indicates a person's evaluation of himself on some specific dimension, say physical attractiveness or intelligence, as distinguished from the more global evaluation of self referred to as self-esteem. Self-esteem is a result of all these specific self-evaluations. As there is no reason to assume that theories of impression formation do not apply to the impression one forms of oneself, a person's self-esteem at any given moment can be conceived of as an average of all these self-evaluations, each weighted by the specific importance attached to it (Anderson, 1965). Thus, the more important a given dimension of self-evaluation for the individual, the closer will be the relationship between self-evaluation on that dimension and global self-esteem. Since rejection-acceptance is one of the major determinants of self-esteem (Coopersmith, 1967; Epstein, 1973) it is likely that individuals' evaluation of their own attractiveness to other people is highly correlated with their self-esteem.

There are few objective standards available for self-evaluation. Hence, most self-evaluation will be arrived at by social comparison with relevant others (reference groups), either through *comparative appraisal,* or through *reflected appraisal* (Festinger, 1954; Jones and Gerard, 1967). In determining his standing on a given attribute dimension a person might compare his own performance to that of other persons (comparative appraisal) or he might find out what others think of him, where they place him on the dimension in question (reflected appraisal). To assess one's professional competence, for example, one can compare one's number of publications, the kind of journals one publishes in, one's teaching, with the achievements of other colleagues (comparative appraisal). Alternatively, competence can be assessed by finding out what colleagues think of one's work (reflected appraisal). One can use indirect cues, e.g. the number of times one is quoted in their publications, invited for talks, asked to review journal articles; or one can use direct cues, e.g. review articles written about one's work, verbal evaluations of one's competence. The difference between the more subtle and the more direct form of reflected appraisal is comparable to the difference between a disguised measure of attitude and a non-disguised measure — and the validity problems are very similar.

Self-evaluation is not an end in itself but a means to get information about our abilities, our strong and weak points. We have to evaluate our past performance realistically in order to predict correctly the *probability of future success or failure.* Such assessment should enable us to approach tasks which match our abilities and to avoid tasks which are far above us and thus offer no chance of success, or tasks which are far below us and thus offer no chance of satisfaction. *The perceived probability of success in a given area should be negatively correlated with perceived task difficulty but positively correlated with a person's self-evaluation on the relevant dimensions.*

II. Self-esteem and the choice of a dating partner

A. THE 'MATCHING' HYPOTHESIS

The expectation that people choose romantic partners who are similar in social desirability has been derived from the principle outlined above by Walster *et al.* (1966), who suggested that the social desirability of a dating choice plays the same role in partner selection as the task difficulty in the selection of tasks. To date a very attractive woman is more difficult than to date a less attractive one, because more attractive women have better chances on the dating market. They are, therefore, likely to be very selective in their dating and the probability of a dating request being accepted should be much lower than the probability of such a request being accepted by a less attractive and less sought after woman. *It is reasonable to assume, therefore, that the perceived and the actual probability of acceptance (success) decreases with increasing attractiveness of the chosen partner (task difficulty).*

The probability of acceptance should further depend on the attractiveness of the person asking for the date. The greater this person's own attractiveness, the lower should be the probability that a given partner would reject him. *Therefore, everything else being equal, the more attractive a person looking for a date, the more attractive should be the dating partner he would finally select.*

A third factor which the attractiveness of the actual dating choice should depend on is the *cost of rejection* by a given other in a given situation. Costs of rejection are psychological costs, such as embarrassment, ridicule, emotional upheaval, unhappiness. The higher these costs the less risk of rejection one should be willing to run. While one might take a little gamble for an attractive partner in a situation in which rejection entails very little embarrassment (e.g. computer dance), one would probably be unwilling to do so when rejection is very embarrassing. *Therefore, everything else being equal, the higher the cost of rejection, the less attractive should be the dating partner one would finally select.*

The cost of rejection will not only depend on situational factors (including role, status, and image differences), but there are also likely to be individual differences. For example, in accordance with esteem theory, low self-esteem individuals have been found to react more negatively to rejection than high self-esteem individuals (Dittes, 1959) and thus should be more likely to avoid it.

B. EMPIRICAL EVIDENCE

Although the matching hypothesis refers to matching with respect to general attractiveness or social desirability, research on matching has focused nearly exclusively on matching of physical attractiveness levels. This restriction has been justified with the argument that physical attractiveness is one of the most important determinants of dating choices among the college students typically serving as subjects. However, the fact that physical attractiveness can be more readily assessed than such vague constructs as a nice personality or a good character has undoubtedly contributed to the popularity of physical attractiveness as a measure of social desirability. This focus on the physical aspects of attractiveness restricts the generality of any conclusion one might draw from these studies.

The first study to test the matching hypothesis was conducted by Walster *et al.* (1966). Subjects in this ingenious field study were first year male and female university students who bought tickets for a computer dance and were completely unaware of taking part in a research project. They expected to be computer matched to a suitable partner on the basis of questionnaires they had filled out. In fact however, the pairing was done on a random basis. The physical attractiveness of all participants had been surreptitiously rated by four judges. During a dance intermission, subjects filled out a questionnaire containing among many other items the question how much they liked their partner and whether they would like to date the partner in future.

The results clearly underlined the importance of physical attractiveness in a dating setting. The more physically attractive a participant was, the more he or she was liked by his or her partner and the greater was the partner's interest in a continuation of the dating relationship. However, neither liking nor intention to date in future were affected by the subject's own physical attractiveness. There was no evidence that unattractive subjects were less interested than attractive subjects in dating attractive others or more interested in dating unattractive others.

Stroebe *et al.* 1971, suspected that the failure of the Walster *et al.* study to support the matching hypothesis was partly due to the fact that their situation contained a number of features which might have minimized subjects' fear of rejection. The fact that every participant had bought a ticket for the computer dance would indicate that he or she was not only unattached but looking for a date. Secondly, before filling out the questionnaire, subjects had already met the partner in a dating context, and thus reduced their fear of rejection. Furthermore, why should subjects try to improve on the matching already done by an all-knowing computer?

We therefore tested the matching hypothesis again in a laboratory experiment in which male or female subjects were shown a picture of a member of the opposite sex, purportedly an earlier participant of the experiment. The picture showed either a highly attractive, moderately attractive, or unattractive other. Subjects, who themselves were divided into three levels of attractiveness on the basis of self-ratings, had to indicate their willingness to consider the other person for a date. It turned out that although everybody was more interested in dating an attractive rather than an unattractive other, there was some evidence for matching. *Within* the general preference for attractive dates, attractive subjects were more willing than unattractive subjects to date attractive others and less willing to date unattractive others. No such matching tendency could be observed, however, when subjects were divided on the basis of external ratings of their physical attractiveness. The correlation between externally rated and self-rated attractiveness was only 0.17, which was probably due to the unreliability of the external ratings (one rater only!).

Further support for the matching hypothesis comes from an innovative study by Kiesler and Baral (1970), who experimentally manipulated the self-esteem of their male subjects by having them either fail or succeed on a fake intelligence test. The subject was then taken to a cafeteria where he was introduced to a female student and then left alone with that student. While great care was taken to make the meeting with the woman appear a coincidence, she was actually a confederate of the experimenters. She was either made up to look very attractive or to look rather mousy and unattractive. She chatted with the subject for about half an hour, while secretly recording all attempts at romantic behaviour made by the subjects, like paying for her coffee, asking her phone number, asking for a date, etc. As predicted, subjects with raised self-esteem showed more romantic behaviour with the attractive confederate, while the low self-esteem individuals behaved more romantically with the less attractive confederate. (It is likely that the self-esteem manipulation did not so much affect the perceived probability of acceptance as the perceived costs of rejection.)

Less clearcut were the results of two further studies conducted by Berscheid and Dion, and Walster and Walster, which were jointly reported in a paper by Berscheid *et al.* (1971). In addition to testing the matching hypothesis these studies also aimed at investigating more directly the process which supposedly mediates the matching tendency.

Matching, it was argued above, is the result of an approach-avoidance conflict. Everybody would prefer a more attractive to a less attractive partner. However, everybody would also like to avoid the unpleasant experience of being turned down, rejected. Thus, people should "pair-off" with a partner of similar attractiveness level, because, from an equity notion, such a partner should be the most attractive person still likely to accept him (or her).

One way to test this line of reasoning directly is to bring subjects into a situation in which the perceived probability of acceptance does not vary with the attractiveness of the prospective partner. Berscheid *et al.* (1971) attempted to achieve this in their two studies by telling half of their subjects that whoever they chose would have to accept the date. The other half were told that the chosen partner could refuse to keep the date if she (or he) did not like the subject. They expected to find matching only in the conditions where acceptance was doubtful, while no matching should occur where acceptance was assured. However, the probability of acceptance manipulation did not affect choice behaviour at all. The matching tendency was equally strong regardless of whether acceptance was assured or not.

The failure of this manipulation to affect choice is perhaps understandable. After all, the embarrassment of having one's invitation for a date turned down is only one of the costs of rejection. In a way, such costs are minimal compared with the costs of realizing after several dates and a great deal of emotional involvement, that one's partner's aim in entering a relationship has been very different from one's own. If one began a relationship in the hope that mutual attraction and mutual trust would develop, it would be more of a hindrance than a help to know that the partner had to come for the first date whether she (or he) liked it or not. Who wants to spend an evening with a date who just sits there, probably wishing to be somewhere else? This would have been what unattractive subjects might have had to be afraid of, if they decided upon the most attractive choice.

Equally ambiguous, though for different reasons, are the results of a study by Huston (1973). He attempted to eliminate the fear of rejection for half of his (all male) subjects by telling each subject that he would only be given a choice of partners who had already seen his picture and had indicated that they were interested in dating him (assured acceptance condition). Thus, even the physically most unattractive subject would be led to believe that the most attractive of the prospective partners had already agreed to date him, after having seen his picture. If it is the fear of rejection which leads the physically less attractive subjects to limit themselves to the less good looking partners, then this manipulation should lessen their restraint. The other half of the subjects had to choose a partner without knowing whether she would accept him (ambiguous acceptance condition). In both conditions, every subject had a choice of the same six females who, from the photographs he was shown, varied from highly attractive to unattractive. As expected, Huston found that subjects decided on more attractive partners when acceptance was assured than when acceptance was ambiguous. Furthermore, he found that subjects who in the ambiguous acceptance condition had to assess the probability of being accepted by that woman for each of the six photographs, rated that probability lower, the lower they rated their own physical attractiveness. However, this relationship could only be demonstrated for self-rated but not for externally rated attractiveness. Furthermore, contrary to expectations, Huston did not find actual matching in the ambiguous acceptance condition. Thus, although subjects rated the probability of being accepted by a prospective partner lower the lower they rated their own physical attractiveness, this did not appear to affect their actual choice of a dating partner from the six photographs.

One explanation for the failure of the Huston study to find evidence for matching in the actual choice of dating partners would have been that rejection had such minimal consequences. Being rejected by the chosen female in the ambiguous acceptance condition would merely imply the loss of a date with somebody whom one had never met and would never meet, unless she accepted. Thus, rejection would entail none of the embarrassment of real life, when one is turned down by somebody whom one likes and respects and whom one might have to continue interacting with for ever after, because she is a colleague or a coworker. However, this cannot be the whole explanation of Huston's failure to find actual matching, since Berscheid *et al.* (1971) reported matching tendencies in a setting in which the consequences of rejection were similarly negligible (the Berscheid and Dion study). Furthermore, as Huston argued, the fact that subjects chose more attractive partners when acceptance was assured than when acceptance was ambiguous would indicate that fear of rejection led to less attractive choices in the latter condition.

C. CONCLUSIONS

What then is the empirical status of the matching hypothesis? Of the six studies (Berscheid and Dion, and Walster and Walster, reported in Berscheid *et al.*, 1971; Huston, 1973; Kiesler and Baral, 1970; Stroebe *et al.*, 1971; Walster *et al.*, 1966) which investigated matching in dating choice, only two did not find any evidence for actual matching (Huston, 1973; Walster *et al.*, 1966). However, the four studies which supported the matching hypothesis reported relatively weak effects which could not be described as a preference for dates of similar attractiveness. Even though a person's own attractiveness level acted as a moderating influence on date selection, the dates finally selected were far above the choosers' own level of attractiveness.

It would have been rather important, therefore, to demonstrate that matching is a function of a person's perception of the probability of acceptance by a chosen partner, which in turn should be a function of the person's physical attractiveness. Of the three studies (Berscheid *et al.*, 1971; Huston, 1973) which attempted to manipulate subjects' perceptions of their probability of acceptance independently of subjects' self-evaluations, none was very successful. While Berscheid *et al.* found matching regardless of whether or not acceptance was assured, Huston did not find any matching under either condition. His failure to find matching even in the ambiguous acceptance condition also lessens the conclusiveness of his evidence that subjects' probability estimates in fact varied with their self-rated attractiveness in the way predicted by the matching hypothesis.

Although some of the principal investigators in this area are females and most of the studies employed subjects of both sexes, it is not quite clear how the matching hypothesis, as formulated above, should apply to women. According to traditional arrangements, male matching takes place through active overtures, which are then accepted or rejected by females. Female matching takes place through rejecting those who request dates. Since the matching hypothesis specifically pertains to whom one asks out, the hypothesis seems to be relevant to males only. Surprisingly, however, neither Berscheid *et al.* (1971) nor Stroebe *et al.* (1971) observed any sex differences in matching tendencies.

One also cannot help but feel exceedingly uneasy about the exclusive focus on physical attractiveness. Physical attractiveness may be an important determinant of partner choice, but even among college students there are many other factors of equal or greater importance. The impact of physical attractiveness in dating studies could have been enhanced by the fact that the samples investigated were already matched with regard to a great many important characteristics (e.g. age, education, socio-economic background) and that other important characteristics elude assessment. For example, as long as one can neither define nor measure an "interesting personality" or a "good character" it is not surprising that physical attractiveness wins out over personality variables. Furthermore, physical attractiveness is bound to come out strong in studies relying on first impressions.

These are obviously not arguments against a matching hypothesis, but merely against the impression that the physical aspects of attractiveness play an exclusive role in matching. The assumption that everybody wants to date Miss World, but that very few are chosen, divides the world into a few beautiful and happy people who get the partners they want, and the average who have to take second best, and thus should according to this view, never be completely happy. While this may be true for one's choice of a car it does not seem to be true for one's choice of a partner.

III. Self-esteem and attribution

A. SELF-ESTEEM AND REFLECTED APPRAISAL FROM INDIRECT CUES

The research reported in the last section provided tentative evidence that a person's self-evaluation affects his perception of the probability of acceptance or rejection by a prospective partner and that people tend to resist approaching a desirable prospective partner when they perceive the probability of acceptance as low. However, asking for the first date or being asked out is only the beginning of a long process of communication where the partners have to learn about their mutual feelings. Each tries to give the right cues and to read the partner's cues correctly. These cues are often so subtle that mistakes can happen easily. Walster *et al.* (1966), for example, observed that the correlation between participants' perceptions of how much their partners liked them and the actual liking after a computer dance was 0.23 for males, and 0.36 for females. Thus the subjects showed "some, though not a great deal of ability in estimating how much the partner liked him" (1966, p. 515). This is actually a problem which goes beyond the dating relationship and is typical for the early stages of any interpersonal relationship (cf. Cook's chapter in Section 3 of this book).

We are probably all fairly certain how our wives, husbands, or close friends feel about us, since we have had many opportunities to learn about their feelings. We are likely to be less sure, however, how a new colleague or a new acquaintance may feel about us. Behaviour of people engaged in the formal interactions typical for the early stages of a relationship is ambiguous with regard to underlying motives. One of the causes of this ambiguity is that formal interactions are strongly determined by various external factors such as a norm to be pleasant or polite (rather than honest). For example, if a man goes out of his way to take home a girl he has just met and is asked to stay for a drink, the offer could be a sign of attraction, but it could as well be mere politeness. Even if behaviour is not normatively determined, different motives could still underlie the same behaviour. For example, if at a cocktail party a relative stranger with whom one talked for a few minutes excuses herself to get a drink and never returns, one may conclude either that she found the conversation rather dull and pretended thirst to get away or that thirst was the true reason for her behaviour.

How does a person make inferences in situations such as these? It is likely, especially in such ambiguous situations, that people rely heavily on relevant past experiences. Thus, if a person felt (rightly or wrongly) that people had often been bored by his conversation in the past, he would consider the probability very high that this was the case in this particular instance as well. He would therefore tend to attribute the cocktail party incident to his dullness and the invitation of his passenger to politeness. To a person who feels that he has generally been witty and charming in the past, it might never occur that the party friend left for any reason other than thirst or that the passenger had any motive other than the desire to continue the conversation.

B. SELF-ESTEEM AND REFLECTED APPRAISAL FROM DIRECT CUES

While it is obvious that with indirect cues used for reflected appraisal attributions would not be easy, it might appear that such problems did not exist in the case of explicit evaluations. After all, a direct appraisal consists of a straightforward statement of a person's attitude, like "you cooked an excellent dinner", "I found your lecture fascinating", or "I don't like your dress", "I found your lectures irrelevant".

Unfortunately, however, such explicit evaluations are frequently even more ambiguous than more subtle reflected appraisals, since conveying evaluations is strictly governed by norms. Positive evaluations are particularly problematic, since it is considered good manners to hide one's true feelings from the target of disapproval. Although it would often be kinder to tell a hostess what one thought of her dinner or her dress (after all, she might improve) one typically does not only refrain from doing so, but even makes explicit statements to the contrary.

The process of inferring feelings from interpersonal behaviour, or more generally, of inferring dispositions from acts, has been thoroughly analysed by a number of theorists (e.g. Bem, 1972; Heider, 1958; Kelley, 1967; Jones and Davis, 1965). The basic assumption which is shared by these attribution theories, is that the degree to which attitude and behaviour are seen as correspondent is a function of the relative weight assigned to internal versus external factors. A person will be perceived as holding attitudes consistent with his behaviour if the behaviour is not seen as coerced by situational pressures.

The inference of attitude from explicit statements of opinion has recently been investigated by Jones and Harris (1967) and Jones *et al.* (1971), who tested a number of predictions derived from correspondent inference theory (Jones and Davis, 1965). In a series of experiments in which subjects had to infer a speaker's attitude towards some issue (e.g. segregation, drug use) from his speech, Jones and his coworkers demonstrated that even if the perceivers were informed that the speaker had been instructed to take a given position, their attributions of his "true" attitude was still affected by the position taken in the speech. A person who gave a favourable speech was perceived as having a more favourable attitude than a person presenting an unfavourable speech (unless the speech was very weak). However, while in the "free choice" condition attributions were fully determined by the position taken in the speech, attribution in the "no choice" condition appeared to be a joint result of the position taken in the speech *and* of the perceivers' "prior expectations" regarding the speaker's attitude. Thus, if the perceivers expected the speaker privately to hold a favourable attitude and he in fact gave a favourable speech, it did not matter for the perceivers' attributions whether the speech was given under "choice" or "no choice" instructions. The speaker was always perceived as holding an extremely favourable attitude. If, on the other hand, the speaker took an unfavourable position, contrary to the private beliefs he was expected to hold, attributions were markedly affected by the instructions under which the speaker was allegedly acting. If he was under "free choice" instruction the perceivers apparently dismissed their prior expectations and attributed an unfavourable attitude correspondent with the direction of the speech. If, on the other hand, the speaker acted under "no choice" instructions, the perceivers were apparently in a conflict whether to rely on the speech or on their prior expectations. They resolved this conflict by attributing a moderately unfavourable attitude.

The results of these studies apply directly to the process of inferring an evaluator's "true" attitude from his evaluation. The norm to be polite, or the power one may have over the evaluator, constitute precisely such situational pressures which coerce people to give positive evaluations. For example, at the end of a dinner party, everybody has to praise the meal, since to criticize it or even to say nothing would be exceedingly rude. The hostess, therefore, cannot assume that her guests really hold the attitude corresponding to their stated opinions.

Extrapolating from the Jones and Harris (1967) and Jones *et al.* (1971) results, the correspondence of the target's inference in such situations should depend on his "prior expectations". What would determine the target's prior expectations in the typical situation where his performance or some aspect of his personality is evaluated? It seems most reasonable to assume that we expect other people to evaluate us as we evaluate ourselves. For example, the dinner hostess's expectations should be determined by her own evaluation of her cooking abilities in general and the meal she prepared in particular. If she considered the meal a success, she should expect her guests to feel likewise and therefore accept the correspondent inference that the compliments reflected their "true" attitudes, while she should make a less corres-pondent inference if she felt the meal was a flop.

A study by Stroebe *et al.* (in press) supported this prediction. Subjects of high or low chronic self-esteem were led to believe that another subject would evaluate them on the basis of a personality questionnaire they had filled out. In fact, they received either a positive or a negative standard evaluation. They were told that the other subject would act either under "sincere" or under "role-playing" instructions. Subjects under "sincere" instructions would write an honest evaluation expressing their own feelings. Under "role-playing" instructions some of the subjects would be instructed by the experi-menter to write a positive evaluation while others would be instructed to write a negative evaluation. It was the subjects' task to decide, from reading the evaluation, under which instructions it had been written. As predicted, low self-esteem subjects felt that the negative evaluation was sincere and the positive one role-playing while high self-esteem subjects came to the opposite conclusions.

C. CONCLUSIONS

The results of the studies of Jones and his coworkers suggest that people who give positive evaluations should be perceived as holding positive attitudes, even though there are normative pressures constraining their evaluations. However, how positive the "true" attitude of the evaluator is perceived by the target person will depend, according to Stroebe *et al.* (in press) on the target's self-evaluation. If the appraisal is consistent with the target's self-evaluation a more extreme attitude should be attributed than if the appraisal is inconsistent with the target's self-evaluation.

Since, unlike the situation created in the Stroebe *et al.* study, situational pressures in real life usually act towards positive appraisal, inferences should typically be more correspondent in the case of negative appraisals. After all, by taking a negative position the evaluator is counteracting situational pressures, and out-of-role behaviour is always more informative than in-role behaviour (Jones et al., 1961). Whether the target will infer, however, that the other person really believes in his judgement, or whether the target will suspect that the negative appraisal is merely used for other purposes (e.g. to humiliate or hurt him), should depend on the specific situation. It appears likely, however, that with an increasing inconsistency between evaluation received and self-evaluation, the target will increasingly tend to assume other motives.

IV. Self-esteem and attraction towards an evaluator

A person's perception of the feelings of others for him is affected by his self-esteem. As argued in the last section, the same actions, even explicit evaluations, may be interpreted as reflecting different degrees of liking or disliking depending on the perceiver's self-esteem. However, self-esteem does not only affect our perceptions of others' feelings for us, it also moderates the affective reactions aroused by such perceptions. There are theoretical reasons to believe that even if high and low self-esteem individuals did not differ in the perceptions of such feelings, they would still differ in their affective reactions. Research on this issue has mostly been guided by two theoretical approaches (esteem theory and consistency theory) from which conflicting predictions derive. Esteem theory postulates a need for a *positive* attitude towards self, while consistency theory assumes a need for a *consistent* self-attitude.

Exchange theory, which also allows explicit predictions regarding the effect of evaluative feedback on attraction, has had surprisingly little impact on research on this issue.

A. ESTEEM THEORY

According to the esteem theory formulated by Dittes (1959), a person's attraction towards other people may be considered a "function of two interacting determinants". Firstly, the extent to which the person's needs are satisfied by these others, and secondly, the strength of these needs. Assuming a multiplicative relation between need and gratification, a person who has a very strong need should react more strongly to instances of need gratification or deprivation than a person whose need is very weak.

The typical need (according to Dittes) which is satisfied in interpersonal relationships, is the need for "social acceptance". The strength of the need for social acceptance, like the strength of any other need, varies as a function of deprivation and satiation. The need for acceptance should be weakened when recently satisfied and strengthened after a period of deprivation. In addition to these short term fluctuations, there are individual differences in need strength due to more chronic deprivation or satiation. People who have a long history of task-related or interpersonal failure may be in more need for positive regard from others than people who have always had a great deal of social acceptance. Since such unsuccessful persons should also have lower self-esteem than people with a history of success, we would expect high self-esteem (HSE) individuals to find acceptance less rewarding and rejection less punishing than low self-esteem (LSE) individuals. Assuming that a person's liking for another person is a function of the amount of reward or punishment he receives from him, LSE individuals should react to positive evaluations with a greater increase and to negative evaluations with a greater decrease in attraction than HSE individuals. Thus, as depicted in Fig. 1, one should expect a linear relationship between the positivity of the evaluative feedback a person receives and the degree of attraction with which he reacts, with the slope of the function becoming steeper the lower the person's self-esteem.

The assumption that LSE individuals are more rewarded by positive evaluations and more punished by negative evaluations than HSE individuals is inconsistent with the judgemental model incorporated in

Thibaut and Kelley's (1959) exchange theory (see La Gaipa's chapter). Although Dittes and Thibaut and Kelley agree that attraction in a relationship is a function of the satisfaction or outcomes a person experiences in that relationship, the theories have discrepant implications for the dependence of satisfaction on self-esteem. According to Thibaut and Kelley, a person's satisfaction with a given outcome will depend on the distance of that outcome above or below the person's Comparison Level (CL) which is an *average value* of all the outcomes known to that person. Since we assumed that HSE individuals have a greater history of task-related as well as interpersonal success than LSE individuals, they should be used to better outcomes and consequently their CL should be higher than that of LSE individuals. It would thus follow that any given outcome would be experienced as less satisfactory by HSE rather than LSE individuals.

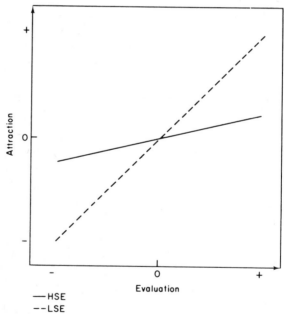

—HSE
--LSE

FIG. 1. The relationship between Self-esteem and affective reactions to positive or negative evaluations according to esteem theory.

That these predictions are inconsistent with Dittes' predictions does not imply that Dittes' model could not be interpreted in judgemental terms. If, inspired by Upshaw's (1969) variable-perspective model, one replaced the notion of a CL (modelled after Helson's (1964) adaptation-level theory) with the assumption that people judge any given outcome against the best and the worst (instead of the modal) outcome they have experienced in the past, then the increase in polarization of judgements with increasing need strength (which Dittes hypothesized) could possibly be accounted for. If judgements of a given outcome are determined by its distance from the most extreme good and bad outcomes (anchors) which a person takes into account when performing his judgements, then positive and negative evaluations could be judged more extreme by LSE rather than HSE judges, provided we assume that LSE individuals take less extreme evaluations into account (have a narrower perspective) when performing their judgements. It would still be difficult to understand, however, why LSE subjects should have a narrower perspective than HSE subjects. Unfortunately, there are no data available on the effect of self-esteem on judgements of the positiveness or negativeness of evaluations.

B. CONSISTENCY THEORY

The consistency position on affective reactions to positive or negative evaluations was originally formulated by Deutsch and Solomon (1959) who suggested "that if an individual evaluates some aspect of himself (as positive or negative) and another evaluates it similarly, the individual will tend to evaluate the other person favourably; if the evaluations are dissimilar, the individual will tend to evaluate un- favourably" (p. 97). For example, if a person thinks himself a good tennis player, he should like people who praise his tennis and dislike people who criticize it. If, on the other hand, he thinks he plays poorly, he should react to criticism with liking and to praise with dislike.

What happens if a person does not only have a low opinion of one aspect of his self, but has quite generally low self-esteem? "According to consistency theory, . . . we should like those who like us only if we like ourselves; if we dislike ourselves, we should dislike those whose feelings about us are positive and thus incongruent with our own" (Berscheid and Walster, 1969, p. 55). Thus, one should expect a monotonic relationship between the degree of approval or disapproval a person receives and the degree of attraction with which he reacts. Self-esteem should affect the slope of this function which should be positive for HSE and negative for LSE individuals.

Such predictions can in fact be derived from a number of consistency theories (e.g. Heider, 1958; Newcomb, 1961; Secord and Backman,

1965), although rejecting the source of a self-inconsistent evaluation is only one of several ways to re-establish consistency. According to Heider (1958), for example, a person P who evaluates (positively or negatively) some aspect of himself, say his gamesmanship, and receives an inconsistent evaluation from another person O, might react by disliking O. However, alternatively, he might change his mind about his gamesmanship or he might reinterpret the other's evaluation to make it consistent with his own. He might even react by differentiating O into a generally nice guy (O_1+) who just does not know a thing about games (O_2-). Which of these strategies a P will use to achieve balance is not specified by these theories, although it seems likely that he will change the weakest (least polarized) link. Since in most studies on affective reactions to evaluations P and O were complete strangers, it seems theoretically reasonable to assume that P should establish balance by adopting a positive attitude towards a consistent evaluator or a negative attitude towards an inconsistent evaluator.

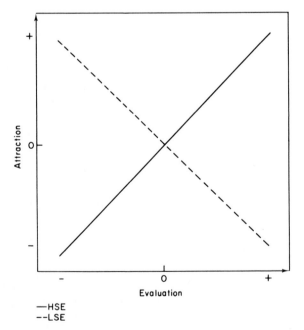

—HSE
--LSE

FIG. 2. The relationship between Self-esteem and affective reactions to positive or negative evaluations according to consistency theory.

C. EMPIRICAL EVIDENCE

The experiments designed to test the theoretical positions outlined above followed a simple paradigm. High and low self-esteem (self-evaluation) subjects received false positive or negative evaluative feedback from another person. They then had to indicate their attraction towards the evaluator. In an attempt to eliminate differences in attribution over the various experimental conditions, great care was taken in all studies to rule out suspicion that the evaluator was under any external pressure or had anything to gain by giving a particular evaluation.

Berscheid and Walster (1969) and Gergen and Marlowe (1970) pointed out that this basic similarity tends to distract from some important differences between these studies. One such difference is that some experimenters varied self-evaluation on some very specific dimension, e.g. task performance or personality trait, while others varied global self-esteem. A second important difference is that the fake positive or negative evaluation from another person consisted in some studies of specific evaluations of performance or trait, while in other studies it consisted of global indications of like or dislike. It is only the studies which combined a variation of specific self-evaluation with a specific evaluative feedback which support the consistency position. Studies which used global self-esteem manipulations typically supported the esteem-theory predictions.

The prototype of the self-evaluation studies is the classic experiment by Deutsch and Solomon (1959). Self-evaluation was manipulated by giving female subjects false feedback about their performance, making it either one of the best or one of the worst of the team. Each subject then received an evaluation from another team member which either evaluated her performance positively, indicating that she was a desirable team member, or negatively, indicating that she was undesirable. The subjects had to indicate their feelings about their evaluator. Subjects with a high self-evaluation liked the positive evaluator more than the negative evaluator while subjects with a low self-evaluation showed no statistically reliable preference for either note-sender.

Deutsch and Solomon interpreted their results as due to a combination of two tendencies, namely a positivity bias to prefer positive evaluations to negative ones, and a consistency bias to prefer consistent evaluations over inconsistent ones. While the two tendencies act in the same direction for subjects with a high self-evaluation, they cancel each other out for subjects with a low self-evaluation. This assumption is reasonable, since positivity effects have been reported in most studies otherwise supporting consistency predictions (e.g. Stroebe *et al.*, 1970).

Further evidence for both a positivity bias and a consistency tendency comes from studies by Berscheid and Walster (1968) and Eiser and Smith (1972). Subjects in the Berscheid and Walster experiment received four personality evaluations which were supposedly written by four subjects, but were in fact composed by the experimenters using self-concept questionnaires the subjects had filled out previously. In these questionnaires subjects had indicated which traits were very typical and which were atypical for them. They had also rated the positiveness of each trait. Each evaluation consisted of eight traits. Two of the evaluations listed only positive traits, while the other two included one negative trait. Crosscutting this, half of the evaluations consisted of traits characteristic for the subjects, while the other half consisted of uncharacteristic traits. When subjects indicated their liking for each of the evaluators, Berscheid and Walster found main effects for positivity as well as for accuracy. Positive evaluators were liked more than negative evaluators and accurate (consistent) evaluators more than inaccurate (inconsistent) ones. Similar results were obtained in the Eiser and Smith (1972) study which used a comparable manipulation, except that their subjects were role-playing the situation.

It is interesting to compare the relative strength of the consistency and the positivity tendencies in these three studies. The effects were of approximately equal strength in the Deutsch and Solomon experiment, while the consistency effect was stronger than the positivity effect in the Berscheid and Walster study and the reverse was true for the Eiser and Smith results.

What determines the strength of these effects? Positive evaluators are preferred over negative evaluators presumably because positive evaluations are more rewarding than negative evaluations. One factor influencing the strength of the positivity effect should therefore be the evaluative difference (difference in scale value) between the two evaluations. Consistent with this expectation, the Eiser and Smith (1972) study which showed the stronger positivity effect also used a greater evaluative distance than the Berscheid and Walster (1968) study.

A second factor which should affect the strength of the positivity effect is the subjects' global self-esteem. Low Self-Esteem subjects should react with greater increase in attraction to positive evaluations and with greater decrease in attraction to negative evaluations than HSE subjects. This prediction has not yet been tested.

The strength of the consistency effect should depend on the degree of inconsistency between subjects' self-evaluations and the evaluation feedback they receive. Support for this assumption comes from a study by Dutton (1972) who manipulated the stability of the self-evaluations of his subjects in an experiment which was basically similar to the Deutsch and Solomon study. Subjects in the stable self-evaluation condition received on repeated trials consistent positive or negative performance feedback. In the unstable self-evaluation condition, subjects either got less feedback or feedback which was somewhat inconsistent from trial to trial. Subjects then received an evaluation which supposedly came from another subject and indicated that the other would like him on a team which was to be formed. While there was a strong preference for consistent evaluators and a minimal positivity effect in the stable self-evaluation condition, the positivity effect was very strong and the consistency effect minimal in the condition in which subjects were least able to establish a stable self-evaluation (fluctuating feedback).

When global self-esteem is varied and the evaluative feedback consists of global indications of like or dislike the question of accuracy or inaccuracy will not arise and thus there should be no consistency effect. There should only be a positivity effect which, for reasons outlined earlier (esteem theory), should be stronger for high than for low self-esteem subjects.

The classic study supporting this assumption has been conducted by Dittes (1959). During a group discussion subjects of high or low self-esteem (as measured by a global self-esteem questionnaire) received false feedback that they were either accepted or rejected by the other members of the group. At the end of the discussion subjects' attraction for the group was measured. As expected, attraction was found to be greater for members who were well rather than poorly accepted by the group, the difference being greater for subjects with low rather than high self-esteem.

Similar results were obtained in two studies by Walster (1965) and Jacobs *et al.* (1971) in which global self-esteem of subjects was manipulated by providing them with false negative or positive feedback about their personality. Subjects were told that personality tests which they had filled out had indicated that they were weak, unoriginal personalities, or great and creative persons. In the Walster (1965) study, the female subjects were approached by a handsome male (confederate) who asked them for a date. It was found that subjects with experimentally lowered self-esteem indicated greater liking for the confederate than subjects whose self-esteem had been raised (Walster also ruled out an explanation in terms of differential response styles by having her subjects rate their attraction to another person as well). In the second study by Jacobs *et al.* the dating skills of male subjects were positively or negatively evaluated by a girl. When attraction ratings for the girl were elicited, subjects with lowered self-esteem liked the accepting girl more and the rejecting girl less than did subjects whose self-esteem had been experimentally raised.

D. UNRESOLVED ISSUES

It is characteristic for solutions to complex puzzles that a few pieces do not seem to fit. The non-fitting pieces in this case are studies which supported esteem-theory predictions, although self-evaluation and specific feedback were varied. In a recent review article Jones (1973) discussed two blatant examples: his own study (Jones, 1966) and the Skolnick (1971) experiment. However, the Jones study differs from other studies in that the subject's attraction response was clearly intended for the people who had evaluated him positively or negatively, while in other studies attraction ratings are intended for the experimenter's eyes only. It is likely that this difference in procedure is responsible for subjects' tendencies to reciprocate in kind. To account for the findings of the Skolnick experiment is more difficult, since Dutton (1972) replicated the Skolnick manipulation in one of his conditions and got consistency results. Thus, of three studies (Deutsch and Solomon, 1959; Dutton, 1972; Skolnick, 1971) which are nearly replications of each other, two supported consistency theory and one esteem theory predictions.

There is another inconsistency, however, which challenges our whole understanding of the concept of self-esteem. Being intuitively convincing it has always been assumed (e.g. Berscheid and Walster, 1969; Crowne and Marlowe, 1964; Dittes, 1959; Gergen and Marlowe,

1970; Rogers, 1959) that self-esteem is negatively related to need for social approval. Unfortunately, several studies, using the Janis and Field (1959) Feelings of Inadequacy Scale as a measure of self-esteem and the Marlowe-Crowne Scale (Crowne and Marlowe, 1964) as a measure of need for social approval, have recently observed the reverse relationship. For example, Hewitt and Goldman (1974), using male subjects only, reported significantly lower Marlowe and Crowne (M-C) scores for subjects who scored low rather than high on self-esteem. Döring and Seipel (1975), using a German version of each scale on a small sample of students, found a significant correlation ($r = 0.46$) for their male subjects SE and M-C scores. Grabitz-Gniech (1971) who did not separate her subjects by sex, reported a correlation of 0.38 for her total sample of nearly 200 college students.

This positive relationship between SE and M-C scores is not even difficult to interpret if one remembers that the M-C scale had originally been designed to identify individuals with a tendency to present themselves in an overly favourable light when answering personality tests. Such persons should also present themselves as competent, self-assured, successful in interpersonal relationships when filling out the self-esteem test and should thus receive a high score for self-esteem.

Hewitt and Goldman (1974) assumed that subjects who scored high on the M-C scale have low self-esteem but receive high scores on the SE scale by answering items dishonestly. Results of their experiment appear to support this interpretation. Those subjects with high scores on SE and M-C scale, reacted to positive or negative evaluations similarly to the LSE subjects (who all had low M-C scores). Both groups of subjects reacted with a greater increase in liking to a positive evaluator and a greater decrease in liking towards a negative evaluator, than the HSE subjects with low M-C scores.

However, if one finds that, contrary to expectations, there are LSE subjects with a low need for approval, is it justifiable still to rule out the possibility (as Hewitt and Goldmann do) that there are likewise HSE subjects with a high need for approval? Maybe the "true" scores of self-esteem and need for approval are unrelated. This possibility cannot be ruled out, since the positive correlation between the two scales could still be accounted for in terms of dishonest responses of those LSE subjects who have a high need for approval. This assumption, however, is inconsistent with our present understanding of the development of both self-esteem and the approval motive.

E. CONCLUSIONS

What then is the empirical status of esteem and consistency theories? Esteem theory predictions have been well supported. In practically all studies reported in the last section, individuals have been attracted to positive rather than negative evaluators. This positivity effect appears to be stronger for individuals with low rather than high global self-esteem, although the latter difference has not been tested in studies manipulating self-evaluation on specific dimensions. Our problem is not in demonstrating but in interpreting these effects, since the findings of Döring and Seipel (1975), Grabitz-Gniech (1971) and Hewitt and Goldman (1974) raise some doubt concerning the precise relationship between self-esteem and need for social approval and thus challenge the assumption of esteem theory.

Consistency theory predictions have only been supported in studies in which a specific evaluation was clearly inconsistent with a specific self-evaluation of the subject. As Mettee and Aronson (1974) argued however, this kind of inconsistency might have made the target of the evaluation suspect that the evaluator did not express his true opinion, due to some external pressure. Thus, when receiving self-inconsistent evaluations the targets might have made less correspondent inferences than in the case of consistent appraisals. This assumption leads to predictions which are discrepant with consistency theory only in the case of negative evaluations. Then consistency theory would predict greater liking for the consistent rather than the inconsistent negative evaluator, while an attribution interpretation would lead to the reverse expectation, since more correspondent (more extreme) attributions would be made in the case of the consistent evaluator. The studies reported in the last section above (Berscheid and Walster, 1968; Deutsch and Solomon, 1959; Dutton, 1972; Eiser and Smith, 1972) have typically reported a preference for the consistent over the inconsistent negative evaluator. Thus, in line with consistency expectations, it appears that people dislike others who make inaccurate evaluations. It is doubtful, though, whether one has to draw on consistency theory to explain such findings. Consistency theory would have been more convincingly supported, if such effects had been demonstrated for self-inconsistent global evaluations.

V. Some final thoughts on the self-concept

In the preceding discussion of the effects of self-esteem on interpersonal attraction it was implicitly assumed that a person's self-concept, though not a complete mirror of social reality, was correlated with the outcomes he has obtained through his experience. Thus, a person's knowledge of the degree of his desirability to the opposite sex would help him to choose the most attactive partner whom he was likely to get (section II above). A person's knowledge of his abilities and interpersonal skills would help him to interpret the actions directed towards him (section III above) and it would influence his reactions to praise or criticism (section IV above).

This conception of the self-concept as a fairly undistorted reflection of social reality, checked and rechecked continuously via social comparison, seemingly contradicts notions such as Rogers' (1959) that people often distort their experience if it is inconsistent with their self-concept; or Aronson's (1969) reformulation of dissonance theory which postulates that dissonance is aroused by the realization that one's behaviour is inconsistent with one's self-concept and the findings that such dissonance is typically reduced by bringing one's perception of the behaviour in line with the self-concept, rather than changing the self-concept.

However, are these assumptions really contradictory? I do not think so. Epstein (1973) recently likened the self-concept to a "theory that the individual has unwittingly constructed about himself as an experiencing, functioning individual", and which is "part of a broader theory which he holds with respect to his entire range of significant experience" (1973, p. 407). Like any theory which has been supported by a great deal of evidence, an individual's "self-theory" is not rejected at the first instance of disconfirming experience. If, for example, I consider myself a good tennis player and I have just lost a game against a beginner, I will not suddenly reject this long-established notion of my playing abilities but look for alternative explanations of my failure, such as bad form or bad equipment. Or if I have considered myself an honest person all my life and I have just told a lie, I will also look for alternative explanations, such as that I did it for a very good purpose or that what I said was not all wrong. Strangely enough, while such behaviour is fully accepted in collecting evidence for scientific theories it is frowned upon for an individual's "self-theories". However, it seems rational and parsimonious since rarely in everyday life can the cause of an event be established beyond reasonable doubt and therefore an individual's "self-theory" should not be rejected with the first instance of contradictory evidence. Only if the "self-theory" is maintained in spite of mounting evidence to the contrary can one speak of an unrealistic self-concept.

It is through attribution processes that one maintains the balance between interpreting events to make them consistent with one's prior experiences and changing one's self-concept to adapt it to inconsistent experiences. As long as these tendencies are well balanced, the self-concept offers the frame of reference for realistic evaluation and interpretation of an ever changing flow of experiences.

5.

The Stimulus-Value-Role (SVR) Theory of Dyadic Relationships[1]

B. I. MURSTEIN

Connecticut College, New London, Connecticut, USA

Stimulus-Value-Role (SVR) Theory is a general theory of the development of dyadic relationships. Designed initially to account for courtship, it has been extended with slight modification to account for friendship and husband-wife relationships as well (Murstein, 1971, 1976).

1. This chapter is a somewhat revised version of the theory set forth in *Who will marry whom? Theories and research in marital choice* (Murstein, 1976).

It is an exchange theory, positing that in a relatively free choice situation, attraction and interaction depend on the exchange value of the assets and liabilities that each of the parties brings to the situation. The kinds of variables that influence the course of development of the relationship can be classified under three categories: stimulus, value comparison, and role. The variables are operative during the entire course of courtship, but they are posited to be maximally influential at different stages of the courtship. Each of the three stages reflects, by its name, the kind of variables most influential during that period (e.g. stimulus variables are most influential in the stimulus stage).

The chief concern here will be the theory's ability to explain marital choice. However, a theory of attraction to a dyadic relationship cannot aspire to perfect accuracy in predicting marital choice for a number of reasons. First, the search for a marital partner is often highly competitive. Individuals with a large number of interpersonal assets generally have many potentially marriageable partners. It is possible, therefore, that any given relationship in which they are involved may be highly successful, but their other relationships, not examined, may be even more successful. Focusing on a given relationship, therefore, might distort the conclusions about the probability of the relationship terminating in marriage.

Second, individuals differ in their desire to marry. An individual who values marriage as a status very highly may be less stringent in his requirements for dyadic compatibility than an individual who is not eager to rush into matrimony.

Although society has traditionally educated its youth to expect that close heterosexual dyadic relationships between unmarried youths will terminate in marriage, it is evident that more individuals than previously are courting longer and cohabitating without the benefit of matrimony. An increasing number (though still but a small fraction of the population) speak of having a close monogamous relationship without marriage. These factors, too, contribute to the imperfectness of dyadic closeness as a prognosticator of marriage.

Other factors influencing the incidence of marriage are timing, critical incidents, and the social network. "The right person at the wrong time" is a plaint often mentioned by individuals who met highly compatible individuals at a time when they were not ready for marriage. Critical incidents such as a job transfer of one member of the couple to another city may precipitate marriage in some courtship couples but terminate it in others, depending on the developmental stage of the relationship. Last, the social network, the relatives, friends, business associates of the couples may influence courtship by their tendency to treat the pair as a "couple" rather than as individuals.

Courtship may be likened to a slowly accelerating conveyor belt whose destination is matrimony. An individual may jump off relatively easily in the early stages of courtship, but as the destination is approached it becomes rather hazardous, interpersonally speaking, to jump off — there would be a great deal of disappointment and embarrassment in explaining the circumstances to everybody. Depending on the pressure applied by the particular network and the courage of the individual, some individuals may be "conveyed" into marriage despite a late discovery of less than desirable compatibility. These various factors contribute to the conclusion that dyadic compatibility and marital choice are not synonymous. Nevertheless, they are sufficiently correlated so that an understanding of heterosexual dyad formation can lead to an understanding of marital choice.

The remaining portion of the chapter will consist of a discussion of the exchange aspects of SVR theory, followed by an elaboration of the kinds of variables which influence both dyad formation and the various stages of courtship.

I. Exchange in courtship

The exchange model of interpersonal transactions involves the use of some elementary economic concepts for explaining social behaviour (Thibaut and Kelley, 1959; Homans, 1974; Blau, 1964; see La Gaipa's chapter here for a discussion of exchange in another context). Essentially, these approaches maintain that each person tries to make social interaction as profitable as possible, *profit* being defined as the rewards he gains from the interaction minus the costs he must pay. By *rewards* are meant the pleasures, benefits, and gratifications an individual gains from a relationship. *Costs* are factors which inhibit or deter the performance of more preferred behaviours. A young man living in the Bronx, for example, might like a young lady from Brooklyn whom he met while both were at a resort. Back in the city, however, he may doubt that the rewards he might gain from the relationship would be worth the costs in time and fatigue of two hour subway rides to Brooklyn.

Closely allied to rewards and costs are assets and liabilities. *Assets* are the commodities (behaviours or qualities) that the individual possesses which are capable of rewarding others and, in return, causing others to reciprocate by rewarding the individual. *Liabilities* are behaviours or qualities associated with an individual which are costly to others.

A man who is physically unattractive (liability), for example, might desire a woman who has the asset of beauty. Assuming, however, that his non-physical qualities are no more rewarding than hers, she gains less profit than he does from the relationship, and, thus, his suit is likely to be rejected. Rejection is a cost to him because it may lower his self-esteem and increase his fear of failure in future encounters (see chapter by Stroebe); hence, he may decide to avoid attempting to court women whom he perceives as much above him in attractiveness.

Contrariwise, he is likely to feel highly confident of success if he tries to date a woman even less attractive than himself where he risks little chance of rejection (low cost). However, the reward value of such a conquest is quite low, so that the profitability of such a move is also low. As a consequence, an experienced individual is likely to express a maximum degree of effort and also obtain the greatest reward at the least cost when he directs his efforts at someone of approximately equal physical attractiveness, assuming all other variables are constant.

So, although his interpersonal experiences push him towards some-one of objectively equal physical attractiveness, it is not necessary that his own perception of his physical attractiveness and that of his partner be equal. A person with high assets might be content if he got a partner whom he perceived as having as high assets as his own. He would be even happier, however, if he believed he were obtaining a partner with perceived assets higher than his own.

It is not necessary for his partner to complement his perception by perceiving him as lower than herself in assets. This is not necessarily a zero sum game with a winner and a loser. Both partners may think they are getting a partner whose assets exceed their own. In fact, it seems reasonable that when two persons each perceive their partner as having more assets than themselves, they should be more satisfied than when they perceive the partner's assets as only equal to their own. There are data that support this conjecture. Kelly (1949) found that marital adjustment was correlated with the tendency to perceive the partner as superior to oneself.

A. COUPLES NEED NOT BE MATCHED ON THE SAME VARIABLE

It is unnecessary for equity of physical attractiveness to be present in order for a viable relationship to occur. Given that a man and woman are sufficiently acquainted with each others' respective assets and liabilities, it becomes possible for the less attractive member to compensate for his "weakness" in a number of ways. Suppose, for example, that the man is unattractive and the woman is attractive. He might render services to his partner far above what she gives him, waiting on her hand and foot. Consistent with this thesis is a study by Dermer (1973) which reports that the greater a woman's attractiveness, the longer the vacations she expected to take when she married, and the fewer hours she expected to work to supplement her husband's income.

The attractive woman "pays" the man back through the status she confers on him by being with him, a cost (loss of status) she incurs in being seen with an unattractive man. Berscheid and Walster (1974a), reviewing the literature, have indicated that individuals perceived to associate with physically attractive persons gain in the esteem in which they are held by others, whereas those persons consorting with unattractive partners lose status. The outsider looking only at the physical attractiveness of the couple may find them terribly unbalanced with regard to their exchange value and wonder what she possibly sees in him. The people who know the couple well, however, know that she exploits him miserably and wonder why he puts up with it. Yet the situation is balanced if all of the variables are taken into consideration.

No mention has been made thus far of the status accruing to an individual solely on the basis of his sex, but men in our society have traditionally enjoyed a greater social, economic, and political status than women (Murstein, 1974). These advantages may be eroding, but they have not disappeared altogether. It follows, therefore, that men should be able to utilize this greater status to extract benefits prior to and during marriage. A physically unattractive man should find it somewhat easier to marry than a physically unattractive woman, and the United States statistics for 1969 indicated that for every 100 men and 100 women aged fifteen years and older, 31.4 men were married as compared to 28.9 women (Vital Health Statistics, 1972).

As women's liberation spokespersons have constantly stated, men are able to arrange marriage so that more of the benefits fall to them and more of the costs fall to women. Research by Knupfer, Clark and Room (1966) supports this contention in that married men were found to be more content and better adjusted than married women.

During courtship, as Waller has indicated through his "principle of least interest" (1938), the person least involved in the relationship can generally control it if the other is deeply involved. Traditionally, the power differential has been expressed by the man's sexual exploitation of the woman and by the woman's economic exploitation ("gold-digging") of the man. Since women acquired more status by *marriage* than men, the lion's share of exploitation in *dating* was enjoyed by men.

II. Factors counteracting equity of exchange

We have considered exchange to be equitable if the profitability of associating for the couple is objectively equal although, subjectively, it may appear to each partner that he or she is getting more than they deserve. This implies that if they perceived that they were getting less than they deserved they would be apt to dissolve the relationship. However, this is not necessarily the case, for a number of reasons.

A. COMPARISON LEVEL FOR ALTERNATIVES

One reason for staying in a negatively inequitable relationship is because the pool of eligibles for marriage is not homogeneously distributed for all possible locales. A person may find himself in a life space where rewarding members of the opposite sex are at a premium. Thibaut and Kelley (1959) introduced the concept of comparison level for alternatives (CL_{alt}) to indicate that before imbalance of exchange can threaten a relationship a viable alternative must exist for at least one member of the couple. A given boyfriend may be a pompous bore in some respects, but if there are no interested superior replacements, the pompous bore may still be preferable to no boyfriend at all. Of course, those who perceive that they have many interpersonal assets may be more risk-taking in this regard than those who perceive that they have few assets.

B. REWARDS AND COSTS OUTSIDE THE DYAD

If an individual's experiences outside of the dyad are highly satisfactory and in some way are related to the dyad, the rewards occurring extradyadically may suffice to balance out the unprofitability of the dyad *per se*. Thus, if a young orphaned woman finds a surrogate, kindly mother and father in the parents of her swain, she may overlook the less rewarding qualities of the swain himself. Likewise, a politician is unlikely to divorce his spouse in an election year even though his wife may have become a virago. A married politician may not gain many votes due to the fact that he is married, but a divorced politician loses some votes solely on the basis of his divorce.

C. REWARDS AND COSTS FROM WITHIN THE PERSON

So far it may seem as if most interpersonal transactions are largely commercial and self-seeking. If a good bargain cannot be obtained directly from the partner or indirectly through him, the dyad may seem to be in danger of breaking up. But, a moment's reflection suggests that much behaviour is not exchange oriented. Consider the heralded saints of antiquity and of modern times: Jesus, Saint Francis of Assisi, Albert Schweitzer, and Pope John XXIII. These individuals not only seemingly worked without an equitable return, but often returned good for evil. Explanations of high CL_{alt} or indirect rewards from others do not readily explain their behaviour.

It is evident that the rewards these individuals received were not external, but internal; hence they cannot, strictly speaking, be considered exchange. These individuals carried a model of appropriate behaviour within themselves, and their ability to emulate this model provided more gratification than any extrinsic reward. For such individuals to repay evil with evil might have achieved exchange equity, but the failure to fulfill the ideal-self image would have resulted in the high cost of guilt.

Internal reward systems are not the exclusive property of saints. Through societal inculcation, many of our roles are defined by inequitable requirements. Mothers dote on their offspring, philanthropists open their purse strings to the needy, and men sometimes offer their seats to women in the subways to fulfill their ideal-self concepts rather than in the hope of recompense.

Personal commitment to the partner also may be subsumed under the rubric of internal rewards. If the individual believed that he is in some way responsible for his partner's welfare or that he has committed himself to marriage by dint of continuing the relationship over a long period, he may remain in it despite inequities of exchange. In general, however, commitment serves to make terms of exchange more flexible rather than to banish exchange from consideration. For example, an undergraduate man and woman may commit themselves to each other, forswearing other heterosexual interests. But, intending to go to graduate school, they may find that the vicissitudes of fate and graduate departments consign them to graduate schools a thousand miles apart. The costs of infrequent contact and infrequent rewards may be augmented by the cost of foregone relationships with other attractive members of the opposite sex. If the costs of the old relationship exceed the rewards by a substantial margin, the commitment may not be enough to avoid the weakening and eventual termination of the relationship.

Some commitments are much more enduring—the commitments of marriage partners to each other, for example. The commitments in this case extend beyond that of concern for the partner. They involve concern over the welfare of the children, the disruption of status, uncomfortable explanations within the network of friends and associates, and possible conflict with religious commitments (Catholics are not permitted to divorce within the Church).

There are additional considerations beyond these external factors holding a relationship together. When an estranged couple earlier had obtained substantial rewards from the relationship, they may find it hard to believe that the costs each now feels will not eventually melt away. Marriages that have endured have undoubtedly had occasions when things seemed inequitable to at least one of the partners (costs exceeded the rewards within the marriage). Learning theory tells us that an intermittent reward system is extremely hard to extinguish. The individual is thus likely to assume that with patience the trouble will pass and things will get better again.

Also, with the passage of time, the feeling of personal commitment for the marriage partner becomes stronger. The individual increasingly internalizes the role of spouse so that it becomes partially free of reward considerations. The feeling of responsibility for the partner involves the cost of guilt if the partner is abandoned, and to this guilt consideration is added his own cost of starting a new life, with its attendant trouble, and necessary adjustment. Thus, breakups should occur more frequently among premarital couples as compared to marital couples, and among marriages of short duration as opposed to those of long duration, and that, in fact, is what happens.

D. REWARDS AS SYMBOLS

In the last part of the last stage in courtship, and in early marriage, individuals may be more interested in rewards as symbols than for their material value. Apples peeled by a spouse may taste much better than those peeled by oneself because the spouse's actions become a symbol for the love between the two.

E. ADAPTATION LEVEL

Exchange becomes even more difficult to assess when it is realized that even relatively "fixed" assets such as beauty or occupation, change with time. The ravages of time may diminish one's beauty. Adaptation level may eat away at one's interpersonal assets and capacity to reward (cf. Kelvin's chapter in section 3). An individual may relish the compliment of being declared a brilliant wit by his beloved, but the maximal delight in that statement occurs when first he hears it from her lips. When she says it again later on, it is somewhat diminished in value because the individual's adaptation level has shifted somewhat: thanks to the rewarding impact of the original compliment, the individual now thinks of himself as wittier than was the case before he received the initial compliment; consequently, with a higher self-perception of wittiness, a compliment of the same magnitude will be less rewarding than the same compliment was when delivered earlier.

Not only is the value of services (compliments are one example of services) a victim of adaptation level, but also our valuation of beauty. Once we perceive ourselves as meriting a beauteous companion, the reinforcement value of the companion diminishes.

If one person's assets are in services, another's are in status, everything is constantly changing in value, and much behaviour is not exchange oriented, can we presume that equity of exchange is a meaningful feature of dyadic attraction? I think the answer may be "yes", depending on the nature of the relationship and its stage of development. Certainly, exchange is generally the paramount concern in business arrangements.

Concerning more personal relationships, equity of exchange seems important in beginning or limited friendships and in budding romances. Friendships and romances are competitive in the sense that, generally, certain individuals choose each other out of a pool of possibilities, and these choices, according to SVR theory, are based on equity of profitability of the relationship.

As the relationship deepens, however, manifestations of exchange behaviour become more complex, symbolic, and finally impossible to evaluate. The individual's satisfactions from the relationship, as indicated earlier, cannot be reduced to exchange. In fact, the tendency to view a close intimate relationship such as marriage from an exchange orientation may often be considered pathological with respect to the relationship.

I have developed an Exchange-Orientation Scale for married couples, which measures the extent to which an exchange philosophy is used in interpersonal relationships. This scale has been shown to be strongly correlated with marital maladjustment such that unhappily married individuals manifest greater Exchange-Orientation scores than happily married ones (Murstein, Goyette and Cerreto, 1975; Goyette, 1975).

In sum, equity of exchange, though a most difficult concept to make operational, should be researched. Its importance in a relationship should be maximal in influencing choice of partner. Once a relationship develops, its role may be somewhat lessened, although it still plays an important role in most cases. The importance of exchange will vary from relationship to relationship depending on the strength of the mediating variables discussed earlier.

III. The stimulus, value and role stages of courtship

To understand the second basic concern of SVR theory properly, that is, the development of the stages of courtship, a few words must be said about the locus in which the relationship unfolds. This context may be categorized into "open" and "closed" fields.

An "open" field encounter refers to a situation in which the man and woman do not as yet know each other or have only a nodding acquaintance. Examples of such "open field" situations are "mixers", a large school class at the beginning of the semester, and brief contacts in the office. The fact that the field is "open" indicates that either the man or the woman is free to start the relationship or abstain from initiating it, as they wish. The contrary concept is the "closed field" situation in which both the man and woman are forced to relate in some manner by reason of the roles assigned to them by the environmental setting in which they find themselves. Examples of "closed field" situations might be that of students in a small seminar in a college, members of a "Peace Corps" unit, and workers in a political campaign. This interaction generally enables the individual to become acquainted with behaviour of the "other", which is then evaluated according to the individual's own system of values. This system is a compendium of values acquired in the process of acculturalization to the traditional or current tastes of society, values acquired from one's peers and parents, values derived from experience, and values resulting from genetically based predispositions, which may be labelled "temperament".

Individuals, of course, may be attracted to members of the opposite sex without necessarily contemplating marriage. The fact that almost all persons in the United States eventually marry, however, suggests that many of the heterosexual social encounters of young adults contain at least the possibility of eventual marriage; consequently, the general heterosexual encounter has been treated as the first step toward possible marriage.

A. STIMULUS STAGE

When two members of the opposite sex are in an open field (for example, a "mixer" dance) there generally has been a considerable amount of incidental screening which has eliminated many of the maritally non-eligible persons. If the mixer is held on a college campus, for example, attendance may be restricted to college students. Such students not only reflect educational homogeneity, but they are apt to show greater than chance similarity on variables which are correlated with education: socio-economic status, age, intelligence, and, to some extent, values. There remains, nevertheless, sufficient variability with respect to some other variables for an active selective process. Variables such as physical attractiveness, temperament and sex-drive, have undergone very little selectivity through the factors which bring individuals to college, and so interpersonal encounters between the sexes may continue to result in widely varying responses from joy to repulsion.

The motives in attending the mixer will vary from person to person. For some, attendance will avoid the isolation of being alone on Friday night. For others it will be an opportunity to find a lover and sex partner. Still others hope for a possible spouse or at least a companion for the evening. Suppose we derive a fictitious example to help us understand an unfolding relationship. We'll call the man Bart, the woman Angie. They do not know each other. Both are sophomores who during their first year at college made no permanent heterosexual attachments — they're still looking.

Both look around the hall where Bert Mustinelli and his Grinding

Millstone Five are playing some music. Each would like to meet someone interesting, but how can they tell who would be interesting and who not? In an open field, information about personality, value consensus, sex drive, and attitudes towards women's liberation is often not available prior to interaction. Therefore, they try to process whatever information they can get and make the best judgement as to the possible enjoyment that interaction with a given person might bring.

The process of approach depends on the reward value of the meeting, the subjective estimate of the probability of success, and the cost to self-esteem of failure. The description of this phase of the relationship has been dealt with elsewhere by a number of writers, including Davis (1973), Huston (1974) and Murstein (1976) but, in the interest of space, it will not be discussed further here. Instead I shall focus on the kinds of variables which, according to SVR theory, are apt to influence this decision process.

The first cues Angie and Bart get which influence their interest in initiating a contact are often prior to any interaction, and I have subsumed these cues under the classification of *stimulus* variables. These include the other's physical attractiveness — is he (she) the right height, well built, good looking? What does Bart's voice sound like? A rich, well-modulated baritone or an accented, nasal tenor? Is he dressed in a relaxed, sexy manner, or is he "establishment" formal?

There is ample evidence that the initial impact in a dating situation depends largely on physical attractiveness (Berscheid and Walster, 1974a). The importance of physical attractiveness resides not only in its being highly valued by society as a status conferring asset and in the fact that it is the only evidence of potential viability of the relationship prior to interaction. One must consider also that all kinds of desirable personality and intellectual attributes are ascribed to the beautiful. They are viewed as "more sensitive kind, interesting, strong, poised, modest, sociable, outgoing, and exciting . . . more sexual, warm, and responsive than unattractive persons" (Berscheid and Walster, 1972, pp. 46, 74).

Initial impressions are not wholly dependent on the senses, however. An individual's stimulus value also may include information about his reputation or professional aspirations, which precede him into the initial contact. That Ronald Rabbitfoot is a star running back for Podunk University may compensate for his less than classic Greek profile.

In sum, initial judgements are formed on the basis of perceptions of the other and/or information about him. These may be obtained without any interpersonal contact whatsoever, or on the basis of brief introductions. It is questionable how much such initial impressions correlate with subsequent marital happiness. Nevertheless, the stimulus stage is of crucial importance in the open field, for, if the other person does not possess sufficient stimulus impact to attract the individual, further contact is not sought. The "prospect" in question might make a potentially exemplary, compatible spouse, he might manifest value consensus and superb role compatibility with the perceiver, but the perceiver, foregoing opportunities for further contact, may never find this out. Consequently, persons with low stimulus attractiveness (especially those who are physically unattractive) are at a considerable handicap in an open field.

Because physical attractiveness is so highly valued it would seem logical that each individual would seek the most attractive partner available when information about other characteristics is not available. Enjoyment of a date when interaction has been relatively brief also would probably be mainly contingent on the attractiveness of one's partner.

There is evidence that this is the case when either of two conditions exist: (a) the individuals have relatively little experience in dating and have not undergone the costs of rejection; and (b) an experimental paradigm is constructed in which the individual is more or less guaranteed a date (Berscheid and Walster, 1974b; Huston, 1973). However, it is estimated that over 90 per cent of the current population will eventually marry, and it is evident that they are not all physically attractive. There is obviously a net decrement in beauty from ideal preference to actual choice. This change, it is postulated, follows the equity of exchange principle. Experienced individuals of equal attractiveness would possess equal rewarding power, in the absence of other information, and would tend to be drawn to each other pending further information about the other.

In short, we expect some tendency towards equity for a given characteristic (physical attractiveness, self-esteem, status, etc.), all things being equal, and in the next breath I must allow that often all things are not equal. A handsome man of low status, for example, might dampen his equity expectations regarding physical attractiveness of a high status woman. The likelihood of finding equity between two individuals for a given variable, therefore, depends on the importance of that variable to the courtship of the individuals concerned. If physical attractiveness is of paramount concern to both men and women, we should expect that a greater than chance equity of physical attractiveness between members of a couple despite the fact that all other things are not equal.

As a result of their experiences, individuals begin to build up an erotic ranking for themselves. They tend to gravitate towards their own level of equity. Movie buffs will recall the Bing Crosby, Bob Hope pictures in which Crosby always got the girl and Hope got the laughs. In a group of males going out together, certain individuals generally end up with the better looking girls and others with those of lesser attractiveness. Consistency in this regard suggests that experience has taught a certain economy of action, so that each individual focuses on the attainable rather than on the ideal.

B. VALUE COMPARISON STAGE

If a couple approximates equality in their stimulus variables, that is, the weighted amalgam of each individual's perceived stimulus attributes (physical attractiveness, status, poise, voice, etc.) is approximately equal, they may progress to the second (value comparison) stage of courtship. It is impossible to fix a specific time limit for passage from one stage to another because the importance of each stage and kinds and rate of interaction between individuals will vary from couple to couple.

Figure 1, however, presents a theoretical average curve for the importance and duration of the three variables. The curves in Fig. 1, strictly speaking, apply separately to each member of the couple. It is possible for one member of the couple to be in the stimulus stage, whereas his partner is in the value comparison stage. For example, he may be reacting primarily to her physical attractiveness, and she may have queried him on what he thought about women's liberation, equal careers, and childless marriage. He may not have found out much about her values so that a disparity exists not only with regard to what each considers important in the relationship, but also with regard to the stage of courtship each is in. This disparity is not necessarily inimical to the relationship so long as each is highly rewarded by the relationship.

For many couples, however, the deepening of the relationship advances in mutual fashion and reciprocity in social penetration is typical. When she asks about his values, she may in turn supply her own views on the topic in question, or he may ask her about these views. Thus, most couples should show some correspondence of movement through the various stages.

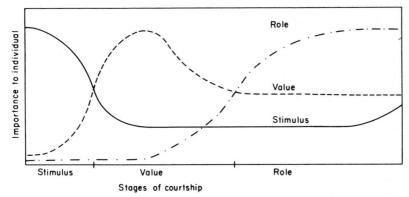

FIG. 1. Stages of courtship starting with Stimulus followed by Value and then by Role. Importance of each class of variable is shown throughout the three stages.

The termination of the stimulus stage may be defined as occurring at the point in the relationship when the stimulus variables, as a group, become less important to the relationship than the value comparison variables. Passage from the stimulus to the value comparison stage might occur in a matter of hours or it might take some weeks. It is also conceivable that such passage might not occur, but I shall deal with this eventuality when we have completed our description of the three stages of courtship.

The label "value comparison" has been used for want of a better name. I use the term value more as an inclusive rubric rather than in the narrow sense of the term. I infer under this term interests, attitudes, beliefs and even needs when they are seen as emanating from beliefs. The primary focus of the value comparison stage, in short, is the gathering of information by verbal interaction with the other.

Verbal interaction will surely be an important feature of the role stage which succeeds the value comparison stage. But in the role stage, the emphasis will be more on the dyadic relationship and will include commitment positions regarding depth of feeling for the other and desire for permanency, confirmation of the self image, and accuracy in predicting the feelings and perceptions of the other.

The value comparison stage occurs when the couple has not as yet developed sufficient intimacy to learn and confess the innermost percepts, fears, aspirations, and concerns that each has. Nevertheless, there is much public and private information that each learns about the other in this period. Information is gleaned about religious orientation; political beliefs; attitudes towards people, parents, friends; interests in sports, the arts, dancing and the like.

The rate of progress through the value comparison stage depends on the rate of social penetration (Altman and Taylor, 1973). The couple exhibits increasingly larger areas of what they think and feel. They evaluate their comfortableness, the acceptance of what they reveal, and the effect of their disclosure on their partner's behaviour. In a successful relationship, the partner evinces acceptance of the values of the individual and discloses his own values. Self-disclosure among individuals promotes reciprocal self-disclosure, and the relationship may proceed to increasingly deeper levels of personality (Cozby, 1973).

A sense of pace is important in the reciprocal disclosure process. To jump too far ahead of what the partner can accept may lead to high cost for the partner, which may outweigh the rewards he perceives himself as obtaining from a relationship to which he is not fully committed. A man telling a long time female friend that watching horses mate "turns him on" (as it did Queen Victoria) may be met with a bemused but accepting smile. Pouring out this confession to a girl on a man's second date with her may lead to raised eyebrows and uncomfortableness.

In the most successful relationships, consensus on the important values intrinsic to the relationship is generally reached. Consensus is important for a variety of reasons. For one thing, it reinforces our perception of the world as correct (Byrne and Clore, 1967). The satisfaction goes beyond simply being "right", because values are introjected into the self and help to define the self-image; hence she who rejects our self-image is often perceived as rejecting us. Moreover, persons with similar values are likely to engage in similar activities thus further rewarding each other.

During the "value comparison" stage, though the stimulus and role variables are also operative, the importance of the stimulus variables has already waned somewhat. The majority of persons of disparate stimulus attractiveness who met, likely as not never developed a relationship. Many who started a relationship have broken up. The relatively few couples of different stimulus who continue their relationship presumably have unusual attractiveness compensating value consensus or role compatibility.

The testing of role compatibility is also underway involving not only intimate verbal communication, but getting to know how to behave *vis-à-vis* the partner as well as knowing what roles the partner can play in satisfying one's own needs: friend, teacher, lover, critic. These roles not only involve the greatest intricacies, they also necessitate a great deal of time to master; hence the rate of growth of role compatibility is slower than that of value comparison, which involves only verbal interaction. There does come a time, however, when role compatibility supersedes value comparison in importance, marking the onset of the role stage, as shown in Fig. 1.

C. ROLE STAGE

When a couple has survived the stimulus and value stages, they have established a reasonably good relationship. Some individuals may decide to marry at this point. However, for most persons, these are necessary but insufficient grounds for marriage. It is also important for the couple to be able to *function* in compatible roles.

Role is defined by English and English as "the behaviour that is characteristic and expected of the occupant of a defined position in a group" (1958, p. 468). Sociologists tend to focus on the "defined position" with the understanding that the role is defined by an individual's culture, and that he adjusts himself into it much as one does in purchasing a ready-made suit. My use of the term "role", however, is much broader and individual-centered.

A wife's role as defined by her husband consists of *his* perception of the behaviour that is expected of a wife. His perception may be in part moulded by his culture, but, part of it may stem from his own idiosyncrasies, which would not be found in his neighbour's definition of the role of wife. In like vein, the wife's definition of the wifely role would consist of *her* perception of what the role should embody.

The role of spouse may be subdivided into specialized functions which the individual is expected to execute in different situations. Thus, the husband's role may be subdivided into his role vis-à-vis his wife in private, in public, and in the family.

A primary feature of the role stage is the evaluation of the perceived functioning of oneself in a dyadic relationship in comparison with the roles one envisages for oneself, and the perceived role functioning of the partner with respect to the roles one has envisaged for him. Personal, intimate behaviours are revealed much more slowly than are values, which can be expressed in more abstract, less intimate fashion. Also, many roles may be included within an overall evaluation of role compatibility, which evaluation therefore may be difficult to make, whereas values are generally simpler to understand.

We can measure role compatibility by comparing expectations and perceptions of the fulfilment of expectation over a wide range of behaviours. Some culturally esteemed behaviours probably may not require measurement of expectations because they are almost universally perceived as rewarding. Individuals with both high social status and high nurturance needs, for example, are generally sought after because such individuals are easy to relate to, rarely self-centred, and sensitive and giving towards others. On the other hand, neurotics are high-cost persons who are difficult to relate to and often offer few rewards through interaction. Role compatibility is probably the most complex of all the stages and is probably never completely traversed, since individuals seem to be constantly adding new roles or modifying existing ones.

D. EXPRESSIVE AND PERCEPTUAL STYLE

In our discussion of the stages and components of courtship so far, we noted that, with respect to stimulus attributes, each person aspired towards his ideal, but the demands of reality tended to force him back towards a person of comparable assets and liabilities. With respect to values, the argument was advanced that homogamy was highly desirable because it signified that the participants were moving towards identical goals. Also, when attitudes are similar, communication should be less stressful, since much would be understood and approved of, and the fear of being misunderstood would be less likely. I should like now to focus on other behaviours, which I have labelled "perceptual outlook" and "expressive behaviour".

Perceptual Outlook

Both the content and style of an individual's perceptions may surely reveal his value system, as the "new look" research demonstrated a quarter of a century ago (Bruner and Postman, 1948). At that time, there was a plethora of experiments in which coins were perceived as greater than objective size by the poor, and ambiguous signs were seen as swastikas by concentration camp victims. A perception, nevertheless, is obviously not completely determined by internal factors, particularly when the stimulus is unambiguous and no pressing needs on the part of the perceiver predispose him to misperceive the stimulus. Individuals under certain circumstances do change their minds and their values when sufficient contrary evidence is brought to bear.

Homogeneity of perceptions between two people, therefore, should be beneficial for a premarital relationship on two counts. Even when the agreement in perception involves no common values, it at least supplies consensual validation from a highly esteemed other: it is rewarding to know that one is in good contact with reality (see also Clore's chapter, section 1; Duck's chapter, section 3). If two campers can agree that the skies portend that a cold wind is coming, they can make appropriate responses even if one believes that it is healthful to be lightly clad, and the other believes it is healthful to be warmly bundled up. If the couple can interpret an experience within similar value systems, homogamy should be even more strongly rewarding. If two naive passengers discover that they have been overcharged by a Parisian taxi driver and they confirm each other's belief that the world is a "jungle", they may feel highly justified in exhibiting suspicious behaviour when future business transactions take place in a Parisian boutique.

Expressive Behaviour

Expressive behaviour is more complex. By expressive behaviour I refer to the *style* and *manner* of interacting with other people or objects rather than to the *content* of what they say; hence talkativeness, querulous, and hyperactivity are three examples of expressive behaviour. To the degree that expressive behaviour reflects similar values, it should be homogamously selective. If two people have a cynical view of the world, they may enjoy each other's humour in spoofing even the noblest of endeavours.

On the other hand, if expressive behaviour reflects a role the individual has adopted, similarity of expressive behaviour is rewarding only to the extent that similarity of the roles is rewarding. For example, a politician who is articulate and likes to talk at the drop of a hat may be benefited by a wife who is equally articulate, independent, and talkative. He thereby gains another campaigner. A man who wishes to play the role of sage patriarch to his wife's "doll house Nora", however, may be discomforted by a wife who boldly enunciates her own views and independence.

In making predictions about the similarity or complementarity of expressive behaviour, therefore, we have to estimate whether the behaviour is most apt to reflect a philosophical position (value), or a role. If it serves the latter, we will have to estimate whether the roles of the partners served by the particular expressive behaviour are similar or complementary.

Not enough is known about perceptual and expressive styles to indicate in which stage they are most operative; consequently, I should assume that they cut across the various stages and I shall not venture any predictions regarding their being especially influential during any one stage of courtship.

IV. Types of courtship and cross-cultural influences

Figure 1 describes what I conjecture to be the typical path of courtship for most middle-class couples in the United States. Variations due to personality, economic, and cultural differences, however, would alter the graph somewhat. "Stimulus" types would hold stimulus variables to be most important over the course of the courtship. For such persons, marrying in the right class or profession would be paramount, and role interaction secondary. One thinks immediately of the exceedingly wealthy class in this regard. Here, values would be relatively unimportant in selection because class selectivity would be great and individual variability much smaller in comparison to class selectivity. In other words, if almost everyone within a class holds similar views, individual selectivity with respect to values does not seem to be a major issue.

The same would probably be true for other societies in which social change was relatively slight and class structure was stable. A Greek peasant might be most influenced by stimulus variables because almost everyone in the village held similar values. Role stratification also might be very rigid, a man's role and a woman's role being clearly defined and differentiated. In that case, the role stage along with the value stage might be of relatively small import.

In our own society, value consensus seems to be of greatest importance within professional and upper-middle-class couples and of least importance in the lower class (Kerckhoff, 1972, 1974). In the lower class, we may presume that the narrowed range of class variability with respect to values and the structuring of roles makes individual selectivity with respect to these dimensions of lesser importance.

Since value comparison in many respects serves as an introduction to role comparisons and role compatibility, it is easier to think of a "value-role" type than of either a separate "value" or a "role" type. This type would include individuals whose greatest rewards come from close interpersonal interaction with people. It would be of interest to determine whether "stimulus" types invariably married "stimulus" types or sometimes "intermarried" with "value-role" types.

V. Distinguishing between similarity and equity

Similarity and equity are often bandied about as if they were equivalent terms. It is necessary however to distinguish between them because equity plays an important role in SVR theory, whereas similarity is of lesser importance. Similarity within the context of our discussion refers to the number of common components or the degree of similar structure two objects may have. If two individuals have similar values, it is meant that if we ranked the values of each in order of preference a high rank order correlation would result.

Equity as used here, refers to equal rewarding power; hence two equitable persons might be totally dissimilar. The beautiful but poor woman who marries the ugly but wealthy bachelor represents an equitable balance of beauty and wealth.

The problem arises when members of a couple are equally represented on a variable so that they are both similar and equitable with respect to it. Generally, similarity functions as an antecedent variable. Individuals possessing similar values are drawn to each other because they receive consensual validation that their views are correct. In some cases, however, logic tells us that two people who share a socially undesirable characteristic may not necessarily be drawn to each other. They may in fact *settle* for each other because it is the best they can do. It is doubtful, for example, that two physically unattractive individuals are drawn to each other because they admire unattractiveness. Rather, they may have learned through experience that if they do not possess outstanding compensating attributes for their unattractiveness, they are apt to be rejected by more attractive persons whom they attempt to court. It is the presence of similars at the bottom of the totem pole which enables us to differentiate similarity as a socially desirable attracting agent from similarity as an equity or exchange factor.

Similarity can be non-rewarding even when the traits involved are socially desirable. Unless similarity leads to a rewarding experience, it may lead to competition and dissatisfaction. When both members of a couple possess strong needs to dominate each other, the couple may function less harmoniously than a tandem of a dominant and submissive member. The strongest interpersonal relationship therefore, does not necessarily occur between the most similar types, but between those with equal rewarding power (equity), even where the variables contributing to these rewards are different for the partners.

A. WHERE IS LOVE?

Up to this point there has been no mention of love, but this does not mean that I perceive marriage as a loveless relationship. Indeed, in Western society everybody marries for "love"; consequently, the term "love" has come to represent a large number of diverse behaviours; we love apple pie, football teams, sex, Uncle Otto, our spouses, sometimes other people's spouses, children, colleagues, and country. Apart from indicating a positive affinity for a diverse series of objects, these "loves" offer little insight into the nature of the relationship. One could also speak of heterosexual love, parental love, conjugal love, and romantic love. These subdivisions only differentiate between the objects of love but do not illuminate the process.

In addition, our understanding of love is further clouded because the word "love" has assumed a high symbolic value, so that it operates as a reinforcement (reward) independent of any overt behaviour. For example, Ephraim Exploitum having just finished a tasty swordfish steak tells his wife tenderly, "Darling, I love you". He then proceeds to the living room to watch the news on television, while his wife who had returned from her job and prepared his meal now turns her attention to the dishes. On the other hand, some persons may engage in what many individuals consider loving behaviour, but for one reason or another do not label their action as "love".

Since love can be independent of behaviour, and since, in any event, definitions of love vary enormously, I prefer to focus on the determinants of close dyadic attraction rather than labelling preferences. Almost all of the subjects in my research loved their partners, but it would seem of greater interest to determine whether the focus of their attraction had to do with stimulus, value comparison, or role variables.

VI. Conclusions

Stimulus-Value-Role theory is a complex theory of dyadic formation. From a transactional framework it is an exchange theory; viewed teleologically it is a sequential, partial filter theory.

From the theory 19 hypotheses were originally formulated and tested (Murstein, 1970, 1971) and later extended to 39 hypotheses (Murstein, 1976). A complete elaboration of the theory and description of the empirical work in it can be found in *Who Will Marry Whom? Theories and Research in Marital Choice* (Murstein, 1976), although a sample is reprinted in section 2 here.

The author of a theory is hardly the most unbiased judge of a theory's worth. However, the data seem to offer support for the exchange portion of the theory. The sequential aspects have been tested only indirectly, and although these data support it, the crucial test of this phase would necessitate a longitudinal study which regrettably has not as yet been undertaken.

Theories of dyadic attraction like most theories in the social sciences, cannot be said to be right or wrong. Rather, they are conceptual arguments for organizing existing data into a meaningful framework and for making predictions. As such they generally have strong points and weak points and they differ in usefulness. Because of the relative youthfulness of SVR theory its heuristic value in understanding dyadic attraction remains to be determined.

6.
Interpersonal Attraction and Social Exchange

J. J. LA GAIPA*
University of Windsor, Ontario, Canada

"Social exchange" represents a general perspective on human behaviour (not just on attraction) which characterizes a whole range of
different specific outlooks. Whilst each is different in emphasis, the
basic premise of the many outlooks is that man forms face-to-face

*I am grateful to Steve Duck for his comments on an earlier draft.

129

relationships in the light of the benefits, costs or "profit" that such associations are expected to bring.

The different outlooks reviewed in the next section define such and other terms in their own ways, but there are two major general features of all social exchange theories which can be specified at the outset. *First,* a characteristic of the social exchange approach is its inter-disciplinary flavour. Even from the above outline it can be seen that the theory, whilst applied to psychology, draws heavily on economic notions and also has some relationship to sociological theory. *Second* this approach, more than many others, concerns reciprocity in relationships (i.e. each person seeks to maximize his rewards, whilst ensuring at the same time that the costs of the Other are not so high as to threaten the existence of the relationship). Exchange, then, involves reciprocal interaction for the purposes of mutual reward. Hence exchange theories are more concerned with the effects of repeated interactions on expectations of future benefit or profit and thus tend to focus more on the subsequent development of stable interpersonal relationships (Homans, 1971), not exclusively on single encounters.

However, "exchange" is not simply the addition of the two processes of giving and receiving (Simmel, 1950). Exchange constitutes a third process that emerges when giving and receiving are simultaneously the cause and effect of each other. It is not adequate therefore to concentrate exclusively on such activities, although much useful work has been done on either "giving" or "receiving" as separate processes (e.g. altruism, Berkowitz, 1972; helping the distressed person, Staub, 1974; or receiving aid from others, Fisher and Nadler, 1974). Whilst giving to others may make individuals feel good (cf. Berkowitz, 1972), accepting aid from others can lead to the development of inequitable relationships (Walster, Berscheid and Walster, 1973). But in any case, such features of interaction are incidental effects on attractiveness rather than major examinations of interpersonal attraction seen in terms of social exchange. In other words (Berkowitz, 1972) they are extrinsic rewards of interaction (i.e. those where individuals direct Others to rewards or benefits in the external environment: for example, relief from pain) rather than intrinsic or social rewards of interaction itself (i.e. those obtainable only in the interaction itself; for example, compliments). This chapter concentrates on intrinsic aspects of social exchange and their relationship to attraction.

At this stage one should note (Walster *et al.*, 1973) the considerable resistance that exists to looking at social relationships in such economic terms (benefit, costs, rewards, etc.). Intimate relationships are often viewed by people as "special", not so mercenary, untainted by "crass considerations" of social exchange. However, Walster *et al.* (1973) argue that "even in the most intimate relations, considerations of equity will influence strongly the viability and pleasantness of a relationship" (p. 170). Nisbet (1970) and the present author agree that the key notion here is that people expect *some* kind of reward to follow their actions — but exchange theories are not limited to any particular kind of reward and they are thus useful at all levels of relationship. Every relationship, even at the most intimate level, has an aspect of exchange insofar as the acts of one person are predicated on the expectation that some kind of reward will flow from the act — if nothing more than an expression of warmth or gratitude.

I. Theories of social exchange

In this section I shall review four kinds of approach to social exchange: behavioural-economic, cognitive behavioural, sociological, and re-source theory. As will become clear, there are very many theories in each category and the treatment here will necessarily be brief. In the presentation of each theory, therefore, I will deal with its major focus, i.e. what it seeks to explain; its critical concepts, propositions and limitations. Hopefully, this method will generate interest in examining each one in greater detail than is possible here and original sources are listed to facilitate this. A short critical review is given of each theory because of the value of this as a learning device: before one can synthesize and develop a better model, it is necessary to be alert to the kinds of things that need improvement. The reader should, however, be cautious about any premature dismissal of any given theory on the bases of the limited comments given here. The theories cited have tried to go a step beyond the poets and the essayists in applying the scientific method to such topics as love and friendship. Although they have achieved varying degrees of success, they have certainly laid the foundation for better theory building and research.

Whilst the primary function of this chapter is to illustrate the theoretical perspective on attraction which Exchange Theories provide, and this requires the listing of certain major approaches as above, I have also considered (below) some wider theoretical issues in social exchange and attraction which transcend the individual viewpoints expounded in the next section.

A. BEHAVIOURAL-ECONOMIC

Theory of Elementary Social Behaviour

Homans (1974) is generally credited with showing the possible relationship between reinforcement theory and some elementary concepts from economics. A full appreciation of the specific content of his theory requires examination of it as part of his overall theoretical strategy since Homans was as much concerned with how to build a theory as he was with social exchange. However, since this context is available elsewhere, the reader is referred to Abrahamsson (1970) for a fuller discussion.[1]

Definition of Key Exchange Concepts: (a). *Activity* Behaviours aimed at deriving rewards.

(b). *Rewards* Anything a person receives, or any activity directed toward him, that is defined by the person as valuable.

(c). *Value* The degree of reinforcement or capacity to meet needs of an activity for an individual — whether his own activity or activity directed toward him.

(d). *Cost* An activity that is punishing, or an alternative reward that is forgone in order to get another reward.

(e). *Investments* A person's relevant past activities (such as skill, education and expertise) and social characteristics (such as sex, age and race) which are brought to a situation and evaluated by both the person and those with whom he is interacting.

(f). *Profit* Rewards, minus the costs and investments, for engaging in a certain activity.

(g). *Distributive justice* Activities involving the calculation of whether costs and investments have led to a "fair" profit by individuals in an exchange.

Basic Propositions: (1) If in the past a particular stimulus situation has been the occasion on which an individual's activity was rewarded, then

---

1. Abrahamsson notes four points that represent Homans' approach. 1. Psychological propositions are the fundamentals of social theory: i.e. that unified social scientific explanation will depend on statements about the behaviour of men as men. 2. Such propositions can explain a large number of social phenomena even in other disciplines. 3. The propositions are quite general in nature, that is, of high level of abstraction. 4. The task of a theoretician is to arrive at a deductive scheme through the inductive method.

the more similar the present stimulus situation is to the past one, the more likely he is now to emit the activity or similar activity.

(2) The more often within a given period of time an individual's activity rewards that of another, the more often the other will emit the activity.

(3) The more valuable to an individual a unit of the activity another gives him, the more often he will emit activity rewarded by that of the other.

(4) The more often an individual has in the recent past received a rewarding activity from another, the less valuable any further unit of that activity becomes to him (because of satiation effects).

(5) The more to an individual's disadvantage the rule of distributive justice fails of realization, the more likely he is to display the emotional behaviour we call anger.

According to an implicit formula, humans assess whether the rewards received from a situation are proportional to the costs incurred in it and the investments brought to it. Distributive justice is thus the expected ratio of investments and costs to rewards.

Limitations Deutsch (1971) has criticized the use made by Homans of Skinnerian propositions and methodology on the grounds that much of the best of Skinner has been ignored. All that is left essentially is the notion of hedonism which underlies both the law of effect and the image of "economic man". Furthermore, Abrahamsson (1970), takes issue with Homans' concern over observable behavioural data and questions whether internal, subjective processes can be ignored. The private way in which an individual experiences the outcome of an act is useful information. Abrahamsson considers such concepts as "meaning" and "definition of the situation" as strategically crucial in any attempt to understand what is going on during social exchange, especially in relation to interpersonal attraction.

Major criticisms of Homans are (1) that the basic propositions are tautological: thus rewards and costs as well as activities and values are defined in terms of each other in ways that lead to circular reasoning (Abrahamsson, 1970; Turner, 1974). (2) Many of the variables employed by Homans are not directly measurable. Homans (1974) admits, for example, that it is difficult to infer or measure "value". Therefore, he turns to the amount of activity expended in the past to obtain a particular reward as an indicator of the value of the activity. But this does not obviate the tautology (Mulkay, 1971), because no evidence is provided for defining value independently of the activity to be explained as products of these values. (3) No adequate method has been developed for assessing the equivalence in value of different commodities (Gergen, 1969). How much approval, for example, should a person get for five minutes of advice? The lack of a common currency for measuring values creates problems for such notions as profit, rate of exchange and distributive justice (Deutsch, 1971) which imply an ability to compare, to add and subtract. (4) Homans has conducted few empirical tests of the adequacy of his theory but instead has attempted to apply his theory to the findings of other research. The empirical imprecision of the variables makes it possible to interpret findings after the event by merely extending a term's coverage in order to fit the facts. (5) Clear deductions are not possible from the propositions offered by Homans because of the problem in defining and measuring rewards (Abrahamsson, 1970) even though the application of the theory ultimately rests on the assumption of specific rewards and costs. It is therefore necessary (see next section) to identify main *classes* of rewards, rather than relying on implicit definitions of rewards and costs.

Emphasis is given to criticisms of Homans' theory here because it is the most frequently cited exchange theory but the measurement problem, for example, is not unique to Homans and applies to the calculation of rewards and costs in any exchange theory (Simpson, 1972). On the other hand, Homans' pioneering efforts in social exchange have stimulated much thinking in this area — particularly attempts to rebut the above criticisms by the development of axiomatic-deductive theories.

B. COGNITIVE-BEHAVIOURAL

The cognitive-behavioural approach to social exchange is part of a larger trend in psychology that seeks to bridge the gap between reinforcement theory and cognitive theories. The various models listed here are thus somewhat heterogeneous.

Equity Theory

Adams' (1965) Equity Theory has generated considerable research because of its implications for applied settings, its derivation from cognitive dissonance theory, and its relatively clear, straightforward propositions. Adams is mainly concerned with the consequences of "imbalance" in social exchange and thus differs in emphasis from Homans (1974) who was primarily concerned with the reinforcement of activities involved in exchange, and secondarily in the notion of distributive justice.

Adams focuses on a person's "inputs" or investments. A person attempts to maintain a favourable ratio between his inputs (e.g. how hard he works, educational level, general qualifications) and outcomes (e.g. pay, fringe benefits, intrinsic interest of the work) as compared to another person. Inequity is likely to be perceived if he feels that, as compared to another, the amounts received are disproportionate to the inputs. Adams cautions that what determines the equity of a particular input-outcome balance is the *individual's perception* of what he is giving and receiving whether or not it corresponds to the perception held by others. Inequity can result from under-reward (causing distress) or over-reward (causing guilt) and motivates an individual to reduce inequity or achieve equity (as dissonance — an antecedent of Adams' view — similarly motivates). Various modes of resolving inequity include changing inputs or outcomes, distortion or withdrawal from the encounter.

Research on equity theory has certain characteristics which emphasize indirect exchange rather than direct exchange in that the source 'of the rewards is typically external to the dyads or interactions (see introduction to this chapter). Many of the field studies have taken place in industrial settings where a third party is responsible for allocation of rewards. There has also been considerable reliance on material rewards rather than intrinsic rewards. In experimental studies, the major task has been that of reward allocation following manipulation of the inputs of the participants.

Adams (1965) was not specifically concerned with the effects of inequity on interpersonal attraction, but in a review article, Walster *et al.* (1973) presented a series of propositions, corollaries and conclusions useful for integrating research in this area by means of an overall conceptual scheme, and more recent research, particularly in regard to physical attractiveness, has drawn heavily on equity theory (cf. Berscheid and Walster, 1974a).

Do both overreward and underreward produce dissatisfaction (i.e. is there the predicted curvilinear relationship between amount of reward and satisfaction)? In a study of 350 college roommates, Howitt and La Gaipa (1975b) asked questions like: "As compared to what *you have given your* roommate, how much understanding have *you received?"* A nine point scale was used, the small numbers indicated receiving "much less", the middle numbers "about the same", and the larger numbers "much more". Two criteria were used—reported level of friendship and feelings of obligation. The predicted curvilinearity was not found using the attraction measure but a strong, linear relationship was obtained. Overreward was associated with higher levels of friendship and underreward with lower levels of friendship.

According to equity theory, overreward should have resulted in feelings of guilt since, to admit to being overrewarded is to suggest that the obligation to return in kind was ignored. To test the curvilinear hypothesis using "obligation" as the criterion, subjects were divided into three groups: those receiving less than they gave; those receiving about the same and those receiving more. Mean ratings of obligation were computed for each group and some support for the curvilinear hypothesis was obtained. More obligation was experienced under equity conditions than either extreme; the lowest obligation was reported for underreward; the next lowest level of obligation was received with the overreward. This latter group, however, was more heterogeneous suggesting that other variables need to be considered when dealing with overreward, such as perceived effort on intentions. When one obtains more than one deserves, the question of the other person's motives become more salient.

Limitations The role of equity in the development of interpersonal relationship has been under-researched. It is plausible that equity is a necessary but not a sufficient condition for the growth of a relationship: equity may be essential for maintaining a relationship and inequity may lead to its disruption. But how important is "fairness" in the desire to increase the level of a relationship? There are two points here: first, Howitt and La Gaipa (1975b) found that perceived fairness was not as good a predictor of the growth of friendship over time as other social exchange variables, such as reciprocity (discussed below). Second, an exchange relationship can be "fair" without being satisfying and there is a need to examine the relationship between equity and satisfaction with the amount of the reward (Gergen, 1969).

The Justice Motive

Lerner (1974a) has developed a theory of social justice whose key concept is the notion of "Personal Contract". The individual is seen as developing a personal contract with himself to give up immediate gratifications on the expectation of getting more desired outcomes later. During the process of socialization there is a shift from living by the "pleasure principle" to living by the "reality principle". This shift entails recognition by the child of the long-term benefits arising from delay of gratification or from incurring "costs" of frustrated impulses as an "investment" of effort on the assumption that more desirable benefits will accrue to him in the future. The child learns that "deserving" (via costs and investments) is an effective way of obtaining desired outcomes.

"Personal Contract" and social justice are proposed as being dynamically interdependent (Lerner, *et al.* 1976). The psychological linkage between the personal contract and the social norms is the recognition of an "equivalence" between himself and others (that is, although the child is aware that he is distinct from others, he views himself as being in a similar "position" in regard to the desired outcomes). He uses them as social referents and models in order to obtain some clarity and to reduce the threat from the uncertainty otherwise attached to the making of judgements of personal deserving. Justice for others is important as assurance of one's own ability to achieve goals by one's own deserving. Any evidence that others do not get what they deserve threatens the viability of the self-sacrificing and "deserving" method of obtaining what one desires. The validity, then, of one's own personal contract depends on other persons' ability to deserve their own outcomes. The personal contract, then, can only be maintained by viewing the world as just (i.e. assuming that people deserve what they get and — more important — get what they deserve).

A major contribution of Lerner's theory is in regard to the delineation of the forms of justice most appropriate for different situations. As part of the socialization process, the child acquires the rules for determining in any given circumstances how resources are deserved and are to be allocated. On occasions, *Marxist principles* obtain and need rather than input is important. On other occasions *equity* obtains (e.g. where the participants perceive each other as nonequivalent but interdependent). Under this condition, an attempt is made to match outcomes with investments. Yet again *parity* is sometimes sought (e.g. when people perceive each other as being a unit, or members of a team): here, all members share equally in the outcome. Unit relations, then, require parity while non-unit relations evoke equity considerations (Lerner, 1974b).

The key concept of "personal contract" differentiates this theory from other theories. This "contract" is not negotiated with a specific other person in a direct, face-to-face relationship, rather, the "contract" is entered into *prior* to forming a relationship. The notion of mutual reinforcement, so basic to exchange theories, is of less relevance to this theory than the idea that failure to reciprocate might invalidate one's own personal contract and, in the very process, make one less deserving. The form of justice employed is thus less a response to the *behaviour* of a specific other than it is to the perception of the category to which the other is to be assigned, e.g. as belonging to a unit or nonunit relationship.

Limitations Lerner's (1974a) application of this theory of social justice to research on interpersonal attraction uses a broad definition of attraction: usually attraction to victims of injustice. Research shows that friends differ from nonfriends in the justice strategy employed (Lerner, Miller and Holmes, 1976), but this is not the same as demonstrating that use of parity facilitates the growth of friendship. Nor have consequences of social injustice on the development and dissolution of intimate relationships yet been demonstrated. A further problem involves the application of this theory to different classes of rewards. The notion of "personal contract" seems more appropriate when dealing with extrinsic than intrinsic or social rewards.

Interaction Outcome Matrix Model

Thibaut and Kelley (1959) independently developed a social exchange theory that is quite similar to Homans' but draws on both reinforcement theory and cognitive theory. Thibaut and Kelley go beyond the simple notion that we are attracted to those who provide us with rewards: the focus of their theory is on the notion of interdependency which rests on *outcome control* i.e. one person's ability to determine directly the outcomes (rewards and punishments) or another, and therefore to exert influence over his behaviour. A relationship will continue if satisfaction in terms of rewards and costs are adequate and as a function of interdependency (reciprocal or mutual control). What is distinctive or unique to Thibaut and Kelley is the concern with identifying those factors that determine reciprocal control. Such outcome control requires some command, then, over reinforcement resources: both parties have power over each other if by varying his behaviour each person can affect the quality of the *other's* outcomes. Power in a relationship is outcome control.

The major analytic technique used by Thibaut and Kelley is the outcome matrix which is formed by taking into account all the behaviours two individuals might enact together. In this matrix each cell represents one of the possible parts of the interaction between the dyad and shows the consequences for each person of what he has done. The matrix resembles the payoff matrices used in economic game theory (see Fig. 1).

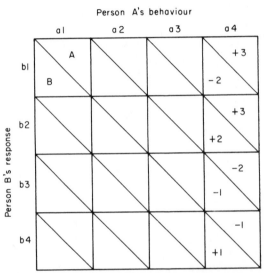

FIG. 1. An example of an outcome matrix. In this diagram person A's behaviour is indicated at the top of the matrix and person B's responses are listed down the side; the outcome for each individual is listed as indicated by A and B, with a full example of outcomes given for the case where A chooses behaviour a4. Thus if person A performs action a4 and person B responds with b3, then both interactors lose a small amount (but B loses less than A). If however B had chosen to respond with response b2 then each interactor would have gained rather than lost, but B would have gained less than A.

Thibaut and Kelley stress that the reward-punishment value of an outcome must be viewed with reference to the expectations of the participants based on two "comparison levels". The first of these is the actor's comparison level (CL) defined as the minimum level of positive outcomes which an individual feels he deserves. CL is the average value of all outcomes known to a person, based on prior history and present situation. The comparison level of alternatives (CL_{alt}) is the evaluation of outcomes a person has in his immediate situation compared with possible outcomes in alternative relations. Thibaut and Kelley suggest that the level of outcomes received relative to CL affects the person's *attraction* to the relationship, whereas the level of outcomes obtained relative to CL_{alt} defines his *dependence* on the relationship. Thibaut and Kelley thus assign greater weight to comparison functions than did Homans (1974): attraction depends on more than the simple ratio of rewards and costs. For example, to be effective — to maximize his outcome — he must take into account not only the various costs involved in what he is doing but also the consequences of his responses for the other person. He tries, then, to produce responses that cost him the least (or yield the greatest pleasure) while trying to get the best outcome available for the other. So routine day-to-day interactions involve both coping with the immediate situation and accomplishing more intermediate instrumental goals. Man is not a simple-minded hedonist seeking to maximize his profits in every exchange episode.

Limitations Though this theory seeks to explain both the growth of interpersonal relations and the antecedent and consequent conditions of interdependency and reciprocal control, little research has been done on friendship formation. Thibaut and Kelley (1959) have limited the testing of their theory to conditions specific to experimental games and bargaining in the belief that it is almost impossible to measure the effects of an individual's reinforcement history on his comparison level. Thus research has been restricted to the study of behavioural contingencies leading to changes in the comparison level that are under the control of the experimenter.

Theory testing has been confined to extrinsic type of rewards (money, points, and other tokens) rather than intrinsic or social rewards. But the psychological impact of such rewards may be vastly different — with consequent problems in generalizing from one kind of reward to another. The rewards used in studies on bargaining and conflict resolution in experimental games may not be psychologically equivalent to the exchange of such rewards as love and esteem (Turner Foa, and Foa, 1971).

Incremental Exchange Theory

Huesmann and Levinger (1976) have developed a formal model to account for the growth of dyadic relationships. An essential feature of social relationships, which is often overlooked, is that they change over time, and Huesmann and Levinger are concerned with what happens as the depth of a relationship (mutual involvement) increases.

This theory assumes an expectation of higher payoffs in inter-personal rewards as the depth of the relationship increases: the expected values of rewards increase with mutual involvement. The second basic assumption is that the growth of a dyadic relationship can be viewed as a sequential movement from one outcome matrix to another. In contrast to the static use of the single matrix employed by Thibaut and Kelley (1959), a relationship is represented instead by a set of systematically linked payoff matrices. The "current outcomes received" largely determine the direction and the amount of the movement from one matrix to the next (Huesmann and Levinger, 1976).[2]

The parameters of incremental exchange theory are generally the same as found in other theories of exchange such as decision making, payoffs and costs, consideration of the future, learning from past outcomes, and the termination of the relationship. The model goes beyond other theories in two ways. The first is that the actor, in assessing his own rewards, considers the *payoff* of the other. The actor, in choosing among his options, is made sensitive to the probable responses of the Other, in order to avoid the "individualistic" orienta-tion of Thibaut and Kelley (1959).

Secondly, incremental exchange theory differs from other exchange theory in its concern with transitions between states of a relationship according to specified rules. An example of a state-to-state transition rule would be: "If both actors' payoff is greater than 5, then move to State$_{t+2}$; if both actors' payoff is greater than 2, then move to State$_{t+1}$. . .". The model also handles changes in the actors' concep-tions of one another over time and transition to a new stage modifies such conceptions in that the actor's immediate behaviour options become located in a new matrix with new payoffs, and, in addition, the actor can look ahead to new possibilities of rewards.

Limitations Among others, Huesmann and Levinger (1976) note the following:

(a) The model itself contains a large number of parameters rendering it complex and making its predictions difficult to disconfirm;

2. This technique is supplemented by computer simulation of growth of relationship using a program called RELATE.

(b) Most of the concepts within the model, such as payoffs, costs or discounts, are extremely difficult to define operationally;

(c) Like other reinforcement approaches, this theory offers no substantive explanation of what constitutes rewards or costs;

(d) Difficulty attaches to use of the model for any given application because of the need to specify states, behaviours, payoffs, costs, probability estimates, discounts and depth of search.

Social Penetration Theory

Altman and Taylor (1973) appear to have developed the most comprehensive, substantive theory seeking to explain the growth of interpersonal relations. This is another theory that draws on the seminal work of Thibaut and Kelley (1959), reinforcement theory and cognitive theory. Reinforcement theory is used to account for the likelihood that a given response will be made; cognitive theory is drawn upon to account for the evaluation of and forecast of reward costs.

An underlying assumption of social penetration theory is that if the level of exchange in a relationship is sustained or increases over time, then both parties must be profiting from the interaction (Taylor, 1968). Though the theory is mainly concerned with the exchange of information, other areas of exchange include the expression of positive and negative affect, and mutual activities. The interpersonal reward/cost experiences are rather loosely defined as compatability, cohesion, liking and mediating cognitive experiences.

The factors seen as accelerating or retarding social penetration processes include reward/costs, personality and situational influences. The degree and breadth of self-disclosure is used as an operational measure of social penetration (Altman and Taylor, 1973) and personality characteristics affecting disclosure are typically measured by the Jourard Self-Disclosure measure (Jourard, 1971) which taps predispositions to reveal intimate information about one's self. The situational factors include the ability to enter and leave relationships freely, and the degree of commitment to another person.

In brief, relationships are hypothesized to proceed in a systematic fashion with interpersonal exchanges gradually moving from superficial, non-intimate areas to more intimate deeper layers of the selves of the social actors. These changes in rate and amount from less intimate to more intimate areas are hypothesized to reflect interpersonal cost factors. According to the framework, individuals are hypothesized to assess the reward/cost balance of the present and past exchanges, and to generate an integrated forecast or extrapolation to reward/cost implications for future interactions.

Two central features, characteristic of social penetration theory, which differentiate it from other exchange theories, include the incorporation of the concept of the self and the high priority given to one kind of activity, i.e. self-disclosure. The metaphor used to describe the personality is that of an onion made up of many layers whose core is the "real self." The growth of a relationship involves penetrating these layers to get to the "real" person. With this view of the personality as structured in terms of layers, the depth of a relationship corresponds to a particular layer that has been penetrated. The metaphor of personality structure in terms of layers is clearly compatible with the role assigned to disclosure.

The second distinguishing feature of social penetration is the emphasis given to *disclosure* as the vehicle for cutting through the layers to reach the inner core. There are two possible problems here. The first is the assumption that the depth of a relationship can be conceptualized or equated with the breadth of information exchange — an empirical question which has not yet been fully examined. Secondly, even if we accept the importance assigned to intimacy as the vehicle of social penetration, the question is whether social penetration is the key phenomenon in friendship formation. In order to establish its relative importance, it is necessary to show firstly the lesser importance of other kinds of phenomenon in the same study. Other activities such as positive regard, authenticity, helping, etc. are treated by Altman and Taylor as providing the proper context for the facilitation of disclosure. Which of these activities is most salient and the relationships among them has yet to be determined.

A beginning in this direction was made by Heilbronn (1975) in a study comparing the predictive value of self-disclosure as postulated by Altman and Taylor (1973) with a multidimensional approach as postulated by La Gaipa (1969) and Canfield and La Gaipa (1970). Heilbronn found that the amount of disclosure as measured in early stages of the acquaintance was not a particularly good predictor of the level of friendship as measured at two later time periods. Actually causal attribution, including the effort made to be revealing, was a much better predictor than the degree to which the subjects reported "communicating on an intimate level to reveal highly personal information about one self to another". This is not to deny that amount of a given reward exchange is a useful parameter: other kinds of rewards were found to be predictive using "amount" as the parameter. The best predictor was similarity facilitation, which is defined as actions designed to "determine and enhance what one has in common with another person (interests, beliefs, personality) in order to increase the amount of social exchange and shared activities".

Limitations Altman and Taylor (1973) have achieved some measure of success in verifying social penetration theory. This is due in part to their ability to provide operational measures of reward as the independent variable as well as operational measures of self disclosure as the dependent variable. They have taken a position common to other behaviourists (e.g. Thibaut and Kelley, 1959) that reward should be defined in terms of what can be manipulated in an experimental setting and have used the procedure of manipulating social approval provided by the experimenter and have then measured amount of self-disclosure. Will other rewards with different psychological properties have the same effect?

Altman and Taylor face a problem common to most of the other exchange theorists in providing independent non-tautologous measures of their variables. At present social penetration is defined in terms of self-disclosure: the stage of relationship is defined in terms of social penetration. However, they point to other indicators, such as the degree of commitment to a relationship. Unfortunately measures of commitment have not been developed and research has not yet indicated the relationship between breadth and depth of self-disclosure and commitment to the other. Altman and Taylor have used sociometric choice and liking as dependent variables but apparently do not consider them to be adequate indicators of social penetration.

C. SOCIOLOGICAL

The sociological approach to exchange focusses on the *consequences* instead of the *nature* of exchange. Social exchange is viewed as one kind of social interaction which is particularly important because of its function in the formation of social units and the cementing of social relations. Thus the sociological approach concentrates on social and cultural factors influencing face to face interactions, particularly in its use of such notions as roles and cultural constraints on exchange.

Structural-functionalism

The most lucid discussion of social exchange may be found in Blau (1964). Unlike Homans, Blau does not go about stating a formal set of propositions of exchange since he was not interested in the construction of a set of axioms for a deductive theoretical system. The objective, rather, was to show the *implications* of treating social behaviour as exchange. Blau employs narrow definition of exchange and although drawing on the basic concepts of exchange theory, such as reward, cost and profits, applies these concepts simply to relations with others from which rewards are expected and received.

The bases of Blau's theory can be traced back to economics and psychology as may Homans', but in a slightly different way, since Blau is more specific than Homans in drawing upon principles from economics such as reciprocity, maximization of profit and diminishing marginal cost and values. Blau attempts to use supply and demand curves to explain social exchange whilst accepting a large part of the behaviouristic approach used by Homans. He places considerable weight on the impact of sociocultural variables such as norms of "reciprocity" and "fairness" (following Gouldner, 1960).

Blau is critical of Homans for tacitly assuming that the principle of "distributive justice" can operate independently of group norms. What gives the notion of justice its specific content and meaning is the system of values and norms in a society. Blau argues that all exchanges are constrained by norms of "fair exchange" which specify the minimal "expectations" that each party in exchange should receive; once exchange relations have been established, norms of "fair exchange" govern the transactions that occur. On the other hand, Blau agrees with Homans that mutual reinforcement is essential for the development of stable social relations.

This tendency to eclecticism is also apparent in the adoption of symbolic interactionist concepts such as "presentation of self" where man seeks actively to impress the other with the value of his own qualities. He tries to create the image that association with him will be gratifying and so the presentation of a favourable self-image is made with the intent of maximizing rewards. Blau attempts to deal with the problem of identifying different kinds of rewards involved in social exchange and he goes beyond Homans in developing an exhaustive categorization of types of rewards. The four generalized reinforcers include money, approval, esteem or respect, and compliance.

Limitations Blau's theoretical scheme has been subjected to relatively few criticisms. The reason is due, in part, to Blau's eclectic attempt to draw on a variety of perspectives — "something for everyone". But Blau has avoided some of the controversy generated by Homans simply by not making explicit sociological laws or axioms and the presentation of exchange concepts and their incorporation into exchange principles is occasionally vague. Indeed the concepts used overlap considerably without pointing very precisely to the phenomena to which they refer. "As such, they can be bent and redefined in an *ad hoc* fashion to fit whatever the facts may dictate (Turner, 1974, p. 290)."

D. RESOURCE THEORY

Resource theory is derived from a structural orientation in sociology and psychology. Structuralists give logical and analytical priority to the whole over its parts and are concerned with the pattern of interrelationships among the variables belonging to a set. A structural model involves the identification of the basic components and the way these elements combine to produce interrelated patterns of behaviour. Most of the theories outlined up until now have looked at rules of exchange and justice at the expense of the types of reward involved, and a repeated criticism of the theories here has been this neglect of resource class. Relatively little effort has been given to showing how exchange rules differ as a function of the properties of resource class (for example, the rules of exchange as they apply to love and status needs are barely examined, Foa and Donnenwerth, 1971). Research has been concerned mainly with the more tangible kinds of rewards on the assumption that any findings will have general application to less tangible rewards. But in order to understand the conditions under which exchange rules apply, it is clearly necessary to develop conceptual schemes that can be used to differentiate *classes* of rewards and thus the *content* of social exchange.

Longabaugh (1963) developed an observational system for coding interpersonal behaviour as social exchange. This system, as applied to observations of mother-child dyads, included the resource classes of information, support and control. In the area of friendship formation, Wright (1969, 1974) and La Gaipa and his associates have also constructed measures of friendship rewards (La Gaipa, 1969; Canfield and La Gaipa, 1970; Lischeron and La Gaipa, 1971; La Gaipa, 1972).

However, Foa and Foa (1971) have developed the most exhaustive taxonomy of resource classes which can be used to describe social exchange regardless of the institution or nature of the relationship. The six resource classes (love, status, information, goods, services and money) are plotted on the conceptual dimensions of particularism and concreteness (see Fig. 2).

Definition of Resource Classes: Love—expression of affectionate regard, warmth or comfort.
Status—expression of evaluative judgement that conveys high or low prestige, regard or esteem.
Information—includes advice, opinions, instruction or enlightenment but excludes those behaviours that could be classified as love or status.
Goods—are tangible products, objects or materials.
Services—involve activities on the body or belongings of an individual that often constitute labour for another.
Money—is any coin, currency, or token that has some standard unit of exchange value.

This classification refers to the *meaning* that people assign to behaviour rather than to the behaviour itself. What a given behaviour means may be contextually specific, while the same meaning may be indicated by different behaviours. For example, it appears that not every type of exchange is permissible in any given institution and the appropriateness of a resource appears to be defined by cultural norms (Foa, 1971). Thus certain kinds of exchange may be characteristic of a given institution: for example, at work the exchange of money and services seem typical, whereas in the school the exchange involves money and information and in the family, love and status appear to be the critical resources.

The Structure of Resources

Two conceptual dimensions (particularism and concreteness) are used to locate the hypothetical structure of the six resource classes. The dimension of *particularism* refers to the degree to which the value of the resource is affected by the particular person who provides it. The most particularistic resource is love since its reinforcing qualities are tied most closely to the person delivering it, whilst money is the least particularistic in that it does not change value as a function of the relationship between the giver and the receiver.

The second dimension of *concreteness* refers to the form or type of expression characteristic of the resources. Concreteness ranges from concrete to symbolic: the most overtly tangible activities, services and goods are classified as concrete; but because information and status are usually conveyed by verbal or paralinguistic behaviours, they are highly symbolic. Intermediate places on this dimension are found for love and money in that these resources are exchanged in both concrete and symbolic forms. This structural model of the cognitive classification of resources is shown in Fig. 2 in the circularly ordered taxonomy.

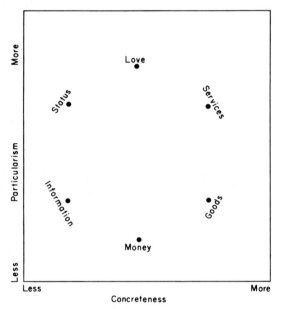

FIG. 2. Positions of the six resource classes plotted on the two dimensions of *particularism* and *concreteness*.

Reprinted from Foa (1971). Interpersonal and economic resources. *Science* **171**, 345-351. © American Association for the Advancement of Science.

Research on resource theory has focused on the effects of exchange involving proximal (i.e. adjacent in Fig. 2). and distal (i.e. not adjacent) resources. A person is more likely to be satisfied with a resource obtained if the resource was from the same resource class or a proximal class than a distal one (Teichman, 1971). In the extreme case, money for love is the least satisfying. Turner, Foa and Foa (1971) tested three hypothesis generated from the proposed order: (1) The similarity-dissimilarity hypothesis was that resources proximal in order will be perceived as similar; (2) The exchange hypothesis was that proximal resources will be preferred to distal ones in exchange; (3) The structural invariance hypothesis was that the pattern of interrelationships among the six resource classes follow their order and invariant with respect to the exchange situation. All three hypotheses were supported.

Advantages of Resource Theory

Why is it so important to provide greater resource specificity of the exchange patterns? A variety of reasons for doing so have been presented: (a) It is important to realize that rewards in each class possess different exchange characteristics. Let us take as examples some differences between love and money. Unlike money, love cannot be saved, stored or deposited for a long time; love cannot change hands very quickly; the rewards resulting from love can be obtained only after a series of encounters. The giving and receiving of money, however, can be done in a hurry. Love is a relatively long-term investment, whereas money can be exchanged in a single encounter. (b) Research on bargaining and conflict resolution in experimental games is more generalizable to everyday social life if payoff matrices are designed to handle differences in the kind or quality of reward rather than simply in terms of different amounts of the same reward. (c) The testability of certain propositions from various exchange theories is also increased to the extent that exchange patterns are specifiable. More precise definition of the rewards thus helps to avoid the confounding of related variables, such as respect and liking.

Limitations of Resource Theory

Some of the possible weaknesses of this model are as follows: (a) Information is lost by the use of broad categories since the content of the exchanges within any given resource class are likely to be quite heterogeneous. For example, examination of the consequences of exchange of information for some other resource class requires attention to a multiplicity of parameters varying from amount, type and intimacy to function. To make comparisons across resource classes some effort would be needed to hold constant the specific parameters involved. (b) The definition of each resource class is quite vague, though varying somewhat in ambiguity from class to class with love being the most difficult to define and money the least difficult to define. (c) The lack of standard units of measurement will make it difficult to assess the consequences of different asymmetrical exchanges.

II. Theoretical approaches to reciprocity

An exchange relationship is reciprocal by definition and the essential feature of exchange is the notion that people will reciprocate beneficial acts and harmful acts. But why do people reciprocate? Three basic explanations have been offered: normative, reinforcement, cognitive. In this section I will deal with the basic assumptions underlying each of these approaches; the research evidence bearing on each approach; and possible limitations.

A. NORMATIVE

The normative explanation postulates that reciprocity is due to social rules of mutual obligation to reciprocate behaviour. The give-and-take of social exchange according to the "norm of reciprocity" is regulated by feelings of obligation or indebtedness incurred by accepting a benefit (Gouldner, 1960) and exchange actions, then, are defined by a generalized moral norm. Though the norm of reciprocity is universal, this does not mean that it operates in all situations and Gouldner has called attention to some of the possible conditions influencing the need to return the benefit received. Essentially, the obligation to repay depends on the value of the benefit received which depends on a variety of factors. The degree of obligation varies with the intensity of the needs of the other; the resources of the donor; the motives imputed to him, and the situational constraints pertaining to intentionality.

Obligation

Does reciprocal behaviour depend on feelings of obligation? Indebtedness can be an aversive state since people like to stay out of debt (Blau, 1964) and if one anticipates not being able to return a favour, he is less willing to ask for help (Greenburg and Shapiro, 1971). Differences in feelings of obligation are not necessarily related to differences in the amount of benefit return (Gergen *et al.*, 1974).

The effect of obligation on reciprocal behaviour also varies according to the nature of the relationship. The source of the favour is important and feelings of obligation are stronger, in some instances, toward a gift received from an enemy than from any ally (Nadler *et al.*, 1974). On the other hand, the gift from an ally is more likely to evoke a positive feeling than a gift from an enemy. The ally was perceived as more humane and generous, whereas ulterior motives were attributed to the enemy.

Intentions

Merely being a recipient of a favour does not activate the reciprocity norm. Indeed, a person may reciprocate less toward one who has provided him with a favour than one who has not, depending on the motives attributed to the donor (Schopler and Thompson, 1968). Indeed knowledge of intentions may operate as situational constraints (Kahn and Tice, 1973) since exposure of intentions restricts the other person's freedom. Freedom is restored by ignoring the other's intentions when reciprocating.

Liking

Does receiving a benefit lead to attraction? The studies just reviewed suggest that being a recipient of aid could be perceived as a threat to one's freedom of action and one implication would be that receiving a gift would decrease attraction. On the other hand, there is some evidence that the influence of aid on attraction depends on whether or not obligation is involved. Persons who received benefits without the need to reciprocate evaluated the donor less positively than those who were obligated to return an equal amount (Gergen *et al.*, 1975). The explanation given was that a benefit without obligation runs counter to the commonly held values of reciprocity. Moreover, such actions could create unrelieved tensions of obligation as well as possible suspicion of the donor's motives.

Liking for a person who has done something for us depends on whether the person intended to provide the benefit (Nemeth, 1970): just receiving a favour is not enough and Nemeth questions the assumption that liking is a mediating variable in reciprocity. In addition, the cost of the benefit to the donor influences liking: the greater the cost, the greater the liking (Tesser *et al.*, 1968). Similarly Gergen *et al.* (1975) found that donors were evaluated more positively when they had meager resources than were donors with considerable resources, but the more affluent donors were more preferred as teammates than those with meager resources.

In a dyadic bargaining situation, different images are generated by violators and nonviolators of the norm of reciprocity as Esser and

Komorita (1975) found by varying the degree of reciprocated conces-
sions. Opponents that showed relatively little reciprocation were
viewed as competitive and exploitative but when the level of reciprocation was 100%, the other was rated as cooperative, reasonable, warm
and fair.

Stage of the Relationship

In a review article on self-disclosure, Altman (1973, p. 258) noted that
"*all* studies on reciprocity conducted to date used strangers as Ss, in
short-term, *ad hoc*, non-recurring relationships". In the model of
disclosure proposed by Altman, the norm of reciprocity plays a more
important role in the early stages than in the later stages of a
relationship: as persons establish meaningful relationships, the pressures decrease to repay a favour immediately. The finding of maximum
reciprocity in experimental studies is consistent with this model, since
reciprocity research has dealt mainly with strangers. A full understanding of the dynamics of reciprocity requires studies where subjects
have a long-term relationship which they cannot easily leave and
Altman has called repeatedly for longitudinal studies of this kind.

In a longitudinal study of college roommates (Heilbronn, 1975),
correlations between feelings of obligation and reciprocity were
examined at three points in time: after one month acquaintance; six
months later and then a year later. The correlations between obligation
and perceived reciprocity were essentially zero at all three points.
Beliefs that the other person would reciprocate was not associated with
feelings of obligation towards him. These results do not support the
Altman model at least at the perception level.

But the more important question may be whether feelings of
obligation are predictive of the growth of a relationship. Examination
of the Heilbronn data indicated that feelings of obligation measured in
early acquaintance did predict the level of friendship nearly eighteen
months later. Feelings of obligation, then, were not associated with the
attraction when measured at the same point in time, but were
associated with *subsequent* measures of friendship.

Is the Concept of Reciprocity Necessary?

Can the effects of social exchange on attraction be explained without
postulating the concept of reciprocity to explain the data? Gross and
Latané (1974) found that receiving led to liking, liking led to giving,
and giving led to liking. The additive main effects of giving and

receiving on attraction indicate that subjects feel more positively toward people who help them *and* more positively toward people they help. The lack of any significant interactive effects raises a question about the need for a concept of reciprocity. To demonstrate the existence of reciprocity, it would be necessary to show that the effects of giving on liking depend on the amount received, or that the effects of receiving on liking depend on the amount given. Neither of these was found.

What is not clearly understood is the relationship between the culturally determined norm of reciprocity and the unique norms that develop within specific dyads as a result of repeated interactions in view of the fact that such interactions lead to expectations of future rewards (Homans, 1961). Howitt and La Gaipa (1975b) asked college roommates (N = 350), after a month's acquaintance, to indicate the likelihood that the other roommate would reciprocate as much of a benefit as was given. We found that for significant numbers of students, living under relatively close relationships, reciprocal relationships had not been established. Any external social norm appears to have been mitigated by situational factors.

What is overlooked in research on the norm of reciprocity is the basic notion that reciprocity is essential for the maintenance and development of a relationship (Thibaut and Kelley, 1959; Altman and Taylor, 1973). What are the consequences, then, of the expectations that another person would reciprocate? We found that these expectations that a reward would be forthcoming following a benefit given when measured in early stages of acquaintance, after six months and after 18 months were predictive of the growth and dissolution of friendship (Howitt and La Gaipa, 1975b; Heilbronn, 1975).

Most of the studies reviewed in this section have dealt with the norm of reciprocity involving some kind of favour and the focus has been on the identification of the mediating mechanisms. But considerable research has also been done on the norm of reciprocity in regard to the disclosure of information by simply establishing the relationship between the amount disclosed by each person. The norm of reciprocity has received considerable support when studied this way (Davis and Skinner, 1974; Derlega *et al.*, 1973; Ehrlich and Graeven, 1971; Worthy, Gary and Kahn, 1969; and Rubin, 1975).

Altman and Taylor (1973) contend that it is not particularly useful to invoke a "norm" of reciprocity as either an explanation or as a description of exchange: postulating a "norm" is not an explanation of reciprocity. The theoretical task involved in explaining reciprocity requires that one determines that the tendency for a person to respond in kind to the actions of another operates through one or more intervening variables. The task, then, is to identify the intervening variables that mediate the effects of reciprocity.

B. REINFORCEMENT

An explanation of reinforcement that is congruent with traditional exchange theory is that reciprocity occurs as an operant process following socially rewarding outcomes of disclosure (Jourard, 1971; Altman, 1973). Indeed, Homans (1971) argues that the existence of a "norm" continues only insofar as adherence to the norm has been found to be rewarding. Reciprocity, on this view, would be shaped by its positive and negative consequences. If disclosure is rewarding to the person disclosing and/or to the person who is the object of disclosure, then this kind of behaviour is likely to be repeated. If a person finds it intrinsically rewarding to receive disclosure, he is likely to disclose himself so as to encourage more disclosure from the other person (Worthy *et al.*, 1969). However, the mechanisms involved in this kind of explanation have yet to be clearly delineated and few direct tests have been made of this kind of orientation (Altman, 1973).

Attraction Is attraction the mediating variable? Do we like a person who tells us intimate details about their lives or who listens to our intimate affairs? Several studies have found a lack of a relationship between intimate disclosure and liking. Ehrlich and Graeven, 1971; Delerga *et al.* (1973) and Rubin (1975) finding no relationship between liking and disclosure, argued that, to the extent that person's statements are determined by demand characteristics and by normative pressures to reciprocate another's confidence, considerations of liking may be irrelevant to exchange of self-disclosure. Some support has been obtained for a curvilinear hypothesis (Cozby, 1972; Kohen, 1972) where both low and high levels of disclosure are associated with less attraction than moderate levels of disclosure. Cozby found that high levels of disclosure are likely to be interpreted as reflecting personality problems rather than as indicating trust.

One way to assess the role of liking as an intervening and mediating variable is to use the partial correlation technique which permits holding attraction constant. Howitt and La Gaipa (1975b) found that perceived reciprocity of input and outcome of disclosure was very high (r = 0.81). When liking was held constant, the perceived reciprocity dropped only to r = 0.70. This drop was not sufficiently large to warrant labelling attraction as an intervening variable.

Trust: Does the amount of trust that we have in another person affect the reciprocation of intimate disclosure? The role of trust as a mediating variable has been frequently mentioned though research has yet to support this hypothesis. Rubin (1975) found that reciprocity was not mediated by trust and in a longitudinal study, Howitt and La Gaipa (1975b) replicated Rubin's findings: trust was not found to be a mediating variable. The correlation between amount of disclosure and level of friendship was not changed by partialling out the amount of trust in the other. This is not to say that trust is unimportant as a determinant of *friendship*: it was just not found to play a role in *disclosure*.

Interaction Style: Does the interaction style of an interview influence self-disclosure? This question is of concern to therapists who seek to facilitate self-disclosure as part of their treatment. In one study (Ellison and Firestone, 1974), subjects listened to potential disclosure targets who had either an intrusive or reflective style. A greater *willingness* to disclose was indicated toward the interviewer with the reflective style than the intrusive style.

Not enough studies have directly tested the relative merits of normative and reinforcement explanations of reciprocity. The reader will recall that a reinforcement explanation relies on consideration of the positive and negative consequences of behaviour but Derlega and her associates have conducted a series of studies concerned with examining alternative explanations. In one study (Derlega *et al.*, 1973), self disclosure increased as a function of intimate input under "low potential consequences" (i.e. if subjects believed their comments would remain private) but not under "high potential consequences". Derlega *et al.* concluded that the norm of reciprocity is less likely to operate under conditions where a person is worried about getting hurt as a result of disclosure.

In a second study (Derlega *et al.*, 1973), the discloser of intimate but deviant information (i.e. a homosexual relationship), was liked less than the discloser of either intimate but nondeviant (a heterosexual relationship) or nonintimate information. The amount of reciprocal disclosure was higher in the deviant-high discloser condition than in the low discloser condition, even though the deviant was liked less than the nondeviant. These results were viewed as supporting the norm of reciprocity — the rewarding qualities of liking were not particularly relevant.

C. COGNITIVE BIAS

A third possible explanation of reciprocity that has been generally ignored by social exchange theorists is that of cognitive biases: cognitive consistency theory and exchange theory have tended to go their separate ways. The "norm" of reciprocity has been tested by behaviouristically-oriented exchange theorists in terms of overt measures of behaviour: indeed Altman and Taylor (1973) argue against the use of questionnaire data to study reciprocity because of the response sets that contaminate the results. But what a behaviourist may discard as "response set" might be the very thing a cognitive psychologist would want to study.

A cognitive bias according to balance theory is a preference for perceiving social structures in particular ways and various cognitive biases have been identified beside that of balance (cf. Taylor, 1970). A reciprocity bias would thus be a preference for perceiving social relationships as reciprocal. Kelley (1971) cautions against interpreting cognitive biases as simply error: such biases, rather, reflect the need to perceive the world as an orderly and predictable place (cf. Kelvin's chapter, section 3 of this book). The notion that giving will lead to receiving implies that a person has some control over the other person's actions.

Cognitive measures are most likely to be used when studying persons in established role relationships where more objective measures would be impractical or likely to affect the process being investigated. Few, if any, studies exist where husbands and wives have been directly observed over extended periods of time to determine the degree to which the amount disclosed by one was correlated with the amount disclosed by the other. A more common practice has been to ask each person to indicate on a rating scale the amount of disclosure characteristic of each person in the dyad.

In a study on disclosure in marriage, Levinger and Senn (1967) found high correlations between *perceived* inputs and outcomes of disclosure for husbands ($r = 0.91$) and for their wives ($r = 0.79$). In a study of a different kind of subjects (roommates), Howitt and La

Gaipa (1975a) found similarly high correlations ($r = 0.81$). Both of these studies support the notion that people prefer to think that a high relationship exists between what they gave and what they received. There is a "strain" to perceive a high level of reciprocity.

But does a relationship exist between the self-reports of one person and the self-reports of the other person in the same dyad? Levinger and Senn (1967) obtained independent measures of each partner's disclosure to the other and found that the correlation between input and outcome was much lower ($r = 0.38$) than that obtained when each person described his inputs and outcomes, i.e. subjects tend to misperceive and overestimate the reciprocity which exists objectively.

Howitt and La Gaipa (1975a) reasoned that one roommate's "give" should correspond to the other roommate's "receive". If Person A reports giving a small amount, then Person B should also report receiving a small amount. However, correlation of only 0.34 was found between inputs and outcomes. Though the size of this correlation suggests that a relationship does exist between one's inputs and the other's outcome, the magnitude of the correlation is far below what is considered acceptable evidence of statistical reliability. The level of "accuracy" increased as the roommates became better acquainted, but never high enough to be considered reliable. This kind of autistic distortion among friends was also found by Newcomb (1961) in his classical study of roommates who also overestimated the true amounts of similarity between them.

The first impression that is evoked by these two studies is that questionnaire-type data are unreliable when agreement among raters in each dyad is used to estimate reliability. Somewhat different results, however, were obtained when an alternate index of reciprocity was used (ratings of "the likelihood that the other would reciprocate"). Now the correlations were quite satisfactory ($r = 0.73$). Few instances were found where members of the same dyad reported different levels of expected reciprocity, as if a dyadic norm had been reached on the extent to which each could count on the other.

It is not as yet clear why the verbal reports of roommates corresponded more highly when indicating what they expected in terms of reciprocity than when reporting the amounts actually given and received. Both measures were valid, however, in predicting the growth of friendship over time as measured by behavioural and cognitive measures. Needless to say, the more reliable measure (expected reciprocity) proved to be a somewhat better predictor.

III. A taxonomy of exchange variables

It should now be evident that a variety of conceptual schemes exist which deal with different aspects of attraction and social exchange although there is some overlap among the models presented. There are some important differences also in the kinds of problems to which one is sensitized by each model. In this section, I will try to provide a framework that helps to view different theories and results within a more common perspective and I will make explicit some unanswered questions raised by the various orientations.

The aim is to provide a scheme useful in seeing the relationships within any one broad class of variables as well as different classes of variables. The usefulness of this scheme can be judged only in terms of the kinds of propositions stimulated by it and eventually by the kinds of research generated by it. The classes of variables included in this taxonomy are as follows: resource class, patterns of exchange, stages of the relationship, social context, transitional processes, and units of change.

A. RESOURCE CLASS

Exchange theorists generally have been reluctant to specify rewards in their formulation of theoretical propositions. Thibaut and Kelley (1959) have been instrumental here in pointing out that, in the absence of any agreed upon system of rewards, there is a danger in trying to explain results by *ad hoc* postulation of rewards. Refinement of resource theory however, may encourage the specification of rewards and more precise predictions may be possible by relating rewards to specific situational contexts (Gergen, 1969).

The exchange theories reviewed differ in the resource classes used (see above). Homans (1974) and Blau (1964) make frequent use of studies on the asymmetrical exchange of *status* (social approval) and *information* (expertise). Research on equity theory (Adams, 1965) relies on *pay* or *money* as reward outcomes, particularly in field studies. Experiments on equity theory also have used points or other tokens possessing similar psychological characteristics of money. The exchange of *love* has also received some attention (Foa and Donnenwerth, 1971; Davis, 1973).

At a different level of comment, research on the justice motive (Lerner, 1974a; Lerner *et al.*, 1976) deal mainly with *universalistic* rather than *particularistic* kinds of rewards (see above, p. 147). In formulating a personal contract, the child willingly delays getting such rewards as "goods", "services" or "money", not status and love. Social penetration theory (Altman and Taylor, 1973) relies rather heavily on the resource class of *information*. Changes from one stage in a relationship to another involve changes along parameters from this resource class. Levinger and Snoek (1972) and Levinger (1974) also assign a high priority to information exchange.

These differences are important for researchers because the choice of resource class has some implications for the mechanisms used by the theorist. Research on the norm of reciprocity involving favours, such as "goods" and "services", has looked at the role of *obligation*. On the other hand, research involving reciprocity of information has been more concerned with *liking* and *trust* as mediating variables.

Important considerations for our conceptualization of acquaintance depend on the types of resource class examined. For example, what is the interaction between resource class and stage of the relationship in regard to the kinds of meanings inferred? Rewards from the same resource class may evoke different subjective meanings depending on the level. For example, doing a favour in an early stage might be interpreted as a desire to establish a friendly relationship. The same act at a later stage might be a token of love and affection, i.e. to reinforce existing relationships rather than to initiate the relationship. Considerable research is needed in order to determine the degree to which findings from experiments involving exchange among strangers can be generalized to more established relationships or to developing ones.

B. PATTERNS OF EXCHANGE

If one assumes that the effects of exchange on attraction depend on the meaning attached to the social acts, then a more holistic or configural approach to acquaintance is called for. Resource theory has drawn attention to the *content* of rewards, but meaning is conveyed by both *context* and *content*. The pattern of interaction in an exchange episode would include all of the following, not just content: sequencing of interaction, rate of exchange, symmetry, direction and rules of exchange. Unfortunately, exchange research has touched on only some of these areas.

Sequencing

Any given exchange episode is part of an ongoing sequence of interaction which possesses formal configural properties of its own. The configural properties of exchange may contain messages which contradict or transcend the message contained in the content of the exchange. A specific exchange act acquires part of its meaning from what preceeded the act and what followed it.

Symmetry

Attention needs to be paid to whether the reciprocated behaviour is in the same resource class ("symmetrical") or in a different resource class ("asymmetrical") from the initial behaviour. Experimental studies (cf. Cozby, 1972) have emphasized the importance of symmetrical exchange, whereas descriptive studies (Homans, 1974; Blau, 1964) have focused on asymmetrical exchange. The antecedent and consequent conditions of asymmetrical exchange are in particular need of further research, though obviously difficult to study. Many of the attacks levelled against Homans (1974) stems from the methodological problems involved in establishing the equivalence of different kinds of rewards (cf. Abrahamsson, 1970). Some unanswered questions for further research are: Does the degree of asymmetrical exchange in a relationship depend on the stage of the relationship? Is the problem of inferring meaning and intentions more difficult under asymmetrical than symmetrical exchange? Are feelings of injustice more likely to be evoked under conditions of asymmetrical than symmetrical exchange?

Direction

The notion of movement from one resource class to another raises interesting possibilities in the context of developing relationships. If observed over time, the movement of exchange could be visualized as being inner-directed or outer-directed: *inner-directed* or core-directed exchange would be movement from the universalistic classes toward the particularistic classes, e.g. decreasing use of goods and services and increasing use of status and love. Similarly *outer-directed* exchange would be characteristic of a relationship where exchanges of love and status become less usual and exchange involving goods and services would be more frequent. A shift from love-love exchange to a love-gifts exchange might be indicative of a deterioration of a relationship. On the other hand, the growth of a relationship would be characterized by increasing incidence of particularistic rewards. The direction of exchange, then, may help to account for movements across stages: particularly the growth or dissolution of relationships.

The Rules of Social Exchange

A major area of research on processes of exchange lies in the conditions under which different "justice strategies" are employed (see above). Some attention has been given to the role of the social context as a mediating factor but relatively little attention has been paid to the stage of the relationship or the resource class involved.

The usual treatment of friendship as the independent rather than as the dependent variable raises a question about the relevance of research on justice strategies to the topic of this chapter, i.e. attraction and exchange. The focus of the major exchange theories has been on the effects of exchange on the formation of social relationships (cf. Blau, 1964). On the other hand research designs that have included the variable of friendship have treated it as a causal variable: examining, for example, whether equity or equality is used in an exchange relationship as a function of the kind of social association. Friends are more likely to divide an object into equal parts to avoid creating a status difference (Lerner, 1974b) and equal sharing or division of a concrete thing is important in friendship among children (La Gaipa and Bigelow, 1972). The extent to which this operation of equal division is important or feasible in the resource classes used by adults is open to question.

Although it is important to know whether the notion of injustice is equally relevant for all resource classes, research on justice strategies has not adequately sampled all of them. Is a person unfair who does not exchange the same amount of intimate information as he received; or does not return "love" with "love"? Is the notion of justice as relevant for resource classes high in particularism as for resource classes low in particularism?

Perhaps the notion of injustice is not equally relevant at all stages of a social relationship — an implicit assumption in much of the writing reviewed in this chapter. For intimate friendships, is an imbalance between inputs and outcomes perceived along the dimension of fairness or along the dimension of commitment?

C. STAGES OF THE RELATIONSHIP

Stages are one way of describing changes in social relationships but whether it is necessary or even desirable to use a stage approach is an empirical question. Altman and Taylor (1973) postulate four stages that differ according to the degree of social penetration: orientation, exploratory affective, affective, and stable exchange. A three-stage level of relatedness model has also been proposed: awareness, surface contact, and mutuality (Levinger and Snoek, 1972; Levinger, 1974) although the last step is further subdivided into three stages varying from minor interaction to total unity. Using more common terms, La Gaipa (1969) has attempted to define four levels of friendship, varying from social acquaintance to best friend.

There are, however, some important questions which attach to any such "stage theory": How do people define the stage they are in? Is the stage defined in terms of the pattern of exchange characteristic of the relationship? Are negotiations involved in defining a stage or do people find themselves operating at a certain level without necessarily intending it? Do transitions reflect changes in the amount and forecast of future reward? A major problem is the nature of the relationship among the variables within a stage and across stages. Are the same variables critical at each stage or do new patterns emerge? Do changes in some variables generate homeostatic mechanisms to restore equilibrium? Do any such compensatory mechanisms have dysfunctional effects, i.e. is stability achieved at the expense of change? Finally, can the degree of equilibrium in a stage be operationalized in such a way to permit deductions as to the consequences of disequilibrium?

D. SOCIAL CONTEXT

No adequate system has yet been developed for classifying the variables essential for defining the social context in which exchange occurs even though one major role assigned to situational variables is that of regulating the exchange processes. Blau (1964) includes normative processes, role relationships and multi-group affiliation as key elements in the situation; Altman and Taylor (1973) postulate four dimensions:formality v. informality, segmental v. holistic, short term v. long term, confined v. non-confined. Related parameters include the "temporal" dimension, such as prior history and future expectations, and "spatial" e.g. physical distance. A second role assigned to situational variables is an interpretative function since the meaning of a social act depends on the context in which it occurs.

Knowledge of the social context has implications for the other parameters already outlined here: the choice of the resource class selected; the pattern of exchange; the definition of the stage and transitions from stage to stage.

Attention to the relationship between social context and resource class may be useful in generating various questions. Let us take a rather obvious example. Can the stability of a relationship be maintained as physical distance leads to increase reliance on the exchange of information rather than "goods" and "services"? More concretely, under what conditions will a close friendship be maintained as there is increasing reliance on the exchange of letters?

E. TRANSITIONAL PROCESSES

The more traditional exchange theories have been concerned mainly with the *maintenance* of social relationships rather than *development* and *change*. The notion of equilibrium or balance is implicit in a variety of such theories, e.g. Homans (1974); Thibaut and Kelley (1959); Adams (1965) and Lerner (1974a). What is common to these theories is the idea that imbalance is uncomfortable and that homeostatic devices are activated to restore balance.

Other exchange theories view social relationships as basically dynamic and tending toward change rather than stability and equilibrium. For example, Blau's (1964) theory of social exchange has some dialectic features, i.e. a view that conflict is inherent in any social system; that internal contradictions lead to change. The dilemmas include the strain for maximum profit versus the strain for reciprocity; the notion of diminishing marginal returns beyond a certain point (increases in a reward is associated with decreases in the value attached to it) and that balance in one social relationship is at the expense of imbalance in another.

Longitudinal models of social exchange deal more specifically with change. Altman and Taylor (1973) postulate social penetration process as the primary mechanism leading to change. Social penetration theory specifies the forces that facilitate or inhibit disclosure. Levinger's (1974) three-level approach includes interpersonal discovery and disclosure, as well as mutual investments. The Huesmann and Levinger (1976) incremental exchange theory postulates anticipated or expected payoffs as influencing transition.

F. UNIT OF CHANGE

It is often useful to identify the units of change most salient in a theory since generally, the mechanisms postulated to account for change depend on what unit of change is viewed as most important. Exchange theorists, however, are not always explicit as to the unit of change. Homans (1974) interprets change in terms of increases or decreases in the amount of profit incurred in the interaction, but repeated interactions lead to changes in expectations of future rewards. Altman and Taylor (1973) are concerned with changes from superficial to more intimate exchange of information: the two major parameters of information are breadth and depth. Huesmann and Levinger (1976) refer to changes in the depth of the relationship where depth is defined in terms of mutual involvement.

IV. Conclusions

This chapter has presented a range of theoretical strategies used to build and test models of social exchange. As should be self-evident by now, the major problem is the lack of adequate operational measures of different classes of theoretical variables. We need measures of different rewards, measures of situational variables, measures of variables involved in transitions from stage to stage, and techniques to study exchange from a longitudinal point of view.

Finally, no one view of man is likely to explain behaviour. Nor can we expect *simple* answers to questions about whether man seeks to maximize his payoffs or to maintain equity. It is likely that more than one motive is involved and so the utility of particular theories under particular conditions needs to be determined, particularly if an overall theory proves to be unworkable. Until this is done, many fruitless debates will continue, as well as reliance on anecdotal evidence and citations by poets and philosophers on the true nature of love and friendship.

7.

Complementarity in Interpersonal Attraction

B. A. SEYFRIED

State University of New York, Oswego, New York, USA

An aspect of the marriage of two of my friends, Sarah and Luke, illustrates rather neatly what is meant by complementary needs in attraction. Luke is a slob; Sarah is not quite as messy as Luke. As a consequence of the difference in filth tolerance, Sarah frequently must pick up Luke's clothes, papers, books, and other belongings for him or nag Luke into cleaning up if she wants to live in a neat household. On one occasion, Sarah sent Luke to pick up the clutter in the living room: Luke picked up some beer cans and books. However, when Sarah walked into the living room, she noticed that Luke had overlooked two newspapers under the coffee table and a pair of old tennis shoes in the middle of the floor.

What ensued was not a fight between the two. Instead, Sarah

jokingly pointed out the items that Luke had overlooked and together they cleaned up the remainder of the living room. Later, they both joyfully related to a guest this story of Luke's selective blindness to disorder.

Ordinarily, one would expect that a series of conflicts over neatness would strain the marriage between Sarah and Luke. However, the attitude of both participants makes the conflict an inherent part of their marriage. Sarah enjoys the nurturant role of looking after her husband, gently nagging him to clean up and teasing him when he proves incompetent at the task. Luke enjoys being looked after, delights in the reputation of slob and enjoys the teasing interaction when he fails to do an adequate job of keeping the house neat.

The example above illustrates how Sarah's nurturance (the desire to look after others) and Luke's succorance (the desire to be helped by others) turns a situation which could result in hostility into a situation that is an asset to a marriage.

I. Theoretical explanations

To understand the role of complementarity in attraction, it is necessary to consider various theories of how dissimilar but congruent behaviour may produce attraction. Theoretical approaches are therefore discussed first and are followed by a discussion of research on complementarity. The two distinct theoretical traditions in explanations of complementarity and attraction emphasize the concepts of need gratification and self concept.

A. NEED GRATIFICATION

Two theoretical approaches emphasize the role of need in attraction: Winch's (1958) complementary needs theory and Schutz's (1960) compatibility theory. Both theories rely on the concept of need gratification as the cause of attraction. In the section which follows, Murray's (1938) concept of need is described, Winch's (1958) and Schutz's (1960) theories are described, and the question of why need gratification leads to attraction is discussed.

Murray's Concept of Need

Murray's (1938) definition of need is one that social psychologists favour in discussing the complementary needs theory. According to

Hall and Lindzey (1957), "no one has subjected the concept of need to so careful an analysis nor provided such a complete taxonomy of needs as has Murray" (p. 172). Consequently, selected aspects of Murray's theorizing provide a basis for thinking about needs, their idiosyncrasies, and their relationship to the complementary needs hypothesis.

Murray (1938) defined *need* as a "construct which stands for a force . . . which organizes perception, apperception, intellection, conation, and action in such a way as to transform in a certain direction an existing unsatisfying condition" (pp. 123 and 124). According to Murray's definition, a need is an internal motivator which pushes an organism into behaving. The operation of a need is inferred from such factors as (a) the end result of behaviour; (b) the pattern, mode, or style of behaviour which a person uses in approaching a goal; (c) selective attention to particular stimulus objects; and (d) expression of satisfaction when a particular goal is achieved or disappointment when a goal is not achieved (Murray, 1938).

Murray differentiated between a number of different aspects of needs. Viscerogenic versus psychogenic, manifest versus latent, focal versus diffuse, and proactive versus reactive are distinctions relevant to the discussion of complementary needs.

Viscerogenic Needs Versus Psychogenic Needs Murray (1938) defined *viscerogenic needs* as those which are linked to organic events. Viscerogenic needs are those which have a biological basis such as the need for air, urination, food, or sex. *Psychogenic needs* are derived from primary needs and characterized by "no subjectively localizable bodily organs" (p. 77). Murray (1938) listed a variety of social needs such as nurturance (the need to help other people), succorance (the need to be helped by other people), dominance (the need to control the sentiments and behaviours of other people) and abasement (the tendency to accept and invite blame). Schutz (1960) pointed out that such interpersonal needs are generally satisfied "only through attainment of satisfactory relationships with people" (p. 15). Psychogenic needs are those of primary concern in the discussion of complementary needs and attraction.

Manifest Versus Latent Needs A second theoretical distinction is made by Murray: between manifest and latent needs. *Manifest needs* are expressed physically or verbally in overt behaviour directed at real objects. *Latent needs* do not influence overt behaviour but may be expressed in desires, fantasy, resolutions for the future, dreaming, play, artistic creation, and watching the exhibition of a need in others (Murray, 1938).

Whether a need is manifest or latent affects how the need influences interactions. Only if a person's need is manifest will it have an impact on other people's liking for him. For example, suppose a man has a manifest need to dominate others: this need might be expressed in overbearing behaviour toward others. The overbearing behaviour could influence a second person's feeling of attraction depending on whether the overbearing behaviour resulted in need gratification or not. However, if a need is latent, the need is not expressed in a fashion which is observable to a second person. Consequently, latent needs are not likely to influence such a person's feelings of attraction.

Focal Versus Diffuse Needs   Another theoretical distinction which Murray made is between focal and diffuse needs. *Focal needs* are needs that can be gratified by only one object or very few kinds of objects. *Diffuse needs* are those which can be gratified by a wide variety of objects.

The main impact of this distinction on complementary needs theory is to point out that some needs may only be gratified in a limited number of social situations while others may be gratified in a wide range of situations.

Proactive Versus Reactive Needs   Murray (1962) further differentiated between *proactive needs* (needs which arise spontaneously from within the person) and *reactive needs* (needs which are activated by an environmental event). He described needs for food, for affection, for knowledge and for artistic creation as examples of proactive needs. Proactions are things a person wants to do (Murray, 1962). Reactions are "more apt to be responses to situations which are unsought, unexpected, and dissatisfying" (Murray, 1962, p. 448). This con-ceptualization of needs points out the importance of considering both the individual and the environment as sources of motivation.

Relationship between Needs and Behaviour   Murray (1938) spent considerable time discussing the question of whether one should talk about human personality in terms of *actones,* patterns of observable behaviour such as physical movement or a run of coherent words, or in terms of needs. He argued for the conceptual advantages of a need based conception of behaviour over an actone based conception of behaviour.

According to Murray, one advantage of the need concept is that it allows for the opportunity of considering observably different types of behaviour as conceptually similar to each other. Murray gave the example of different types of organisms using different actones to attain the same goal, food: "Some organisms kill their prey with teeth and claws, others by injecting venom" (p. 57). Murray also felt that at every stage of the life history of an individual the same needs may be gratified but the actones that are used to gratify the needs may themselves evolve. "The embryo assimilates food through the umbilical vessels, the infant sucks it from the tendered breast of the mother, the child eats with a spoon what is put before him, and the adult has to work, or steal, to get money to buy food" (Murray, 1938, p. 57).

According to Murray's (1938) view, the concept of need provides a useful construct for explaining behaviour. Using the concept of need one can categorize different types of behaviours as expressions of the same need. For example, the need for nurturance might lead a woman to select nursing as a career, to spank her son for running heedlessly into the street, or to try and cheer up a sick neighbour. All the behaviours can be expressions of the same need.

Interrelationships Among Needs Murray described a large number of needs such as the need for abasement, aggression, dominance, exhibitionism, nurturance and autonomy. Because of the large number of interpersonal needs which may influence an individual's behaviour, some organizing principles were needed to explain how an individual managed to coordinate the process of need gratification.

Murray described four different types of relationships which may exist between different needs: prepotency, scheduling, need subsidation, and need fusion. *Prepotency* refers to the principle that among needs there is a need hierarchy in which needs highest in the hierarchy are satisfied before needs lower in the hierarchy. According to Murray, when two or more needs are elicited simultaneously, the prepotent need is gratified first.

Scheduling is a second concept which Murray used to explain how need satisfaction is patterned. *Schedules* (Hall and Lindzey, 1957) represent strategies for reducing conflict among competing needs and goal objects by arranging for the expression of different needs at different times. For example, consider the viscerogenic need to urinate. When the need to urinate arises, most people manage to control when and where they express such a need rather than spontaneously expressing the need immediately it arises. Such scheduling allows for need gratification to occur in an organized and coordinated fashion.

Need subsidation occurs when one need is used to gratify a second need. For example, when a woman expresses her need for nurturance by spanking her child for running into the street, she is using behaviour gratifying to her aggressive need in order to gratify her nurturant need.

Need fusion arises when a single action gratifies more than one need at the same time. Murray (1938) gave the example of an exhibitionist person who is paid to sing a solo in public. According to Murray, this person's exhibitionistic needs and acquisitive needs are being gratified at the same time.

Prepotency, scheduling, need subsidation, and need fusion are all strategies for dealing with conflict between needs. When these mechanisms fail, a person must make a difficult choice between two courses of action. According to Murray (1938), motivational forces in such a conflict are generally equal in power and push the person in two mutually exclusive directions.

Complementarity and Equivalent Concepts

Winch's Theory Winch (1958) and his coworkers argued that when the needs of two people combine in a complementary fashion, attraction results. According to this view (Winch *et al.*, 1954), person A's and person B's needs will complement each other when (a) the needs are different in type, but of the same intensity (*Type I complementarity*) and (b) when the needs are of the same type, but different in intensity (*Type II complementarity*). An example of Type I complementarity arises when a person with a high need for nurturance (the need to look after people) is attracted to a person with a high need for succorance (the need to be looked after by others). An example of Type II complementarity arises when a very dominating person is attracted to a person with a low need for dominance who can be controlled.

Winch's answer to the question of which needs create a complementary need relationship and which do not has never been fully adequate.

Originally, Winch (1958) classified needs as complementary on the basis of a combination of common sense and "Freudian derived psychologies". A later factor analysis of the research data (Winch *et al.*, 1955) indicated two empirically derived dimensions of complementarity: nurturance-receptivity and dominance-submissiveness. Winch (1967) also felt that there was a suggestion of an achievement-vicariousness dimension in his data.

Schutz's Theory Schutz (1960) constructed the concept of compatibility, which is similar to Winch's concept of complementarity. *Compatibility* is defined as a "property of a relation between two people . . . that leads to mutual satisfaction of interpersonal needs and harmonious coexistence" (p. 105). According to Schutz (1960), the greater the amount of compatibility in a group, the greater the likelihood that group members will prefer continued personal contact with each other. However, Schutz (1960) does not feel that compatibility necessarily leads to increased liking, merely to an increased desire for group members to remain together.

The difference between Schutz's (1960) and Winch's (1958) theorizing is that Schutz focused attention on group cohesion and Winch focused attention on interpersonal attraction. Group cohesion and attraction are two related but not equivalent concepts. Cartwright (1968) defines group cohesion as the resultant of all forces which keep a person within a group — and one measure of group cohesion is liking between individual members of the group. Group cohesion has also been measured by asking people how they evaluate the group as a whole, how much they want to stay in the group, and how closely they identify with the group. In short, interpersonal attraction is merely one of several measures of group cohesion.

Despite the difference in the theoretical statements that the two theorists make, Schutz's concept of compatibility is generally talked about in relationship to interpersonal attraction (Kerckhoff and Davis, 1962; Levinger *et al.*, 1970).

Schutz (1960) specified three different types of compatibility: originator compatibility, interchange compatibility, and reciprocal compatibility. *Originator compatibility* is defined as agreement between an interacting pair of people as to who should originate interaction and who should be the receiver of an attempt to originate interaction. For example, a person who likes to invite other people to join him in an activity but is uncomfortable when others try to get him involved in their activities is compatible with a person who enjoys being invited to join in activities but does not care to be the initiator. When two initiators or two receivers are paired with each other, incompatibility arises.

Interchange compatibility is defined as compatibility over the amount of interaction which occurs. According to Schutz (1960) people differ in the amounts of interaction they like to engage in. For example, some people enjoy a great deal of affectionate interaction with their spouses, others are embarrassed by too much affection. People who are similar in the amount of interchange they desire are compatible with each other. People who are dissimilar in the amount of interchange they desire are incompatible.

Reciprocal compatibility refers to compatibility of the behaviour that a person likes to express and the behaviour desired by the person he is interacting with. If person A likes to express affection and person B likes to receive affection, then persons A and B have reciprocal compatibility.

Schutz (1960) argued that originator, interchange and reciprocal compatibility may be found in three different need areas: inclusion, control, and affection. *Inclusion* is defined as "the need to establish and maintain a satisfactory relation with people with respect to interaction and association" (Schutz, 1960, p. 18). A person with strong needs to express inclusion enjoys such activities as associating with other people, belonging to clubs and other social organizations and entertaining other people. A person with a strong need to receive inclusion behaviour enjoys being invited to do things, being invited to participate in discussions and being invited to participate in other activities. *Control* is defined as "the need to establish and maintain a satisfactory relation with people with respect to control and to power" (Schutz, 1960, p. 18). People with a strong urge to express their need to control derive satisfaction from such activities as taking charge of things, influencing other people's action and having others obey them. People with a strong need to be recipients of controlling activity like others to make decisions and take charge of things. *Affection* is defined as "the need to establish and maintain a satisfactory relation with respect to love and affection" (Schutz, 1960, p. 20). A person with a strong need to express affection enjoys being friendly and having close, personal relationships with others. A person who likes to receive affection prefers others to act friendly and behave in a close, personal fashion.

Why Need Gratification Leads to Attraction Winch's (1958) need gratification theory appears to fall within a reinforcement model best described by Lott and Lott (1960). According to these authors (cited in Byrne, 1969), people are discriminable stimuli to which responses may be learned. When a person is rewarded, he reacts to the reward with an implicit affective response; the response to reward is then conditioned to any objects present at the time of the reward, including people. Through repeated pairings, a person eventually comes to elicit the implicit affective response without the presence of the reward.

Where theorists differ is over the behaviours that are viewed as rewarding. Byrne and Clore (1967) on the one hand argue that agreeing and disagreeing attitude statements are rewarding. Winch (1958, 1967) on the other hand suggested that behaviours which result in gratification of specific needs such as nurturance, dominance, or achievement are rewarding.

One shortcoming of Winch's thinking is that he only discussed the reinforcing properties of dissimilar behaviour. However, there is no intuitive reason why similar behaviours cannot be complementary: for example, interaction between two people who are high in need for affiliation leads to mutual need gratification just as interaction between a person high in nurturance and a person who is high in succorance. In each case, personality needs of two interacting people may be mutually gratified. Logically, therefore, the theory of complementary needs should offer an account of similar as well as dissimilar "complementary" needs.

B. SELF CONCEPT

Secord and Backman (1964b) rejected the concept of need complementarity. Instead, they suggested that dissimilar behaviours may lead to attraction because of congruent self-concepts and argued that when the behaviours of two people are congruent with each other, attraction results. No drive need be satisfied: congruency involves the self-concept rather than a drive state.

According to Secord and Backman (1964b) congruence exists when a person perceives another person as behaving in a way that confirms his self-concept. To quote the authors "If a person perceives himself to be a dominant individual, the behaviour of others who permit him to dominate them is likely to be perceived as congruent. This state of congruency is thought to produce liking for that other person" (p. 116). In the terms of this approach, therefore, congruency is independent of similarity or dissimilarity. Instead, congruency may arise when (a) both self and friend are both high on the same need; (b) self is high and friend is low on the same need; or (c) self and friend are both high on certain interdependent needs.

Secord and Backman (1964b) placed heavy emphasis on social perception in the research procedures which they used to study congruency, by asking 152 subjects to complete ranking scales for ten needs. Subjects ranked the importance of ten needs for themselves and then answered the same questionnaire in the way in which they thought their best, same sexed, friend would answer the questionnaire. The results showed six significant correlations between the two sets of rankings which indicated support for the similarity hypothesis. The need pairings were nurturance-nurturance, exhibition-exhibition, deference-deference, autonomy-autonomy, achievement-achievement and aggression-aggression. The authors also categorized four need pairings as indicating support for the congruency hypothesis: nurturance-succorance, deference-nurturance, autonomy-autonomy, and achievement-achievement. The overlap of two need pairings in the results supporting similarity and congruency hypotheses arose because Secord and Backman (1964b) felt that the positive relationships between autonomy-autonomy and achievement-achievement were both similar and congruent. Other need pairings found significant were incongruent relationships, dissimilar relationships, and unknown relationships.

Centers (1972) also felt that the self-concept is an important variable influencing when dissimilar patterns of behaviour produce attraction. He pointed out that the selection of friends on the basis of congruent behaviours is mediated by self-evaluations and perceptual comparisons of oneself with others. These perceptions mediate the relationship between the congruent behaviour of two people and attraction. Centers pointed out that the perception of a need may be inaccurate. Consequently, a person may inaccurately feel that he is interacting with a person whose needs are congruent to his own.

Secord and Backman's (1964b) theorizing has both weaknesses and strengths. One shortcoming of the theorizing is that it provides no explanation of why congruent patterns of behaviour may lead to attraction. At the risk of committing the nominalist fallacy, one possible explanation is to hypothesize a need to behave consistently with one's self concept. This approach argues that need reduction results from being treated in a way that is consistent with how we think of ourselves.

A second hypothesis is that the self-concept influences a person's choice of schedules for the gratification of his needs. For example, a person who regards himself as a good friend may choose to gratify his need for nurturance in his friendships. A person who regards himself as a good parent, may choose to gratify his nurturance need in his relationship with his children. In the example above, one's self-concept influences the patterning of need gratification.

The strength of Secord and Backman's (1964b) theory is that it emphasizes the importance of social perception in defining what constitutes congruent behaviour. Centers (1972) pointed out that one possible implication of this theoretical statement is that relative rather than absolute levels of congruency will result in attraction. In other words, if a person perceives himself as more dominating than a second person, attraction may result due to complementary needs even though the absolute level of the first person's dominance is low. Centers (1972) also provided research support for this hypothesis. He found that there was no relationship between the absolute levels of one's own abilities and perceived abilities of one's fiancé. However, a significant percentage of males and females rated their fiancé higher relative to themselves on many abilities.

A second strength of Secord and Backman's (1964b) approach is that it emphasizes the role of cognition in attraction rather than just the affective processes assumed to be present in Winch's need gratification theory.

Secord and Backman's thinking also suggests that there may be other variables which interact with the need gratification process.

II. Research on complementary needs

Research on complementary needs has tended to contrast a "similarity hypothesis" with the complementary needs hypothesis. The similarity hypothesis in this context predicts that people with similar personality characteristics will be attracted to one another. The complementary needs hypothesis predicts that complementary patterns of need gratification will lead to attraction.

A. SUMMARY OF RESEARCH

Research comparing the validity of the two hypotheses has had mixed results. Some research has supported the complementary needs hypothesis (Rychlak, 1965; Wagner, 1975; Winch, 1955a, 1955b;

Winch *et al.*, 1954, 1955), some has supported both the complementary needs hypothesis and the similarity hypothesis (Beier *et al.*, 1961; Centers, 1972; Katz *et al.*, 1960; Secord and Backman, 1964b; Seyfried and Hendrick, 1973a), some has supported the similarity hypothesis (Banta and Hetherington, 1963; Cattell and Nesselroade, 1967; Izard, 1963; Miller *et al.*, 1966; Mehlman, 1962; Palmer and Byrne, 1970; Pierce, 1970; Thompson and Nishimura, 1952; Van Dyne, 1940), and some has supported neither the complementary needs or the similarity hypothesis (Bowerman and Day, 1956).

B. RESEARCH SUPPORTING THE COMPLEMENTARY NEEDS THEORY

Winch's Research

The most frequently cited study supporting the complementary needs theory is Winch's original study. In this study, Winch selected 25 young married couples who were homogeneous with respect to race, social class, lack of ethnic ties, length of marriage, and lack of children. At the time of the study, at least one member of each couple was an undergraduate student at Northwestern University.

Winch had subjects answer questions designed to elicit information about their interpersonal needs, provide information for a case history, and provide responses to an eight card Thematic Apperception Test (TAT). These three measures were elaborated into five measures: a content analysis of the need interview; a holistic, clinical oriented analysis of the need interview; a holistic analysis of the case history; a holistic analysis of the TAT; and a final set of ratings by a conference of five people of the needs expressed on all three measures. Winch and his coworkers then proceeded to perform several different analyses of these data.

In studying the results of the need interview analysis, Winch *et al.* (1954) hypothesized that 344 interspousal correlations involving two different needs would be positive (Type I complementarity) and 44 interspousal correlations involving the same trait would be negative (Type II complementarity). Winch and his coauthors found that the number of significant correlations supporting the complementary needs hypothesis exceeded the number expected by chance.

Winch (1955a) tested the complementary needs hypothesis a second time by comparing the average correlation between the needs of married couples with the average correlation of randomly matched

couples on the two need interview measures and on the final conference rating. The average correlation between married couples was
significantly lower than the average correlation of the randomly
matched couples on the two need interview measures but not on the
final conference rating. Winch argued that this finding provides
further support for the complementary needs hypothesis.

Winch *et al.* (1955) performed a crude cluster analysis of the two
need interview measures and the final conference rating. Results
showed an assertiveness-receptivity dimension in married couples.
More assertive people (either male or female) married more receptive
people. Ktsanes (1955) factor analyzed the need interview results and
found four main factors which he labelled Yielding Dependency,
Hostile Dominance, Mature Nurturance, and Neurotic Self-Deprecia-
tion.

Criticisms of Winch's Research

Winch's research has been criticized for a variety of reasons. Tharp
(1963) pointed out that the 388 correlations predicted to be related to
each other were not independent of each other. The implications of
this lack of independence is best illustrated in the following example.
If trait A is correlated with trait B and trait B is correlated with trait
C, then trait A would be correlated with trait C even though there may
be no necessary relationship between the traits A and C. Lack of
independence would therefore inflate the number of correlations one
would expect between two variables by chance. Therefore, the number
of correlations used as an estimate of chance in one of Winch's data
analysis (Winch *et al.*, 1954) is too low. The low estimate biases the
experiment in the direction of finding statistically significant results,
although not necessarily results supporting the complementary needs
hypothesis.

Another criticism (Tharp, 1963) of Winch's research is of the
interpretation of the data. There are five sets of data and, according to
Winch (1955), three of the data sets support the complementary needs
hypothesis and two do not. Actually, the five data sets are not
independent of each other. The need interview was a contributing
factor in three of the measures. The only ratings showing results
supporting the complementary needs hypothesis were those based
entirely or in part on the need interview. The need measures based on
the case history interview and the TAT showed no effect for complementary needs. According to Tharp (1963), only one set of Winch's

data supports the complementary needs theory and two sets of data do not support the complementary needs theory.

Katz *et al.* (1960) questioned the need ratings themselves. Since "each judge rated all the characteristics of a given subject", Katz *et al.* argued, support for the complementary needs hypothesis may be a reflection of the implicit personality theories of the raters rather than actual need relationships.

Wagner's Study

Another study showing strong support for the complementary needs hypothesis is Wagner's (1975) recent study. Subjects were counsellors at three camps who had been working together for at least a month. All subjects were male and between the ages of 18 and 22. Needs of the counsellors were measured in three ways:(a) interviews with counsellors themselves about how they handle various situations such as making an important decision; (b) interviews with staff members in which each counsellor described the behaviours of other counsellors that he knew well; and (c) an interview with the camp director in which the director indicated who was high and low on the eleven needs studied. The need measures were combined into a single ordering of counsellors at each camp based on how much of the eleven needs each counsellor possessed. The measure of attraction was the counsellors' own ratings of how well they worked with each of the other counsellors.

Wagner hypothesized that counsellors who were compatible working companions would be complementary on six pairs of needs. Need pairings were selected based on compatibility of the needs with the role of counsellor. Wagner found that compatible counsellors were complementary on the need pairs of nurturance-succorance, aggression-abasement, responsibility-nurturance, exhibition-deference, and dominance-autonomy in at least two out of the three camps studied. The only prediction not confirmed was a hypothesis about the relationship between affiliation and dissociation.

C. INTERACTING VARIABLES

Other than the two studies just described, most research indicates either mixed support or no support for the complementary needs theory. This difference may be due to a variety of factors. Winch (1967) pointed out that his measure of needs was based on content analyses of interviews about how needs are expressed in actual situations rather than responses on self-report paper and pencil tests.

He also pointed out that there is no evidence that Edwards' Personal Preference Schedule, a frequent self-report measure of needs used in this type of research, is a valid measure of the needs that it purports to measure.

The failure of the research to indicate stronger support for the complementary needs theory may reflect the action of factors interacting with the complementary needs relationship or of methodological factors. Factors which may interact with the relationship between complementary needs and attraction are the degree of intimacy between two people and the nature of the role relationship between two people. Methodological factors may arise out of inadequacies in how the complementary needs hypothesis is conceptualized.

Intimacy

One limitation on the relationship between complementary needs and attraction may be the length of acquaintance between two people. Kerckhoff and Davis (1962) suggested (and supported with research findings) the idea that similarity is an important factor in attraction during the early phases of courtship and that complementarity is an important variable influencing attraction during the later stages of courtship.

Kerckhoff and Davis (1962) conducted a study in which 103 women and the men to whom they were engaged, pinned, or going steady filled out two questionnaires. The value measure asked subjects to rank in order of importance 10 standards by which family success can be measured. A second questionnaire was Schutz's FIRO-B scale, a scale which measures the types of behaviour that a person likes to express and wants to receive from others in the areas of inclusion, control, and affection.

Analysis of the results showed that for short term relations, value consensus was significantly related to progress toward permanence in a relationship. In long term relationships, progress toward permanence in a relationship was significantly related to complementarity in the areas of inclusion and control.

Levinger *et al.* (1970) replicated the Kerckhoff and Davis study on two additional samples at the University of Massachusetts and at the University of Colorado. The study showed no evidence that value consensus or complementarity in the areas of inclusion, control, or affection influenced progress toward permanence in a relationship in the same fashion as in the Kerckhoff and Davis study. The

Massachusetts sample showed that high value consensus and high inclusion need complementarity were related to progress toward permanence in a relationship. These two relationships were not found in the Colorado sample. In an attempt to reconcile the conflicting results between Kerckhoff and Davis' study and the more recent study, Levinger *et al.* suggested that there may have been major shifts in the nature of the population attending college between 1959 and 1966 or that the population studied had passed the point in their relationship where the filtering process was relevant.

This research is interesting because it raises the question that the mate selection process may be a filtering process, i.e. that different variables may be important at different points in the mate selection process. Similar views have been suggested by Murstein (1970 and section 1 of this book), Levinger and Snoek (1972) and Duck (1973b and section 3 of this book).

Role Relationships

A variety of theorists have suggested that role expectations may determine the circumstances under which dissimilar behaviours lead to attraction (Murstein, 1967; Seyfried and Hendrick, 1973b; Tharp, 1963; Wagner, 1975; Winch, 1967). According to Winch (1967), compatibility of both personality and role are necessary to produce attraction.

A variety of studies indicate that people seek different patterns of need gratification in different role relationships. Rychlak (1965) asked groups of six subjects to solve two problems. After the groups had had an opportunity to interact, subjects were asked to indicate who in their group they would most and least like for a boss, most and least like to have as an employee, and most and least like to have as a neighbour. Results of the study indicated that different patterns of needs were preferred for the three different role relationships: boss, employee, and neighbour.

Rychlak (1965) found that highly nurturant subjects preferred a highly succorant subject for the most liked neighbour role. However, nurturance was not related to succorance in the boss or employee role relationships.

Rychlak also found that subjects with a high need for order preferred a boss with a low need for change over a boss with a high need for change. However, the same subjects preferred a dissimilar neighbour with a high need for change.

Schutz (1960) also found that different patterns of compatibility characterized different role relationships. Members of a fraternity at M.I.T. completed a questionnaire measuring their needs for inclusion, affection and control. The subjects also answered a sociometric questionnaire on which they indicated which three men in the fraternity that they would select for roommates next semester and which three men they would select as companions with whom to travel west by car. Schutz (1960) found that roommates showed greater than chance amounts of all three types of compatibility: reciprocal, interchange, and originator compatibility. For travelling companions, interchange compatibility was not important. Instead, subjects showed greater than chance amounts of reciprocal and originator compatibility.

Schutz (1960) also studied different areas of compatibility. He concluded that for the role of roommate, affection compatibility was the most important area of compatibility. In contrast, for the role of travelling companion, control compatibility appeared more important. According to Schutz (1960), different types of role relationships require different types of compatibility.

Hendrick and Brown (1971) also reported relationships between personality characteristics and role relationships. They asked subjects to complete the Maudsley Personality Inventory which measured introversion-extraversion. Subjects were then presented with the questionnaires of two other people: the questionnaire was answered in an extraverted fashion on 20 out of the 24 questions: on the second questionnaire, 20 out of the 24 questions were answered in an introverted fashion. Subjects were asked how much they thought they would like the person, how interesting the person would be to talk to at a party, how ideal the person's personality is, how much they would prefer this person as a leader of a group to which they belonged, how similar the person was to themselves, how reliable a friend the person would be, and how honest and ethical the person would be. A variety of role relationships are covered in these questions: party goer, leader, reliable friend, and honest and ethical person. Extraverts perceived similar extraverts as more attractive than dissimilar introverts in the role relationships of reliable friend, party goer, and leader. There was no significant difference in their ratings of the extraverted and introverted stimulus person on honesty and ethicality.

The introverted subjects perceived the dissimilar extravert as more attractive as a fellow party-goer and as a leader. However, they preferred the similar introvert as a reliable friend and felt that the similar introvert would be more honest and ethical than the dissimilar extravert.

The pattern of results in the studies cited above (Hendrick and Brown, 1971; Rychlak, 1965; Schutz, 1960) suggests that different patterns of need gratification may arise in different role relationships. Wagner (1975) took this factor into account in conducting his study of complementary needs. He selected only complementary need pairings consistent with the role of counsellor in his study and he pointed out that complementary relationships inconsistent with the role of counsellor would probably not arise.

The status of the concept of role, like that of the self concept, is unclear in regard to the complementary needs hypothesis. One possibility is that roles may influence how people schedule need gratification. In other words, complementary patterns of need gratification may emerge only when they are consistent with role relationships because people choose to schedule their need gratification in such a fashion.

A second possibility is that people seek out role relationships which are consistent with the needs they must gratify. For example, if a person possesses a strong affiliative need, he may arrange his life so that he has frequent opportunities to associate with others (he might select a career as a salesman, for example). On the other hand, if a person's affiliative needs are low, he may select roles that do not provide frequent opportunities to associate with others.

Conceptual Problems

Selectivity of Interaction One problem which research on complementary needs does not appear to take account, is the selectivity which occurs in interaction. When conflicts arise between the needs of two people, the conflicts are not always enacted. For example, in the situation described at the start of this chapter, Sarah and Luke could have handled the conflict through argument, nagging, and recrimination. Instead, the conflict was handled with nurturance and friendly teasing.

Or consider the interaction situation which arises when two highly dominating people interact. Complementary needs theory predicts that two such people would attempt to dominate each other, frustrate each other's attempt at need gratification and end up hating each other. What this thinking fails to consider is that interaction is selective. Instead of confronting each other with hostility, what is more likely to happen is that one or both people will withdraw from the confrontation and express their need to dominate others elsewhere. Thibaut and Kelley (1959) use the concept of comparison level for alternatives to explain this type of phenomena (see La Gaipa's chapter here). The *comparison level for alternatives* is "the lowest level of outcomes a member will accept in the light of available alternative opportunities" (p. 21). People compare their outcomes or anticipated outcomes in a particular relationship to possible outcomes in other relationships. If the level of outcomes received falls below the comparison level for alternatives, a person leaves the relationship.

Because of this selectivity in interaction, the naturalistic research approaches to complementary needs which do not involve actual observation or manipulation of complementary relations, may not adequately test the complementary needs hypothesis. The reason is that incongruent interaction is probably avoided.

Similarity and Complementarity Together In studying the complementary needs hypothesis, one frequently-used approach is to pit the similarity hypothesis against the complementary needs hypothesis. If correlations between personality needs on the same personality traits are positive for highly attracted couples, then the results support the similarity hypothesis. If the correlations are negative, then the results support the complementary needs hypothesis. The procedure is adequate if one realistically feels that it is the case that *either* similarity *or* complementarity must be present alone. An alternative possibility is that *both* similarity *and* complementarity principles are operative at the same time. If both processes are operative, then the procedure for testing the complementary needs hypothesis is not adequate.

The problem is best illustrated in an experiment conducted by Seyfried and Hendrick (1973a) and which is reprinted in section 2 of this book. Seyfried and Hendrick (1973a) found a pattern of results expected only if both complementarity and similarity effects were present at the same time. The results suggest that similarity and complementarity effects may be cancelling each other out. Support for the complementary needs hypothesis would have been undetectable without a control group that was both similar and complementary and without a dissimilar control group that was neither complementary nor similar. Such groups are generally not included in most tests of the complementary needs hypothesis.

III. Summary

Theorizing on complementary needs falls into a reinforcement model of attraction: behaviours that gratify needs are rewarding and rewards elicit implicit affective responses in people. The implicit affective responses become associated with any objects present, including people. Through pairing of rewards and specific people, people become conditioned stimuli capable of eliciting the implicit affective responses generally associated with the rewards.

Complementary needs theory argues that behaviours which result in mutual need gratification act as rewards. What behaviours result in need gratification is still vaguely defined. Winch (1967) argues that assertiveness-receptivity, nurturance-succorance, and achievement-vicariousness are dimensions along which one would find complementary need gratification. Schutz (1960) argues that originator, interchange, and reciprocal compatibility in the areas of inclusion, control, and affection will increase the desire of groups of people to associate with each other.

Research on the complementary needs hypothesis shows only moderate support for the hypothesis. Strongest support comes from studies by Winch *et al.* (1954), Winch (1955b), and Wagner (1975). A variety of reasons exist for the weak support for the complementary needs hypothesis. Intimacy of a relationship, self concept, and role relationships may interact with the relationship between complementarity and attraction. Other factors which might interfere with findings supporting the complementary needs hypothesis are failure to take into account the selective nature of interaction in research and failure to consider the possibility that both similarity and complementarity may be present at the same time in designing research.

Empirical Studies in
Interpersonal Attraction

8.

*Knowing, Feeling, and Liking
A Psychophysiological Study of Attraction[1]

G. L. CLORE

University of Illinois at Urbana-Champaign, USA

and

J. B. GORMLY

Rutgers University, USA

*First published in Journal of Research in Personality, 1974 **8**, 218-230. Copyright 1974 by Academic Press, Inc. Reproduced by permission.

1. Some of the data discussed here were presented previously in a paper read to the Psychonomic Society, St. Louis, November, 1969. The research was supported by Grant MH-14510 from the National Institute of Mental Health, Public Health Service. The authors wish to thank J. McV. Hunt for the physiological recording facilities, Richard J. Rose for generous expert advice, Barbara Baldridge, Howard McGuire, and Stuart Itkin for help in analyzing the data, and Michael G. H. Coles, Martin Kaplan, and Marilee Sargent for comments on the manuscript.

Skin conductance and heart rate were recorded during verbal exchanges in which subjects were either agreed or disagreed with on a variety of issues. The manipulation of attitude similarity had significant effects on interpersonal attraction, perceived competence, and skin conductance, but not on heart rate. Disagreement produced higher skin conductance than agreement, and speaking was more arousing than listening. The correlations between arousal and attraction showed that heightened arousal was associated with both attraction toward agreers and dislike toward disagreers. As predicted, the linear relationship between attitude similarity and attraction increased in slope (0.00, 3.75, 8.75) with increasing levels of conductance (low, medium, high). The failure of subjects to prefer agreers to disagreers under conditions of low arousal suggests that information without affect does not influence attraction.

Those who hold attitudes similar to our own are generally more liked than those who do not. Regardless of whether one is exposed to the written responses of bogus strangers for a brief period (Byrne and Clore, 1966) or to the overt behaviour of actual people during a week or more of confinement (Griffitt and Veitch, 1974), attitude similarity has a positive influence on interpersonal attraction. There are several kinds of explanations for this finding; some emphasize informational factors (Kaplan and Anderson, 1973), while others stress affective processes (Clore and Byrne, 1974). According to the latter conception, subjects respond affectively when their own attitudes are confirmed or disconfirmed by others; so that attraction and dislike depend not only on what one knows about another person (information) but also on what one feels about that information (affect).

To date only a few studies have been explicitly concerned with the role of affect in attraction (e.g. Gouaux, 1971; Gouaux *et al.*, 1972). Hence, the purpose of the present research is to determine whether or not affective arousal (measured physiologically) does in fact accompany attraction toward another person. Two physiological measures were taken, skin conductance and heart rate. Although the meaning of heart rate measures is currently in dispute (Coles, 1972; Elliott, 1969; Lacey, 1967), the sensitivity of skin conductance to affectively relevant stimulation is generally acknowledged (e.g. Lazarus, 1968).

Beyond the specific concern with whether affect accompanies attraction, two questions were asked: (1) How do agreement and disagreement influence skin conductance and heart rate, and (2) how are those indices of physiological arousal related to attraction and dislike?

Arousal and Agreement-Disagreement

Despite a growing tendency for personality and social psychologists to collect physiological information (Shapiro and Schwartz, 1970), few investigators have done so in studies of interpersonal attraction. One experiment (Burdick and Burnes, 1958), frequently cited as support for balance theory, did find more Galvanic Skin Responses (GSRs) for subjects confronted by a liked person who disagreed (imbalance) than by one who agreed (balance). However, the difference reached only the 10 per cent level of confidence. Several other experiments also report higher physiological arousal in response to disagreement than to agreement. This result has been found when arousal was measured by muscular tension (McNulty and Walters, 1962) as well as when GSR was used (Cooper, 1959; Dickson and McGinnes, 1966; Gormly, 1971; Katz *et al.*, 1965; Smith, 1936; Snoek and Dobbs, 1967; Steiner, 1970). Moreover, related research found more GSRs in response to failure than success (Shapiro and Leiderman, 1967) and higher heart rate and muscle tension after criticism than after praise (Malmo *et al.*, 1957).

However, some studies have failed to find greater arousal to disagreement, dissimilarity, or criticism. Murray (1963) noted no higher heart rates when subjects were insulted than when the interaction was friendly. Similarly, Dimascio *et al.* (1957), in therapeutic interactions scored according to Bale's system, found no relationship between the amount of "disagreement" and measures of heart rate and finger skin temperature. Finally, Hirschman and Katkin (1971) report that their subjects gave more nonspecific GSRs while listening to similar than to dissimilar strangers. With these few exceptions, a review of previous research suggests that disagreement should lead to higher levels of skin conductance than agreement, but it provides little basis for a prediction concerning heart rate.

Arousal and Attraction

With respect to the second question concerning the relationship between arousal and attraction, there is little existing evidence. One physiological study shows that the presence of strangers is more arousing than the presence of friends when arousal is measured by GSR (Kissel, 1965) or free fatty acid levels in the blood (Back and Bogdonoff, 1964). These data suggest a negative relationship between physiological arousal and attraction such that one is least aroused in the presence of those one likes most.

In contrast, several other experiments have found that attraction is an interactive function of arousal and degree of attitude similarity rather than a simple linear product of arousal (Byrne and Clore, 1967; Stapert and Clore, 1969; Weiner, 1969). Although these studies used only self-report measures of arousal (Effectance Arousal Scale), they suggest that arousal intensifies both attraction toward agreers and dislike toward disagreers.

In line with those data, the reinforcement-affect model of attraction (Clore and Byrne, 1974) also suggests an interaction. The model distinguishes between the affective and informational stimulus components of attraction experiments. For example, informational elements are especially salient in impression formation studies, while studies of attraction typically incorporate affective elements as well. One possibility suggested by the model is that the slope of the line describing the relationship between the proportion of positive stimuli and attraction should increase with the affective involvement of the subject. Since skin conductance is sensitive to affective stimulation (Lazarus, 1968), the conductance data collected here allowed a test of the slope prediction.

I. Method

A. DESIGN

The study was a $2 \times 2 \times 2$ design varying Level of Agreement and Speaking Order and Sex of Dyad. Speaking Order seemed potentially important because it determined the subject's role. Speaking first put the subject in the position of being agreed or disagreed with by his partner, while speaking second put him in the role of agreer or disagreer. The effects of these manipulations were assessed on two questionnaire variables (attraction and perceived competence) and two physiological variables (skin conductance and tonic heart rate). In addition, for the physiological measures there were two sets of data for each subject (Speaking and Listening).

B. SUBJECTS

The subjects were 48 students (28 females, 20 males) at the University of Illinois. They were randomly selected by computer from a large pool of introductory psychology subjects on the bases of sex and availability.

C. PHYSIOLOGICAL MEASURES

Skin conductance and tonic heart rate (frequency) were recorded on a

Beckman Type RB Dynograph. Conductance was measured directly using a constant voltage source of approximately 0.2 V. Silver-silver chloride electrodes, 0.75 cm in diameter, were centred on the volar fingertips of the first and third fingers of the nonpreferred hand. The electrodes were plated with silver chloride in a manner described by Lykken (1959) to minimize electrode polarization. Heart beats were recorded beat-by-beat from the right and left inner-forearms with a ground on the right back-forearm. Both skin conductance and average heart rate were scored for the 5s intervals after the subject began speaking (Speaking data) and after the accomplice began speaking (Listening data). The highest conductance recorded during each of these 5s periods was used as the skin conductance data. The physiological data for each subject were corrected for his own range of response as described below.

D. QUESTIONNAIRE MEASURES

Two questionnaires were administered, a Survey of Attitudes and the Interpersonal Judgment Scale. The Survey of Attitudes consisted of 12 topics presented in a six-point format with alternatives ranging from mild to extreme on each side of the issue. The items included such issues as interracial marriage, homosexuality, marijuana, birth control, religion, and the American way of life. The Interpersonal Judgment Scale provided measures of attraction and perceived competence. The scale asks the subject to respond to a target person on six 7-point scales including judgements of his intelligence, knowledge of current events, morality, and adjustment. The final two items ask how much the subject likes or dislikes the other person and whether or not he would like to work with him as partners in an experiment. When added together, these items form a 2- to 14-point scale of attraction which has been used extensively in previous work on interpersonal attitudes (Byrne, 1971). In addition, the first two items on the scale were also combined in this experiment. The sum of these items (intelligence and knowledge of current events) formed a 2- to 14-point scale of perceived competence.

E. PROCEDURE

When he arrived at the laboratory, each subject met an accomplice of the experimenter. The accomplice was always the same sex as the subject and was introduced as another subject from introductory psychology. The first task was to fill out the Survey of Attitudes.

After completing the attitude survey, the oscillograph was demonstrated and the subject's range of response on the physiological measures was assessed. The range assessment was made by having the subject close his eyes and rest for 5 min., after which the experimenter asked him to open his eyes and then proceeded to clap his hands three times in front of the subject's face. This procedure, adapted from Rose (1966) provides low and high points of arousal so that each subject's arousal level can be corrected for individual differences in range of responding.

The correction formula for conductance is

$$sc_i = \frac{\text{skin conductance } (i) - \text{low point of skin conductance}}{\text{range of skin conductance}},$$

where i is any given data point. The same general formula was used on the heart rate data.

The goal of the study was to assess the subjects' physiological reaction to the accomplice's opinions on a trial-by-trial basis. An exchange of opinions was arranged by enlisting the subjects' help in making tape recordings supposedly to be replayed in future versions of the experiment in which other subjects would listen to the opinions expressed and make judgements about the speakers. In order not to confuse these later listeners, the subjects were asked to respond in a fixed order. In half of the cases the real subject spoke first (*Subject First Condition*), and in the other half he gave his opinion after the accomplice (*Accomplice First Condition*). In addition to being told that they would be rated by others at a later time, the participants were also informed that they would be asked to make judgements about each other.

The subject and accomplice were seated face-to-face as they made the tape recording, separated only by a 10-in. high partition. Each was given a blank copy of the Survey of Attitudes, and on each trial the experimenter announced a topic and asked first one and then the other subject to state his position by reading one of the six alternatives under each issue. A given statement was of the general form: "I feel that students who smoke marijuana are (are not) being foolish". The stronger versions of the statements included the words "I strongly feel", while the milder forms began "I feel that perhaps". The accomplice's copy of the attitude scale was actually a cue sheet that had been prepared during the 5-min. rest period. To increase realism, the positions expressed were determined by the constant discrepancy method (Byrne, 1971). By this method the accomplice never gives the exact same response as the subject when he agrees nor the exact opposite when he disagrees.

At the conclusion of the attitude exchange and after making some other ratings, the accomplice was taken to a different room to allow the subject to make his ratings on the Interpersonal Judgment Scale in private.

II. Results

A. CORRELATIONAL RESULTS

The most interesting relationships to emerge from the experiment are those between skin conductance and attraction ratings. Recall that skin conductance was recorded on each trial at two different times, as the subject spoke (*Speaking*) and as he heard the accomplice speak (*Listening*). The range-corrected form of these data was analyzed using skin conductance summed over the last six trials. The last six trials were used because the pattern of agreement and disagreement was essentially the same for both Agree and Disagree groups on the early trials. The cumulative percentage of agreement begins to differ for the two conditions only after Trial 6.

To determine the strength of the relationship between arousal and attraction, several sets of correlations were computed. Overall attraction was completely unrelated to conductance either during Speaking ($r = -0.02$) or during Listening ($r = -0.08$). However, when subjects in the Agree and Disagree conditions are considered separately, the two variables are clearly related. The correlations are positive for Agree subjects ($r = 0.67$, $p < 0.01$, while Speaking; $r = 0.55$, $p < 0.01$, while Listening) and negative for Disagree subjects ($r = -0.24$, while Speaking; $r = -0.38$, $p < 0.05$, while Listening). When the conditions are further broken down into Order-of-Speaking groups (Subject First v. Accomplice First) this pattern is maintained. The eight component correlations based on cell sizes of 12 are surprisingly large, half of them exceeding 0.50 and almost two-thirds of them significant at the 0.05 level. All of them are positive in the Agree condition, and all but one are negative in the Disagree condition. Further, the strength of these correlations is not dependent on the fortuitous choice of a particular set of trials for analysis. The results are the same if the last three trials, the last six trials, or all trials are considered. Under any of these conditions the same correlations with attraction are significant, and the same pattern of signs is maintained.

To make explicit the test of the slope hypothesis, these same conductance data were treated as though they were an independent variable in an analysis of variance. To obtain lines for different arousal groups, the distributions of conductance scores in the present study were trichotomized to form low, medium, and high groups with equal n's. Figure 1 shows, in conformity with the prediction, an increase in the slopes of the similarity-attraction lines (0.00, 3.75, 8.75) with increasing skin conductance. The differences among the slopes of the lines in Figure 1 were tested by the Agreement × Conductance interactions from two analyses of variance, each with two levels of Agreement and three levels of Conductance. The interaction was significant for both Speaking ($F(2,42) = 5.17$, $p < 0.01$) and Listening data ($F(2,42) = 5.28$, $p < 0.01$).

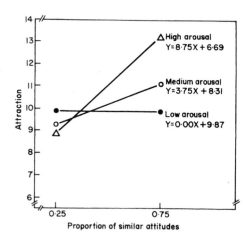

FIG. 1. The relationship between attitude similarity and interpersonal attraction expressed for groups with high, medium, and low skin conductance while speaking.

Ratings of the partner's competence were also correlated with skin conductance. A pattern of positive and negative correlations was found similar to those found for attraction. However, the only correlation with competence to reach significance at the 0.05 level occurred when skin conductance was recorded as the subjects listened to the accomplice disagree with them in the Subject First condition ($r = -0.57$).

Finally, correlations between tonic heart rate and attraction were generally uninformative. None reached significance.

B. EXPERIMENTAL RESULTS

Skin Conductance A comparison across all trials of the two sets of data showed Speaking ($M = 0.47$) to be more arousing than Listening ($M = 0.38$) ($t(47) = 9.53$, $p < 0.001$) even though the measures taken at these two times were highly related ($r = 0.93$). Corrected conductance was also analysed on a trial-by-trial basis in two $2 \times 2 \times 2 \times 12$ analyses of variance with two levels of Agreement, two Orders of Speaking, Sex of Dyad, and 12 trials (issues). Significant main effects for Trials were found for Speaking ($F(11,440) = 16.28$, $p < 0.001$) and Listening conductance ($F(11,440) = 13.83$, $p < 0.001$), reflecting habituation in the first few trials.

Figure 2 shows the effect of Level of Agreement on Speaking conductance. A significant main effect ($F(1,40) = 5.57$, $p < 0.02$) indicates that subjects who *disagreed* with the accomplice were more aroused ($M = 0.52$) during the exchange of opinions than those who *agreed* with him ($M = 0.42$). In the Listening data the difference in arousal between the Agree ($M = 0.35$) and Disagree conditions ($M = 0.42$) is consistent but not quite significant when analysed either across all trials ($F(1,40 = 2.30$, $p < 0.14$) or across the last six trials (Agree $M = 0.33$, Disagree $M = 0.41$) ($t(24) = 1.79$, $p < 0.10$).

Heart Rate Heart rates were recorded as the subject spoke (*Speaking*) and as the accomplice spoke (*Listening*). There was a nonsignificant tendency for Speaking to be accompanied by faster corrected heart rates ($M = 0.60$) than Listening ($M = 0.49$). As in the case of conductance, the heart rate measures at these two times were highly related ($r = 0.76$). The $2 \times 2 \times 2 \times 12$ analyses of variance produced significant main effects only for Trials, showing habituation effects in both Listening ($F(11,440) = 3.56$, $p < 0.001$) and Speaking data ($F(11,440) = 2.85$, $p < 0.001$). Although disagreement generally led to higher heart rate than agreement, the differences were not significant.

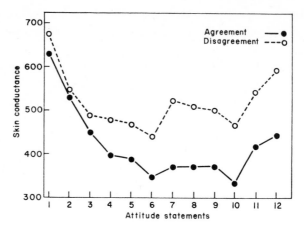

FIG. 2. Skin conductance shown as subjects in the Agreement (75% agree) and Disagreement (25% agree) groups express their opinion on each of 12 issues.

Questionnaire Measures Interpersonal attraction and perceived competence were each analysed in a 2 × 2 × 2 (Percentage of Agreement × Order of Responding × Sex of Dyad) analysis of variance. A significant main effect of Agreement on attraction ($F(1,40) = 8.75$, $p <0.005$) shows that agreers ($M = 11.42$) were more liked than disagreers ($M = 9.83$). Similarly, the analysis of perceived competence also reveals a significant main effect for Agreement ($F(1,40) = 4.38$, $p <0.04$) indicating that subjects attributed more competence to agreers ($M = 10.79$) than to disagreers ($M = 9.83$). There were no other significant effects in the two analyses.

Effects of Range Correction To assess the range-correction procedure, the raw skin conductance data were also analyzed. Corrected and raw conductance measures were not highly related (Speaking $r = 0.36$; Listening $r = 0.37$), but the analyses of variance showed effects of comparable magnitude. The corrected conductance data during *Speaking* were somewhat cleaner (fewer higher-order interactions) and showed a stronger Agree-Disagree effect (corrected $F(1,40) = 5.57$, $p <0.02$; raw $F(1,40) = 3.65$, $p<0.06$). However, the same comparison in the corrected *Listening* data was slightly weaker ($F(1,40) = 2.30$, $p <0.14$) than in the raw form ($F(1,40) = 3.00$, $p<0.09$). The clearest comparison comes from the correlational data. Average correlations between conductance and attraction were notably higher when the range correction was applied (Agree raw $r = 0.38$; corrected $r = 0.61$;

Disagree raw $R = 0.12$; corrected $r = -0.31$). Hence, the suggestion of Lykken, Rose, Luther and Maley (1966) that the correction represents an improvement over the use of uncorrected scores was supported.

The range correction was also applied to the heart-rate data. The procedure seemed less appropriate for heart rate in that changes in level during the experiment sometimes exceeded the range estimations established at the beginning. Comparison of the analyses of variance showed no significant effects in either raw or corrected data other than the trials effects. Hence the data do not allow an informative assessment of the range correction as applied to heart rate.

III. Discussion

A. EXPERIMENTAL RESULTS

The skin conductance results show that it was more arousing to speak than to listen, more arousing to be disagreeable than to be agreeable, and somewhat more arousing to be disagreed with than to be agreed with. In addition, initiating the exchange on an issue (Speaking First) was more arousing than responding (Speaking Second) but only in the early trials before initiators could anticipate a trend in their partners' positions.

The Speaking v. Listening result is consistent with a previous finding showing greater heart-rate increases when subjects were in an active rather than a passive conversational role (Murray, 1963). The Agreement v. Disagreement effects also support the findings of previous investigations, including those of Gormly (1971) and Steiner (1972). The fact that disagreement was more arousing than agreement is also consistent with some nonphysiological research on attraction. Several studies have reported evidence for disagreement-produced arousal using both self-report (Byrne and Clore, 1967; Stapert and Clore, 1969) and performance measures (Lombardo *et al.*, 1972).

While skin conductance was strongly related to several other dependent variables, heart rate was not. The failure of heart rate to emerge as an interesting measure is clarified somewhat by a recent study published since these data were collected. Burdick (1972) also found heart rate to be uninformative, but demonstrated that heart-rate variability is a relatively good predictor of attitudinal variables. Thus, variability appears to be a preferable cardiac measure for future investigations.

The primary questionnaire results show that Attitude Similarity affected both attraction and competence ratings. Consistent with previous attraction research (Byrne, 1971), agreement led to greater attraction and greater perceived competence than disagreement. The other variable manipulated in the design was Speaking Order (initiating v. responding). It had no general effects on either of the self-report measures, but an inspection of the competence data did disclose one anomalous cell. A Scheffé test confirmed that subjects spoke first (and thus had their opinions contradicted) attributed more competence to their partner than did subjects who themselves had the last word (p < 0.05). A power relationship thus seems to have emerged in the Disagree condition on the basis of Speaking Order, even though the order was dictated by the experimenter. The result was a sort of "last word phenomenon" that may bear further study.

B. CORRELATIONAL RESULTS

The most notable finding was that reports of more extreme attraction and rejection followed higher levels of skin conductance during an exchange of opinions. The relatively large correlations obtained are interesting chiefly because they provide evidence of convergent validity (Campbell and Fiske, 1959) for the Interpersonal Judgment Scale (Byrne, 1971), a frequently used measure of attraction. Physiological and questionnaire measures presumably have little error variance in common; hence, the similarity of findings across these two methods of measurement is more meaningful than if two questionnaire measures had been used. Interestingly, the present correlations are stronger than those of previous studies employing questionnaire measures of similar variables (e.g. Byrne and Clore, 1967).

Affect The hypothesis that the slope of the attraction function would increase with level of affective arousal was supported. Slopes increased (0.00, 3.75, 8.75) as level of arousal increased (low, medium, high). According to the reinforcement-affect model (Clore and Byrne, 1974), attraction depends not only on the positive or negative information about a target person, but also on affective reactions to that information. The zero slope in the low arousal group is especially interesting because it indicates that subjects who did not respond affectively to the other person's attitudes did not prefer agreers to disagreers. If one assumes that skin conductance indicates affective involvement, then the results imply that liking occurs only to the extent that feeling (skin conductance) accompanies knowing (agreement-disagreement).

Clore and Byrne's model actually assigns a causative role to affect, asserting that persons are liked when they are associated with positive affect and disliked when they are associated with negative affect. However, the correlational nature of the arousal-attraction relationship obtained here does not allow a test of that aspect of the hypothesis. Also the use of the analysis of variance model to test the differences in slopes should not be taken to mean that skin conductance was manipulated as an independent variable. Previous studies have successfully manipulated affect and produced changes in attraction. For example, Gouaux (1971) has obtained ratings of strangers associated with elating and depressing films, and Griffitt and Veitch (1971) have performed attraction experiments in which subjects were tested in hot and crowded rooms. However, neither of those studies obtained physiological measures of affect arousal.

Attention This discussion has focused on the sensitivity of conductance to affective elements in the situation, but the arousal-attraction relationships could reflect variations in attention as well. For example, according to an attentional hypothesis the correlations would indicate that the extreme attraction responses were made by attentive (aroused) subjects and the neutral ones by subjects whose attention wandered (nonaroused). However, that hypothesis is not a strong one because the experimental situation provided little opportunity for individual differences in attentiveness to manifest themselves and no room for boredom. Conductance was measured during a brief face-to-face encounter in which subjects gave only one sentence statements of their positions on 12 issues. Moreover, the data show clearly that the arousal-attraction relationships were as strong while speaking (when attention was presumably maximal) as while listening (when more individual variation could be expected).

Information The importance of informational factors in attraction is highlighted by viewing the arousal-attraction relationships in another way. Arousal and attraction were positively related when subjects saw a similar stranger and negatively related when they encountered a dissimilar stranger. As a consequence, attraction cannot be predicted from physiological arousal alone; in fact, the overall correlation between the two variables is close to zero. However, good predictions can be made by considering physiological arousal in combination with agreement and disagreement. These findings are consistent with an attribution analysis of emotion (Schachter, 1964). According to that position, one feels an emotion such as joy or sadness, not on the basis of physiological response alone, but only in combination with a relevant interpretation of the physiological response. Presumably the subjects themselves cannot know whether they like or dislike the stranger merely from an awareness of their own autonomic activity; they must interpret those responses in light of the knowledge that they have been agreed or disagreed with. They must know not only that they are excited (aroused) but what they are excited about (information).

9.

*Effects of Information on Interpersonal Attraction: Similarity versus affective value[1]

ICEK AJZEN

University of Massachusetts, Amherst, USA

The affective value (positive or negative) of personality traits describing another person (O) was manipulated independently of their similarity (similar or dissimilar) to traits describing the subject. This procedure was also simulated under role-playing conditions. Results showed a significant ($p < 0.01$) main effect of affective value on attraction toward Person O, as predicted by an expectancy-value theory of attitude formation. Attraction was not significantly influenced by the manipulation of similarity. In a second study it was shown that information about another person's

---

*First published in *Journal of Personality and Social Psychology* 1974, **29** 374-380. Copyright©1974 by the American Psychological Association. Reprinted by permission.

1. This research was supported in part by National Institute of Mental Health Grant MH 20182-01. The author is grateful to Thomas J. Thieman and William Holmes for their assistance and to Martin Fishbein and George Levinger for critical comments on an earlier draft.

opinions, rather than personality traits, also had evaluative implications which correlated significantly ($p < 0.01$) with attraction. It is suggested that similarity is usually found to be related to attraction because of the empirical association between similarity and affective value.

To account for the consistent finding of a positive relationship between similarity and interpersonal attraction, Byrne (1969, 1971) has argued that information about another person's opinions, interests, or personality traits is reinforcing to the extent that these characteristics of the other person are similar to those of the perceiver. Being associated with these reinforcing events, the other person becomes attractive as a direct function of the proportion of similar characteristics.

While there can be little doubt concerning the empirical association between similarity and attraction, direct evidence in support of Byrne's reinforcement position is scarce (cf. Fishbein and Ajzen, 1972). Consistent with theories proposed by Fishbein (1963), Rosenberg (1956), and others, it is here suggested that a subject's attitude toward another person is determined by his beliefs that the person has certain attributes, multiplied by his evaluations of these attributes. This theory is presented in symbolic form in Equation 1 (where A = attitude toward a person; SP_i = subjective probability that the person possesses attribute i; V_i = subjective value of attribute i; and n = number of attributes):

$$A = \sum_{i=1}^{n} SP_i V_i \tag{1}$$

The Byrne paradigm permits subjects to form beliefs about a stranger's attributes. For example, information that the stranger believes in God may increase the perceived likelihood that he is religious. Depending on the subjective values of these attributes, the information leads to the formation of a positive or negative attitude toward the stranger. Since similar attributes tend to be evaluated more positively than dissimilar ones (e.g. Stalling, 1970), subjects come to hold more favourable attitudes toward a similar than a dissimilar stranger.

The present study investigated this alternative account of the formation of interpersonal attraction in the Byrne paradigm. To separate the effects of similarity and the effects of the information's affective value, subjects were given personality feedback about themselves and about another person. It was predicted that attraction toward the other person increases with the desirability of the personality traits used to describe him, irrespective of the degree to which these traits are similar to those describing the subject himself. Similarity between descriptions of the subject and the stranger was expected to have little effect on attraction.

Most research on the similarity-attraction relationship has used opinion statements rather than personality traits. A second study was therefore conducted to demonstrate that information about another person's opinions can be used to form beliefs about his characteristics. It was expected that these beliefs, multiplied by the values of the attributed characteristics, are related to interpersonal attraction, as specified in Equation 1.

I. Study 1: personality traits

A. METHOD

Study 1 was conducted under traditional experimental procedures and under role-playing procedures. Subjects in the role-playing condition were asked to respond like a person who had been in the situation described, while subjects in the experimental condition were actually put into that situation.

Experimental Condition

Subjects A total of 48 introductory psychology students, 25 males and 23 females, were tested in individual sessions in the experimental condition.

Procedure The experiment was described as a study of impression formation. Subjects were told that they would receive information about another person in the form of feedback on a personality inventory which this person had been administered. First, however, they were asked to complete the same personality inventory so that they could also be given feedback on their own personality.

At this point the subject was given a questionnaire containing 100 self-descriptive items selected at random from the Minnesota Multiphasic Personality Inventory. After completing this inventory, the subject was asked to wait a few minutes while the experimenter went into an adjoining room, ostensibly in order to analyse the inventory using "some standardized scoring keys". As the experimenter returned to the subject's room, he tried to make some comment about one or two of the items the subject had checked on the inventory, such as "I noticed you checked that you like to cook" or "very few people will admit that they cry easily". This was done in an effort to assure the subject that the experimenter had in fact scored his responses.

Personality feedback for the other person and for the subject was presented on 12 six-point bipolar adjective scales. (See Table 1 for a list of the adjectives used.) A check mark was placed on each scale indicating the other person's standing or the subject's standing on the dimension in question. The subjects were given as much time as they needed to study first their own profile and then that of the fictitious other person whose name on top of the page was covered by a piece of tape, apparently in order to conceal his identity.

Subjects in the control groups went through exactly the same procedure except that they were not given feedback about themselves. Although they did complete the personality inventory, they were told that this was done mainly to give them an idea of the basis for the other person's personality feedback. Control subjects, therefore, read only through one personality profile, that profile describing the other person.

At this point, all of the subjects completed a questionnaire to be described below which contained measures of the dependent variables. At the end of the experiment, the subjects were asked to indicate whether they thought that the test had adequately assessed their personality and whether they had compared themselves to the other person in terms of the personality feedback. Finally, all of the subjects were completely debriefed with reference to the deception and the purpose of the experiment. Experimental sessions lasted about 30 minutes.

Role-Playing Condition

Subjects Sixty-one introductory psychology students served as subjects in the role-playing condition. Subjects were tested in two groups of approximately 30 each. Data for one subject selected at random were omitted in order to equalize the number of subjects in the different experimental treatments. Thus, a total of 60 subjects were left, 30 males and 30 females.

Procedure Instructions and materials were assembled in self-contained booklets and distributed to the subjects. The front page informed subjects about the general purpose of the experiment, which was the same as in the experimental condition described above. On the second

TABLE 1. Personality descriptions.

Item	Descriptions of subject (or Tom)				Descriptions of other person	
	Column 1 75%[a]	Column 2 25%[a]	Column 3 75%[b]	Column 4 25%[b]	Column 5 75%[c]	Column 6 25%[c]
Selfishness	−2	−1	+2	+1	+2	−2
Imagination	−3	−3	−2	−2	+1	−1
Efficiency	−1	+2	−3	−3	−1	−3
Friendliness	+2	−2	+2	−1	+3	+1
Reliability	+1	+1	+1	+2	+1	−2
Fairness	+1	+3	+1	−1	+2	+2
Cooperativeness	+2	−1	−2	+2	+3	−3
Rationality	−1	+1	+3	−2	−2	+3
Kindness	+2	−2	−1	+3	+2	−1
Tolerance	−2	+1	−1	+1	−3	−2
Politeness	+3	+3	+2	+2	+3	−3
Maturity	−2	−2	−2	−2	+3	−3
Sum	0	0	0	0	+14	−14

[a] Percentage of similarity created by combining this column and column 5.
[b] Percentage of similarity created by combining this column and column 6.
[c] Percentage of positive traits describing other person.

page they read that Tom, a student, had recently filled out an extensive personality inventory and had then received feedback on his own personality traits. Subjects read through Tom's personality profile presented on the 12 bipolar adjective scales, just as in the experimental condition. They were then told that Tom had also received information about another student, Bob, who had filled out the same personality inventory, and were given Bob's personality profile to study.

Control subjects again went through identical procedures except that they were given no feedback about Tom; they studied only Bob's personality profile. At this point, all of the subjects completed the same questionnaire used in the experimental condition. However, role-playing subjects were asked to answer most questions the way they thought Tom had answered them.

Questionnaire

The first part of the questionnaire consisted of Byrne's (1966, pp. 41-43) six-item Interpersonal Judgment Scale. In the role-playing condition, "this person" was replaced by "Bob", and "I" or "me" were replaced by "Tom". The items asked the subject to rate the other person's intelligence, knowledge of current events, morality, and adjustment and to indicate his liking for the other person and whether he would enjoy or dislike working with him. Consistent with research by Byrne and his associates, the last two items were summed to yield a measure of attraction toward the other person. High scores indicated high attraction.

The Interpersonal Judgment Scale was followed by five 7-point evaluative semantic differential scales. Endpoints of the scales were: harmful-beneficial, foolish-wise, dirty-clean, bad-good, and sick-healthy. In the experimental condition, the concept rated was "This person is", while subjects in the role-playing condition rated the concept "Tom thought that Bob is". The scales were scored from 1 to 7 and summed. High scores again indicated high attraction.

The next item on the questionnaire had the subject rate the similarity between himself and the other person in the experimental condition, and between Tom and Bob in the role-playing condition. Ratings were made on a 7-point bipolar scale ranging from extremely similar to extremely dissimilar.

Finally, all subjects rated the desirability of each of the 12 traits used in the personality profiles on a single 7-point scale ranging from desirable to undesirable.

Experimental Design

Similarity and affective value were manipulated by varying the personality descriptions of the two persons involved. Check marks were placed on each of the 12 adjective scales. The endpoints of each 6-point scale were adjectives of opposite meaning. For example, the first scale ranged from selfish to unselfish. The numbers in Table 1 indicate positions of the check marks, where + 3 is the positive and − 3 is the negative end of each scale. Descriptions of the subject (or of Tom) in columns 1 and 2 of Table 1 were each combined with the 75%-positive description of the other person in column 5. Similarly, columns 3 and 4 were each combined with column 6. The resulting pairs of descriptions were 75% similar or 25% similar, and the other person's description was 75% or 25% positive. Thus, all four possible combinations of similarity (similar versus dissimilar) and affective value (positive versus negative) were created.

In Table 1 it can also be seen that descriptions of subjects (or of Tom) were 50% positive and that the sum over all 12 traits was always zero. The positive description of the other person summed to + 14 while the negative description summed to − 14.

Control subjects received, of course, only the two descriptions of the other person; one control group read the 75%-positive profile while a second control group received the 25%-positive profile.

Overall, then, six groups (four experimental and two control) were employed in the experimental condition, and the same design was used in the role-playing condition. The number of subjects in each group was 8 in the former condition and 10 in the latter. Males and females were distributed approximately equally across the cells of the design.

B. RESULTS

Manipulation Checks

Similarity As planned, the two focal persons (subject and other, or Tom and Bob) were perceived to be significantly (F = 5.694, $p < 0.01$) more similar in the similar condition (M = 4.506) than in the dissimilar condition (M = 3.433). The mean of the control groups (M = 3.658) was between those of the experimental groups. The affective value of the other person's description showed no significant main effect or interaction on perceived similarity. These results held for the experimental as well as for the role-playing procedures; that is, procedure had no significant main effect on perceived similarity nor did it interact with other variables.

Personality Feedback about Self In the experimental procedure, the subjects were asked to indicate their reactions to their own personality feedbacks. Only six subjects expressed some doubts about the accuracy of the feedback, and most of these subjects indicated that their responses had nevertheless taken the feedback into account. All of the subjects were retained for statistical analyses.

Interpersonal Attraction

Measures of attraction were submitted to four-way analyses of variance with the following main effects: procedure (experiment versus role play), affective value (positive versus negative), similarity of personality profiles (similar versus dissimilar versus control), and sex. Since sex had few significant effects, this variable is omitted in reporting the results.

Table 2 presents the means for the two attraction measures (the Interpersonal Judgment Scale and the semantic differential), and Table 3 presents the analyses of variance. Considering first the Interpersonal Judgment Scale, it can be seen that the affective value of the other person's personality description had a highly significant effect on attraction ($F = 25.456$, $p < 0.01$). The positive description

TABLE 2. Means of attraction measures.

Attraction measure	Positive description		Negative description	
	Experiment	Role play	Experiment	Role play
Interpersonal Judgment Scale				
Similar	10.567	8.500	7.250	6.625
Dissimilar	8.400	6.200	6.333	6.000
Control	9.167	9.417	3.750	5.600
Semantic differential				
Similar	26.568	24.500	21.083	18.708
Dissimilar	25.800	21.100	20.300	17.400
Control	27.917	26.625	15.625	18.600

TABLE 3. Analyses of variance.

Source	df	Interpersonal Judgment Scale		Semantic differential	
		MS	F	MS	F
Similarity (A)	2	21.199	2.841	20.762	1.672
Affective Value (B)	1	189.963	25.456**	1134.518	91.334**
Procedure (C)	1	6.658	< 1	73.156	5.889*
A × B	2	25.031	3.354*	71.467	5.754**
A × C	2	15.154	2.031	27.319	2.199
B × C	1	16.426	2.201	22.608	1.820
A × B × C	2	0.094	< 1	10.725	< 1
Error	84	7.463		12.422	

* $p < 0.05$
** $p < 0.01$.

led to a mean attraction score of 8.708, while the mean attraction for the negative description was 5.926. Although there was a tendency for the similar stranger to be more attractive ($M = 8.235$) than the dissimilar stranger ($M = 6.733$), this effect of similarity on attraction was not significant. Further, the significant Similarity × Description inter-action appeared to be attributable mainly to differences between experimental and control groups (for which similarity was irrelevant) rather than to the difference between similar and dissimilar experi-mental groups, as can be seen in Fig. 1. Indeed, an analysis of variance

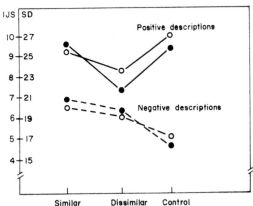

FIG. 1. Effects of similarity and description on attraction measures.

performed on the Interpersonal Judgment Scale attraction measure, but excluding the control groups, showed no significant interaction between similarity and description ($F = 1.273$, $df = 1/56$).

It can thus be concluded that attraction was strongly influenced by the affective value of information used to describe the other person. In contrast, similarity had no significant effect across levels of affective value. Very similar results were obtained for each of the other four items on the Interpersonal Judgment Scale but are not presented here due to space limitations.

More important, the results for the semantic differential measure confirmed the above conclusion. The Interpersonal Judgment Scale and the semantic differential measures of attraction correlated 0.692 ($p < 0.01$; $N = 108$). The analysis of variance for the semantic differential presented in Table 3 shows much the same results as were obtained for the Interpersonal Judgment Scale. The difference between positive description ($M = 25.418$) and negative description ($M = 18.619$) groups was highly significant ($F = 91.334$, $p < 0.01$). In contrast, the effect of similarity did not reach statistical significance ($F = 1.672$). The mean of the similar condition was 22.715, the mean of the dissimilar condition 21.150, and the mean of the control groups 22.192. The Similarity $\times$ Description interaction was again significant ($F = 5.754$, $p < 0.05$), and the pattern of means was very similar to the Interpersonal Judgment Scale attraction measure, as can be seen in Fig. 1. An analysis of variance excluding the control groups again revealed a nonsignificant Similarity $\times$ Description interaction ($F < 1$, $df = 1/56$). In addition, the semantic differential showed a significant procedure effect, indicating that attraction was generally higher in the experimental conditions than in the role-playing conditions. (See Table 2.)

Attitude Formation in Study 1

It is recalled that each subject rated the desirability of the 12 traits used in the personality descriptions. These ratings were scored from +3 to −3. Also available were the descriptions of the other person provided to the subject, again scored from +3 to −3 (see Table 1). These two sets of values were multiplied for each trait, and the sum across the products served as an estimate of the subject's attitude toward the other person, as suggested in Equation 1. As expected, this estimate was found to correlate significantly with the Interpersonal Judgment Scale measure of attraction ($r = 0.476$, $p < 0.01$) and with the semantic differential measure of attraction ($r = 0.567$, $p < 0.01$). These findings lent some support to the validity of the attitude model represented by Equation 1. Also of relevance to this model are the results of Study 2.

II. Study 2: opinions

A. METHOD

The booklet given to the 61 subjects in the role-playing condition of Study 1 contained a second part designed to assess the effects of another person's opinions on the formation of attitude toward that person. A total of 36 opinion items were constructed dealing with religion, college life, foreign policy, domestic politics, and racial relations. Each item was followed by five lines labeled strongly agree, agree, undecided, disagree, and strongly disagree. The 36 items were divided at random into three sets of 12 items each. The three sets were distributed equally among three different subgroups of subjects. Check marks were placed on the response scale of each item by throwing a die.

The 12-item opinionnaire was described to the subjects as responses provided by another student. On the basis of his responses, subjects were asked to answer several questions concerning the other person. First, each subject was asked to indicate which of 100 adjectives were descriptive of the other person by checking either yes, no, or ? (undecided) for each adjective. The 100 adjectives were selected from Anderson's (1968) list of 555 personality trait words and represented the whole range of likeability. Subjects then rated the hypothetical student on the Interpersonal Judgment Scale and the semantic differential described earlier.

B. RESULTS

It was expected that information about the other person's opinions would allow the subject to form an attitude toward the other person. To test this hypothesis, the subjects' responses to the adjective check list were scored as follows: A yes was scored $+1$, a no -1, and 1 ? was scored zero. These values for each trait were multiplied by Anderson's (1968) likeability values for the same traits. The resulting products were summed as an estimate of the subject's attitude toward the other person. This estimate correlated significantly with the Interpersonal Judgment Scale measure of attraction ($r = 0.676$, $p < 0.01$) as well as with the semantic differential measure ($r = 0.663$, $p < 0.01$).

These results, then, provided empirical evidence in support of the claim that subjects can use information about another person's opinions to attribute personality traits to him. The affective values of these traits can then provide the basis for the formation of attitude toward the other person.

III. General discussion

Attempts to provide an explanation for the observed similarity-attraction relation have recently led to a controversy between advocates of an information integration model (Anderson, 1971; Kaplan and Anderson, 1973) and advocates of a reinforcement model (Byrne et al., 1973; Byrne and Lamberth, 1971; Clore and Byrne, 1974). The attitude theory employed in this paper (see Equation 1) is quite consistent with an information-processing approach. The findings reported above suggest that similarity is usually found to be related to interpersonal attraction merely because similarity tends to be correlated with the affective value of the information about the stranger provided to the subject. An orthogonal manipulation of these two aspects of information showed that similarity as such had little effect on attraction.

At least two recent studies have also raised some doubts about the effects of similarity on attraction. Using a correlational design, Tesser (1969) found that although similarity was significantly related to attraction, the correlation was rather low and depended at least in part on the information's affective value. Using personality traits as unconditioned stimuli in a classical conditioning experiment, Stalling (1970) found a significant effect on the traits' affective values, but no significant effect of their perceived similarity to the subject. These findings are quite consistent with the results of the present study.

In contrast, McLaughlin (1971) recently reported an experiment in which affective value as well as similarity of another person's personality traits were found to have significant effects on attraction. His findings are difficult to interpret, however, since the affective value of the traits used to describe the other person was confounded with the affective value of the traits which subjects could use to describe themselves. This problem was avoided in the present study since the affective value of the personality feedback given to the subject was the same in all of the experimental conditions (see Table 1), namely, neutral.

One possible problem of the present study is worth mentioning. It will be recalled that in the experimental condition of Study 1, subjects received contrived personality feedback about themselves. This procedure raises the question of the feedback's believability. It is for this reason that the role-playing condition was included in the study. While the role-playing situation is somewhat artificial, it avoids the problem of providing a subject with feedback about himself. The procedural difference had a main effect only on the semantic differential measure of attraction. More important, it did not interact significantly with any of the other variables, indicating that the effects (or lack thereof) of similarity and affective value did not differ under experimental and role-playing conditions. The present findings, therefore, cannot be attributed to any suspicions which the subjects may have harboured about their own personality feedbacks. Further, it is recalled that postexperimental inquiry revealed little suspicion with respect to that feedback. A post hoc control group was run to examine the possibility that in the experimental condition, description of the other person's personality profile was confounded with the subject's desired-self profile. Thirty-seven male and female undergraduates were asked to describe themselves on the 12 bipolar adjective scales used in Study 1 (see Table 1). Responses were scored from -3 to $+3$ and summed over the 12 scales. As might be expected, subjects rated themselves quite favourably ($M = +10.03$), but significantly ($t = 3.21$, $p < 0.01$) lower than the positive other's description ($+0.14$). These findings argue against a serious confounding effect. It should also be noted that the neutral personality feedback given to subjects in Study 1 is likely to have lowered their perceived-self profile, thereby further reducing the probability of a confounding effect.

10.

Effects of Physical Attractiveness, Attitude Similarity, and Sex on Various Aspects of Interpersonal Attraction*

WOLFGANG STROEBE, C. A. INSKO, V. D. THOMPSON, And
B. D. LAYTON

University of North Carolina, Chapel Hill, USA

Male and female subjects' attraction to opposite-sex others of either high, medium, or low physical attractiveness and of either similar, moderately similar, or dissimilar attitudes was measured in terms of subjects' liking for other, of his or her preference for other as a coworker, and of the probability that he or she would consider other as a dating or marriage partner. The major results indicated that subjects' attraction was

*First published in *Journal of Personality and Social Psychology* 1971, **18**, 79-91. Copyright © 1971 by the American Psychological Association. Reprinted by permission. Stroebe is now at University of Marburg, West Germany.

greater to physically attractive rather than unattractive and to similar rather than dissimilar others. Similarity had a greater effect for females than males on liking and working, while physical attractiveness had a greater effect for males than females on working, dating, and marrying. Comparisons among the dependent variables revealed that physical attractiveness had a greater effect on dating than on liking or marrying for male and female subjects, although the difference was greater for males. Self-rating of attractiveness was found to be related to date selection. Relative to subjects who rated themselves as attractive, unattractive subjects were more likely to consider unattractive others and less likely to consider attractive others as a date.

Since being attractive to and attracted by members of the opposite sex are important aspects of our social life, everyday psychology is rich in notions about the important determinants of opposite-sex attraction. One of the well-accepted beliefs on this issue, often deplored by females, is that males are mainly attracted by physical appearance. Females, on the other hand, though they too are attracted by "good looks", are believed to place more importance on less "skin-deep" qualities.

To investigate this notion we had male and female subjects indicate their attraction to opposite-sex others who were of either high, medium, or low physical attractiveness and were in their attitudes either similar or dissimilar to the subjects. Ratings of subjects' liking for other, of his or her preference for other as a coworker, and of the probability that he or she would consider other as a dating or marriage partner were used as dependent measures of attraction. Rephrasing the above commonsense notion in terms of our design, we hypothesized a Sex × Physical Attractiveness interaction, a Sex × Attitude Similarity interaction, and possibly even a Sex × Physical Attractiveness × Similarity interaction.

The few studies which have investigated the effects of physical attractiveness and similarity on opposite-sex attraction tend to show only some of the predicted sex differences. In a study which manipulated attitude similarity and physical attractiveness of same- and opposite-sex others, Byrne *et al.* (1968) found that while similarity had a greater effect on females than on males, there was no sex difference in the effects of physical attractiveness. Their failure to find a sex difference in the effects of physical attractiveness may have been due to a failure to create enough difference between the two levels of physical attractiveness. In this study physical attractiveness was manipulated by presenting the male and female subjects with pictures of either physically attractive or unattractive same- or opposite-sex others. These pictures were selected from yearbook pictures on the basis of male and female judges' ratings. While the pictures chosen for the unattractive conditions appeared to have been near the extreme end of the attractiveness dimension — Byrne *et al.* described them as a "distinctly nonappealing group in terms of physical appearance" (p. 269) — the attractive males and females were merely "nice looking people", but "no rivals to Elizabeth Taylor or Rock Hudson". The difference in physical attractiveness between the two levels was possibly diminished further by the use of Xerox reproductions of the glossy prints rated by the judges. Xerox reproductions of photographs are generally not very faithful, and a person who looks attractive on a photograph usually looks much less attractive on a Xerox copy of that photograph.

Walster *et al.* (1966) investigated the effects of physical attractiveness, personality, aptitude, and implied liking on liking and subsequent dating. Subjects in this experiment were male and female students of the University of Minnesota who had purchased tickets to a "Computer Dance". When buying the tickets, each subject was surreptitiously rated by four judges on a scale of physical attractiveness. Subjects believed that a computer was going to match the partners for the dance on the basis of questionnaires filled out at the time the tickets were purchased, while, in fact, subjects were randomly paired. During the dance intermission, subjects answered a questionnaire containing questions relating to how much the subject liked his date and whether he would like to date the partner again. How much partners actually dated was determined with a 4-6 month follow-up interview. The results indicated that the only important determinant of a subject's liking for his (or her) date and his (or her) willingness to date again was the date's physical attractiveness. Intelligence scores and various personality measures (obtained either when the tickets were bought or from the university records) were uncorrelated with attraction.

Walster *et al.* (1966) interpreted their data as showing no sex differences in the effects of physical attractiveness on attraction. They expressed their surprise about the absence of a sex difference and pointed out that they "had assumed that physical attractiveness would be a much less important determinant of (women's) liking for men than for (men's liking for) women. However, it appears that it is just as important a determinant" (pp. 513-514). However, they did not report a test of the Sex × Physical Attractiveness interaction. Fortunately, they did report several correlations between ratings of the date's physical attractiveness and how much they were liked. For example, the correlation between the individuals' rating of the dates' physical attractiveness and their liking for the dates was 0.78 for males and 0.69 for females. The difference between these two correlation coefficients is significant ($z = 2.51$, $p < 0.012$).

In discussing their failure to find any effects of implied liking or personality, Walster *et al.* stated that perhaps the generality of their results is limited to large-group situations where young people (18-year-olds) are in brief contact. It appears very likely indeed that the apparent absence of additional effects as well as the overriding effect of physical attractiveness for both sexes may have been due to certain peculiarities of the situation. Since the subjects were exposed to each other for only a few hours, the overpowering effect of physical attractiveness was possibly caused by a relative lack of additional information on which interpersonal attraction could be based. In addition, the context of a dating situation may increase the importance of physical attractiveness and decrease the importance of other factors. The decision to date a person is possibly not only affected by the degree of attraction to that person, but also by the anticipated status effects of being seen with that person. Thus, a dating situation may greatly magnify the effect of physical attractiveness to the point where it "swamps out" other normally operating variables.

In the Walster *et al.* (1966) study, the questionnaire assessment of liking was administered by the same people who organized the dance. In the context of the assessment, the liking responses may thus have more closely reflected willingness or intention to date than is ordinarily the case. It is therefore not surprising that the overriding effects of physical attractiveness were observed on both measures of attraction, liking and dating.

In a more neutral situation, physical attractiveness will possibly have differential effects on dependent variables such as liking, dating, and marrying. We explicitly hypothesized that dating is more strongly affected by physical attractiveness than is either liking or marrying. As suggested earlier, the decision to date someone is not only affected by liking for that person, but also by considerations of possible status gains or losses incurred through being seen with her or him.

Finally, we hypothesized that similarity has a greater effect upon marriage than dating. In the consideration of a long-term relationship like marriage, factors such as similarity, which determine the expectations of rewards and costs of future interaction, should be much more powerful than in the dating situation.

I. Method

A. SUBJECTS

The subjects were 100 male and 100 female students from the introductory course at the University of North Carolina. Of these, 90 male and 90 female students were used for the experiment proper, while 10 male and 10 female students participated in the preliminary experiment, conducted in order to select photographs which would represent the three levels of physical attractiveness.

B. PICTURE SELECTION

Three male and three female photographs, representing the three levels of attractiveness (high, medium, and low), were selected on the basis of ratings made in a preliminary study. Thirty male and 30 female pictures were selected from college yearbooks by the authors, so as to cover the total range of attractiveness. Particular care was taken to include extremely attractive and extremely unattractive pictures in the sample.

The 30 female pictures were then rated by male judges, and the 30 male pictures, by female judges on an 11-point scale of physical attractiveness, ranging from extremely unattractive (Category 1) to extremely attractive (Category 11). Each judge was presented with the set of 30 opposite-sex pictures in a different random order, and his ratings were recorded by the experimenter. The judges were told that they should feel free to use all the categories, but that they would not have to place an equal number of photographs in each category.

To represent the high, medium, and low levels of attraction, three male pictures with mean ratings of 9.3 (SD = 1.55), 6.0 (SD = 1.67), and 2.0 (SD = 1.0), respectively, and three female pictures with mean ratings of 9.1 (SD = 1.04), 6.0 (SD = 1.09), and 1.9 (SD = 0.83) were selected.

C. INDEPENDENT VARIABLES

The three independent variables in this experiment were attitude similarity (high, medium, or low) between the opposite-sex other and the subject; physical attractiveness (high, medium, or low) of the other; and sex of the subject and other (male-female, female-male).

Attitude similarity was manipulated by having the other appear similar to the subject on either eight out of eight, four out of eight, or zero out of eight items on an attitude questionnaire. (In the four out of eight condition, the four items that were similar for one subset of subjects were dissimilar for another subset.)

The physical attractiveness of the other was manipulated by attaching his or her picture to the attitude questionnaire. The picture was one which had been rated as high, medium, or low in physical attractiveness.

In additional analyses subjects were divided into three groups of high, medium, or low physical attractiveness, either on the basis of subjects' self-ratings or on the basis of the experimenter's ratings of the subjects' physical attractiveness.

The self-ratings were obtained by having subjects rate themselves on a "Self-Rating Inventory", which consisted of twenty 7-point semantic differential scales. Included in these were scales related to physical attractiveness (good-looking-plain; appealing-unappealing; attractive-unattractive). On the basis of responses to these three scales, the subjects were divided into three groups of as nearly equal size as possible. The "low" group consisted of subjects with a sum of 13 or less on the three 7-point scales; the "medium" group consisted of subjects with a sum of 14 or 15; and the "high" group consisted of subjects with a sum of 16 or more.

The experimenter rated the subjects on a 6-point scale ranging from "very unattractive" to "very attractive". On the basis of these ratings, the subjects were divided into three groups of as nearly equal size as possible. The low group consisted of subjects rated 3 or less; the medium group consisted of subjects rated 4; and the high group consisted of subjects rated 5 or more.

D. PROCEDURE

The subjects were scheduled in groups of 3-7 individuals. On arrival each subject was asked by the experimenter to sit down in one of seven small rooms and to put on a pair of earphones. All instructions were tape-recorded and given through the earphones.

As soon as the last subject arrived, the subjects were informed that they were participating in an experiment on person perception, and that they would have to make judgements about another person on the basis of limited information. They were told that since their own attitude and personality characteristics would affect their judgements, it was necessary that they fill out some attitude and personality assessments in the first part of the experiment, before actually judging the other person.

As soon as these instructions were given, the experimenter gave each subject an "Attitude Inventory", which consisted of the 8 items needed for the similarity manipulation plus 37 filler items. (The 8 items selected were the ones which had shown the greatest diversity of opinion in a pretest.)

After finishing the questionnaire, subjects were asked to fill out the Self-Rating Inventory and a "Personality Inventory". The latter consisted of 42 items from the MMPI and served solely to keep the subjects busy while the experimenter prepared the 8-item attitude questionnaire, supposedly filled out by the other. For each subject the proportion of similar attitude items was either 0, ½, or 1. The "constant discrepancy" pattern (Byrne, 1969) was used to fake similarity or dissimilarity.

As soon as the experimenter had finished marking the others' attitude questionnaires for all subjects, he collected the two inventories. The subjects were then instructed through the earphones that they would receive a questionnaire which was completed by another person and a photograph of that person.

E. DEPENDENT VARIABLES

Approximately 3 min. after the subjects had received the questionnaires and the pictures, they were given an eight-item "Interpersonal Judgment Scale" (IJS) and were asked to rate the other person (other) on each of those eight items. The IJS contained the six items originally used by Byrne (1969) and two additional items. Four of the eight items were filler items, and four assessed the four dependent variables. Two of the dependent measures have been repeatedly used by Byrne. They assessed liking for and the preference for working with the other. The other two dependent measures were as follows: "If you were looking for a date and you knew this girl (boy), how likely would it be that you would consider her (him)?" and "if you were thinking of getting married and you knew this girl (boy), how likely would it be that you would consider her (him)?" Different forms were given to male and female subjects. Following Byrne's precedent, subjects responded to the liking and working items by marking one of seven alternatives. For the dating and marrying items, the seven alternatives ranged from "I definitely would consider her (him)" to "I definitely would not consider her (him)". High scores indicate high attraction.

II. Results

A. THREE-FACTOR MULTIVARIATE ANOVA

Mean effects of similarity, physical attractiveness, and sex on each of the four dependent variables, liking, working, dating, and marrying, are presented graphically in Figs 1a, 1b, 2a, 2b, 3a, 3b, 4a, and 4b, respectively. High scores indicate high attraction. The effects of

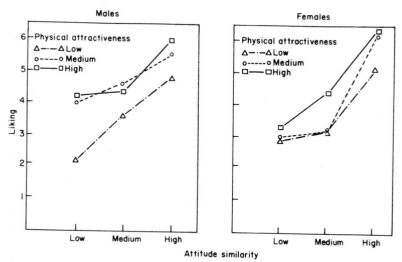

FIG. 1. Mean effects of similarity and physical attractiveness for males (a) and females (b) on liking.

similarity are indicated by the slopes of the curves; the steeper the slopes, the greater the similarity effects. The effects of physical attractiveness are indicated by the distance between the curves; the greater the distance between the curves, the greater the effects of attractiveness.

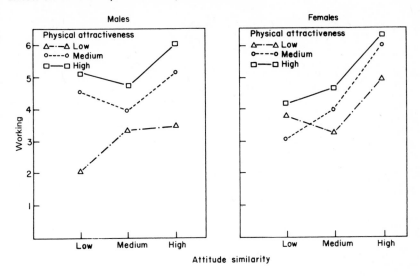

FIG. 2. Mean effects of similarity and physical attractiveness for males (a) and females (b) on working.

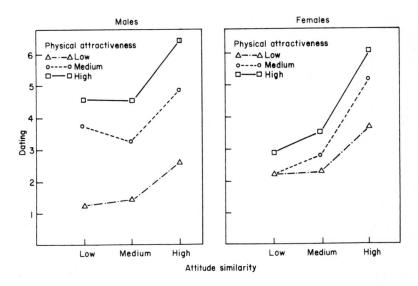

FIG. 3. Mean effects of similarity and physical attractiveness for males (a) and females (b) on dating.

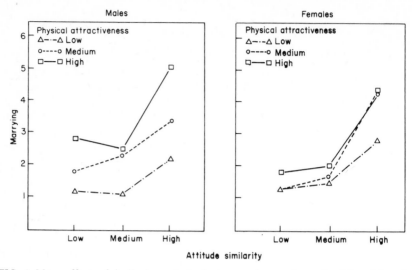

FIG. 4. Mean effects of similarity and physical attractiveness for males (a) and females (b) on marrying.

Table 1 summarizes a three-factor (Similarity × Physical Attractiveness × Sex) multivariate ANOVA. As expected, both similarity and physical attractiveness were significant for all four dependent variables. Subjects liked more, preferred to work with, and considered as a dating or marriage partner similar rather than dissimilar and attractive rather than unattractive others.

On three of the dependent variables (working, dating, marrying), the effects of physical attractiveness were stronger for males than for females (Attractiveness × Sex interaction). As can be seen from the graphs, the distance between the lower and the upper curve in Figures 2a, 3a, and 4a is greater than the distance in the corresponding Figs 2b, 3b, and 4b. (However, in an analysis of just the females' responses, attractiveness was still found to have a significant effect on working, $F = 8.75$, $p < 0.01$; dating, $F = 13.72$, $p < 0.01$; and marrying, $F = 6.88$, $p < 0.01$.)

In addition, there was a significant Similarity × Attractiveness × Sex interaction on working. Relative to females, males were less influenced by similarity when physical attractiveness was high, and equally influenced (approximately) by similarity when physical attractiveness was low. If we compare Fig. 2a and 2b, it is apparent that while the slope (similarity effect) of the lower curve (low physical

TABLE 1. Multivariate analysis of variance of the mean effects of similarity, attractiveness, and sex on liking, working, dating, and marrying.

Source	Univariate df	Liking		Working		Dating		Marrying		Multivariate F
		MS	F	MS	F	MS	F	MS	F	
Similarity (A)	2	95.66	67.76**	42.65	30.37**	75.74	44.37**	73.17	61.67**	17.54**
Attractiveness (B)	2	20.21	14.32**	44.52	31.70**	88.34	51.76**	30.34	25.57**	12.25**
Sex (C)	1	1.42	1.01	1.61	1.43	1.25	—	1.09	—	1.61
A × B	4	.31	—	.84	—	1.92	1.26	3.19	2.69*	1.31
A × C	2	4.82	3.42*	5.84	4.16*	4.55	2.67	1.91	1.61	1.58
B × C	2	2.61	1.85	8.04	5.72**	16.02	9.38**	4.71	3.97*	4.05**
A × B × C	4	2.31	1.63	4.30	3.06*	1.07	—	1.32	1.11	1.74*

*p < 0.05.
**p < 0.01.

attractiveness) in Fig. 2a is about equal to the slope of the corresponding curve in Fig. 2b, the slopes of the middle and the upper curves (medium and high physical attractiveness) are flatter in Fig. 2a than in Fig. 2b. (In an analysis conducted separately for each sex, the Similarity × Physical Attractiveness interaction did not reach acceptable levels of significance for males, $F = 1.57$, $p < 0.20$; or females, $F = 2.29$, $p < 0.10$.)

All the significant effects described above reached acceptable significance levels for both univariate and multivariate Fs. There are, however, several significant univariate Fs not accompanied by significant multivariate Fs. One of these is a Similarity × Attractiveness interaction on marrying. The effects of similarity were greater for attractive rather than unattractive others. The remaining univariate Fs are the Similarity × Sex interactions on liking and working. Females were more influenced than males by similarity.

B. MULTIVARIATE TREND ANALYSIS

Mean effects of similarity on the four dependent variables (liking, working, dating, marrying) are presented graphically in Figs 5a and 5b. Table 2 summarizes trend analyses of the similarity effects (collapsing sex) on the four dependent variables. Both the linear and

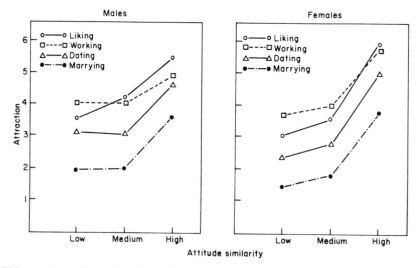

FIG. 5. Mean effects of similarity for males (a) and females (b) on liking, working, dating, and marrying.

TABLE 2. Trend analyses of the effects of similarity on liking, working, dating, and marrying (collapsing sex).

Source	Liking		Working		Dating		Marrying	
	MS	F	MS	F	MS	F	MS	F
Linear component	177.63	125.88*	72.07	51.32*	122.01	71.48*	118.01	99.47*
Quadratic component	13.61	9.64*	13.22	9.42*	29.47	17.26*	28.33	23.88*

*$p < 0.01$, $df = 1/162$.

the quadratic components for all four dependent variables have significant univariate Fs. The multivariate Fs are also significant for both linear ($F = 34.95$, $p < 0.01$) and quadratic components ($F = 6.19$, $p < 0.01$). In an additional analysis, following Byrne's precedent of summing, liking and working resulted in both a significant linear component ($F = 107.73$, $p < 0.01$) and a significant curvilinear component ($F = 12.07$, $p < 0.01$).

Although the multivariate F for the Similarity $\times$ Sex interaction was not significant (see Table 1), we feel that the significant univariate Fs for this interaction on liking and working justify separate trend analyses for the two sexes. These analyses are summarized in Tables 3 and 4.

For males, only the linear components were significant for liking and working, whereas both the linear and the quadratic components were significant for dating and marrying. For females, both the linear and the quadratic components were significant for all four dependent variables and for the liking and working sum. (All significant univariate Fs are accompanied by significant multivariate Fs.)

C. FOUR-FACTOR MULTIVARIATE ANOVA

We also did a multivariate ANOVA using self-rating of own attractiveness as an additional factor. Since such a breakdown of the data produced missing cells, it was impossible to extract the highest order interaction. This analysis resulted in a significant Self-Rating $\times$ Physical Attractiveness interaction on dating (univariate $F = 4.66$, $p < 0.01$; multivariate $F = 1.86$, $p < 0.05$). The means for this interaction are presented in Table 5. Relative to subjects with high self-ratings, subjects with low self-ratings were more likely to consider dating unattractive and less likely to consider dating attractive others. All univariate Fs which were significant in the three-factor multivariate ANOVA were also significant in the four-factor multivariate ANOVA. The sole discrepancy is that the significant multivariate F for the Similarity $\times$ Sex $\times$ Attractiveness interaction in the three-factor analysis was not significant ($p < 0.10$) in the four-factor analysis.

A similar four-factor multivariate ANOVA utilizing the experimenter's rating of subject's attractiveness did not produce a significant Rated Attractiveness $\times$ Physical Attractiveness interaction. Self-rating of own attractiveness and the experimenter's ratings of subject's attractiveness correlated trivially, but significantly (0.17, $p < 0.05$).

TABLE 3. Trend analyses of the effects of similarity on liking, working, dating, and marrying (male subjects).

Source	Liking		Working		Dating		Marrying	
	MS	*F*	*MS*	*F*	*MS*	*F*	*MS*	*F*
Linear component	60.00	34.61**	14.02	7.78**	32.27	14.12**	40.02	26.64**
Quadratic component	1.42	—	2.94	1.63	13.89	6.08*	12.27	8.20*

*$*p < 0.05$, $df = 1/81$.
$**p < 0.01$, $df = 1/81$.

TABLE 4. Trend analyses of the effects of similarity on liking, working, dating, and marrying (female subjects).

Source	Liking		Working		Dating		Marrying	
	MS	F	MS	F	MS	F	MS	F
Linear component	123.27	113.20*	68.27	67.76*	98.82	87.57*	81.67	93.17*
Quadratic component	16.12	14.88*	11.76	11.67*	15.60	13.83*	16.20	18.48*

*$p < 0.01$, $df = 1/81$.

TABLE 5. Mean effects of self-rating and attractiveness on dating.

Attractiveness of other	Self-rating of own attractiveness		
	Low	Medium	High
Low	2.68	2.05	1.89
n	22	19	19
Medium	4.46	3.12	3.62
n	15	24	21
High	3.94	4.86	5.04
n	18	22	20

D. DEPENDENT VARIABLE ANALYSIS

In order to gain information about differences among our four dependent variables, we selected three orthogonal contrasts (marrying versus dating, marrying versus working, dating versus liking), and used these as separate dependent variables in a multivariate ANOVA.[1] Table 6 summarizes the analysis.

Similarity had a greater effect on marrying than on working, and on liking than dating (similarity main effect on marrying versus working and dating versus liking). It can be seen from the graphs that in general the slopes of the curves in Figs 4a and 4b (marrying) are steeper than the slopes of the curves in Figs 2a and 2b (working). The same is true if we compare Figs 1a and 1b (liking) with Figs 3a and 3b (dating).

Physical attractiveness had a greater effect on dating than on marrying and on dating than liking (attractiveness main effect on marrying versus dating and dating versus liking). The distance between the lower and the upper curve in Figs 3a and 3b (dating) is greater than either the distance between the curves in Figs 4a and 4b (marrying), of Figs 1a and 1b (liking).

The marrying versus dating and the dating versus liking effect for physical attractiveness was greater for males than for females (Attractiveness × Sex interaction on marrying versus dating, and dating versus liking). The difference in the distance between the lower and the upper curve in Fig. 3a (dating for males) and the distance between

1. The comparisons of dating with marrying and liking were selected in order to check our assumption, regarding the greatest importance of physical attractiveness for dating. Given these two comparisons, the third comparison had to involve working and could not involve dating.

TABLE 6. Dependent variables analysis.

Source	Univariate df	Marrying v. dating		Marrying v. working		Dating v. liking		Multi-variate F
		MS	F	MS	F	MS	F	
Similarity (A)	2	.02	—	4.24	3.94*	4.12	3.60*	3.88**
Attractiveness (B)	2	15.14	16.04**	1.36	1.09	24.72	21.56**	7.88**
Sex (C)	1	.01	—	5.34	4.27*	.01	—	2.12
A × B	4	.98	1.04	1.69	1.35	1.61	1.40	1.37
A × C	2	.62	—	1.17	—	1.91	1.66	.91
B × C	2	5.50	5.83**	3.09	2.47	9.24	8.06**	4.19**
A × B × C	4	1.50	1.59	4.72	3.78**	1.11	—	1.78*

*p < 0.05.
**p < 0.01.

the corresponding curves in Fig. 4a (marrying for males) is greater than the difference in the distance between the lower and the upper curve in Fig. 3b (dating for females), and the distance between the corresponding curves in Fig. 4b (marrying for females). Likewise, the difference in the distance between the lower and the upper curve in Fig. 3a (dating for males) and the distance between the corresponding curves in Fig. 1a (liking for males) is greater than the difference between the lower and the upper curve in Fig. 3b (dating for females), and the distance between the corresponding curves in Fig. 1b (liking for females). (For females only, the multivariate F for the attractiveness effects on marrying versus dating and on dating versus liking was not significant, $F = 2.05$, $p < 0.10$; the univariate F for marrying versus dating was significant, $F = 5.42$, $p < 0.01$. For males only, the multivariate F for the attractiveness effects on marrying versus dating and dating versus liking was significant, $F = 8.90$, $p < 0.01$; the univariate F for marrying versus dating was significant, $F = 3.46$, $p < 0.01$, as was the univariate F for dating versus liking, $F = 27.87$, $p < 0.01$.)

III. Discussion

Byrne (1969) presented a great deal of experimental evidence that individuals like more and prefer to work with others who hold similar rather than dissimilar attitudes. Our results extend Byrne's findings even further by showing a significant main effect of attitude similarity on all four dependent variables. Relative to dissimilar others, similar others are not only liked more and preferred as co-workers, but they are also more likely to be considered as probable dating or marriage partners. However, our findings do not support Byrne in one respect. Byrne and Nelson (1965a) proposed as a tentative law of interpersonal attraction that "attraction towards X is a positive linear function of the proportion of positive reinforcements received from X" (p. 662). Byrne and Nelson found that a plot of the mean attraction scores for 11 different similarity proportions suggested linearity. For this plot Byrne and Nelson utilized, in addition to the data from their own study, results of five published studies (Byrne, 1961a, 1961b, 1962; Byrne and McGraw, 1964; Byrne and Wong, 1962) and of two unpublished studies. Our data, on the other hand, show both significant linear and curvilinear relationships between the proportion of similar attitudes and attraction, measured in terms of all four dependent variables, whereas male subjects show both linear and curvilinear relationships on only dating and marrying. For male subjects, liking and working were linearly, and not curvilinearly, related to the proportion of similar attitudes. Descriptively, the linear *F*s were markedly larger than the curvilinear *F*s for both sexes and all four dependent variables.

In agreement with the results of both the Byrne *et al.* (1968) and the Walster *et al.* (1966) study, we found a significant main effect of physical attractiveness on all four dependent measures of interpersonal attraction. Both males and females felt more attracted to physically attractive rather than unattractive opposite-sex others.

Byrne *et al.* (1968) reported a Similarity × Sex interaction on their dependent variable, which was a sum of the subjects' scores on the liking and working scales. We, too, found that relative to males, females are more affected by similarity in their liking for others and their preference for others as co-workers. However, this interaction reached an acceptable significance level only for the univariate *F*s and not for the multivariate *F*. Nonetheless, the fact that the Similarity × Sex interaction replicates a previous finding gives the effect somewhat greater credibility. (We also found that the interaction is significant when Byrne's precedent of summing liking and working is followed.) We thus claim qualified support for the original prediction of a Similarity × Sex interaction.

But why was the Similarity × Sex interaction not found for dating and marrying? The absence of a sex difference in the effect of similarity is perhaps easier to understand for marriage than for dating. Marriage, after all, is a long-term commitment, and it should be apparent for both males and females that similarity (or compatibility) is an exceedingly important selection criterion. However, regarding the selection of a date, we had clearly expected that females would be more affected than males by similarity. It appears that our stereotypes about sex differences in interpersonal attraction were oversimplified; or perhaps our experimental situation was not realistic enough.

The sex difference in the effect of similarity on working is further modified by a significant Similarity × Attractiveness × Sex interaction. Relative to females, males are less affected by similarity when physical attractiveness is medium or high, but approximately equally affected by similarity when physical attractiveness is low.

Contrary to our expectations, we did not find an Attractiveness × Sex interaction effect on liking. However, for the other three dependent variables (working, dating, and marrying), the effects of physical attractiveness were stronger for males than for females. We pointed out earlier that Byrne *et al.'s* (1968) failure to find an Attractiveness × Sex interaction may have been due to the relatively small difference between their two levels of physical attractiveness. Since we obtained the interaction for working but not for liking, it is possible that by summing the working and liking scores, Byrne *et al.* "swamped out" a possible Attractiveness × Sex interaction on working. However, in our study the interaction was significant even when we summed the liking and the working scores.

Unfortunately, the interpretation of the sex difference on the effects of physical attractiveness is somewhat problematic. For obvious reasons, different sets of pictures had to be used to manipulate the attractiveness of opposite-sex male and female others. Thus, the stronger effect of physical attractiveness for males could be due to a greater difference in physical attractiveness among the female than male pictures. Since the two physical attractiveness scales may differ in origin and unit size, the fact that the male and female pictures selected for each level of physical attractiveness received nearly identical ratings does not exclude this possibility. However, if the Attractiveness × Sex interaction were actually caused by unequal differences in the physical attractiveness between the two sets of pictures, it would be difficult to understand why this interaction effect did not occur for liking. In addition, our extreme pictures represent the most unattractive and the most attractive males and females that could be found in college yearbooks. Since it can be assumed that yearbooks reflect the range of physical attractiveness represented on campus, our extreme pictures should represent this range with respect to males as well as with respect to females. The Physical Attractiveness × Sex interaction can therefore be interpreted as indicating that for the range of physical attractiveness represented among college students, physical attractiveness is a more important determinant of opposite-sex attraction for males than for females.

The four-factor multivariate ANOVA using subject's self-rating of own attractiveness as a fourth factor resulted in a significant Self-Rating × Physical Attractiveness interaction for dating. Compared to subjects who perceive themselves as attractive, subjects who think they are unattractive are more likely to consider dating unattractive and less likely to consider dating attractive others. This, at least partly, supports the Walster *et al.* (1966) hypothesis that "one's romantic feelings and choices are affected both by the objective desirability of the romantic object and by one's perception of the possibility of attaining the affection of the other" (p. 508). As in any bargaining situation, participants in the dating game have to learn the range of outcomes available to them. Being turned down or never asked for a date is embarrassing and frustrating, and the less attractive individuals, in order to avoid further frustration, possibly learn to stop trying for the most desirable but unavailable dates. Initially, we were puzzled that the Self-Rating × Physical Attractiveness interaction was significant for dating but not for marrying. It seems so obvious that attractive others who are unavailable for less attractive persons as dates are also unavailable as marriage partners. However, the absence of a significant Self-Rating × Physical Attractiveness interaction for marrying is perhaps not quite so surprising if one considers that physical attractiveness is of much less importance regarding marriage than dating. Given other good qualities, a physically less attractive person may not be very popular as a date, but may still have good prospects as a marriage candidate.

Walster *et al.* found no evidence that unattractive subjects were less likely than attractive subjects to date attractive others and more likely to date unattractive others. There are a number of differences between the Walster *et al.* study and our study which could account for this difference in the results. For example, the dependent variable in our study was whether subjects would consider the other for a date, whereas in their study subjects had already met at a dance and were asked whether they would date the same partner again. Whatever restrains a person from considering someone for a date may be less important after he (or she) has already socially met that person. Furthermore, the fact that the partner bought tickets for a computer dance indicates that he (or she) is not yet "going steady" and indeed is looking for a date. An additional consideration is that we obtained the interaction only for self-perceived attractiveness and not for independently judged attractiveness. Walster *et al.* only tested for the interaction with independently judged attractiveness. (They could have used their perceived "popularity" scores for a related test.) It makes good sense that self-perceived attractiveness rather than rated attractiveness is the more appropriate variable. Walster *et al.* (1966) appear in agreement with this statement when they referred to the "perception of the possibility of attaining the affection of the other" (p. 508).

In order to test whether the three independent variables had the predicted differential effects on our four dependent variables, we selected three orthogonal contrasts (marrying versus dating, marrying versus working, dating versus liking) and used these as separate dependent variables in a multivariate ANOVA. Since most of our predictions are relevant mainly to the marrying versus dating and the dating versus liking comparisons, we will discuss these first.

We predicted that similarity would be more important for marrying than dating. Contrary to expectation, similarity had no differential effects on dating and marrying. Our failure to find differential similarity effects on dating and marrying is even more puzzling in view of the fact that differential similarity effects were found with respect to dating and liking. Relative to dating, liking was significantly more affected by similarity. This suggests that our predictions regarding the similarity effects on dating and marrying are incorrect, not because we underestimated the importance of similarity for date selection, but because we overestimated its importance for the selection of marriage partners.

Physical attractiveness had a greater effect on dating than on either marrying or liking. This differential effect is further qualified by a sex interaction. The difference in the effects of physical attractiveness on dating and either marrying or liking is greater for males than for females. Further analyses indicated that for females only, physical attractiveness has no differential effect on dating and liking and only a marginally differential effect on marrying and dating. This suggests that at least with respect to the dating versus liking comparison, the attractiveness main effect mentioned above reflects differences mainly for male subjects. Our prediction of a greater physical attractiveness effect on dating than on either marrying or liking was based on the assumption that the decision to date someone is not only affected by liking for that person, but also by considerations of possible status gains or losses through being seen with him or her. Thus, central to our interpretation is the assumption of a differential effect of physical attractiveness on dating and liking. The fact that such a difference was observed only for males invalidates or qualifies our interpretation.

Regarding the comparison of marrying and working, similarity had a greater effect on marrying. More interesting is that this difference was modified by a Similarity × Attractiveness × Sex interaction. The triple interaction seems to be due to the fact, as mentioned earlier, that relative to females males are less affected in co-worker preference by similarity when physical attractiveness is medium or high, but approximately equally affected by similarity when physical attractiveness is low. Since this is not true for males' as compared to females' selection of marriage partners, the interaction results.

With some exceptions, our findings are fairly consistent with everyday observations of opposite-sex attraction. It nevertheless is an open question whether the factor which affects preference for a date or preference for a marriage partner would have the same effect on actual date selection or marriage-partner selection. It also remains to be seen how much our findings are affected by factors which are unique to Southern culture. Nonetheless, our results strongly suggest that the various dimensions of interpersonal attraction have unique aspects, so that generalization from one to the other may not always be warranted. In this respect Byrne's (1969) procedure of summing liking and working does not appear advisable.

11.

*Perceived Congruence Among Premarital Couples as a Function of Neuroticism[1]

B. I. MURSTEIN

Connecticut College, USA

The traditional psychoanalytic position favours unconscious perception in the choice of marital partner which leads to the conclusion that neurotics choose each other in marriage. Stimulus-value-role theory, on the other hand, states that neurotics "settle" for each other because of their limited rewarding power for others. It was hypothesized therefore that neurotics will be less satisfied with a neurotic partner than will normals with a normal partner. Perceptual congruence was also predicted to be greater for nonneurotics than neurotic couples. Conflicting evidence was obtained for the first hypothesis, but the second was clearly supported.

*First published in *Journal of Abnormal Psychology* 1973 **82** 22-26. Copyright © 1973 by the American Psychological Association. Reprinted by permission.

1. This research was sponsored in part by National Institute of Mental Health Grant 08405.
   The kindness of Regina Roth in reading the manuscript and offering criticisms is greatly appreciated. The assistance of Jerry C. Lamb with computer analysis is also gratefully acknowledged.

The literature on marriage sometimes conveys the impression that everyone marries in accordance with his perceived fulfillment of his needs, and that each individual succeeds in finding another individual either admirably or maliciously suited for him. Psychoanalysts in particular have never ceased to stress that neurotics seek each other out (Mittelman, 1944). Kubie (1956), in fact, claims that almost every marriage is unconsciously determined to some degree, and the individual only deludes himself into believing he married for consciously arrived at reasons.

The psychoanalytic approach is quite at variance with a theory of marital choice recently developed called stimulus-value-role (Murstein, 1970). This theory favours the idea that each individual possesses assets and liabilities in the marriage market which determine the kind of spouse he will be able to obtain. Assets are any commodities which are valued by others and include good looks, interest in others, socioeconomic status, and freedom from neurotic traits. Liabilities are those qualities which are negatively valued by others and include such qualities as physical unattractiveness, a lack of education, and indifference to others. There also may be detriments to a relationship which are not actual qualities of the other such as the physical distance necessary to see a girlfriend or restrictions placed on the relationship by parents.

Although an individual may at first be unaware of his assets and liabilities, he becomes increasingly aware of them as a result of his interactions with the opposite sex. Initially, like many inexperienced youths, he may attempt to court someone whose assets outnumber his own and whose liabilities are fewer. Such action on his part, however, increases his probability of being rejected proportionately to the degree that he overshoots his own marital rank.

On the other hand, to focus on someone of lower rank is to maximize his success but minimize his satisfaction; accordingly, his best combination of probability of success and maximum of satisfaction is achieved when he approaches someone of his own nubile status.

Moodiness, inability to make decisions, dislike of the self — in sum, the components of neurosis — are all obviously liabilities which make a person less attractive. It should be expected, therefore, that neurotic individuals should not be as likely to entice nonneurotics into marriage as neurotics, not because these neurotics are drawn to each other as their primary choices, but because having more liabilities than the average individual they can only attract those with an approximately equal net worth.

The possession of neurotic liabilities does not necessitate that a neurotic marry another neurotic. A female neurotic may be beautiful, thus balancing off her liability with an important asset, or her boyfriend may be exceedingly corpulent, thus balancing off her liability with one of his own. All things being equal, however, neurotics are more likely to marry neurotics than nonneurotics as has been demonstrated in another study with the present population (Murstein, 1967).

The traditional psychoanalytic stance thus appears to lead to different conclusions than does stimulus-value-role theory regarding the perceptions of neurotic members of a couple about each other. If the neurotics are unconscious of their reasons for marrying each other, as psychoanalysts claim, there is no reason for them to denigrate their partner or to perceive them as less than optimal. From stimulus-value-role theory, however, it may be concluded that neurotics do not *choose* each other so much as *settle* for each other. In that case, it is hypothesized that neurotics should be less favourable in their perceptions of their partner than nonneurotics. A second hypothesis is that neurotics should show less congruence in their perceptions of themselves and their partners than will nonneurotics. The basis of this hypothesis is the belief that neurotics tend to misperceive themselves and their partners as a function of their neurosis. Their perceptions are also more deviant from the norm, and hence the perceptions of neurotics regarding different aspects of themselves as well as in comparison with those of their partner are less likely to show agreement than are the perceptions of persons free from neurosis.

I. Method

A. SUBJECTS

The S population consisted of 99 couples who were "going steady" or were engaged and who had volunteered to participate in the study for which they were paid $15 per couple. The sample was largely drawn from three Connecticut colleges or universities, only 13 of the 198 Ss indicating that they were neither students nor college graduates. The average ages of the men and women were 21.1 ($SD = 2.2$) and 19.8

(SD = 1.5), respectively. Background questionnaires revealed that the sample was a relatively homogeneous, upper-middle-class one.

Neuroticism was determined by means of the "neurotic triad" of the MMPI. The scales of Hysteria, Hypochondriasis, and Depression were summed considering the K correction factor to yield the neurotic triad score. Neuroticism was arbitrarily defined as being in the upper third of the distribution for one's given sex. For the neurotic group, each S had to be in the upper third of the distribution as did his partner with respect to her sex's distribution. The "healthy" group consisted of persons who were not classified as neurotic and whose partner also did not fall within the neurotic classification. By this method of classification, 13 neurotic couples and 37 nonneurotic couples were obtained, and these constituted the groups compared in the present study.

B. TEST

To test the hypotheses, a modified version of the Edwards Personal Preference Schedule[2] was employed. The standard test consists of paired sentences representing different needs roughly equated for social desirability with the intention that S be forced to express his personal choice rather than the more socially acceptable one. Unfortunately, Corah *et al.* (1958) have shown that the social desirability factor has not been removed, while Horst and Wright (1959) found that the paired comparisons of the test are less reliable than the items considered individually. For the present study, therefore, the items were considered singly, and for each one a 5-point scale ranging from "very frequently" or "very important to me" to "almost never" or "almost no importance" was used.

The Ss were tested on any one of several testing dates and took the revised form as part of a larger battery of tests and questionnaires. The tests were coded to assure anonymity, and the couples sat apart and were not allowed to communicate with anyone except the administrator.

Because in the present study the revised Personal Preference Schedule was used as a general measure of personality, the specific need scores were not utilized. Instead, each S took the revised Personal Preference Schedule under four different "sets" systematically balanced to avoid sequence effects. These were self, ideal self, perception of

2. The Edwards Personal Preference Schedule used in the research was modified and reproduced by permission. Copyright 1953 by the Psychological Corporation, New York, New York. All rights reserved.

boyfriend (girlfriend), and ideal spouse. Each set was correlated with every other set. Since there were eight sets per couple (4 for each member), there were 28 correlations computed per couple ($n(n-1)/2$). Of these correlations, 12 may be classified as intraperceptual (6 for men, 6 for women) in that two sets from within each person were compared. These were self, ideal self; self, perception of partner; self, ideal spouse; ideal self, perception of partner; ideal self, ideal spouse; perception of partner, ideal spouse. The remaining 16 correlations were interperceptual in that they compared sets coming from different persons.

The mean of each correlation was obtained for the neurotic group and for the nonneurotic group and a t test computed for the difference. An example will illustrate the procedure. The self and ideal-self correlations of the men of the neurotic group were converted to Fisher's Z in order to work with a more normal distribution. The mean Z of this group was compared with the mean Z of the nonneurotic group for the self, ideal-self correlation. The t value of 2.29 favouring the nonneurotic group was significant for the one-tailed test ($p < 0.05$). In like manner, the means for each of the 27 other correlations were compared.

II. Results

Of the 28 correlations, 8 were found to significantly differentiate the neurotic and nonneurotic couples at the 0.05 level or better (one-tailed test). For these significant correlations, the mean r for each group and the t value are shown in Table 1.

Hypothesis 1 called for the normal Ss to be more satisfied with their partner than the neurotic Ss. Because the correlations measure perceptual congruence, and because perceptual congruence might be taken to be highly related to satisfaction, it might be presumed that the 28 correlations as a whole reflect satisfaction; however, 2 of the 28 correlations bear more strongly than any of the others on this question. These are the correlations between the man's perception of his partner and his ideal-spouse concept and the woman's perception of her partner and her concept of ideal spouse. Neither of these, however, was even remotely close to a significant difference (mean rs for neurotic men and nonneurotic men were 0.80 and 0.84; for neurotic and nonneurotic women, 0.79 and 0.80). Hypothesis 1 therefore is rejected.

Hypothesis 2 called for greater perceptual congruence among the nonneurotic Ss than for the neurotic ones. Because the same Ss appear in each comparison, the usual criteria for chance levels of significance for multiple tests of significance do not hold. If these tests had been wholly independent, it would be expected that 1.4 of the 28 comparisons would be significant by chance. Although it is impossible to make an exact statement of the significance of the findings, the fact that the number of significant t values reported was about six times the expected rate suggests confirmation of Hypothesis 2.

TABLE 1. Significant t values between neurotic and non-neurotic couples using the Revised Personal Preference Schedule items.

Variables compared	Neurotic mean r	Non-neurotic mean r	t
Self$_M$, ideal self$_M$	.71	.82	2.29*
Self$_M$, boyfriend$_W$	$-.13$	.03	1.71*
Ideal self$_M$, self$_W$	$-.15$	.05	2.33*
Ideal self$_M$, ideal spouse$_W$	$-.07$	.09	1.72*
Ideal spouse$_M$, ideal spouse$_W$	$-.27$	.02	3.18**
Ideal spouse$_M$, boyfriend$_W$	$-.23$	.03	3.22**
Girlfriend$_M$, ideal spouse$_W$	$-.19$	.01	2.64**
Girlfriend$_M$, boyfriend$_W$	$-.19$	$-.02$	2.03*

Note. The subscripts M or W indicate whether the man or woman is doing the perceiving.
*$p < 0.05$ for one-tailed test.
**$p < 0.01$ for one-tailed test.

III. Discussion

The failure to support the first hypothesis and the fact that the differences in correlation between the neurotic and nonneurotic groups appear slight, although some reached statistical significance, may make it appear as if perception as measured here is minimally related to neurosis. There is reason to believe, however, that a number of biases caused the data to underrepresent the true difference between the perceptions of neurotics and nonneurotics.

First, the data were drawn from a volunteer population who took a number of surveys asking very personal questions. It might be assumed that the typical volunteer would be very self-assured to be willing to participate in such a study and that he would be more apt to be nonneurotic than neurotic. This fact is confirmed in that a clinician well versed in the MMPI[3] who examined the profile sheets of the *S*s without knowledge of their diagnosis judged 61 men and 73 women to be essentially free of "disturbance" and only 21 men and 20 women to show evidence of even slight disturbance. These figures suggest that we had a constricted sample for this variable and that our "neurotics" were more comparable to the average population at large than to true neurotics. Obviously, it is difficult to find differences within such a constricted sample.

Second, it is to be expected that individuals who are thinking seriously of marriage will tend to alter their perceptions of themselves and their partners in a socially desirable manner. Our culture does not generally countenance "marriages of convenience". An individual is supposed to be in love when he marries, and there is obviously a tendency for both neurotics and nonneurotics to idealize their partners as the high perceived partner, ideal-spouse correlations clearly show. Indeed, this idealization as reflected in the great magnitude of these correlations may have prevented any differences between the neurotic and nonneurotic groups from reaching significance because of a "ceiling" effect. It is conceivable, therefore, that Hypothesis 1 would not have been rejected with a group less advanced in courtship or a test less amenable to social desirability.

In fact, with the aid of hindsight. Hypothesis 1 was reexamined by correlating the neurotic triad score with the men's and the women's perceived partner, ideal-spouse correlation, treating the latter correlation as a score after converting it for each couple to Fisher's *Z*. The correlation for men was -0.26 and for women -0.27, both modest in size but statistically significant ($p < 0.01$). Neuroticism, in short, was inversely related to satisfaction when the total population was used.

It is possible to argue that neurotics are not really more dissatisfied with each other than are nonneurotics; they just complain more. According to this hypothesis, a person who gets a high neurotic triad score evinces a tendency not only to complain about himself but about his partner as well; thus he should manifest a lower partner satisfaction correlation than the nonneurotic (a non-complainer) shows with respect to his partner.

The veridicality of the "complaining hypothesis" might be tested by comparing partner satisfactions for the case in which a neurotic was courting a normal person. To make this test, all cases in which a

3. The author is grateful to Philip A. Goldberg, who served as the judge.

neurotic man (upper third of male neurotic triad score) was going with a healthy woman (lowest third of female neurotic triad score) and in which a neurotic woman was going with a healthy man were compiled. There were 11 of the former and 10 of the latter, making 21 cases in all.

The partner satisfaction mean for all neurotics, combining men and women, was compared with the partner satisfaction mean of the normals. If the complaining hypothesis were true, the neurotics ought to be less satisfied with their partner than the normals. According to stimulus-value-role theory, however, a normal courting a neurotic ought to be as satisfied with the neurotic as the neurotic is with him. Presumably, in order for the relationship to function well, the neurotic being deficient in personality adjustment would be higher than his normal partner in some other desirable asset. A t test between the two groups was clearly nonsignificant ($t = 0.27$); hence the neurotics did not complain more about their partner than the normals and the complaining hypothesis received no support.

It might be thought, however, that perhaps the differences in perceptual congruence between neurotics and nonneurotics are due to the difference in perception of needs for the self, ideal self, spouse, and ideal spouse. To test this possibility, t tests were computed for each of the 15 Edwards Personal Preference Schedule need scores over each of the 4 perceptual "sets", yielding a total of 60 t tests for each sex. Neurotic and nonneurotic men differed significantly ($p < 0.05$) on only 3 of the 60 t tests, and neurotic and nonneurotic women differed on 1 of 60 tests, findings which are consistent with chance expectations. It can be concluded, therefore, that the present population does not possess very different expectations for themselves and others for the various needs. It was a general overall difference in perceptual congruence that differentiated the groups.

Regarding this difference, Table 1 indicates that apart from the self, ideal-self correlation for the men, all of the other significant differences between the neurotic and nonneurotic groups resulted from negative correlations for the neurotic group and zero-order correlations for the nonneurotic group. In truth, therefore, it is not so much the perceptual congruence of the nonneurotic group which separates them from the neurotics as it is the latter's conflicting perceptions compared to the former's noncorrelated perceptions. This is exactly the same differentiation earlier reported by Murstein (1966) for couples making poor and good courtship progress. In that study with the same Ss, Ss making poor courtship progress showed factor scores which were incompatible with each other (negatively correlated), whereas Ss making good courtship progress showed essentially no relationship between their factor scores. Presumably, therefore, healthy relationships are marked by an absence of conflicting perceptions rather than necessarily by very similar ones.

In sum, the data support the notion that neurotics going with other neurotics are perceptually less congruent than nonneurotics courting nonneurotics. Regarding whether neurotics are less satisfied with their neurotic partner, the issue is more clouded, different answers having been obtained with different analyses. Future research might well clarify this question. Such research ideally should include more demonstrably neurotic persons than those so classified in the present study. The test used should perhaps be more specific to the concerns of premarital couples than the more general Edwards Personal Preference Schedule. In fact, a test which would avoid the vast overestimation of the partner one may marry which social propriety seemingly calls for would be most welcome. Surely in the United States there must be *some* marriages of convenience.

12.

Testing a Multidimensional Approach to Friendship[1]

J. J. LA GAIPA
University of Windsor, Ontario, Canada

The studies reported here represent a programme of research which, by its very nature changed in emphasis and direction as studies were completed. The following sections reflect these emphases and changes: first, the need to construct indices of friendship dimensions; second, some inventories that we researched, particularly those measuring different conceptions of friendship at different stages of relationship; third, a series of longitudinal studies where we were particularly concerned with identifying variables predicting friendship growth and whether different variables are as important at different stages in a relationship. The research findings will be presented in more or less detail as is appropriate to the argument and will be reported in approximately the order in which they were obtained.

1. This chapter reports a series of studies of friendship formation conducted at the University of Windsor between 1968 and 1975. I would like to thank the following who served on thesis and doctoral dissertation committees for the research reported here: Meyer W. Starr, William L. Libby, Akira Kobasigawa, Roland Engelhart, and in particular Theodore M. Newcomb, my own thesis advisor and a source of inspiration for much of this research. I am grateful to Steve Duck for his comments on the original draft of this chapter.

One particular focus of our work was the examination of inter-personal attraction within the social context where it occurs (Kerckhoff, 1974) and thus identifying cultural definitions of what a good friend "ought" to be like. In this work we found it useful to think of friendship in terms of a hierarchy ranging from casual acquaintances to best friend (Canfield and La Gaipa, 1970a) and to look at role expectations for each (both as providers of anticipatory qualities in interaction as well as an "ought" quality: Secord and Backman, 1964), since people's expectancies are themselves normative and help to define characteristics of different stages of intimacy (Levinger, 1974). Knowledge that two persons define themselves to be at a certain level of friendship allows the outsider to make certain predictions about the evolution of the relationship, although the fact that one examines role expectations does not lead to the concentration only on *behaviour*. What seems to be prescribed by role expectations is of a cognitive rather than a purely behavioural nature and the shared expectations include intentions and motives also. This suggests that social norms do not simply operate to define behavioural patterns but also provide a basis for evaluation and interpretation of behaviour, and (since evaluation of the adequacy of performance is particularly dependent on labelling processes) a basis for attributions about the other and his continued potential as a friend for the future. This latter theoretical point has important practical implications since friends presumably make attributions which allow them to assess the rewards to be expected if the relationship continues (cf. La Gaipa's chapter in section 1 of this book). This in turn particularly requires that the researcher develops not only indices of rewards and benefits derived from or causing friendship (Wright, 1965) but also indices of degree of friendship likely to be predicated on such rewards.

I. Measurement of friendship dimensions

A. IDENTIFICATION OF FRIENDSHIP EXPECTANCIES

A group project on the "Meaning of Friendship" was carried out by ten college students enrolled in an undergraduate course in Social Psychology at the University of Windsor in 1968. The students conducted over 150 open-ended interviews while home during the holidays and personal data was collected on age, sex, nationality and occupation.

While no claim is made that the 150 subjects were a cross section of the larger society, the data do not simply reflect the student subculture.

The study was designed to find out what expectations people have of others at different levels of friendship and instructions were to describe "critical incidents" that "explain or illustrate why you consider this person to be your . . . best friend?"

The subjects were instructed to think of friends of the same sex at five different levels of friendship. Each level was briefly defined as follows: *Best Friends* (Your very closest friends, perhaps one or two persons); *Close Friends* (A rather select group of 10 or 12 persons with whom you have established a close relationship); *Good Friends* (A larger group of people who you seek out and prefer, but with whom you are not particularly close); *Social Acquaintances* (People you interact with at school, at work, drinking coffee, getting together for a bull session); *Casual Acquaintances* (People that you barely know — with whom you just have a "nodding" acquaintance).

A content analysis of over 1800 friendship statements served to identify the major friendship themes at each level. The resulting 152 items were listed by level of friendship, and administered to 30 judges. The instructions were to rate each of the items on a one to nine scale, ranging from "Definitely Not Essential" to "Definitely Essential" according to the specified level of friendship. The items retained were those that were rated as essential and that have evoked high inter-judge agreement. At this point the Casual Acquaintance level was dropped because of the lack of satisfactory items.

The remaining 80 items covering the four remaining friendship levels were administered by means of a Likert-type questionnaire. A total of 1167 high school and college students, comprising four groups, rated each statement for one of the four levels of friendship. Each subject read the four definitions of friendship and then rated each of the 80 items for the level of friendship assigned to his group using a 5 point scale ranging from "Definitely Not Essential" to "Definitely Essential".

Ratings, then, were obtained from different groups of subjects responding to the four levels of friendship. Separate factor analyses were conducted (La Gaipa, 1969) using the principal component technique with rotation to simple structure. A total of 11 factors was identified from the responses to the four levels of friendship. The eight major factors were: *Self-Disclosure* ("feeling free to express and reveal personal and intimate information"); *Authenticity* ("openness and

honesty in the relationship; being real, genuine and spontaneous");
Helping Behaviour ("expressing concern for one's well being; giving
help readily without being asked; providing psychological support");
Acceptance ("acknowledging one's identity, integrity and individuality;
not taking advantage of another"); *Positive Regard* ("providing ego
reinforcement; enhancing one's feeling of self worth; treating one as
deserving of respect and as an important, worthwhile person");
Strength of Character ("striving to achieve and conform to the
objective value system of the society"); *Similarity* ("possessing similar
points of view; expressing agreement on controversial issues; possessing
similar attitudes and interests"); *Empathic Understanding* ("interpreting accurately the feelings of another person; understanding how
one really feels; really listening to what one has to say") and *Ritualistic
Social Exchange.*

What is particularly interesting about these four factor analyses is
that the same factors were not always isolated at all levels of
friendship. Some factors emerged only at one level, others were found
at two or three levels and others still at all four levels. These findings
suggest that there are differences in the way friendship is perceived at
each stage of development (Canfield and La Gaipa, 1970b). Subsequent
factor analytic studies have replicated this finding and generally from
four to seven factors are typically isolated for any given level of
friendship. It is assumed on the bases of the procedures used to
construct the scales that the factors do measure shared *beliefs* or
expectancies about friendship. These friendship dimensions, however,
are also likely to reflect shared *values*. Conceptually, there is a
difference between expectations and values, though, in practice, the
two are highly interrelated (McGuire, 1960). Theoretically, a person
might consider two dimensions equally essential but rate one as more
desirable to him than the other.

Since expectancies and values do not necessarily correspond, a form
of the friendship inventory was developed to tap values. This involved
a slight modification in the instructions for the Friendship Inventory
above: "Read each statement and indicate how *important* you consider
the characteristic to be for friends at the level assigned to you." The
five-point Likert-type scale was described as follows: Slightly Important,
Rather Important, Quite Important, Very Important and Extremely
Important.

The friendship inventory of values was administered to a total
sample of 2361 college students; 1002 in U.S. universities and 1359 in

Canadian universities. The objectives of this part of the study were to determine the reliabilities of the scales (data not reported here);[2] conduct further factor analytic studies, to identify any major group differences, and to obtain normative data for interpreting individual friendship profile scores.

Figure 1 presents bar graphs portraying the means and standard deviations of data on six of the scales by level of friendship. These data are limited to the Canadian sample (the sex differences were so minor here that the two groups could be combined; overall, however, the U.S. data[3] corresponds quite closely to what is shown in Fig. 1). With few exceptions, the differences between means were less than one integer apart.

Comparisons *across friendship dimensions* should be made with caution since we do not know the extent to which any observed differences are due to scale artifacts. One can, however, be more confident about differences *across levels of friendship* on the same dimension of friendship. Keeping this reservation in mind, the data in Fig. 1 suggest that differences in the importance assigned to each scale vary with the level of friendship. Most of the differences between means were highly significant except for a few adjacent levels such as between close friend and best friend.

An interesting contrast can be made between Self Disclosure and Authenticity. Self Disclosure has received considerable attention in research on interpersonal attraction (see La Gaipa's chapter in section 1), in part, because of the ease of operationalizing this dimension. Authenticity, on the other hand, has received relatively little attention. The data in Fig. 1 suggest that for many people Self Disclosure does not become very important until the relationship is defined as Close and Self Disclosure is not very discriminating at the lower levels of friendship. Although most acquaintances occur at the levels of social acquaintance and good friend, Self Disclosure does not appear to be a critical factor in defining this vast area of social relationships. On the other hand, Authenticity seems to be an essential condition at *all* levels of friendship: to be a "phony" is not tolerated at even the lower levels.

2. Details of these data may be obtained from the author (Editor).

3. In the U.S. sample, females made more distinction than males between Close and Best Friend and between Social Acquaintance and Good Friend. Females also assigned higher value to Best Friend than did males and lower value to Social Acquaintance on most scales employed.

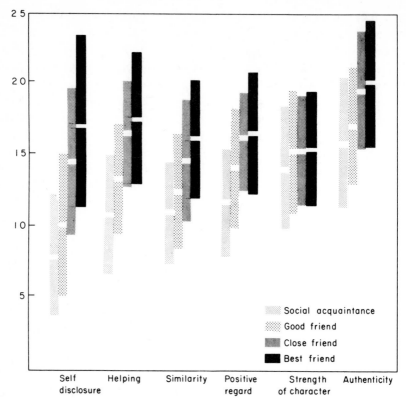

FIG. 1. Variability of scores by friendship scale and level of friendship. (One standard deviation above and below the mean.)

These cross-sectional data involve *value* statements about hypothetical friends. Heilbronn (1975) conducted a longitudinal study involving *amount of rewards*. At the end of the 18 month period, all of the friendship dimensions were found to discriminate friends from nonfriends in terms of amount of rewards received.

Heilbronn also examined amount of rewards reported at three points in time. Self Disclosure showed little change over time, perhaps because it was not too important at the levels of friendship established. Authenticity showed a considerable decrease. Examination of written comments revealed that females, in particular, complained about the lack of effort made by the former roommate to maintain the social relationship. A common term used to describe the former roommate was that she was a "phony". Jones and Davis (1965) have suggested that "out of role" behaviour provides more information about real intentions than "in role" behaviour. Perhaps, in these cases, acts that had previously been defined as "acts of friendship" were now reconstrued simply as "ought" behaviour as roommates.

The data in Fig. 1 suggest the hypothesis that level of friendship serves to define the importance attached to any specific dimension of friendship and the same dimensions do not appear to be involved as one moves from one level of friendship to the next. Movement from Social Acquaintance to Good Friend probably can occur along any of these dimensions and approximately the same increase was found on all scales. Movement from Good Friend to Close Friend was most pronounced on two dimensions, i.e. Self Disclosure and Helping. A change from Close Friend to Best Friend was most evident on Self Disclosure. Long term longitudinal studies are necessary to examine these possibilities further.

B. VALIDATION STUDIES

Friends versus Non-Friends

I have tried to show that the value attached to various friendship dimensions varies with the level of friendship. The ratings used to support this proposition involved hypothetical persons located at different positions in a friendship hierarchy. The question therefore arises whether actual persons chosen as friends in real life relationships differ from persons not chosen as friends in terms of these dimensions. The format of the friendship inventory of values was slightly revised and called the Friendship Description Inventory. The instructions now were to rate each of the 35 items as being slightly, rather, quite, very or extremely descriptive of an acquaintance. Wengreniuk (1971) conducted a study of male, Canadian college students living in off-campus housing run by the University. Each of the four houses contained eating facilities and accommodation for approximately ten men.

The subjects were instructed to describe two persons living in his own house, the most preferred and the least preferred friends, by means of the Friendship Description Inventory. The most preferred friend was to be someone that the subject was actually close to rather than someone that was popular or desirable as a friend. The least preferred friend was to be someone that the subject knew well enough to describe adequately.

The data were subjected to analysis of variance. The Most-Least Friend ratings had a highly significant main effect ($F = 350.93$, p

<0.001). A significant interaction was also found between Most-Least Friend ratings and Friendship Scales ($F = 12.16$, $p < 0.01$). This suggests that there are differences in ratings of most and least preferred friends as a function of the friendship dimension involved. In order to identify which friendship scales were accounting for this interaction, a further analysis was made. For each subject a difference score was obtained separately for each scale in terms of his ratings of his most and least friend. A treatments by subjects analysis of variance was done of the mean differences. The major source of the interaction was that the Strength of Character dimension showed less difference between most and least preferred friend than any of the other scales. All seven scales discriminated, but there were relative differences in their effectiveness. The Helping Scale was the most differentiating scale. The other scales, in decreasing order of discrimination were Authenticity, Similarity, Positive Regard, Acceptance, and Self Disclosure.

Interpersonal Distance

Hansvick and La Gaipa (1974) examined the relationship between Self Disclosure scale of the friendship inventory and interpersonal distance as measured by the Comfortable Interpersonal Distance Scale (CID) developed by Duke and Nowicki (1972). These two instruments were administered to 40 college female roommates. Analysis of variance indicated that the amount of self disclosure had a significant main effect on physical distance ($F = 5.54$, $p < 0.05$). But no main effects were found for either level of friendship or the importance attached to self disclosure. Instead a significant interaction was found between level of friendship and importance ($F = 6.55$, $p < 0.05$). When Self Disclosure was rated as low in importance, level of friendship was unrelated to interpersonal distance. When Self Disclosure was rated as high in importance, the lower the level of friendship, the closer the interpersonal distance. The Argyle and Dean (1965) equilibrium model was used to interpret the results. If a person believes that self disclosure is important, an attempt may be made to compensate for low levels of interpersonal intimacy by decreasing physical distance with the other. This probably occurs only under conditions of forced interaction such as in a nonvoluntary roommate relationship.

Psychiatric Patients

An assumption underlying the construction of the friendship scales is that persons with atypical view of friendship are likely to encounter problems in interpersonal relationships. Emotionally disturbed persons are often deficient in the ability to develop and maintain satisfactory relationships. We predicted that psychiatric patients would differ from normals in their orientations to intimate relationships (Engelhart *et al.*, 1975).

The friendship scales were administered to 174 psychiatric patients of both sexes in treatment as hospital inpatients or outpatients, or private psychiatric outpatients. The sample consisted of 70 schizophrenics, 48 neurotics, and 56 with personality disorders. Beside diagnostic information, data were collected on background factors and degree of interpersonal adjustment. A so called "normal" comparison group was used consisting of 366 males and 267 females on whom standardization data were available. None of the differences found could be accounted for by any background differences. The friendship scales were administered with instructions to respond in terms of how important they considered each item to be as a characteristic of a "best friend of the same sex".

More significant differences were found between the neurotics and the normals than between the psychotics and the normals, contrary to expectations. Differences were more apparent when comparisons were made by sex. The female schizophrenic places more value than the "normals" or other psychiatric groups on Strength of Character. The male schizophrenics place less value than normals on Similarity.

As compared to the normative sample, the neurotic male emphasizes friendship characterized by Self Disclosure of intimate material, and Authenticity whereas the neurotic female deemphasizes these same traits as compared to normal females. There was a tendency for the neurotics to resemble their respective opposite-sex normal group. This finding suggests a possible confusion as to role definition and sexual identity within neurotic patients. Such confusion could lead to both intrapersonal conflict with regard to role identification and to difficulties in interpersonal adjustment. In the present instance, the findings appear to indicate the presence of a tender, feminine-like receptivity in male neurotics, while female neurotics deemphasize the importance of friendship-type behaviour, or protest their independence and self sufficiency apart from others. The internal conflicts thus generated may be responsible in part for the symptomatology seen in neurotic patients.

Patients with personality disorders (mainly passive-aggressives and alcoholics) were not too different from the "normal" population. A higher value was assigned to Self Disclosure and a trend was also found for Helping with the results again being more dramatic for the males than for the females.

The major differences between the psychiatric groups and the "normal" group appear to be in regard to Strength of Character and Similarity. Strength of Character was consistently rated as more important and Similarity as less important. Perhaps, this is due to the relatively poor self concept in this population and the desire to avoid friends with similar kinds of problems (cf. Novak and Lerner, 1968).

Factor analysis of the friendship items suggests possible differences in the cognitive structuring of friendship qualities. The factor structure isolated for the schizophrenic sample was surprisingly similar to that obtained with the "normal" sample. On the other hand, the factor structure for the neurotic group was quite different. Self Disclosure typically accounts for much of the variance in "normal" groups. For the neurotic group, however, Authenticity emerged as the main factor and Self Disclosure emerged as the sixth factor.

Personality Factors Earlier in this chapter, a distinction was made between psychological and cultural factors in friendship orientation. The data presented so far have dealt with individual differences in adherence to cultural values. Now let us examine the possible impact of psychological factors.

In an early study (La Gaipa, 1972b) a variety of personality tests and the friendship scales of value were administered to samples ranging in size from 150 to 300, for a total of 2651 subjects. Extreme groups were identified on each of the friendship scales (i.e. the upper quartile and the lower quartile) and significance tests were then computed on the difference between means on each of the personality measures. The reason for using extreme groups was that it was assumed that the values of persons in these groups would reflect personality rather than adherence to cultural norms. Where the samples were small, product moment correlations were computed on the entire sample. The size of these correlations,[4] however, suggest that personality factors are relatively unimportant as determinants of friendship values. The amount of variance accounted for by the personality tests was seldom

---

4. Each subject completed between 1 and 3 personality tests and thus very large numbers of correlations were obtained. Specific details may be obtained from the author whose comments here are limited by considerations of space (Editor).

over 10%. Similarly, a significant relationship between the friendship scales and the Rokeach Value Survey (Rokeach, 1972) suggest that a person's generalized values have some input into what is valued in friendship. But the size of the correlations permit relatively low level predictions.

Howitt and La Gaipa (1975a) examined the role of personality variables on a self-other attributional model of friendship formation. The California Psychological Inventory (Gough, 1964) was administered to 160 college roommates. Various patterns emerged as to the contribution of specific personality variables to different components of the friendship model.

Friendship Values The ratings as to the importance assigned to each of the seven friendship dimensions was positively associated with Responsibility (CPI). This suggests that greater importance is assigned to these friendship values, the more a person describes himself as conscientious, responsible and having a dependable disposition and temperament.

Exchange of Rewards Ratings were also obtained on the amount of reward obtained and the amount of reward given on each of the seven scales. Positive Regard, Helping and Similarity were positively associated with Socialization. This appears to indicate that the perceived amount of reward given or received varies with the social maturity, integrity, honesty and sincerity of the person. Authenticity and Empathic Understanding were related to Sense of Well Being. Such persons minimize their worries and complaints and are relatively free from self-doubt and disillusionment. Flexibility was negatively correlated with self rating of Strength of Character, as well as with the amount of self-disclosure given to the other. This suggests that persons who are inflexible or rigid, deliberate, cautious and pedantic are likely to attribute more favourable character traits to themselves as well as to reveal more intimate information to others.

Causal Attribution The subjects also rated their effort and ability in providing rewards, as well as the effort and ability of the other. The degree of ability attributed to self was associated with Self-acceptance. Persons, then, are more likely to assign greater ability to themselves, the more they have a high sense of personal worth, self confidence and capacity for independent thinking and action. The attribution of ability to the other was associated with Responsibility. The degree to which effort was attributed to self varied with Socialization, whereas attribution of effort to other varied with Sense of Well Being.

Expectancy of Growth The subjects estimated the likelihood that the friendship would develop into a more intimate relationship with the passage of time. It was found that Flexibility was negatively correlated with subjective probability of success. The more rigid the person, the higher the expectancy.

As compared to the findings on friendship values, somewhat higher predictions were obtained when personality variables were correlated with either the perceived ability or the perceived effort made to provide the other with friendship benefits. By using several CPI dimensions, a multiple R of 0.49 ($p < 0.001$) was obtained with self ratings of ability and a multiple R of 0.40 ($p < 0.001$) with self ratings of effort. This finding suggests that role-taking capacity might be more predictable than a person's value-orientation. The reason for calling attention to this result is that earlier findings have suggested that what really matters is not simply what a person views as important, but rather his ability to perform in the friendship role in a way that is consistent with the other person's expectations.

II. Longitudinal research

A. PREDICTIVE VALIDITY OF THE FRIENDSHIP INVENTORY

The first of a series of longitudinal studies was conducted by Lischeron and La Gaipa (1971) in an attempt to assess the predictive validity of the friendship scales. It was hypothesized that the effects of reward outcome on friendship formation depend on the reinforcing value of the rewards provided. An index of expectancy confirmation was derived from two ratings: (1) the degree of importance ascribed to the friendship item in maintaining a "close friendship" and (2) the degree to which the roommate's behaviour was characterized by each of the items.

The subjects consisted of 76 male college roommates. The data were collected in two time periods. The first (Time One) was after five to six weeks acquaintance. The second (Time Two) occurred after rooming together for six months.

The correlation between expectancy confirmation and level of friendship at time two ranged from an r of 0.34 for Strength of

Character to an r of 0.67 for Similarity, all significant at 0.01 level. A change score was also computed between the levels of friendship as measured at two points in time. Expectancy confirmation at Time Two was predictive of changes in level of friendship, ranging from a nonsignificant r of 0.17 for Self Disclosure to a significant r of 0.46 for Similarity (p <0.01). Expectancy confirmation at Time One was associated with level of friendship at Time One, but was unrelated to either the level of friendship at Time Two or the change in friendship.

The role of actual similarity in friendship formation was also examined in view of an earlier finding by La Gaipa and Werner (1971) that agreement on friendship values predicted attraction toward an anonymous stranger. Lischeron and La Gaipa (1971) found a mean r of 0.04 between the actual similarity of friendship values on the seven scales and the growth of friendship. This finding suggests that confirmation may be more important than role consensus in determining friendship.

This study indicated that the growth of friendship can be predicted using these friendship scales, that some scales are more predictive than others, and that there is a need to be cautious in generalizing from results obtained in early stages of an acquaintance.

B. ATTEMPTS TO BUILD A MODEL OF FRIENDSHIP

Theoretical Structure

In the construction of a theoretical model, it is necessary to identify the kinds of theoretical variables likely to be relevant, and to specify the functional relationships among the variables. The major source of theoretical input has been Heider's (1958) theory of interpersonal relations.

In seeking to build on an Heiderian structure, we have drawn on three extensions of Heider's theory: (1) the balance principle as used by Newcomb (1961); the attributional model of motivation as developed by Weiner (1972), and (3) the role of intentionality in the perception of beneficial acts as discussed by Jones and Davis (1965). Instead of casting the many variables generated by these theorists into a broad taxonomy, we turned to the Weiner model as the focal point around which the other variables could be assessed and integrated into a larger and more comprehensive model.

The Attributional Model of Motivation Weiner (1972) postulates that stimuli arouse cognitions (about the causes of a behavioural outcome) which in turn determine affective responses and goal expectancies as well as subsequent behaviours. It is assumed that individuals attribute the causes of success and failure to four elements: ability, effort, task difficulty and luck (see Heider, 1958). When assessing whether the person or environment "caused" the behaviour ("locus of control") ability and effort are the internal or personal forces, whereas task difficulty and luck are external determinants. When assessing the stability of the behaviour, ability and task difficulty are the stable factors, and effort and luck the unstable factors. Locus of control is postulated as determining affective responses (valence), whereas the stability dimension is more important in determining expectancy of change.

The cognitive model specifies a temporal order of events: attribution of causality precedes expectancy change and affect. The effect of reward outcomes on expectancy-valence is mediated by causal ascriptions, so expectancy and valence has a multiplicative effect on behaviour. Indeed, the Expectancy × Valence component of the Weiner model, adopted from expectancy theory, provides an essential motivational element to the model. Within an affiliative context, the motivation to engage in instrumental acts of friendship would be zero if a person assigns high value to forming the friendship but has zero expectations as to the likelihood of achieving success.

Applying the Weiner model to an affiliation context from an achievement context may require certain modifications. In an achievement task the affect generated by success or failure may depend largely on causal attribution about self. In an affiliation context, however, a dyadic relationship is involved: the person is not responding simply to his own behaviour; both self and other attributions are involved. It is necessary to determine what additional psychological processes and components are thus necessary for a cognitive model of friendship formation.

The first basic assumption in expanding the Weiner model is that cognitive biases are involved in the perception of variables such as causal attribution, reward exchange and the level of friendship. The second assumption is that social exchange variables may be necessary insofar as the persons involved in a dyad evaluate the amount of reward given and received in terms of such criteria as equity and reciprocity. The third assumption is that different factors may be important at different stages of the relationship.

Methodology

Subjects There were different numbers of subjects in each phase of the study. A total of 446 students enrolled at the University of Windsor were involved at Time One, the first phase of the study. Of these 446 subjects, 350 continued on to the second stage, Time Two, 176 males and 174 females. Howitt (1975) analysed the data of the 350 Ss at Time One and Time Two.

In the third stage of the study, Time Three, a total of 102 subjects remained, 55 females and 47 males. Heilbronn (1975) analyzed the data on these 102 subjects across all three points in time.

Procedure and Instruments Students living in double rooms in the university dormitories were asked to participate in a study on room-mate compatibility. The only requirement was that they did not know each other prior to the beginning of the academic year. The first administration (Time One) took place about one month after the beginning of the academic year; the second administration (Time Two) took place about six months later; the third administration took place about a year later. By this time 80% of the roommate relationship had terminated and the Heilbronn (1975) study, then, was in part a follow up of students who had largely moved elsewhere after the completion of the academic year.

The "Roommate Compatibility Questionnaire" (Howitt and La Gaipa, 1975b) was administered at three points in time. This questionnaire contains 240 items making up a variety of scales, some of which are described below.

Friendship Rewards Inventory This form of the friendship scale taps amount of rewards received and amounts given (see above). The 35 items in each version tap seven dimensions: Self Disclosure, Helping, Authenticity, Empathic Understanding, Positive Regard, Strength of Character and Similarity. Each item was rated by means of a seven point scale in terms of the frequency of the behaviour ranging from "never" to "always". The instructions were to describe by means of these scales (1) what the person had contributed to the relationship (Reward Input) or the amount of each dimension given, and (2) what the person had received from the roommate (Reward Outcome) or the amount of each dimension received.

Reciprocity Ratios Two scales were used to measure the perceived relationship between what one received and what one gave. For each of the seven friendship rewards, the subjects were instructed to indicate on a nine-point scale: (1) How much they had received as compared to what they had given (Give/Receive), and (2) How much they had given as compared to what they had received (Receive/Give). The scales were described as "Much Less", "About the Same" and "Much More".

Reciprocity Expectancies The instructions were to indicate the chances or likelihood that the target person would reciprocate the behaviours described by the friendship reward scales. The rating scale tapped probabilities ranging from 1 in 10 to 9 in 10.

Perceived Equity Four different estimates of fairness were obtained by means of nine point rating scales.

Expectancy of Growth The subjects indicated on a single nine point rating scale the likelihood that the friendship would increase within the following year. These expectancy scales ranged from low probability to high probability.

Valence Two measures of valence were used: (1) Desire to increase the level of friendship and (2) Affect, a five item semantic differential scale that includes such items as pleasant-unpleasant.

Causal Attribution After responding to the 70 items specifying amounts received and given, each of the seven scales was briefly defined. Then, the instructions were to rate their roommate in terms of the four causal dimensions used by Weiner:

1. Ability — "How good is your roommate potentially at being understanding?"

2. Effort — "How hard did he/she try to be understanding?"

3. Task Difficulty — "How difficult do you think it would be for most people to be understanding?"

4. Luck — "How lucky do you think you were in the assignment of roommates in terms of understanding?"

This was followed by self ratings on both Ability and Effort.

Semantic Different Scales Several pilot studies involving factor analysis led to the isolation of a series of bi-polar scales. Six factor scores were computed on each individual: Affect, Trust, Obligation, Tension, Self-Assurance, and Popularity.

Mutual Activities Checklist Ten activities were rated in terms of frequency of occurrence by means of a five point scale ranging from "never" to "very often". The items included such activities as: "play cards together", "go out evenings together", and "invite him/her to my family home".

Level of Friendship The subjects indicated on a nine-point friendship ladder, the level of friendship that had been established. The ladder was described in terms of four levels: social acquaintance, good friend, close friend, and best friend. The definition of each level was provided for the subject, as described earlier in this chapter. The ladder was used to describe both self-ratings of friendship and estimate ratings of other person.

At Time Three, final friendship, other dependent measures included: (1) factor score: friendship index based on both the friendship ladder and mutual activities; (2) future forecast of friendship; (3) interdependency; and (4) uniqueness.

Results

Causal Attribution Causal ascription appears to play a different role depending on the stage of the relationship. The effort attributed to other and the difficulty of the task had a direct effect rather than an indirect effect in the early stage of the relationship contrary to the Weiner model. The relationship between reward outcome and expectancy-valence was not reduced when partial correlation was used to control for causal ascription. On the other hand, causal ascription did serve as mediating variables in the intermediary and final stages of the relationship. We did find at these time periods that the effects of the amount of reward depends on how much effort was ascribed to other and the perceived difficulty of the task.

The significance of the stage of the relationship in regard to causal ascription is not clearly understood. One possibility is that causal data are unreliable in the early stages of a relationship: certain amounts of interaction may be necessary to make reliable judgements as to intentionality. Another possible interpretation can be made in terms of the social context. The forced interaction as roommates may have enhanced the desire to form a friendship. This may have led to the deemphasis of the possible intentions of the other or a distortion of the motives attributed to other. With additional information with the passage of time, any such distortions might have been corrected by "reality-testing".

Some support was found for the Expectancy × Value component of the Weiner model. Desire for growth and expectancy of growth had an interactive effect on level of friendship as predicted by the model ($F = 5.23$, $p < 0.05$). This relationship, however, was found only at Time Two. Desire and expectancy had an additive effect on friendship at Time One.

Cognitive Biases Taylor (1972) recommends the use of a multiple regression strategy for testing out some of the implications of balance theory. Taylor notes that cognitive consistency theories represent a type of statistical interaction and that regression analysis can separate out the main and interaction effects. Reciprocity bias is a two-way interaction. Balance bias is a three-way interaction.

A significant interaction effect on Expectancy of Growth for Time Two was obtained for ratings of Effort of Self and Effort of Other $(F = 6.11, p < 0.001)$. This interaction simply means that if Person rates himself low in the amount of effort he has expended, then the effort made by Other is less important in estimating the chances that the friendship will grow. Though this finding may seem rather obvious, it should be noted that this reciprocity bias was not found for Time One, nor when other criteria were used such as Level of Friendship.

A significant three-way interaction indicating a balance bias was found when Affect was measured at Time Two. The interactions involve Effort of Self, Effort of Other and Level of Friendship $(F = 10.25, p < 0.001)$. At low levels of friendship, differences between effort made by self and by other had a greater impact on positiveness of feelings than at high levels of friendship. This finding suggests that once a friendship has become established, there is less concern with whether each person is trying equally hard.

A balance bias was obtained at Time One in regard to the Trust ascribed to the other person. The variables included the Ability and Effort attributed to other as well as the Affect level $(F = 8.54, p < 0.001)$. If Person likes Other but thinks that he was not trying as hard as he could in terms of his capability, then less trust is expressed.

A reciprocity bias was found at Time Two when Expectancy was used as the dependent variable: Ability and Effort of Other had an interactive effect $(F = 14.39, p < 0.001)$. This suggests that estimates as to the growth of a friendship do not depend solely on the effort by other: the ability of other is also taken into consideration. The lowest expectancy of growth was found with high ability and low effort a finding that is consistent with the Thibaut and Kelley (1959) social exchange theory (see La Gaipa's chapter in section 1 of this book).

The exchange of social rewards was also found to be subject to reciprocity and balance biases, though only for Time Two data. Reward input and outcome had an interaction effect on Expectancy of Growth $(F = 7.87, p < 0.001)$ suggesting that the influence (on expectancies) of the amount given varies with amount received. A balance bias was found in regard to Level of Friendship ($F = 7.94$, p <0.001) for Input, Outcome and Affect. If Person gets less than he gives, the effect on friendship depends on whether he has a positive or negative affect toward Other. One possible interpretation is that a person with a positive affect toward another may be receiving less than he gives because of his own deliberate actions. He may be over-rewarding the other in the hope that he will reciprocate and increase the level of friendship.

Finally, a reciprocity bias on Trust was found at Time Two involving reciprocity of attraction ($F = 11.95$, p <0.001). The degree of Trust or Sincerity expressed by Person was influenced by the discrepancy between how he would rate the level of friendship, and his estimate of how Other would rate it. The lower the perceived reciprocity, the lower the trust.

There is some support for the hypothesis that causal ascriptions are subject to cognitive biases. Weiner's cognitive model needs modification in this respect when used to understand friendship formation. It should be noted, however, that reciprocity biases were found more often than balance biases, that Expectancy of Growth was the dependent variable most subject to bias, and that biases seem to occur more often at Time Two than Time One.

Social Exchange Variables Reciprocity ratios were found to be critical variables by both Howitt (1975) and Heilbronn (1975). The Give/Receive ratio is a measure of the degree to which Other has reciprocated. The Receive/Give ratio is a measure of the degree to which Self has reciprocated. The significance of these reciprocity indices is that they served as both direct and indirect variables and were found to differ in importance as a function of the stage of the relationship.

The stage of the relationship appears to influence the saliency of the reciprocity standard employed. In the Howitt study (1975), the beta weights for both Time One and Time Two were several times as great for Receive/Give as for Give/Receive. After most of the roommates had gone their separate ways by Time Three, the reverse was found by Heilbronn (1975). The path coefficients at Time Three of the Give/Receive ratio on Friendship was 0.64 as compared to 0.01 for the Receive/Give ratio.

One possible interpretation can be made in terms of the finding that the desire to increase the level of friendship is more important in the earlier stages than in the later stage. What a person gives as compared to what he receives may reflect his own level of motivation. The amount given may provide a clue as to how one feels about another: Persons love those whom they benefit more than those who benefit them (Blau, 1964). Tedeschi (1974) has observed that an obvious cyclical relationship exists between the actor and self-attribution. "The more benefits provided, the more actor should infer self-liking for the other person . . . (p. 203)."

Overreward can also serve as a deliberate strategy to motivate other to reciprocate (Blau, 1964). But such tactics are less relevant or meaningful once the expectations of growth have dropped, as they did from Time Two to Time Three. In the early stages, it seems that one's own behaviour may be critical. In later stages, however, once the relationship has stabilized, the behaviour of other may become salient. The results suggest, then, that after the transitions between stages slows down, a person is more alert to the rewards he receives as compared to what he has given. Thus, causal ascription and reciprocity appear to be dynamically interrelated and each seems to serve as a possible mediating variable for the other, though these two variables differ in their contribution to the dependent variable. Perhaps, the impact of effort depends on the assessment of the relationship as reciprocal. If a person believes he is getting less than he gives, then the other person's level of effort may not be enough. Beyond a certain point, good intentions may become irrelevant.

Predicting Change in Level of Friendship Werts and Linn (1970) have developed a general linear model for studying growth in which impact of "growth" is analyzed by conventional least-squares regression models. This procedure avoids treating "gain scores" or "residual" measures of change as the dependent variable. Instead of using a difference score as the criterion, then, final status is used as the dependent variable and initial status is included on the right side of the equation along with the other predictors. This linear growth model was used both by Howitt (1975) and Heilbronn (1975).

Multiple regression equations were used to assess the relative importance of different predictors of friendship at Time Three from data collected at three points in time (Heilbronn, 1975). At Time One, the best predictor was the Desire to form a close relationship. At Time Two, six months later, the emphasis shifted to the amount of reward input and outcome, mutual activities and the effort made by other. At Time Three, a year later, reciprocity is critical, i.e. the ratio of the amount received compared to the amount given.

Heilbronn (1975) also used path analysis for studying the direct and indirect effects of variables within the same time period and across stages. As a regression technique, path analysis can be employed as a general linear model (Werts and Linn, 1970) to examine changes over time. Path analysis provides a technique for rationally inferring causal relationship in complex situations even though experimental manipulation is impossible (Darlington, 1968). The major outcome from path analysis is a path diagram which displays all of the variables included in the analysis and the path coefficients between variables and arrows indicating the direct and indirect paths from variable to variable.

A longitudinal path analysis included the key variables identified at each of the time periods. Various routes are possible leading from Time One predictors to level of friendship at Time Three, the validity of which depends in part on the size of the path coefficients. A causal explanation involving one of the shorter routes is as follows. The greater the desire to form a closer friendship (T-1), the more frequent the mutual activities at Time Two, and the greater the effort attributed to Other. These two factors influence the amount of reward given Other (T-2). The effect of reward input (T-2) on friendship at a later date depends on the reciprocity (Give/Receive) that Person feels was provided by Other at Time Three.

Summary

The findings in regard to causal ascription are that attribution intervenes specifically between friendship reward exchange and such dependent measures as expectancy-valence and level of friendship. Attribution, however, operates in different ways according to the particular stage of the relationship. The Weiner model was supported in the later stages of the relationship, but not in the early stages. The Weiner model, then, may need modification in terms of temporal effects when applied to affiliative behaviour.

The need to consider the stage of the relationship in explaining the role played by causal ascription as well as the role of other social exchange variables is consistent with the "filtering theory" (Kerckhoff and Davis, 1962). This theory postulates that value consensus is important in the early stages of courtship and need complementarity is important in later stages of courtship. Levinger *et al.* (1970) failed to replicate this proposition but were loath to discard it. We suggest that the filtering theory may have some validity using different theoretical variables than employed by Kerckhoff and Davis. The present study would indicate that such variables as causal ascription and reciprocity may have different impacts depending on the stage of the relationship.

Strong support was found for an interface between attribution theory and social exchange theory in accounting for friendship. A variety of statistical techniques revealed that the social exchange variables (input, outcome, reciprocity ratios) account for much of the variance at intermediate and later stages of friendship. The role played by social exchange variables changes as a function of time.

A cognitive approach to social exchange also is supported by the results of these studies. Reward input and outcome appear to be insufficient to account for the growth of friendship. Attributional and social exchange variables appear to be essential components in any comprehensive model of friendship formation.

13.

Need Similarity and Complementarity in Interpersonal Attraction*

B. A. SEYFRIED *and* CLYDE HENDRICK

Kent State University, USA

An attempt was made to test the merits of the complementary needs and similarity hypotheses as determinants of interpersonal attraction. Subjects were divided into four groups on the basis of scores on nurturance and succorance scales of the Edwards Personal Preferences Schedule. The basic design of the experiment, replicated for both male and female subjects, was 2 × 2 factorial using all combinations of subjects high and low in nurturance and high and low in succorance. Subjects then rated on several measures two stimulus strangers, one highly nurturant and one highly succorant. The design allowed each stranger to be rated for attraction in terms of similarity of needs relative to the subjects' need combinations, in terms of complementarity of needs, or both. The results showed strong effects due to need similarity, but only slight effects due to need complementarity.

*This report is based on a Masters Thesis completed at Kent State University by the first author under the direction of the second author. First published in *Sociometry* 1973, **36**, 207-220. Copyright © 1973 by the American Sociological Association. Reprinted by permission. Seyfried is now at Suny, Oswego, NY, USA.

One of the more intriguing areas of social research concerns the determinants of interpersonal attraction. To date, the preponderance of research evidence indicates that similarity on a variety of attributes is the best predictor of attraction (Newcomb, 1961; Byrne, 1969). Dimensions of similarity which have been related to attraction include attitudes (Byrne and Nelson, 1965a), economic background (Byrne et al., 1966), defense mechanisms (Byrne et al., 1967), and self-concept (Griffith, 1966; Hendrick and Page, 1970). The positive similarity-attraction relation is perhaps the best established result in social research.

Since people are not all carbon copies of each other, it is important to understand the circumstances in which dissimilar individuals are attracted to each other. One attempt to specify such circumstances is Winch's (1958, 1963) theory of complementary needs. According to the theory, mutual need reduction is the basis of attraction. Winch suggests that there are two types of complementary needs. Two people may possess dissimilar but interdependent needs of the same intensity (e.g. a highly dominant person and a highly submissive person), or two people may possess different intensities of the same need (e.g. high and low levels of a need for exhibition). Some research has supported the complementary needs hypothesis (Winch et al., 1954; Rychlak, 1965; Kerckhoff and Davis, 1962), but other research in this tradition has supported the similarity hypothesis (Banta and Hetherington, 1963; Pierce, 1970), and some studies have not supported either hypothesis (Becker, 1964; Katz et al., 1960).

In the present study, an attempt was made to create a situation in which the joint effects of both need similarity and need complementarity on attraction could be assessed. Previous work has tended to rely on correlating personality test scores of such related persons as friends and spouses. Such correlations are open to a variety of interpretations. The present study attempted to avoid the problems of such correlational data by creating "standard strangers" (Byrne, 1969) who were high in certain need states. Subjects were preselected so that they varied in their own need states relative to the need states of the standard strangers. More specifically, subjects evaluated the attractiveness of two stimulus strangers. One stranger was highly nurturant and the second was highly succorant. Subjects were either high in both nurturance and succorance, low in both, or high in one need and low in the other. The design allowed assessment of whether attraction to the strangers was based on need similarity, need complementarity, or both.

I. Method

A. DESIGN

Subjects initially completed the nurturance and succorance scales of the Edwards Personal Preference Schedule (EPPS). These needs were defined as the desire to help others, and the desire to be helped by others, respectively. The EPPS is constructed so that the nurturance and succorance scales are relatively independent factorially, allowing all possible combinations of subjects (high and low in nurturance and high and low in succorance) to be selected for study. This approach was used with subjects' nurturance (high or low) and succorance (high or low) constituting two between-subject independent variables. The four groups of subjects resulting from this 2 × 2 factorial design were designated as (1) high nurturance-high succorance, (2) high nurturance-low succorance, (3) low nurturance-high succorance, and (4) low nurturance-low succorance.

After completing the EPPS, subjects were engaged in an "interpersonal judgement task" modeled after Byrne's (1969) methodology. All subjects rated two bogus strangers on several evaluative measures. One stranger had completed the nurturance scale of the EPPS in a highly nurturant fashion, and the second stranger had completed the succorance scale in a highly succorant fashion. The nurturance-succorance of the two stimulus strangers was considered as a *within-subject* independent variable.

Two important characteristics of the design should be noted. First, it was felt that inclusion of the high nurturance-high succorance and low nurturance-low succorance subject groups represented an improvement in design over previous research in this area. Prior research (e.g. Hendrick and Brown, 1971; Palmer and Byrne, 1970) did not consider the possibility of both similarity and complementary needs effects occurring at the same time. Such experiments have included only groups of subjects either similar or complementary to a stimulus stranger. As a consequence of such a design, if both similarity and complementary needs effects occurred in equal strength, there would be no difference in attraction between similar and complementary subjects. If both effects occurred, but one was stronger, an erroneous conclusion would be drawn that attraction was based only on similarity or only on complementarity. This problem may be handled by including all possible combinations of need states in a symmetrical factorial design. Such an analysis of variance design allows assessment of the possibility of *both* similarity and complementarity, as either additive or interactive effects.

The second point to note is that the complete design potentially allowed assessment of similarity or complementarity (or both) effects in two different ways. One approach involved comparisons of the four subject groups' attraction ratings of each stimulus stranger, considering each stranger separately (*between-subject* design). The second approach involved comparison of relative attraction for the two stimulus strangers for each of the four subject groups (*within-subject* design). The *within-subject* design may be justified only when the average overall desirability of the two stimulus strangers (i.e. the grand means) is equal. Inequality of the grand means results in a confounding of critical interaction effects, rendering their interpretation ambiguous. Unfortunately, such a difference in overall desirability did occur between the two stimulus strangers. Therefore only *between-subject* comparisons were made separately for each stimulus stranger. The logic of the *between-subject* comparisons is described below.

Table 1 shows the need states of the four groups of subjects. The need relationship existing between each group of subjects and the two stimulus strangers is shown in the body of the table. If subjects high in nurturance (groups 1 and 2) were more attracted to the nurturant stranger than subjects low in nurturance (groups 3 and 4) then subjects would be basing their attraction ratings of the nurturant stranger on need similarity. Likewise, if subjects high in succorance (groups 1 and

TABLE 1. Conceptual design of the experiment.

Need Combination of Subjects			Need State of Standard Strangers*	
Group	Nurturance (A)	Succorance (B)	Nurturant Stranger	Succorant Stranger
1	High	High	Similar to A and complementary to B	Similar to B and complementary to A
2	High	Low	Similar to A and dissimilar to B	Complementary to A and dissimilar to B
3	Low	High	Complementary to B and dissimilar to A	Similar to B and dissimilar to A
4	Low	Low	Dissimilar to A and dissimilar to B	Dissimilar to A and dissimilar to B

*The entries in the columns under the nurturant and succorant strangers show the need relation between the stranger and a given group of subjects.

3) were more attracted to the succorant stranger than subjects low in succorance (groups 2 and 4), then subjects would again be evaluating on the basis of similarity. In each case, these results are shown statistically by a main effect of subjects' nurturance in the analysis of the nurturant stranger, and a main effect of subjects' succorance in the analysis of the succorant stranger.

On the other hand, if groups 1 and 3 were more attracted to the nurturant stranger than groups 2 and 4 (and if groups 1 and 2 were more attracted to the succorant stranger than groups 3 and 4), then subjects would be basing their attraction ratings on need complementarity. Statistically, these results are shown by a main effect of subjects' succorance in the analysis of the nurturant stranger, and a main effect of subject's nurturance in the analysis of the succorant stranger. Finally, if both main effects were significant for the analysis of each stimulus stranger, the implication would be that subjects based their attraction ratings on both similarity and complementarity.

B. SUBJECTS

The subjects were 185 students enrolled in psychology courses at Kent State University. Twenty students were initially deleted before subjects were divided into groups: eleven, because they did not complete the questionnaires; two, because they had participated in a similar experiment; and seven, because they said the experiment dealt with liking of similar and dissimilar others.

Subjects were assigned to the four groups via a median split on their nurturance and succorance scores. Assignments were made separately for each sex because of sex differences in mean level of the two needs. The median nurturance scores were 15.22 for females and 11.45 for males. The median succorance scores were 11.29 for females and 9.25 for males. After the median splits, all subjects who fell on the median ($N = 22$) were dropped from the sample; an additional 23 subjects were discarded to equalize the N in the four conditions. These deletions were made on the basis of subjects nearest the median. The final sample consisted of 60 males and 60 females, 15 of each sex in each of the four subject groups. The mean nurturance and succorance scores are shown in Table 2 for each group. Inspection of these means indicates (and supplementary analysis of variance confirmed) that the composition of the groups on the two needs was completely adequate in order to assess the two hypotheses.

TABLE 2. Subjects' mean nurturance and succorance scores.*

Measure	Subjects' Sex	Type of Subjects			
		High Nurt. High Succ.	High Nurt. Low Succ.	Low Nurt. High Succ.	Low Nurt. Low Succ.
Nurturance	Male	19.07	16.67	8.33	5.73
score	Female	21.73	19.93	9.93	9.87
Succorance	Male	13.67	6.73	14.60	4.87
score	Female	15.40	7.93	17.20	7.67

*The higher the mean, the higher the nurturance or succorance scores.

C. MATERIALS

The materials consisted of a modified form of the EPPS (labeled the "Self Evaluation Questionnaire"), and stimulus booklets with a nurturance scale purportedly completed by one stranger, and a succorance scale purportedly completed by a second stranger. The dependent variable forms for each stranger followed his completed scale.

The Self Evaluation Questionnaire, used to divide subjects into groups, consisted of all 56 items on the EPPS used to measure nurturance and succorance, plus twelve filler items. The complete EPPS consists of 225 forced choice items measuring 15 different needs (Edwards, 1959). Two statements measuring one need are paired with two statements measuring another need, for each of the 14 other needs. For this reason, a high score on one need means that subjects preferred that need relative to the 14 other needs; and a low score means that a subject preferred the 14 other needs relative to the need in question. A low scorer on a particular need is therefore not the opposite of a high scorer, but he is dissimilar to the high scorer. Thus, as shown in Table 1, a subject had to be high in a need relative to the other need possessed by a stimulus stranger in order to be considered complementary to the stranger. Subjects low in a need relative to the stranger's need were simply considered as dissimilar.

The nurturant stimulus stranger was presented by a bogus questionnaire which consisted of all 28 items measuring nurturance on the EPPS. Twenty-five of the 28 statements favouring nurturance were circled. This questionnaire was described as "Short Form Y" of the Self

Evaluation Questionnaire. The succorant stimulus stranger was presented by a bogus questionnaire which consisted of all 28 items from the EPPS measuring succorance, and which was labeled "Short Form X" of the Self Evaluation Questionnaire. Twenty-five of the 28 items favouring succorance were circled.

The dependent variable questionnaire for each stranger consisted of eight questions measuring liking and admiration, four questions measuring perceived similarity and eight trait adjectives. The attraction questions asked the subject to rate such items as how likeable, interesting to talk to, enjoyable to be with, admirable, and close to one's ideal that he found the stimulus stranger. The similarity ratings included perceived similarity in personality, interest and values, and how much the subject thought he would agree with the stranger in a discussion. Each rating was made on a 9-point scale with endpoints appropriately labeled. For half the subjects the nurturant stranger was presented first in the booklet; for the other half, the succorant stranger was first.

D. PROCEDURE

Data were collected from groups ranging in size from 11 to 44. Subjects were told the experiment was a study in person perception, and some background material was discussed. The measure of the subjects' nurturance-succorance (Self Evaluation Questionnaire) was then introduced as a measure of self perception. After completing this questionnaire, manila envelopes containing the stimulus booklets were distributed. The envelopes were marked male or female, and subjects were asked to take an envelope appropriate to their sex. Both stimulus strangers were of the same sex as the subject. The nature of the booklets and rating scales was explained, and subjects were asked to rate the stimulus strangers in the order they were presented. After the ratings were completed, subjects wrote on the back of the booklet their impressions of the experiment and what they thought the hypotheses were. Afterwards they were given a complete explanation of the experiment.[1]

1. After about half of the data were collected, the Marlowe-Crowne Social Desirability Scale was administered to the subjects after the main part of the experiment was completed (Crowne and Marlowe, 1960). The mean social desirability responses did not differ across sex or the four groups of subjects and therefore will not be considered further in this paper.

II. Results

The rating data were analyzed by analysis of variance. Separate analyses were conducted for male and female subjects because of the mean differences in nurturance and succorance between the two sexes. Data for each stimulus stranger were analyzed separately as well. Although the EPPS presumably controls for social desirability of response alternatives, the nurturant stranger was apparently much more desirable generally than the succorant stranger. The nurturant stranger was more attractive ($F = 275.18$, $df = 1/112$, $p < 0.001$), and was perceived as more similar ($F = 123.12$, $p < 0.001$). These effects appear to be perceptual in nature, rather than because of differences of actual similarity. For example, as shown in Table 2, low nurturance-low succorance males had a mean nurturance score of 5.73 and a mean succorance score of 4.87, yet they rated the nurturant stranger 17.73 in similarity, while the succorant stranger was rated only 11.13. Because of this apparent bias in favour of the nurturant stranger, the hypotheses were tested separately for each stimulus stranger.[2] Each analysis of variance followed a 2 × 2 factorial design with subjects' actual nurturance (high or low) and succorance (high or low) constituting the two independent variables.

The results are presented separately for preliminary manipulation checks, the ratings of perceived similarity, and ratings of attraction.

A. MANIPULATION CHECKS

Ratings on two of the trait adjectives served as a check on the veridicality of the subjects' perceptions of the stimulus strangers. Given

2. The statistical basis for separate analysis for nurturant and succorant strangers is described in the method section. Ideally, both sexes would have been combined within a single analysis for each stimulus stranger. However, as noted, medians differed between the sexes for the nurturance and succorance measures. Combining the data for both sexes would have resulted in cases in which, for example, a male subject with a nurturance score of 14 would have been assigned to the high nurturance group; but a female with an identical score would have been assigned to a low nurturance group. Thus, combining data for both sexes in a single analysis did not seem statistically defensible. Only one of the Newman-Keuls comparisons shown in Table 3 would have changed, had the error terms for an overall analysis been used instead of the error terms from the four separate analyses. The difference between low nurturance-high succorance and low nurturance-low succorance males in ratings of perceived similarity to the succorant stranger was significant in the overall analysis. Since no conclusions were affected by this minor change, the more conservative approach was taken of analyzing the data separately for each sex and stimulus stranger.

the nature of the responses attributed to the two strangers, the nurturant stranger was expected to be rated higher on *helpful* and lower on *dependent* than the succorant stranger. On *helpful*, the nurturant stranger was rated 8.04 and the succorant stranger was rated 3.37 ($F = 519.10$, $df = 1/112$, $p < 0.001$). On *dependent*, the nurturant stranger was rated 5.33 while the succorant stranger was rated 7.32 ($F = 34.75$, $p < 0.001$). These differences indicate that the two stimulus strangers were correctly perceived.

Perceived Similarity. The four questions measuring perceived similarity were highly intercorrelated for both the nurturant stranger (median r of 0.76) and the succorant stranger (median r of 0.72). The four questions were summed to form a single measure of perceived similarity. The mean similarity ratings are shown in Table 3 for each stimulus stranger. The means indicate that the two groups of subjects high in nurturance perceived the nurturant stranger as more similar than the two groups of subjects low in nurturance (for males, $F = 25.04$, $df = 1/56$, $p < 0.001$; for females, $F = 32.02$, $df = 1/56$, $p < 0.001$). Comparable although weaker results were obtained for the succorant stimulus stranger. Subjects high in succorance rated the succorant stimulus stranger more similar (columns 1 and 3 in the bottom panel of Table 3) than subjects low in succorance (columns 2 and 4). The effect was significant for both males ($F = 7.20$, $df = 1/56$, $p < 0.01$) and females ($F = 8.24$, $df = 1/56$, $p < 0.01$). The Newman-Keuls tests of specific comparisons for the succorant stimulus stranger indicated that not all of the expected differences between means were significant, although the mean similarity ratings were all in the proper direction. Nevertheless, the significance of the main effect of similarity noted above for both males and females indicates that the manipulation, although weaker than for the nurturant stranger, was adequate to provide a basis for comparison of attraction scores between groups of subjects.

B. ATTRACTION

The median correlations between the eight questions measuring attraction were 0.70 for the nurturant stimulus stranger, and 0.73 for the succorant stimulus stranger. Therefore the eight questions were summed to form a single measure of attraction for each of the stimulus strangers. The mean attraction ratings are shown in Table 3.

For the nurturant stimulus stranger, mean ratings of attraction

TABLE 3. Mean ratings of the nurturant and succorant stimulus strangers on attraction and perceived similarity.*

Measure	Subjects' Sex	High Nurt. High Succ.	High Nurt. Low Succ.	Low Nurt. High Succ.	Low Nurt. Low Succ.
		Type of Subjects			
Nurturant Stimulus Stranger					
Perceived Similarity	Male	24.80 a	25.47 a	17.07 b	17.73 b
	Female	28.73 a	28.27 a	20.33 b	18.13 b
Attraction	Male	54.60 a	54.60 a	42.40 b	44.73 b
	Female	60.60 a	58.73 a, c	49.33 b, c	42.80 b
Succorant Stimulus Stranger					
Perceived Similarity	Male	17.07 a	12.60 a, b	15.87 a, b	11.13 b
	Female	13.73 a, b	10.40 b	16.87 a	10.27 b
Attraction	Male	36.33 a	26.13 b	26.07 b	20.20 b
	Female	27.47 a	19.73 a	27.73 a	21.13 a

*Each mean is based on 15 subjects. Within each row means having no superscripts in common differed at the 0.05 level by the Newman-Keuls test.

showed a strong main effect favouring the need similarity hypothesis for both males ($F = 10.49$, $df = 1/56$, $p < 0.002$) and females ($F = 16.51$, $df = 1/56$, $p < 0.001$). The other main effect for ratings of the nurturant stimulus stranger did not offer any support for the complementary needs hypothesis ($F < 1$ for males; $F = 1.57$ for females). Thus the attraction data for the nurturant stranger indicated that subjects were attracted to this stranger entirely on the basis of need similarity.

For the nurturant stimulus stranger, mean ratings of attraction showed females showed only a main effect supporting need similarity ($F = 4.48$, $df = 1/56$, $p < 0.04$). However, both main effects were significant for males, supporting both similarity ($F = 5.97$, $df = 1/56$, $p < 0.02$) and complementarity ($F = 6.07$, $df = 1/56$, $p < 0.02$). Newman-Keuls comparisons shown in the bottom of Table 3 indicate that these latter two effects were due to the relatively high attraction mean of the high nurturance-high succorance group which differed significantly from the other three groups. None of the individual comparisons for females reached significance, although the directions of the mean differences (and the significant main effect noted above) clearly supported the need similarity hypothesis.

III. Discussion

Our results may be summarized simply: (a) there was a consistent positivity bias toward the nurturant stranger, (b) male subjects showed a slight effect for complementary needs in attraction ratings of the succorant stranger, and (c) subjects strongly preferred stimulus strangers with similar needs.

The positivity bias toward the nurturant stranger is probably best attributed to variation in social desirability of different traits in the culture. Comparable findings have been reported previously. Palmer and Byrne (1970) found a preference for a dominant stranger over a submissive stranger. Hendrick and Brown (1971) found that extroverts were preferred over introverts. Why such cultural differences in trait preferences exist is, of course, quite a different type of research question.

Support for the complementary needs hypothesis was quite weak, consisting only in the fact that high nurturance-high succorance males were significantly more attracted to the succorant stranger than the other three groups of males rating the succorant stranger. This result suggests that a complementary need relation may enhance attraction only if a subject is both similar and complementary to a stranger. This restriction and the fact that none of the results for female subjects favoured complementarity indicates only very marginal support for that hypothesis.

The data indicated rather overwhelmingly that subjects were attracted on the basis of need similarity. Explication of this result requires some further consideration of the notion of complementarity. The complementary needs hypothesis is a variant of a general need gratification theory (Winch, 1958, 1963). However, if need gratification is the crucial variable, there is no reason why both similar and complementary need pairings cannot lead to mutual attraction (Secord and Backman, 1964). Thus there could be four possible need pairings between two people: similar needs leading to need gratification, dissimilar needs leading to gratification (Winch's concept of complementary needs), similar needs not leading to gratification, and dissimilar needs not leading to gratification. This analysis suggests that need similarity-dissimilarity is independent of the amount of reward (and presumably attraction) in a relationship. However, subjects in the present study strongly preferred strangers similar in need states. What do these results imply for the notion of need gratification? It seems unlikely that similar need pairings result in anticipated need gratification. Two highly succorant individuals constantly seeking help from each other are likely to frustrate rather than reward each other. The problem remains, then, of specifying why similarity of need pairings did lead to increased attraction.

One answer may be that subjects were responding in terms of a type of attitude similarity. That is, subjects may have treated the strangers' responses as if they represented the strangers' attitudes about their personality traits. The difference between response to another's "need state" and response to his "attitude about need states" may be considerable; and in some cases, may yield opposing results. For example, suppose that dominant person A gives a speech expressing the attitude that dominating others is desirable. Another dominant person, B, hears the speech, interprets it as a statement of attitude, and is highly attracted to A because of attitude similarity about the domination of others. However, if B interprets the speech as an habitual way of relating to people, B might conclude A would try to dominate him, and accordingly dislike or reject A. Thus, depending on possible interaction possibilities, A's communication may lead to high attraction via perceived attitude similarity, or low attraction via perceived frustration of need gratification if further interaction were to occur.

This analysis suggests that attraction may be based on complementary needs only when the possibility of need gratification can be strongly activated in some way. One possibility for such activation is to lead subjects to expect to engage in future interaction. A second possibility is to use a situation which engages reciprocal role behaviours as the basis of attraction, rather than complementary personality traits. It may be relatively easy for subjects to anticipate potential need gratification when they respond to stimulus strangers in terms of well-learned role expectancies. For example, Seyfried and Hendrick (1973b) found that when subjects responded to stimulus strangers who differed in their sex-role attitudes, there was a tendency to prefer strangers of the opposite sex who exhibited appropriate (complementary) sex-role attitudes relative to the subject. These results suggest that attraction based on complementarity often may be based on reciprocal role relationships, rather than complementary personality needs.

The basic unanswered question is why similarity of attitudes or traits *per se* leads to greater attraction. Several answers are possible, but none are completely satisfactory. Newcomb (1953) suggested that a need for consistency between cognitions of similarity and attraction leads to attraction between similar people. Byrne and Clore (1967) suggested that belief similarity satisfies an effectance motive. Both consistency and effectance may be viewed as cognitive need states. When such states are satisfied, the positive affect resulting therefrom may be attached to the relevant stimulus persons, resulting in greater attraction.

14.

Continuity between The Experimental Study of Attraction and Real-life Computer Dating[1]

DONN BYRNE, JOHN LAMBERTH

Purdue University

and

CHARLES R. ERVIN

University of Texas

As a test of the nonlaboratory generalizability of attraction research, a computer dating field study was conducted. A 50-item questionnaire of attitudes and personality was administered to a 420-student pool, and 44 male-female pairs were selected on the basis of maximal or minimal similarity of responses. Each couple was introduced, given differential information about the basis for their matching, and asked to spend

1. This research was supported in part by Research Grant MH-11178-04 from the National Institute of Mental Health and in part by Research Grant GS-2752 from the National Science Foundation. The authors wish to thank James Hilgren, Royal Masset, and Herman Mitchell for their help in conducting this experiment.

First published in *Journal of Personality and Social Psychology*, 1970, **16**, 157-165. Copyright © 1970 by the American Psychological Association. Reprinted by permission.

30 minutes together at the Student Union on a "coke date". Afterward, they returned to the experimenter and were independently assessed on a series of measures. It was found that attraction was significantly related to similarity and to physical attractiveness. Physical attractiveness was also significantly related to ratings of desirability as a date, as a spouse, and to sexual attractiveness. Both similarity and attractiveness were related to the physical proximity of the two individuals while they were talking to the experimenter after the date. In a follow-up investigation at the end of the semester, similarity and physical attractiveness were found to predict accurate memory of the date's name, incidence of talking to one another in the interim since the coke date, and desire to date the other person in the future.

A familiar but never totally resolved problem with any experimental findings is the extent to which they may be generalized to the nonlaboratory situation. At least three viewpoints about the problem may be discerned. First, and perhaps most familiar, is instant generalization from the specific and often limited conditions of an experiment to any and all settings which are even remotely related. This tendency is most frequently seen at cocktail parties after the third martini and on television talk shows featuring those who popularize psychology. Second, and almost as familiar, is the notion that the laboratory is a necessary evil. It is seen as an adequate substitute for the real world, only to the extent that it reproduces the world. For example, Aronson and Carlsmith (1968) ask, "Why, then, do we bother with these pallid and contrived imitations of human interaction when there exist rather sophisticated techniques for studying the real thing?" (p. 4). They enumerate the advantages of experiments over field study, but emphasize that good experiments must be realistic in order to involve the subject and have an "impact" on him. Concern with experimental realism often is expressed in the context of positing qualitative differences between the laboratory and the outside world; it is assumed that in moving from simplicity to complexity, new and different principles are emergent. Third, and least familiar in personality and social psychology, is a view which is quite common in other fields. Laboratory research is seen not as a necessary evil but as an essential procedure which enables us to attain isolation and control of variables and thus makes possible the formulation of basic principles in a setting of reduced complexity. If experiments realistically reproduce the nonlaboratory complexities, they provide little advantage over the field study. Continuity is assumed between the laboratory and the outside world, and complexity is seen as quantitative and not qualitative. To move from a simple situation to a complex one requires detailed knowledge about the relevant variables and their interaction.

Application and the attainment of a technology depend upon such an approach.

With respect to a specific psychological phenomenon, the problem of nonlaboratory generalization and application may be examined more concretely. The laboratory investigation of interpersonal attraction within a reinforcement paradigm (Byrne, 1969) has followed a strategy in which the effect of a variety of stimulus variables on a single response variable was the primary focus of interest. A model has evolved which treats all relevant stimuli as positive or negative reinforcers of differential magnitude. Attraction toward any stimulus object (including another person) is then found to be a positive linear function of the proportion of weighted positive reinforcements associated with that object. Attitude statements have been the most frequently employed reinforcing stimuli, but other stimulus elements have included personality variables (e.g. Griffitt, 1966), physical attractiveness (e.g. Byrne *et al.*, 1968), economic variables (Byrne *et al.*, 1966), race (e.g. Byrne and Ervin, 1969), behavioural preferences (Huffman, 1969), personal evaluations (e.g. Byrne and Rhamey, 1965), room temperature (Griffitt, 1970, and sexual arousal (Picher, 1966).

Considering just one of those variables, attitude similarity-dissimilarity, why is it not reasonable to propose an immediate and direct parallel between laboratory and nonlaboratory responses? One reason is simple and quite obvious, but it seems often to be overlooked. Laboratory research is based on the isolation of variables so that one or a limited number of independent variables may be manipulated, while, if possible, all other stimulus variables are controlled. In the outside world, multiple uncontrolled stimuli are present. Thus, if all an experimental subject knows about a stranger is that he holds opinions similar to his own on six out of six political issues, the stranger will be liked (Byrne *et al.*, 1969). We cannot, however, assume that any two interacting individuals who agree on these six issues will become fast friends because (*a*) they may never get around to discussing those six topics at all, and (*b*) even if these topics are discussed, six positive reinforcements may simply become an insignificant portion of a host of other positive and negative reinforcing elements in the interaction. A second barrier to immediate applicability of a laboratory finding lies in the nature of the response. It is good research strategy to limit the dependent variable (in this instance, the sum of two 7-point rating scales), but nonlaboratory responses may be as varied and uncontrolled as the stimuli. The relationship between that paper-and-pencil measure of attraction and other interpersonal responses is only beginning to be explored (e.g. Byrne *et al.*, 1969; Efran, 1969). The third barrier lies in the nature of the relationship investigated. For a number of quite practical reasons, the laboratory study of attraction is limited in its time span and hence might legitimately be labeled the study of first impressions. Whether the determinants of first impressions are precisely the same as the determinants of a prolonged friendship, of love, or of marital happiness is an empirical question and one requiring a great deal of research.

In view of these barriers to extralaboratory application of experimental findings, how may one begin the engineering enterprise? The present research suggests one attempt to seek a solution. Specifically, a limited dating situation is created in which the barriers to application are minimized. Independent variables identified in the laboratory (attitude similarity, personality similarity, and physical attractiveness) are varied in a real-life situation, and an attempt is made to make the variables salient and to minimize the occurrence of other stimulus events. Even though similarity has been the focus of much of the experimental work on attraction, the findings with respect to physical attractiveness have consistently demonstrated the powerful influence of appearance on responses to those of the opposite sex and even of the same sex. Both field studies (Megargee, 1956; Perrin, 1921; Taylor, 1956; Walster *et al.*, 1966) and laboratory investigations (Byrne *et al.*, 1968; McWhirter, 1969; Moss, 1969) have shown that those who are physically attractive elicit more positive responses than do those who are unattractive. The laboratory response measure was retained so that a common reference point was available, but additional response variables were also used in order to extend the generality and meaning of the attraction construct. Finally, in this experiment, the interaction was deliberately limited in time so that it remained close to a first-impression relationship. Given these deliberately limited conditions, it was proposed that the positive relationship between the proportion of weighted positive reinforcements and attraction is directly applicable to a nonlaboratory interaction. Specifically, it was hypothesized that in a computer dating situation (*a*) attraction is a joint function of similarity and physical attractiveness, and (*b*) the greater the extent to which the specific elements of similarity are made salient, the greater is the relationship between similarity and attraction.

The variety of ways in which similarity and attraction could be investigated in a field situation raises an interesting question of strategy. It should be kept in mind that there is no magic about the similarity effect. Similarity does not exude from the pores; rather, specific attitudes and other characteristics must be expressed overtly. It would be relatively simple to design a computer dating experiment in which no similarity effects would be found. For example, one could lie about the degree of similarity, and in a brief interaction, the subjects would not be likely to discover the deception. Another alternative would be to provide no information about similarity and then to forbid the subjects to talk during their date. Negative results in such studies would be of no importance as a test since they are beyond the boundary conditions of the theory. Another possible study would give no initial similarity information and then require an extended interaction period, but that has already been done. That is, people in the real world do this every day, and numerous correlational studies indicate that under such conditions, similarity is associated with attraction. The strategy of the present research was frankly to maximize the possibility of securing a precise similarity attraction effect in a real-life setting; in subsequent research, the limiting conditions of the effect may be determined.

I. Method

A. ATTITUDE-PERSONALITY QUESTIONNAIRE

In order to provide a relatively broad base on which to match couples for the dating process, a 50-item questionnaire was constructed utilizing five variables. In previous research, a significant similarity effect has been found for authoritarianism (Sheffield and Byrne, 1967), repression-sensitization (Byrne and Griffitt, 1969; Byrne et al., 1967), attitudes (Byrne, 1961, 1969), EPPS items,[2] and self-concept (Griffitt, 1966). Each variable was represented by 10 items which were chosen to represent the least possible intercorrelations within dimensions; the rationale here was the desire to maximize the number of *independent* scale responses on which matching could be based.

B. SIMULATED STRANGER CONDITION

In order to provide a base line for the similarity effect under controlled conditions, a simulated stranger condition was run in which the other

2. Unpublished data collected by Donn Byrne and John Lamberth.

person was represented only by his or her purported responses to the attitude-personality questionnaire. The study was described as an investigation of the effectiveness of the matching procedures of computer dating organizations. Subjects were told, "Instead of arranging an actual date, we are providing couples with information about one another and asking for their reactions". The simulated scales were prepared to provide either a 0.33 or 0.67 proportion of similar responses between stranger and subject. The subject was asked to read the responses of an opposite-sex stranger and then to make a series of evaluations on an expanded version of the Interpersonal Judgment Scale. This scale consists of six 7-point scales. The measure of attraction within this experimental paradigm (Byrne, 1969) consists of the sum of two scales: liking and desirability as a work partner. This attraction index ranges from 2 to 14 and has a split-half reliability of 0.85. In addition, four buffer scales deal with evaluations of the other person's intelligence, knowledge of current events, morality, and adjustment. These variables are found to correlate positively with attraction, but they have somewhat different antecedents and are included in the analysis simply as supplemental information. Three new scales, added for the present study in order to explore various responses to the opposite sex, asked the subject to react to the other person as a potential date, as a marriage partner, and as to sexual attractiveness. Finally, a tenth scale was added in order to assess a stimulus variable, the physical attractiveness of the other person. In addition, the physical attractiveness of each subject was rated by the experimenter on the same 7-point scale on which the subjects rated one another.

C. COMPUTER DATING CONDITION

Selection of Dating Couples

The attitude-personality questionnaire was administered to a group of 420 introductory psychology students at the University of Texas, and each item was scored in a binary fashion. By means of a specially prepared program, the responses of each male were compared with those of each female; for any given couple, the number of possible matching responses could theoretically range from 0 to 50. The actual range was from 12 to 37. From these distributions of matches, male-female pairs were selected to represent either the greatest or the least number of matching responses. There was a further restriction that the male be as tall as or taller than the female. Of the resulting pairs, a few were eliminated because (*a*) one of the individuals was married, (*b*) the resulting pair was racially mixed, or (*c*) because of a failure to keep the experimental appointment. The remaining 88 subjects formed 24 high-similar pairs, whose proportion of similar responses ranged from 0.66 to 0.74, and 20 low-similar pairs, whose proportion of similar responses ranged from 0.24 to 0.40.

Levels of Information Saliency

The experiment was run with one of the selected couples at a time. In the experimental room, they were introduced to one another and told:

> In recent years, there has been a considerable amount of interest in the phenomenon of computer dating as a means for college students to meet one another. At the present time, we are attempting to learn as much as possible about the variables which influence the reactions of one individual to another.

In order to create differential levels of saliency with respect to the matching elements, subjects in the salient condition were told:

> Earlier this semester, one of the test forms you filled out was very much like those used by some of the computer dating organizations. In order to refresh your memory about this test and the answers you gave, we are going to ask you to spend a few minutes looking over the questions and your answers to them.
>
> The answers of several hundred students were placed on IBM cards and run through the computer to determine the number of matching answers among the 50 questions for all possible pairs of male and female students. According to the computer, the two of you gave the same answers on approximately 67% (33%) of those questions.

In the nonsalient condition, they were told:

> Imagine for the purpose of the experiment that you had applied to one of the computer dating organizations and filled out some of their information forms. Then, imagine that the two of you had been notified that, according to the computer, you match on approximately 67% (33%) of the factors considered important.

All subjects were then told:

> For our experiment, we would like to create a situation somewhat like that of a computer date. That is, you answered a series of questions, the computer indicated that you two gave the same responses on some of the questions, and now we would like for you to spend a short time together getting acquainted. Specifically, we are asking you to spend the next 30 minutes together on a "coke date" at the Student

Union. Here is 50¢ to spend on whatever you would like. We hope that you will learn as much as possible about each other in the next half hour because we will be asking you a number of questions about one another when you return.

Measures of Attraction

When they returned from the date to receive their final instructions, an unobtrusive measure of attraction was obtained: the physical distance between the two subjects while standing together in front of the experimenter's desk. The distance was noted on a simple ordinal scale ranging from 0 (touching one another) to 5 (standing at opposite corners of the desk). The subjects were then separated and asked to evaluate their date on the Interpersonal Judgment Scale.

Follow-up Measures

At the end of the semester (2-3 months after the date), it was possible to locate 74 of the 88 original subjects who were willing to answer five additional questions. Each was asked to write the name of his or her computer date and to indicate whether or not they had talked to one another since the experiment, dated since the experiment, and whether a date was desired or planned in the future. Finally, each was asked whether the evaluation of the date was influenced more by physical attractiveness or by attitudes.

II. Results

A. SIMULATED STRANGER CONDITION

The mean attraction responses of two simulated stranger conditions[3] which were run separately from the computer dating experiment are shown in Table 1. Analysis of variance indicated that the similarity

3. Originally, the plan was to run the simulated stranger groups just after the computer dating groups. An unexpected finding was that almost all of the responses were positive and that the subjects were attired more attractively than is usual among undergraduates reporting for experimental sessions. From anecdotal olfactory evidence, even the perfume and shaving lotion level was noticeably elevated. In retrospect, it seemed clear that because the computer dating study was widely discussed and because this experiment was so labeled, the overwhelming majority of the 34 subjects were expecting to go on a date as part of their task. It then became necessary to rerun the simulated stranger groups at the end of the semester when the expectations of dates had diminished. The two levels of similarity were run under two different experimental titles, "Computer Dating" and "Evaluational Processes". The data reported in this paper are from these latter two experiments.

TABLE 1. Mean attraction responses toward similar and dissimilar simulated strangers with two different titles for experiment.

Title of experiment	Proportion of similar responses	
	.33	.67
Evaluational processes	9.47	10.78
Computer dating	10.21	11.33
M	9.84	11.06

Note. The mean attraction responses were 10.12 and 10.77 for the evaluational processes and computer dating experiments, respectively.

variable yielded the only significant effect ($F = 4.00$, $df = 1/46$, $p =$ approximately 0.05).

On the remaining items of the Interpersonal Judgment Scale, the only other significant similarity effect was on the intelligence rating ($F = 7.30$, $df = 1/46$, $p < 0.01$). Interestingly enough, there were several differences between the differently labeled experiments on the other Interpersonal Judgment Scale items. More positive responses were given in the "computer dating" experiment than in the "evaluational processes" experiment with respect to knowledge of current events ($F = 8.07$, $df = 1/46$, $p < 0.01$), adjustment ($F = 6.10$, $df = 1/46$, $p < 0.02$), and desirability as a marriage partner ($F = 6.57$, $df = 1/46$, $p < 0.02$). The sexual attractiveness item yielded a significant interaction effect ($F = 4.93$, $df = 1/46$, $p < 0.03$), with the dissimilar stranger rated as more sexually attractive in the computer dating experiment and the similar stranger as more sexually attractive in the evaluational process experiment. While these latter findings are gratuitous, they suggest the importance of minor variations in the stimulus context and the sensitivity of the Interpersonal Judgment Scale items to such variations.

B. PREDICTING ATTRACTION IN THE COMPUTER DATING CONDITION

The mean attraction responses for male and female subjects at two levels of information saliency and two levels of response similarity are shown in Table 2. Analysis of variance indicated the only significant effect to be that of proportion of similar responses ($F = 13.67$, $df = 1/40$, $p < 0.001$). The attempt to make the matching stimuli differentially salient did not affect attraction, and there were no sex differences.

TABLE 2. Mean attraction responses of males and females with similar
and dissimilar dates at two levels of saliency concerning matching information.

Level	Proportion of similar responses	
	Low	High
Male Ss		
Information		
Salient	10.00	11.91
Nonsalient	10.56	11.38
Female Ss		
Information		
Salient	10.73	11.82
Nonsalient	10.33	12.15

The other variable which was expected to influence attraction was the physical attractiveness of the date. It is interesting to note in the simulated stranger condition that while the manipulation of similarity influenced attraction, it had no effect on guesses as to the other person's physical attractiveness ($F < 1$). Thus, data in the computer dating condition indicating a relationship between attractiveness and attraction would seem to result from the effect of the former on the latter. Two measures of attractiveness were available: ratings by the experimenter when the subjects first arrived and by each subject of his or her own date following their interaction. The correlation between these two measures was significant; the correlation between the experimenter's ratings of male subjects and the females' ratings of their dates was 0.59 ($p < 0.01$) and between the experimenter's ratings of female subjects and the males' ratings of their dates was 0.39 ($p < 0.01$). As might be expected, the subject's own ratings proved to be better predictors than did the experimenter's ratings. In Table 3 are shown those correlations between physical attractiveness ratings and Interpersonal Judgment Scale responses which were consistent across sexes.

Thus, the first hypothesis was clearly confirmed, but there was no support for the second hypothesis.

With respect to the prediction of attraction, it seems likely that a combination of the similarity and attractiveness variables would provide the optimal information. In Table 4 are shown the mean attraction responses toward attractive (ratings of 5-7) and unattractive (ratings of 1-4) dates at two levels of response similarity. For both

TABLE 3. Correlations between ratings of physical attractiveness of date and evaluations of date

Variable	Attractiveness of date Rated by *Ss*		Attractiveness of date Rated by *E*	
	Male *Ss*	Female *Ss*	Male *Ss*	Female *Ss*
Attraction	.39**	.60**	.07	.32*
Dating	.66**	.57**	.21	.33*
Marriage	.56**	.55**	.18	.34*
Sex	.77**	.70**	.53**	.44**

*$p < 0.05$.
**$p < 0.01$.

sexes, each of the two independent variables was found to affect attraction.[4] The physical attractiveness variable was significant for both males ($F = 3.85$, $df = 1/39$, $p < 0.05$) and for females ($F = 10.44$, $df = 1/40$, $p < 0.01$). The most positive response in each instance was toward similar attractive dates, and the least positive response was

TABLE 4. Mean attraction responses of males and females with similar and dissimilar dates who are relatively attractive and unattractive.

Physical attractiveness of date	Proportion of similar responses	
	Low	High
Male *Ss*		
Attractive	10.55	12.00
Unattractive	9.89	10.43
Female *Ss*		
Attractive	11.25	12.71
Unattractive	9.50	11.00

4. The use of the term "independent variable" for physical attractiveness may be a source of confusion. In this experiment, there was obviously no manipulation of physical appearance, but attractiveness was conceptualized as one of the stimuli determining attraction. In other experiments, attractiveness has been successfully manipulated as an independent variable (e.g. Byrne *et al.*, 1968; McWhirter, 1969; Moss, 1969). In the absence of any evidence that attraction determines perception of physical attractiveness (and some evidence to the contrary), it seems reasonable to consider attractiveness as an antecedent variable in studies such as the present one and that of Walster *et al.* (1966).

toward dissimilar unattractive dates. An additional analysis indicated no relationship between an individual's own physical attractiveness (as rated by the date) and response to the other person's physical attractiveness.

C. OTHER EFFECTS OF SIMILARITY AND ATTRACTIVENESS

On the additional items of the Interpersonal Judgment Scale, similarity was found to have a significant positive effect on ratings of the date's intelligence ($F = 4.37$, $df = 1/40$, $p < 0.05$), desirability as a date ($F = 8.92$, $df = 1/40$, $p < 0.01$), and desirability as a marriage partner ($F = 4.76$, $df = 1/40$, $p < 0.05$).

The simplest and least obtrusive measure of attraction was the proximity of the two individuals after the date, while receiving their final instructions from the experimenter. If physical distance can be considered as an alternative index of attraction, these two dependent variables should be correlated. For females, the correlation was -0.36 ($p < 0.01$) and for males, -0.48 ($p < 0.01$); in each instance the greater the liking for the partner, the closer together they stood. Another way of evaluating the proximity variable is to determine whether it is influenced by the same independent variables as is the paper-and-pencil measure. For both sexes, physical separation was found to correlate -0.49 ($p < 0.01$) with similarity. Thus, the more similar the couples, the closer they stood. Because similarity and proximity are necessarily identical for each member of a pair, it is not possible to determine whether the males, the females, or both are responsible for the similarity-proximity relationship. When the physical attractiveness measure was examined, however, there was indirect evidence that proximity in this situation was controlled more by the males than by the females. For females, there was no relationship between ratings of the male's appearance and physical separation ($r = -0.06$). For males, the correlation was -0.34 ($p < 0.05$).

In the follow-up investigation at the end of the semester, 74 of the 88 original subjects were available and willing to participate. For this analysis, each subject was placed in one of three categories with respect to the two stimulus variables of similarity and attractiveness. On the basis of the same divisions as were used in the analysis in Table 4, subjects were either in a high-similarity condition with a physically attractive date, a low-similarity condition with a physically unattractive date, or in a mixed condition of high-low or low-high. To maximize the possible effect, frequency analysis was used in comparing the two homogeneous groups ($N = 40$).[5] In response to the question about the date's name, the more positive the stimulus conditions at the time of the date, the more likely was the subject to remember correctly the date's name ($\chi^2 = 8.47$, $df = 1$, $p < 0.01$). With respect to talking to the other individual during the period since the experiment, the relationship was again significant ($\chi^2 = 4.95$, $df = 1$, $p < 0.05$). The same effect was found with regard to whether the individual would like or not like to date the other person in the future ($\chi^2 = 5.38$, $df = 1$, $p < 0.05$). The only follow-up question which failed to show a significant effect for the experimental manipulation was that dealing with actual dating; even here, it might be noted that the only dates reported were by subjects in the high-similarity, high-attractiveness condition.

The only other question in the follow-up survey represented an attempt to find out whether the subjects could accurately verbalize the stimuli to which they had been found to respond. Of the 74 respondents, about one-third indicated that both attitudes and physical attractiveness determined their response to the partner, while about one-sixth of the subjects felt they had responded to neither variable. With the remaining half of the sample, an interesting sex difference emerged. Physical attractiveness was identified as the most important stimulus by 14 of the 18 males, while attitudes were seen as the most important stimulus by 16 of the 19 females ($\chi^2 = 14.30$, $df = 1$, $p < 0.001$). The present subjects seemed to have accepted Bertrand Russell's observation that "On the whole, women tend to love men for their character, while men tend to love women for their appearance". In contrast to these verbal sentiments, it might be noted that the date's physical attractiveness correlated 0.60 with attraction responses of female subjects and only 0.39 among male subjects. A further analysis compared the similarity-attraction effect and the attractiveness-attraction effect for those subjects who indicated one or the other stimulus variable as the more important. The similarity-attraction effect did not differ between the two groups ($z < 1$). It has been reported previously that awareness of similarity is not a necessary

5. When the 33 individuals who were heterogeneous with respect to similarity and attractiveness were included in the analysis, they fell midway between the similar-attractive and dissimilar-unattractive groups on each item. The probability levels were consequently reduced to the 0.02 level on remembering the date's name and to the 0.10 level on the talking and desire to date items.

component of the similarity effect (Byrne and Griffitt, 1969). There was, however, a difference in the attractiveness effect. For the subjects identifying attractiveness as the major determinant, physical attractiveness correlated 0.63 ($p < 0.01$) with attraction responses; for the subjects identifying similarity as the major determinant, attractiveness correlated -0.04 (ns) with attraction. The difference was a significant one ($z = 2.16$, $p < 0.05$).

III. Conclusions

Perhaps the most important aspect of the present findings is the evidence indicating the continuity between the laboratory study of attraction and its manifestation under field conditions. At least as operationalized in the present investigation, variables such as physical attractiveness and similarity of attitudes and personality characteristics are found to influence attraction in a highly predictable manner.

The findings with respect to the physical distance measure are important in two respects. First, they provide further evidence that voluntary proximity is a useful and unobstrusive measure of interpersonal attraction. Second, the construct validity and generality of the paper-and-pencil measure of attraction provided by the Interpersonal Judgment Scale is greatly enhanced. The significant relationship between two such different response measures is comforting to users of either one. In addition, the follow-up procedure provided evidence of the lasting effect of the experimental manipulations and of the relation of the attraction measures to such diverse responses as remembering the other person's name and engaging in conversation in the weeks after the termination of the experiment.

The failure to confirm the second hypothesis is somewhat puzzling. It is possible that present procedures, designed to vary the saliency of the elements of similarity, were inadequate and ineffective, that the actual behavioural cues to similarity and dissimilarity were sufficiently powerful to negate the effects of the experimental manipulation, or that the hypothesis was simply incorrect. There is no basis within the present experiment on which to decide among these alternatives.

In conclusion, it must be emphasized that striking continuity has been demonstrated across experiments using paper-and-pencil materials to simulate a stranger and to measure attraction (Byrne, 1961a), more realistic audio and audiovisual presentations of the stimulus person (Byrne and Clore, 1966), elaborate dramatic confrontations in which a confederate portrays the stimulus person (Byrne and Griffitt, 1966), and a quasi-realistic experiment such as the present one, in which two genuine strangers interact and in which response measures include nonverbal behaviours. Such findings suggest that attempts to move back and forth between the controlled artificiality of the laboratory and the uncontrolled natural setting are both feasible and indicative of the potential applications of basic attraction research to a variety of interpersonal problems.

15.

Personality Similarity and Friendship Choice: Similarity of What, When?[1]

S. W. DUCK

University of Lancaster, Lancaster, England

The theoretical and practical values of devoting research efforts to the study of interpersonal attraction and friendship formation have dictated that a diversity of studies would be carried out with a consequent identification of a large number of relevant factors (Berscheid and Walster, 1969; Byrne, 1969; Senn, 1971). Such findings might be expected to have a direct application in the solution of a wide variety of problems associated with interpersonal relationships, such as identification of potentially effective work partnerships, advice on the suitability of marital choices and understanding some

1. My thanks are due to John Moulton of Sussex University for his valuable comments on a previous draft of this paper and for his help in the collection of the pilot data.

First published in *Journal of Personality* 1973, **41**, 543-558. Copyright © 1973 by Duke University Press. Reprinted by permission.

causes of failure in interpersonal relationships as a possible antecedent
of emotional disturbance. The possibility of applying the results of
research to such areas can be extended by studying both attraction (as
an early predictor of an ultimate outcome) and friendship (as a
paradigm of a developed relationship). It is somewhat perplexing,
therefore, to find that comprehensive theoretical explanations of
attraction and friendship as parts of a unitary process have not been
explicitly advanced. Nor has the nature of links between the two been
thoroughly pursued.

Inevitably, details of such links may be obscured by the sharp
differences in methodology which characterize studies in the two areas.
On the one hand, studies of attraction tend to concentrate on
attraction to strangers (Byrne, 1969) and perforce to adopt an
experimental paradigm. Previously unacquainted subjects who have
completed attitude profiles are led to understand that given amounts
of similarity exist between them on these profiles. The dependent
variable is then the levels of attraction which are expressed towards
strangers as a result of the manipulation of similarity levels. The
relationship between attraction and similarity of attitudes is explained
in terms of consensual validation (Byrne, 1961a). In other words, an
individual is seen as seeking for his acquaintances those whose
attitudes are similar to his own and therefore provide some evidence
for the validity of his views.

On the other hand are studies which concentrate on instances of
naturally-occurring relationships, such as friendships (Izard, 1960a) or
marital partnerships (Maslow, 1953). In such studies a correlational
method is typically adopted, and attention is usually directed to
similarity on some personality dimension or profile (Izard, 1960b). In
contrast to the studies on attitudes, personality similarity studies have
been based on no consistent theoretical assumptions (Miller et al.,
1966). Furthermore, the divergence of the two areas is enhanced by the
unequal progress made in each, for while the relationship between
attitudes and attraction has become increasingly clear (Byrne, 1969),
the evidence on personality and friendship has been somewhat
equivocal (Hoffman and Maier, 1966).

Despite these disconcerting empirical differences, intuition dictates
that some form of relationship between the two areas is entirely
reasonable. For it may be held that part of the value of studying
attraction to strangers lies ultimately in its claim to be an early part of
a developing process. Thus prediction about later outcomes would be

facilitated by a close attention to the preliminary stages of a potentially developing relationship. Its study may thus present us with a ready key to some of the later and more complex problems which occur in deeper personal relationships. This argument rests on the belief that continuity between attraction and friendship can be demonstrated and that factors relevant in one case are equally relevant in the other. Yet continuity studies have been rare.

Byrne, Ervin and Lamberth (1970) argued that one factor which has been related consistently to attraction (namely, similarity of attitudes) may be predictive of patterns of dating. This assumption underlies the arrangement of partnerships by computer and the authors designed an experiment to reflect this assumption. Potential dates were selected for subjects on the basis of various levels of attitude similarity and their levels of attraction to one another were measured after "coke dates" and again in a follow-up some months later. The authors were also interested, at this later stage, in whether dating had continued, and if so with what frequency. It was found, as predicted, that similarity of attitudes was associated with greater attraction and with higher frequencies of dating after the first meeting. However, the pairs of subjects were inevitably given many chances to interact with each other during the period between the coke date and later testing. This introduces the possibility that other factors than initial levels of attitude similarity may have had some influence on the higher incidence of continued dating in similar pairs. It is not clearly established by this study therefore that similarity of attitudes does more than lay the ground for a developing relationship. Warr (1965) found that proximity was a factor not only in positive but also in negative sociometric choices and this suggests that such variables may be necessary but not sufficient factors in developing friendship. This distinction may also apply to attitude similarity and suggests a kind of analysis which may help to clarify the links between attraction and friendship.

It may be that developing relationships are characterized not by persistent and immutable similarities but by specific and progressive changes in emphasis which provide extended scope for consensual validation. For example, once a partner's attitudes on particular issues are known, it is of considerable value to find out how these attitudes are structured and interrelated. Tesser (1971) has presented evidence that structural similarity in attitudes is positively related to attraction. This may be because dissimilar others "are less predictable and look at the world in ways which are different from our own" (Tesser, 1971, p. 96).

But even this may be a necessary rather than a sufficient condition for further development of a relationship, and deeper knowledge of another individual may cause further emphases to arise. For example, after detailed discussion with another person, more knowledge is available about gross characteristics of his personality. Perhaps it is the case that individuals in this position would be attracted to one another as a function of personality similarity. However, critical to this argument is the time at which such similarity is measured; for it is necessary that the individuals achieve some outline of gross personality characteristics without having the opportunity of a full test of the detail of that personality. For in real life a picture of an acquaintance's personality is perforce built up in slow stages, first at a relatively crude level and then in more detail (Argyle and Little, 1972). Such a constraint may suggest a possible factor in the failure of Hogan and Mankin (1970), and Hoffman and Maier (1966) to discover a relationship between "clique" attraction and personality similarity. In these studies, erstwhile strangers were allowed to interact for formal discussion periods: six 75-minute sessions, with possible informal meetings in the Hogan and Mankin study; and 2-hour sessions at various stages of a 14-week term in the Hoffman and Maier study. However, it may be that these formal interactions, while themselves controlled, may have been affected by intervening informal meetings and may in any case have extended over too long a period before attraction levels were assessed. In terms of the present hypothesis, this time may have allowed individuals to pass the stage at which such similarity was relevant. Part of the hypothesis of the present study is therefore that gross personality similarity, assessed at a very early stage of acquaintance, may mediate the attraction choices expressed at that time.

Would increasing interaction lead to concentration on an individual's deeper and more personal evaluations? This analysis suggests that it would and may thus serve the dual purposes of discovering the characteristics of the other's cognitive outlook, and of deciding whether they were the same as one's own. It has been argued (Duck, 1972) that Kelly's (1955, 1970) theory of personal constructs provides an appropriate measure of personality at this level. Constructs are the individual's personal hypotheses about the world and everything in it, and are deep conceptual components of his way of life. Duck and Spencer (1972) have claimed that such constructs may be appropriate for test against other individuals' constructs: in other words, a test of the validity of a construct is provided by the extent to which it is shared by others. This argument is an extension of Byrne's (1961a) proposition that consensual validation of attitudes underlies attraction and it provides a theoretical link between the areas of attraction and naturally-occurring friendship.

Despite the fact that close friends have been shown to have similar personal construct content (Duck, 1973a), it remains unclear whether this similarity is exclusive of similarity on other dimensions, as the above analysis suggests it will become. Clearly, any hypothesis of the above type requires an answer to this point before its potential for further elaboration can be decided.

It may be obvious why Kelly's (1955) Reptest will figure in a test of this hypothesis, but it may be less clear what other test offers a suitable comparison by means of which to evaluate the argument that emphasis on similarity of personality may change its type in the progressive development of friendship. However, the CPI (California Psychological Inventory) is a personality test where subjects express agreement or disagreement with certain provided statements and profiles are then derived which give some indication of the subject's gross personality traits. Yet the present analysis has argued that developing friendships pass on from concern with grosser personality characteristics to finer and more personal ones. As the relationship develops, similarity on this type of personality test should thus cede any differentiating power as similarity of *personal* constructs becomes more salient.

It is therefore hypothesized that when applied to just-formed acquaintanceships, the CPI will differentiate attracted pairs from those who are not attracted to one another. However, when already-established friendships are studied, the CPI will not there differentiate friendship pairs from other, nominal, pairs in the same acquainted population. On the other hand a test of personality which reflects the minutiae of personal experience will prove more appropriate to the stage of friendship then reached and will thus have that differentiating power.

I. Method

A. SUBJECTS

Since the effects of sex differences in friendship and attraction are by no means clearly delineated (Stroebe *et al.*, 1971; Duck, 1973a), a single-sex pool of subjects was decided upon. Accordingly the subjects were 42 females aged between 18 and 21 years. The study requires two categories of subject: namely, one set of unacquainted subjects and one set of established friendship groups. University halls of residence characteristically contain both kinds of subjects during the first days of a new academic year. Accordingly, subjects were recruited in such a population, and 21 of them were previously unacquainted with one another while the remaining 21 subjects had lived in the hall for at least a year. Since the hypothesis required the identification of established friendship pairs in this latter subset of the subject pool, preliminary screening and a subsequent reliance on a sociometric test were used to ensure that this precondition had been met.

B. PROCEDURE

In view of the fact that different sociometric and associated measures were to be used on the two subsets of the subject pool, each subset was dealt with separately.

However, in each case, the subjects began by completing the CPI and followed the instructions issued with the standard question booklets which comprise the test (Gough, 1964). No additional instructions were given at this stage, but during the course of the experiment it proved necessary to explain some of the American usages employed in the test, such as "hooky" and "deportment marks", which were unfamiliar to some subjects.

Subjects then went on to complete a form of the Reptest (Kelly, 1955) where they were enjoined simply to generate constructs and no "structural" measures were taken here (Duck, 1973b). When a 16 × 18 form of this test had been completed, sociometric techniques were used in the following ways as appropriate to each subset of the subject pool. On the one hand, the subset of acquainted subjects was instructed to generate a list of "friends in this city". Subjects were not instructed to restrict their choices to members of their hall of residence, nor was it indicated that these were the names of most interest to the experimenter. When this task was completed, this subset of the subject pool had finished the experiment. On the other hand, when the unacquainted subset reached the sociometric part of the experiment, the following procedure was adopted. The subset was split into 7-woman groups and each group was given a series of evaluative items for discussion. Items included were: "The best way to combat the drug problem is for the present laws to be made even stricter" and "No individual is justified in committing suicide". Groups were instructed to reach unanimous verdicts on the items. This device was to introduce groups of unacquainted subjects to one another in a way which would ensure some participation by all members of the group and would perforce necessitate the display of some gross outline of personality. The success of this procedure was verified during debriefing. After twenty minutes had been allowed for these deliberations, each subject was asked to record the names of those other persons in the group to whom she felt attracted. When subjects had recorded their lists, they were thanked and debriefed.

C. ANALYSIS

Data from each subset of subjects were prepared separately but were treated in the same fashion. It is clearly a precondition of meaningful analysis that some suitable criterion be adopted for treating some pairings as friendship pairs and some as "nominal pairs" (i.e. pairs of subjects who did not choose one another, although members of the same acquainted population). In both subsets the criterion adopted was mutual choice; i.e. "friendship pairs" were those where the two subjects each chose one another; "nominal pairs" were those where neither chose the other, or where the choice was a one-sided, unreciprocated affair. In the subset of acquainted subjects, all possible pairings were scrutinized and assigned to one of the two categories "friendship" or "nominal"; but in the subset of previously unacquainted subjects it made sense only to scrutinize pairings within a given discussion group and to assign these pairings to the relevant category. The reason is plain enough. For in the previously-acquainted subset all possible pairings have had the chance at some time to assess each other's attractiveness, since all subjects knew all other ones. However, in the unacquainted subset this opportunity has been afforded only to the respective members of each discussion group.

Given these criteria, it was possible to construct sociometric matrices for subsequent reference in the later stages of the analysis. This procedure also serves to meet two possible criticisms of the methodology used in the case of the acquainted subset. For it might be argued that artificial groups could be arrived at if a single person was made the centre of choices by other subjects. While all the "peripheral" subjects may choose the central person (it may be held) it is possible that these "peripheral" subjects may not choose one another and an apparent group would, in reality, disappear if the central popular person were removed. Against this is the finding that reciprocated choices were the rule and unreciprocated choices the exception, which also vindicates the original selection procedures. The second argument which might be advanced is that having all subjects in a single room during the sociometric test may have increased the chances of the subjects choosing from within the pool. To counter this is the view that if this were the case then one would have expected more unreciprocated choices because of a certain randomness which would be infused. On the contrary, however, one finds several distinct but internally coherent groups of a fairly consistent size where all members choose all other members. Furthermore, other evidence, from comments made by subjects during post-experimental debriefing and from the methods used in subject-selection strongly suggest that such criticisms can be rejected.

The analysis then proceeded to the derivation of the 18 dimensions of the CPI, in the standard way described by Gough (1964), and went on to reduce the scores obtained to a unitary summary of the amount of similarity of personality existing between two subjects. To perform this analysis each subject's data in turn took on the role of "comparison data" and her score on the dimension concerned was subtracted from every other subject's corresponding score in turn. Each of the resulting difference scores was classified into one of two categories according to whether this pair of subjects had chosen each other on the sociometric test or not. Thus for each subject, two categories of scores for each dimension were derived, one from the friendship pairs of which she was a member and one from the nominal pairs. Using the scores derived at this stage it is possible to reduce the CPI measures to one unitary measure. In order to effect this reduction one score for the friendship category and one for the nominal category was computed for each subject in turn. This was effected by averaging the scores previously assigned to each category on each dimension (Hogan and Mankin, 1970), the legitimacy of which procedure rests on the fact that mean differences between scores on different dimensions and not the raw scores themselves were being averaged.

The final part of the analysis was then devoted to the Reptests as follows. Each Reptest was first considered on its own, and all constructs which exactly and literally repeated another on the same Reptest were erased, so that only one instance of each construct remained. This was because the constructs themselves and not their frequency was being studied. When this had been done for all Reptests, the instance of each construct used by a given subject was compared with instances of constructs on all other grids and was rated "similar" or "not similar" to each. There are two intuitive criteria for similarity: *literal similarity* (when exactly the same words are used, e.g. Good-Bad, Good-Bad) and *conceptual similarity* (when two constructs express the same concept, but not necessarily in the same way. Thus "say what they feel—tends to hide emotions" was counted similar on this criterion to "express feelings readily—reserved in expression of feelings"). The class of "conceptually similar" constructs of course includes the class of literally similar constructs. It has been found that the literal criterion is the most appropriate measure of similarity in the case of incipient friendships and the conceptual criterion is most valuable when studying firmly established friendships (Duck and Spencer, 1972), and the criteria were applied in that manner. Three independent raters achieved a reliability as measured by Kendall's coefficient of concordance (w) on rating for construct similarity of $w = 0.7684$ ($p < 0.01$) in the case of the conceptual criterion, and $w = 0.791$ ($p < 0.01$) when using the literal criterion.

The number of similarities between the relevant pairings of subjects in each of the subsets (see above) was recorded and the mean similarity scores for each subject were derived and classified in exactly the same way as the previously-derived CPI scores (i.e. into scores originating from friendship pairs and nominal pairs). Both sets of derived scores are amenable to paired t tests, the results of which are given below.

II. Results

For each subset of the subject pool, the above analysis yielded two sets of scores in similar form; one set from the CPI and one from the Reptest; and each set comprised a pair of means for each subject. What did the pairs of data represent and what significant differences did they show?

In the case of the CPI data, one component of each pair of data was the mean overall difference between a subject's scores on the personality dimensions and those of her "friends"; the other component was the mean difference between her and those she had *not* chosen. If similarity of personality (measured by the CPI) were a basis for friendship or attraction, then it should be found that there are smaller differences (and thus greater similarity) between the scores of the friendship pairs than between the scores from the nominal pairs. Each subset of data was therefore submitted to a paired t test and the results are given in Table 1. In the previously unacquainted population, similarity of personality, as measured on the CPI, strongly differentiates friendship and nominal pairs ($t = 2.8591$, $df = 20$, $p < 0.01$), while in the acquainted population it does not ($t = -0.2046$, $df = 20$, ns). These results were predicted by the hypothesis.

TABLE 1. Comparisons of the mean similarity/difference scores derived from the nominal pairs with those derived from the friendship pairings.[a]

	CPI data (differences)	Reptest data (similarities)
Previously unacquainted subset:		
$\overline{X}$	1.2752	0.4309
$SD\overline{X}$	2.0438	1.2455
t	2.8591**	1.5859 ns
Previously acquainted subset:		
$\overline{X}$	-0.0290	0.2300
$SD\overline{X}$	0.6494	0.4696
t	-0.2046 ns	2.2460*

*$p < 0.05$, $df = 20$.
**$p < 0.01$, $df = 20$.
[a] In the case of the CPI data, mean differences between subjects are considered, while the Reptest data represent mean similarities between subjects (see text).

In the case of the Reptest data, one component of each pair of data was the mean number of similarities between a subject's constructs and those of her friends; the other component was the mean number of similarities between her and those she had *not* chosen. In this instance, therefore, the larger scores indicate greater similarity, whereas in the previous case the smaller scores did so. The results of the t tests here yielded the finding that similarity of personality, measured by the Reptest, strongly differentiates friendship pairs from nominal pairs in the acquainted subset ($t = 2.246$, $df = 20$, $p < 0.05$) but not in the unacquainted subset ($t = 1.5859$, $df = 20$, ns). These results were also predicted by the hypothesis.

These analyses constituted the main treatment of the data and the main test of the hypotheses advanced earlier. However, they do not provide for a direct comparison of the differences between the acquainted and unacquainted groups in similarity, on CPI and Reptest measures. Accordingly the data were next submitted to an analysis based on a 2 × 2 ANOVA design, with Level of Acquaintance (Acquainted v. Unacquainted) and Level of Friendship (Friendship vs. Nominal) constituting the factors compared. One such test was completed for the CPI data and one for the Reptest data. The results are given in Table 2.

TABLE 2. Subanalysis using 2 × 2 ANOVA design comparing effects of level of acquaintance (Acquainted vs. Unacquainted = A vs. U) and level of friendship choice (Friendship vs. Nominal = F vs. N).

	MS	F
CPI data		
Rows (F vs. N)	8.1545	5.602**
Columns (A vs. U)	17.8770	12.282***
Interaction	8.9298	6.135**
Error	1.4556	
Reptest data		
Rows (F vs. N)	2.2936	4.018*
Columns (A vs. U)	1.3072	2.290
Interaction	0.2115	0.3705
Error	0.5708	

$*p < 0.05.$
$**p < 0.025.$
$***p < 0.001.$

In the case of the CPI data the F ratio for Rows (Friendship vs. Nominal) was significant ($F = 5.602$, $df = 1,80$, $p < 0.025$) and this indicates that, overall, the gross similarity between newly acquainted "friends" is in this case higher than between nominal pairs. However, the interaction was also significant ($F = 6.134$, $p < 0.025$) and this confirms the previous analysis (see Table 1) that the effect in this instance is contributed mainly by the Unacquainted subset as predicted. The significant difference between subsets (Column effects, $F = 12.28$, $p < 0.001$) is superficially a puzzling finding, but is clarified below by the further analysis.

In the case of the Reptest data, the F ratio for Rows (Friendship vs. Nominal) was also significant ($F = 4.018$, $df = 1,80.$ $p < 0.05$) and again indicates that, overall, established friends were more similar in construing than were nominal pairs. The column effects and interaction effects were not significant. The nonsignificance of the interaction in this test seems to suggest that both subsets are contributing to the finding that friends are more similar than are nominal pairs. Indeed review of the results in Table 1 shows that the effect (friends more similar than nominal pairs) is present in both the Acquainted and the Unacquainted subset, but is significant in the Acquainted subset ($p < 0.05$) and only barely tends to significance in the other subset ($0.2 > p > 0.1$). These results do not conflict with the experimental hypotheses but merit discussion later.

However, it may be argued that the ANOVA analysis, while providing some useful pointers to the detail of the data, is nevertheless an inappropriate analysis in this instance. Therefore, to clarify these results further and to satisfy the above doubts, the amounts of similarity in the two subsets were compared also by means of Student's t test for the unpaired case. The results are given in Table 3 and indicate that the level of similarity in the two subsets did not differ significantly in the case of the Reptest data ($t = 0.5808$, ns, for friendship pairs in the two subsets; $t = 1.69$, ns, for the nominal pairs in each). In the case of the CPI data the previous difference between the two subsets can be seen to be due to differences in similarity

TABLE 3. Comparison of the amounts of similarity in the two subsets.

	Reptest data	CPI data
Friendship pairs		
^{x}A	3.089	4.933
^{x}U	2.940	5.203
^{SD}A	0.573	0.622
^{SD}U	0.994	1.030
t	0.5808 ns	1.004 ns
Nominal pairs		
^{x} A	2.860	4.904
^{x} U	2.510	6.479
^{SD}A	0.434	1.400
^{SD}U	0.818	1.913
t	1.690 ns	2.970*

$^*p < 0.01$, $df = 20$.

between nominal pairs ($t = 2.97$, $p < 0.01$) with greater similarity existing in the Acquainted subset. There was no significant difference in the case of data from the friendship pairs ($t = 1.004$, ns). This clarifies the ANOVA finding and offers some support for the claim of Duck & Spencer (1972) that similarity and acquaintance have a two-way interacting relationship with one another. This claim predicts on the one hand that members of populations will become more similar as acquaintance progresses, due to normative effects; and on the other hand that similarity is itself an attractive principle which both causes and maintains friendship. However, given that similarity levels in construing are comparable between the two subsets, the main interest of these experimental results lies with the differences *within* each subset which offer the most exciting implications and which support the hypotheses most strongly.

III. Discussion

The present results indicate that when a newly acquainted population is considered the CPI is able to differentiate friendship pairs from nominal pairs; but that at the stage of formed (as opposed to incipient) friendships, the CPI has ceded its differentiating power to the Reptest. This finding is of interest for two main reasons: *first,* because it suggests a possible explanation for previously equivocal findings in the area of personality similarity and acquaintance; and *second,* because it provides for the erection of a theoretical framework in which the links between attraction and friendship might be shown more clearly. In one case this study prompts the view that care must be taken in the choice of personality tests used in this area, and in the other case, that the similarity which mediates acquaintance may change in character over time. These two suggestions are by no means mutually exclusive and may be seen to be linked, but while one of them is clearly resultant from this study alone, the second is somewhat more speculative and can gain support from comparison with other studies.

The present test sought to demonstrate that different kinds of personality test may be more useful at different times in the acquaintance process. The contrast was between a provided-statement measure and one where the individual is invited to supply his own personal cognitive dimensions. The results support the view that, at the level of established friendships, an individual's own articulations of his apparent circumstances are of importance and it is commonality of these which ultimately excludes the previous importance of similarity on general issues. Duck and Spencer (1972) have shown that such commonality is relevant in some form quite early in an acquaintance, and the previous analysis suggests that it may be present even from the start as a factor in eventual choices, for differences between friendship and nominal pairs were found in the Unacquainted subset, too, and although well below significance level ($p > 0.1$), were nevertheless clearly in the right direction. These findings thus point to the value of the Reptest at several levels of acquaintance as a measure of the basis of friendship choices. However their greatest value lies in the making of the major point that some of the bewildering equivocation of past results may be accountable to the application of inappropriate measures of personality. The present finding is that in the study of acquaintance temporal appropriateness is an important stricture on the productiveness of the personality measures employed.

When put into the perspective provided by other studies in this area, the results give rise to hopes of finding a theoretical suggestion to provide links between attraction and friendship. (It is not claimed, however, that these results do any more than point to its possibility.) For the change in the effectiveness of the CPI at different stages in friendship (new acquaintances vs. established pairings) may depend on its differential ability to measure the emphasis which predominates at different points in a developing acquaintance. The contention that a relationship is characterized by progressive changes in emphasis is one which has previously been somewhat neglected, despite the fact that acquaintance is usually referred to as a *process*. Such a view does not invalidate a continuity between attraction and friendship. It merely places the emphasis somewhat differently from the view which claims unconditional continuity in the effects of cues which may mediate the development of positive regard.

Such suggestions might be dismissed as speculative were it not for the startling similarity of other findings on various other stages of attraction. Lischeron and La Gaipa (1970) have found that early attraction depends on evaluations of interaction style, while later attraction moves in the direction of dependence on cognitive similarity. This result was mirrored by the study of Hogan and Mankin (1970) on constructed groups which were allowed brief discussions; by that of Stroebe, Insko, Thompson and Layton (1971) on reactions to photographs and attitudes of strangers; and by that of Duck and Spencer (1972) on friendship pairs. The theme of all these studies has been a changing emphasis with developing acquaintance, but the key difference has been the level at which acquaintance was tapped. The theoretical suggestions above claim an increasing selectivity and specialization in the cues attended to with the development of acquaintance along a time scale. Thus can the above findings be integrated within a framework and some of the previous discrepancy between "attraction" and "friendship" be explained in terms of a failure to consider such changes in emphasis at appropriate points on a time scale.

While caution must be exercised in interpreting these results in any theoretically meaningful way, it is justified to offer tentative suggestions for a theoretical framework in which they might be explained. The present results contain the seeds of further study into an integration of the literature in terms of a series of "filters". This hypothesis would suppose that individuals evaluate others on a progressively more specialized and specific set of criteria as a relationship develops. It may be that such a view could incorporate and integrate findings in other areas, too (e.g. person perception) which might be seen as providing insight into the cues which are appropriate at early points of new acquaintances. The hypothesis would regard evaluation on all these cues as a "filtering" procedure by which the population of potential friends could be progressively reduced and defined, until the discovery of similarity of personal constructs set some kind of seal. Elaboration and support for such an hypothesis must clearly await the answers to some of the empirical questions which it suggests.

Aside from such possibilities, it becomes clear from the previous argument that the tests used to examine the relationship of attraction, acquaintance and friendship to personality or other cognitive factors must be carefully considered for "appropriateness". Clearly, qualitative differences in the development of acquaintance require considerable research before the nature of appropriateness is clearly apparent. Nevertheless, some recognition that such differences occur, and some understanding of the possible contaminating effects of ignoring them, can only improve a general comprehension of the nature of the links between attraction and friendship.

IV. Summary

The equivocal results in previous studies of the relationship between personality similarity and acquaintance might be accounted for by examining their failure to distinguish different points of developing friendships on a time scale. It is argued that some points lend themselves to investigation by one kind of personality test but later ones require a more "personal" measure. The CPI has previously been used on recently-acquainted subjects to demonstrate facets of the similarity-attraction relationship, but was predicted to lose this power in favour of the Reptest if established friendships were examined. A test of this hypothesis on one unacquainted and one acquainted population showed that similarity of personality (CPI) mediated attraction in the unacquainted population but only similarity of constructs, and not of CPI dimensions, was an adequate predictor of established friendship choices. It is claimed that care needs to be taken in the choice of personality-tests used in this area to ensure that they are appropriate to the emphasis reached in the relationship. The recognition that these changes of emphasis occur is argued to be a precondition of a satisfactory theoretical explanation of the links between attraction and friendship.

The Place of Interpersonal Attraction in Psychological Theories

16.

The Social Skill Model and Interpersonal Attraction

MARK COOK

University College of Swansea, Wales

At this, I cheered up a little. Either Diana was semi-consciously groping for the sixty-four-cent question, the ultimate bit of balls which I would pass the test by letting her get away with, or she was just running out of material . . . .

Even before she spoke I could see that after mounting a series of short but cumulatively valuable ladders, I had just gone sliding down a major snake. But, as in the substantial form of the game, so too in the version Diana and I were playing, there can be certain parts of the board where a single throw can restore everything lost on the previous turn, and more.

The Green Man — Kingsley Amis.

This quotation from Amis illustrates the point that there is more to attraction than the variables traditionally thought important by psychologists, such as similarity (or complementarity) of personality, intelligence, attitudes, social background, proximity, or for that matter the variables thought important by the lay man, such as appearance or money. These may well be necessary conditions, but are not sufficient — being similar, available, nice-looking, and rich doesn't guarantee a person friends or lovers; attractive people may not enjoy the rich social and sexual lives they are in a sense entitled to, because they lack *social skill,* that is, the ability to get on with other people. Making friends with someone is not an instantaneous process and does not occur magically or automatically, given similarity, proximity, etc., it depends on a complicated, drawn out sequence of moves, directed by a general plan, and triggered by what each person's previous actions were. As Amis remarks, the effect is something like a game of snakes and ladders.

I. The social skill model

The idea of social skill is an old one, and not even special to psychology, but the social skill *model* is a more recent development. It depends on an analogy between social behaviour and such motor behaviours as typing or operating machine tools. As a model or analogy it has no predictive power, but should be judged by its fruitfulness (and in particular by its ability to provide a conceptual framework) for a large and diverse body of research. It appeals particularly to those who want to regard social psychology as just a part of psychology in general, coming under the same principles (and is accordingly disliked by, for example, Harré and Secord, 1972, who argue that social behaviour needs its own conceptual framework.)

Making friends with someone is a skilled performance, in the same sense that driving a car, or playing tennis, or turning a chair leg are skilled processes. All have goals or purposes. All depend on seeing the initial state of the object — road ahead, the tennis ball, the piece of wood, or the other person — and on continuing to see them, in a systematic way. All depend on knowing what to do next to bring the object or person nearer the desired state; then doing it; then observing the effect. The analogy between motor and social skill was first explicitly drawn by Argyle, Kendon and Crossman (Argyle and Kendon, 1967) in the form of a diagram of a feedback loop (Fig. 1). It postulates four basic processes or headings. The operator perceives the other person (perception) and considers what to do in the light of his "goal" (translation). He does what he has decided is appropriate (response) and then observes the result (perception again). For example, a man's goal might be to persuade a girl to have intercourse. He sees that the girl is unwilling, because (he thinks) she is afraid of the possible consequences so he assures her that he has contraceptives. He observes continued unwillingness which he now attributes to a fear that she will acquire a bad reputation, so he assures her—almost certainly falsely—that he won't tell anyone. Continuing unwillingness may lead the man to give up (i.e. change his goal) or possibly to resort to further methods like professing love for the girl, or even suggesting they become engaged. (These examples are taken from accounts of their courtship methods volunteered by American college men.)

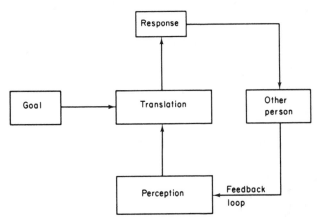

FIG. 1. A simple social skill model, after Argyle (1967).

Argyle (1972) distinguished two levels at which the social skill mechanism operates: a higher level of conscious "plans" and a lower level of automatic habitual responses (a distinction corresponding roughly to that between choosing a way of getting to know someone—by "being nice to them"—and putting it into effect, by smiling, agreeing, deferring, etc.).

In his various discussions of the model Argyle (1967, 1969, 1972; Argyle and Kendon, 1967) makes little reference to attraction, and does not discuss whether his model might apply better to some relationships than to others. However, a distinction can be drawn between goals that are "extrinsic" to an encounter (e.g. getting information, giving it, borrowing money) and goals that are "intrinsic" (e.g. making friends with someone for the sake of being friends, talking to someone for the sake of talking). Interpersonal attraction generally comes into the "intrinsic" category (although sexual encounters may be an exception) but it also includes many 'extrinsic' forms, such as getting married as an end in itself, or having someone available for support, advice, or material help.

Most of the examples cited by Argyle (see for example, 1969, p. 181) are short term encounters and little attention is paid to longer term relationships. Clearly, a person who lacks the social skills that are relevant *initially* will correspondingly have difficulty establishing any *long term* relationships also, but what of the person who already has friends, and a spouse? How does the social skill model apply to them? Presumably he or she will not cease to operate at the lower, automatic level within the relationship: perceiving reactions, desire to speak, etc. although this will proceed perhaps with greater certainty because the signs have become so familiar. Clearly they will also operate at the higher "planning" level (at least sometimes): thinking how to break bad news, how to negotiate a difficult decision or how to avoid an argument. One wonders whether close friends or married couples ever "come out from the control room", so to speak, and act naturally, saying what they think and feel and want, and what they think the other thinks, feels and wants, instead of waiting, watching and scheming, as the model seems to imply. Of course within the terms of the model, being perfectly frank is a response made like any other, because it seems to fit the situation.

However, social skill seems to be most important in the early stages of the relationship, and could be viewed as a first filter (Duck, 1973b) in that people who lack it will not get much further. Once a relationship is established, social skill factors do not seem to lead to relationships breaking up: relationships break up because the people find they have incompatible attitudes, personalities, or role expectations, or because they get bored with each other. However, if a class of person in whom social skill deteriorates — through senility or psychosis, perhaps — were identified, it might be possible to show that breakdown of social skill will disrupt a relationship.

Looking at attraction in the light of the social skill model usually leads to the objection that people are not aware of going through the moves of assessing the other, and then choosing a tactic from a repertoire, according to a goal. This is a familiar but irrelevant objection; most perceptual processes work so fast the perceiver couldn't perceive them as well as perceiving the field itself. In fact one could argue that the "social skill" model is merely the minimum necessary model to explain how making friends, and other social encounters, happen. The skill model provides a convenient set of headings for studying the formation of relations, and by the same token a set of headings for investigations of why some people have trouble translating similarity and opportunity into friendship.

A. PERCEPTION

The first "box" in the social skill model is "perception", a topic extensively written about and researched on in social psychology. The truism that man responds to what he sees the situation to be, not as it really is, or to the person he perceives, not the "real" person, receives lip service but given the size of the difference that often exists between the two the distinction is vitally important. It has in fact received some attention in research on attraction and personality. The actual similarity of personality and outlook in married couples is really rather small, but the degree of similarity they themselves think exists is much greater. A representative finding by Byrne and Blaylock (1963) found an *actual* correlation between husbands and wives (on the Rokeach Scale for dogmatism) of 0.30 to 0.44, but *assumed* similarity of dogmatism ranging from 0.69 to 0.89, indicating that couples shared fewer opinions than they thought.

In the social skill model, perception really takes two forms — first impressions and feedback. The first impression takes in a number of things. In most but not all relationships people look for someone who is attracted to them, with the possible exception of short term sexual relations where sexual willingness matters more. Some preliminary assessments of personality, outlook, social background — an attempt to "place" the other — will be made. Also a more subtle evaluation often gets made — whether the other person falls into the same status range as the perceiver. Zetterberg (1966) coined the term 'secret ranking' for the sexual version of this, but the same happens in non-sexual encounters. A relatively unattractive or unpopular person who tries to make friends with — or a sexual partner of — someone much more attractive or popular is likely to suffer a rebuff. Part at least of the "secret ranking" is fairly visible; several studies (Murstein, 1972; Silverman, 1971) have shown that married couples match each other roughly in physical attractiveness. (Berscheid and Walster, 1974a, note that beauty is not wholly in the eye of the beholder; there is a reasonable consensus on standards of appearance.)

The "secret ranking" — together with the factors of social similarity, proximity and so on — allow one to make an indirect estimate of who is likely to be a suitable friend or lover. It is in fact quite possible that two people who are similar in almost every possible respect, as well as physically close, might dislike each other all the same; there is still a lot of variance left unaccounted for. When two people meet they can start trying to decide if the other actually likes them — partly using the non-verbal cues to be discussed later. Sociometric research early on started looking at how good people were at perceiving attraction. Tagiuri (1958) summarised a series of studies noting that people can generally perceive who likes them, but are less good at seeing who dislikes them. In fact people tend to assume that anyone they like returns their liking. Later research on *how* liking is communicated will be reviewed in the 'response' section.

In sexual encounters perception of sexual willingness becomes very important. At a party or dance a predatory male — who generally takes the initiative, see the section on "rules" — "sizes up" the available females. The work of Kinsey *et al.* (1948, 1953) and of many others since (reviewed by Cook and McHenry, 1976), enables some account to be given of reliable cues to sexual willingness (in terms of age, nationality, personality habits and so forth) but systematic data on how good people are at using this information is lacking: many cases of rape are caused by serious misperceptions of sexual willingness. Contact between cultures also sometimes leads to misunderstanding: Cohen (1971) reports that Arab boys in the Israeli-occupied territory imagine that Israeli girls are sexually uninhibited and have intercourse readily with Israeli but not with Arab boys.

First impressions are often similarly stereotyped. Stereotypes can be based on race and nationality: as in the famous case of the "religious", "ignorant" "cruel" Turks documented by Katz and Braly (1935). They can be based on occupation: Skipper and Nass (1966) found that medical students thought nurses sexually promiscuous, and went on to suggest that the prophecy to some extent became self-fulfilling. Some stereotypes are based on appearance: Secord (1958) in a series of studies found that certain faces — those that seem to an outside observer to depart from the all-American ideal — were disliked and distrusted. More specific (and false, or only partly true) predictions are made on the basis of appearance. McKeachie (1952) found that a girl wearing a lot of lipstick was seen as more frivolous and flirtatious, while Thornton (1944) found that men wearing glasses were judged more intelligent. (Subsequently Jahoda (1963), demonstrated that this was one of the stereotypes that had a grain of truth, and later still Argyle and McHenry (1971) found that the stereotype was limited literally to first impressions, vanishing after as little as five minutes interaction.) Gibbins (1969) found that people were prepared to make quite specific predictions about girls wearing different types of clothing, including whether they smoked or not. McHenry (1971) suggested that such expectations — often gross oversimplifications — occur simply because it is impossible to remember every detail of behaviour about everyone one meets, while at the same time one needs to have some sort of expectation about how people will behave.

B. FEEDBACK

Perception is not usually a "one-off" process, although most person perception research has treated it as though it were. In real encounters people do not usually make a single judgement or form a single impression, and then stop, particularly when perceiving moods, intentions, reactions, etc. One of the most useful features of the social skill model is that it takes account of the *sequential* nature of perception, in the concept of "feedback". The initial impression leads to an initial response that has some effect on the other person; and this effect is observed and acted on, producing further changes; and so on. The process is continuous and circular for as long as the interaction lasts. Indeed many responses are made specifically to produce a response in the other that can be perceived; for example questions are asked to clear up uncertain points, and situations created in order to evoke behaviours. Furthermore perception and response tend to occur simultaneously. One of the features of skilled performance — motor or social — is the development of overlapping perception and response; while the operator is responding to what he has just seen, he is already looking ahead to the next part. Seymour (1966) documented this overlapping during the operation of a capstan lathe: Argyle and Cook (1976) discuss the use of gaze in human social interaction to do several things at once, collect information about the other person, tell the listener that the speaker is or is not about to finish speaking, and to convey the speaker's opinion of the listener.

Regulation and Maintenance of Interaction

"Feedback" during a social encounter occurs on a number of levels. At the lowest level (low in terms of length, and probably also low in consciousness) is what Argyle and Kendon (1967) term "regulation", or the "maintenance" of the interaction. Gaze and postural cues, principally, but other cues as well, are used to start the encounter as well as to finish it. Melbin (1972) remarks on the use by one person, e.g. a charity collector, of gaze to get another person's attention, and on the avoidance of gaze by someone who doesn't want to get involved. Several authors from Casanova to Margaret Mead have remarked on the use of gaze in courtship. Recently Rubin (1970), found that couples who scored high on his "Love Scale" looked each other in the eye more than low scorers. Kendon and Farber (1973) found a standard sequence of greeting and recognition in a field study at an open air party; eye contact was made at a distance, accompanied by a wave, then broken until just before the host and guests met to embrace or shake hands.

Presumably these interchanges are learned, although one or two are sufficiently general to permit the suggestion that they might be innate. Eibl-Eibesfeldt (1975) has found the "eye-brow flash" — a swift raising and lowering of the eye-brow — to occur as a sign of greeting or recognition in many cultures.

Another form "regulation" takes is the interchange of the role of the speaker. A well-known study by Kendon (1967) showed that a speaker approaching the end of his utterance looks up at the other person and remains looking steadily. If on the other hand he has merely paused for thought and hasn't finished, he doesn't look up. Kendon's data showed that looking up was a definite signal; when the speaker neglected to give it, the other took significantly longer to realise it was his turn to speak. Most people are unaware of reacting to the other person's gaze patterns in the ways described above but this is not surprising: most people are unaware of the perceptual processes involved in *motor* skills, too. In fact calling people's attention to the role of gaze in "regulation" makes them very self-conscious, having the same disruptive effect that is often produced by making someone think about a tennis shot or gear change. The rapidity with which perception of regulatory signals occur, and the fact of it being largely below the level of awareness has led Argyle and Kendon to postulate an entirely separate channel for such activity, giving a more complex social skill model (Fig. 2).

Gaze also plays a key part in a third type of regulation — the maintenance of emotional equilibrium. Argyle and Dean (1965) postulate that there is an appropriate "level of intimacy" for any given encounter or type of encounter. Thus one should remain fairly detached at a formal party—remaining at the level of small talk. A domestic row on the other hand was a completely different atmosphere. Argyle and Dean suggest that the right level of intimacy is both communicated and maintained by non-verbal behaviour: the distance the people are from each other and the angle between them, the amount of time they look at each, what they talk about, whether they touch each other all set the emotional tone. A person who wants to make friends—and particularly someone who wants to put relations on a sexual footing—will be working towards increasing the emotional tone, whereas a person who wants to remain relatively formal will try to negate the other's moves, in the ways documented by Argyle and Dean and others since. Thus greater distance may be countered by reduced eye-contact (Argyle and Dean, 1965) or increased smiling by reduced eye contact (Kendon, 1967).

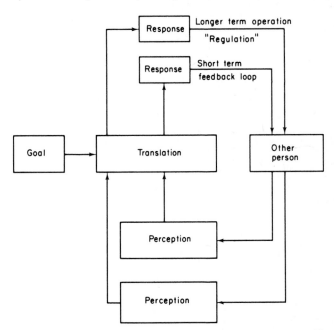

FIG. 2. The two-channel social skill model, after Argyle (1967).

If the use of gaze and other cues in regulation is important in attraction and is learnt, then the possibility is opened that some people fail to learn and will thus be at a disadvantage. They may have difficulty striking up acquaintance with people because they do not react to smiles and eye contact, or fail to make the right reply because they have not learned how to gaze and posture and use the other signals that mediate change of speaker. Their interactions are thus full of interruptions and embarrassing silences. An additional perceptual and feedback failure may mean that they do not realise what type of encounter they are involved in and respond in inappropriate ways. Argyle, Trower and Bryant (1974) studied a series of young people whose personal difficulties were thought to stem from inadequate social skill, and found, among other things, that 52% of them showed "abnormalities of gaze", two thirds looking too much and the other third not looking at all.

Formation of expectancies

The next level of feedback during interaction is generally above the level of awareness — the perception of moods, emotions, reactions, and the anticipation of what the other person is going to do next. Both have received extensive study, very little of it however done in an interaction context. Thus research on facial expression has relied on still photographs as stimuli and asked people to name the emotion expressed using a check list or rating scales (Cook, 1971). Research on tone of voice has used tape-recordings of standard sentences, e.g. "they have bought a new car" (Liberman, 1965) — or of "content free speech". The objections to this type of research have been stated more than once (Cook, 1971; Argyle, 1969); perhaps the most serious is subjects are probably being asked the wrong questions. Extreme emotions, like disgust, fear, anger, probably figure less in building up social relations than relatively subtle variations in approval, interest and animation. Certainly non-verbal behaviour can be shown experimentally to play a major role in determining one person's response to another. Argyle *et al.* (1972) found that the way a message was said accounted for three times as much of the variance in impression formed as did the content; the message was one expressing friendly interest or its opposite.

The prediction of what someone is going to do next — vital for any encounter — similarly has not been studied in interaction setting. Cline (1964) developed a "Behaviour Postdiction Test" in which judges had to predict which of four responses a person would make, in for example a violent argument. Dailey (1971) used a similar task and found that his judges could make on average 50% correct predictions in answers to three choice questions, not much above chance level.

Refining First Impressions

The third level of feedback during interaction has been studied quite extensively in married couples, engaged and courting couples and friends — namely the refining of the first impressions of each other's personality. It is generally held that friends and married couples tend to match each other on personality, attitude and intelligence variables but such similarities — modest as they are — are established experimentally using psychological tests. On the other hand, couples who meet outside the laboratory have to sum each other up without the benefit of questionnaires, relying instead on their own ability to observe and interpret how the other behaves.

Most research on the way people interpret each others' character has painted a depressing picture of partial or total misunderstanding (Cook, 1971), yet there are some grounds for expecting friends and married couples to do better than judges in the typical laboratory study, for they presumably have not only greater incentives to assess the other accurately but also better opportunities. However the evidence does not show that friends and married couples see each other particularly clearly. For example in a study by Clements (1967) married couples were asked to rank the upset caused to their marriage by various problems — selected as significant by the subjects not by the experimenter — such as sexual demands or one partner "not listening" to the other. Husbands' and wives' rankings agreed only 0.35. A study by Katz *et al.* (1960) employed the Edwards PPS to see how well fiancé(s) could perceive each other's personality. For men describing their fiancée's personality, accurate predictions accounted for less than a tenth of the variance, while the assumption of the fiancée's similarity with the fiancé's self accounted for nearly one fifth. The rest of the variance was not accounted for. The girls did slightly better but were still very inaccurate.

Perhaps these samples include a lot of unhappy marriages or ones fated to break up, a suggestion that has been pursued with limited success. Clements's study failed to find any difference between happy and unhappy couples. An earlier study by Dymond (1954), using 55 selected MMPI items, found happy couples could predict 38 of each other's answers correctly, compared with an average of 33 for the unhappy group, and a chance expectation of 27 or 28. Murstein (1970) found that married couples saw each other more accurately than engaged couples, the implication being that some engagements broke up because the couples misperceived each other. To summarise, compatibility does not seem to be able to explain much of the inaccuracy of perception in established relationships.

The survival of relationships between people who misperceive each other can be explained in various ways — some of which will emerge later in the section on rules. The fact of so much misperception can also be explained in several ways. Occasionally the misperception is so extreme as to constitute a psychiatric symptom; Todd *et al.* (1971) reported on a sample of married men who were convinced, generally wrongly, that their wives were unfaithful to them because they thought, again generally incorrectly, that their penes were undersized. An elaborate study by Stephan *et al.* (1971) showed that sexually aroused men rated an attractive girl as more attractive and as more sexually receptive. Schulman (1971) reviews a number of studies on idealisation in engaged and married couples and adds data of his own showing that well over half of a sample of engaged couples failed to realize the extent of disagreement between the man and woman partners.

The list of things to be perceived before and during talking to someone is long and diverse, so it is not surprising to find that people who are good at observing one thing are not necessarily good at perceiving another. What is perhaps surprising is that there seems hardly any transfer from one type of perception to another. Cline & Richards (1960) found modest correlation — the highest correlation out of 21 being 0.44 — between different perceptual tasks, all completed after seeing a filmed interview, while Crow and Hammond (1957) found no correlation at all between ability to judge opinions and personality, and ability to perceive attraction in a group.

C. GOAL

The suggestion that social encounters have goals is an idea that strikes many as cold and manipulative. Some encounters have fairly specific goals (e.g. getting or imparting information) but others have vaguer and more long term aims, like making friends. A number of tests have been constructed to measure the extent and nature of a person's desire to relate to his fellow. For example, the "Fundamental Interpersonal Relationships Orientation" (FIRO), devised by Schutz (1960) yields measures of inclusion, affiliation and control wanted and given. Schachter (1959) has established developmental differences in the strength of people's desire to be with other people; first born and only children like company more than do later born children.

In sexual encounters the goal is more obvious, at least in a superficial sense, namely marriage and/or sexual satisfaction. If one asks why people want to get married or otherwise pair off the answer is again sexual satisfaction, plus the same sort of thing that people get from friendship (Cook and McHenry, 1976). Probably more nonsense has been written about human sexual motivation than about any other topic in psychology. Some men do probably seek a succession of joyless mechanical seductions because they are uncertain of their own virility, but the obvious reason why men seduce women and vice versa is because they enjoy it. Despite the efforts of psychoanalysis not a lot seems to be known about human sexual motivation — apart from the obvious fact there are large individual differences, and that hormone levels do not have much to do with it. A recent study by Larsen (1971) found that length of deprivation hardly correlated with sexual tension experienced or with arousal by a pornographic film. Amount of (pleasant) previous experience, measured by a short questionnaire, containing items like "I find a variety of different partners makes sex more interesting", did correlate moderately with tension and arousal.

Goals enter into attraction at a less general level also. "Affiliative motivation" in practice reduces to some specific aim — getting someone to agree to accompany one somewhere, to remain in one's presence, or in a sexual context, to agree to a progression of sexual intimacies. It is a feature of social skills, like motor skills, that behaviour can be viewed hierarchically with small component sequences of skilled behaviour linking up to form larger sequences and so on.

D. TRANSLATION AND RESPONSE

Every person has a repertoire of social responses: different responses are appropriate for different occasions or different types of people. Thus Inbau (1942), in a standard manual of police interrogation methods, points out that appeal to conscience or attempts to minimise the seriousness of the offence will work on first offenders but will cut no ice with professional criminals, who can only be made to confess by playing on the fear that their accomplices will confess first — the so-called prisoner's dilemma. This illustrates the concept of "translation and mistranslation" — knowing lots of things to do, but doing them in the wrong situation or with the wrong people.

Kirkendall (1961) interviewed a number of young men about their methods of establishing relations with girls and found one man who had got it to a fine art. It is worth describing some of his repertoire to illustrate sequence and strategy in courtship. Kirkendall's informant started by locating a partner and creating a good first impression; working in a woman's clothes shop took care of the former and possessing a good wardrobe of smart clothes ensured the latter (Kirkendall's data was collected in the 1950s; clothes probably matter less today). On the first date he impresses the girl by his car, his experience of motor racing, by demonstrating how many friends he has. He asks the girl for small favours and takes willingness to oblige as a good sign. By the second date he has succeeded in getting the girl in the right frame of mind to steer the conversation to more intimate topics and soon after that, but not before, to start sexual advances. Some of Kirkendall's other informants used cruder and more offensive tactics, ranging from accusing an unwilling girl of being dominated by her parents to threatening to blacken her reputation. A series of studies by Kanin (1969) found that many American college men resorted to force quite readily; 56% of girls reported experiencing repeated acts of "sex aggression".

More systematic experimentally-based accounts of the response side of social skill have been offered by Argyle (1969) or Berscheid and Walster (1969). Argyle emphasises particularly the role of non-verbal behaviour. Liking can be communicated by standing closer to the other person, looking at him or her more (Exline and Winters, 1965; Argyle *et al.*, 1974; Cook and Smith, 1975), smiling (Argyle *et al.*, 1972) "openness" of posture (Mehrabian, 1969) as well as in less obvious or deliberate ways: Hess (1965) suggests that pupil dilation — an involuntary response, of course — can indicate liking or sexual interest. Ekman and Friesen (1969) introduce the concept of "leakage"; attempts to suppress feelings, such as dislike, are not always successful and fragmentary expressions of the person's true attitude may "leak out". Thus Haggard and Isaacs (1966) found "micromomentary" facial expressions, detectable only by slow motion films: these changes — occuring during psychotherapy — were thought to indicate repressed hostility breaking — or "leaking" — through. It has even been claimed by Comfort (1971) that humans attract each other sexually by "pheromones" or sexual odours, as some species of animals and insects do.

Some non-verbal cues can be used to communicate interest in someone other than the person one is talking to. Gaze of course is one such; according to Scheflen (1965) posture can do the same. A man or woman talking to one person can indicate his or her greater interest in someone else by angling the lower part of their body towards the third person rather than towards the speaker. Scheflen also claims that "palm presentation" — facing the palm outwards — is used by American middle class women to indicate sexual availability.

Just as someone who fails to react to the cues that someone else gives will have difficulty striking up a relationship, so someone who himself fails to give appropriate non-verbal cues will find it more difficult to get on with others, to establish rapport as Reiss (1960) terms it. Argyle *et al.* (1974) found that video-taped feedback, assertion therapy, role playing and similar techniques appeared to produce significant improvements in a significant proportion of a group of people complaining of difficulty in getting on with people.

Of course non-verbal behaviour is not the only way to communicate — or create — attraction. More elaborate sequences of behaviour have been described and experimentally studied, including the research on ingratiation by Jones (1964), which demonstrates that the most obvious tactics for winning favour may not always work precisely because they are obvious. An example of a subtle way of making oneself liked may be derived from the 'pratfall' experiment (Aronson *et al.*, 1966). It was reasoned that while people prefer others of superior ability and accomplishments, they are also a little wary of them and hence Aronson *et al.* derived the prediction that if a superior person were humanized by being seen — heard in fact since a tape-recording was used — to make a clumsy blunder then he is seen more favourably. The experiment supported the hypothesis: the clumsy but accomplished person was seen more favourably than an accomplished careful person. The same was not found for a person of average ability, who lost esteem by committing a blunder.

A similarly ingenious study by Walster (1965) has examined the role of self-esteem in courtship. It is a reasonable hypothesis that the higher a girl's opinion of herself the more particular she will be about accepting invitations. Walster found that "failing" a test made a girl much more favourably inclined towards a man she met shortly afterwards, indicating that passing mood — open to manipulation — partly determines the attractiveness of others. A series of studies by Walster *et al.* (1973) showed that "playing hard to get" was not — contrary to folklore — a good tactic for girls. Men were not attracted to girls who were reluctant to accept invitations, nor likely to return to a prostitute who told her clients she only accepted men she liked!

II. Rules and social behaviour

A person making a chair leg is free to use whatever methods he thinks best, but there are serious limits on people's choice of response, when seeking to attract a friend, mate or sexual partner. The restrictions — imposed by custom or even law — are perhaps more obvious in the latter case. Ford and Beach (1952) document a number of restrictions on the form sexual invitations may take, some of them fairly widespread: the most direct approaches in particular tend to be forbidden. Most cultures require men to cover their genitals and virtually all require women to do so. Most cultures again forbid direct requests for sexual favours, although there are a few exceptions: Balinese and Lepcha men can simply ask a girl if she will have intercourse; the men of Jaluit in the Marshall islands are almost as explicit, asking for intercourse by pronouncing the name of the sexual organs; Siriono men can ask directly but must whisper. Women too are almost universally forbidden to ask men to have intercourse; one exception is Bali again, while Lepcha women often do ask directly although they are not supposed to. In most human cultures, however, invitations to seduction or courtship must be made in vague, symbolic or non-verbal ways. A striking example of the former is the custom of "love magic" observed in a number of cultures (Rosenblatt, 1971). The man sets about attracting a girl by acts of magical significance performed *in the girl's presence or to her knowledge,* so that he communicates his interest indirectly. In our society a man asks a girl — or vice versa — to come to see a particular film, not because he especially wants to see it himself, or even because he thinks she wants to, but as a conventional indirect invitation.

It seems odd at first sight that humans — having the gift of language — should use vague, symbolic, easily-misunderstood signals to attract each other. Animals, who must rely on posture, vocalization, smell, etc. to attract mates, at least have instinct to ensure that the signals are understood. In fact the very feature of vagueness is a great advantage in courtship and in attraction in general. The point about direct verbal invitations or statements is that they tend to require direct verbal answers which either commit the speaker or offend the one who asked. Invitations given by non-verbal communication or in symbolic form are not binding on either party and can be withdrawn or refused without causing affront or loss of self-esteem. Naturally this principle will only work if certain other rules are observed too. A person whose invitation to see a film or whatever is refused, should not really press the point too far, for fear of making the rejection personal. (Paradoxically some persistance is often required, especially in heterosexual encounters; part of social skill lies in deciding whether reluctance is real or feigned.) Another, much stronger rule, first remarked on by Goffman (1956), forbids one to comment on non-verbal behaviour in particular or on the interaction in general. A piece of behaviour — a smile, or moving away — may often be just about as clear as the spoken word, but the "taboo on second-order interaction" as Goffman termed it, forbids one to comment on it. It is not done to say things like "why have you moved away, don't you like me" or "why smile if you're not interested". This taboo safeguards the essential feature of non-verbal communication — its vagueness, lack of commitment, the fact that things cannot be "taken down in writing and given in evidence". Goffman's taboo of course has unfortunate consequences for people who are unaware of their own non-verbal behaviour, and inadvertently give off cues to boredom, anxiety or hostility; they are unlikely to find out — without skilled intervention — where they are going wrong.

A particularly striking rule in sexual attraction — again documented by Ford and Beach — concerns who shall take the initiative. In most human societies, the male is required by custom to approach the female, not vice versa. There are few exceptions; Maori women try to attract a man by pinching or scratching his hand — surreptitiously. Among the Kwoma in New Guinea the men are afraid of offending the girl's family by unwanted attentions, so they leave the initiative to her. In a few South Sea islands no distinctions are made and either sex can initiate courtship. Sometimes the prohibition on female initiative is taken literally — the Mbundu in Africa consider the slightest sign of interest by a girl to be shameful — but generally they work to restrict the ways a girl can try to attract a mate to non-verbal ones. The rule about initiative does not apply to non-sexual attraction.

There are also rules about the sequence of events in forming a relationship, which differ widely from culture to culture. For example being asked to someone's home does not signify very much in Britain or the U.S.A. but in some countries, e.g. France, shows much greater involvement and is likely to follow later in a relationship. Sexual relationships also follow sequences; in the West a man who tries serious advances without going first through preliminaries — however perfunctory — of kissing and embracing would be thought crude and aggressive. The Crow Indians of North America had radically different customs;

the man seeking a mate by crawling up to a tent at night and trying to find a woman inside, whose genitals he then stimulates. Sometimes the customary sequences observed in particular cultures — or subcultures — seemed to have developed partly to avoid outsiders being involved by mistake. This is particularly true of deviant sexual groups like homosexuals or wife-swappers. Such groups use private codes (constantly up-dated as they become public knowledge) meet in special places and follow particular dialogues. For example, a male homosexual pickup in London some time ago described by Wildeblood (1956) started by asking for a light and giving a smile; continued with remarks about marriage, why the man was out at that time, and the offer of a drink; and ended its first stage by noting that the pub lacked a friendly atmosphere and naming one that did not — a known homosexual pub. Another more detailed account of such encounters in the U.S.A. is given by Humphrey (1970).

III. The other person

The last box in the social skill model contains, so to speak, the other person whose reactions to one's own responses are perceived. However this is where the analogy with motor skill is not quite correct. The other person is not a passive object — like a tennis ball, a piece of wood, or a motor car — but is an agent, perceiving, selecting a response according to his or her own goal, before making the response. This complicates things but does not make the model invalid. Each person in a dyad has to take into account what the other person will think of his or her responses, what inferences they will draw about his or her goal, etc. One consequence of this has been noted already: the most obvious way of making someone like one is often ruled out, because it is too obvious and will be seen as ingratiation.

A more elaborate analysis — theoretical rather than empirical — is offered by Jones and Gerard (1967) of the cognitive processes that might occur at a first meeting between boy and girl. Figure 3 assumes that the girl has a behavioural repertoire of three responses while the boy has a repertoire of only two, and also assumes that the responses have reward and cost values on an arbitrary scale for the two people. The reward however depends on the joint outcome; a warm smile by the girl coupled with a smile from the boy is rewarding to both, whereas a smile by the girl met by a blank stare from the boy is a definite rebuff to the girl and a positive reward to the boy. According to exchange theory (see chapter by La Gaipa in section 1 of this book) each person predicts what response his move might get from the other and calculates accordingly. Given the — arbitrary — values filled in Fig. 3, this leads to the prediction that the couple will not start an interaction because the potential rewards of being friendly are outweighed by the risk of unreciprocated friendliness. Hostility on the other hand is safe, and may even offer a slight reward if the other blunders and is friendly. This analysis offers some insight but also has a number of limitations. The "rewards" and "costs" filled in are arbitrary, so until a way of measuring them is devised, the model cannot predict anything. It is not clear whether the model will hold for alternating sequences envisaged, rather than simultaneity, reminiscent of childrens' games of scissor, stone and paper. If the boy smiles first, the girl can safely do the same and maximise rewards for both. Finally the scheme seems to ignore the role of rules or norms. Politeness requires people in most contexts to smile at strangers, rather than ignore or scowl at them.

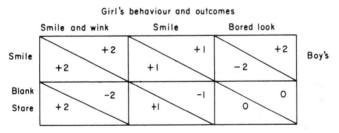

FIG. 3. An example of a "pay-off" matrix (modified from Jones and Gerard, 1967). The behaviour which the girl can adopt is shown at the top of the figure; the boy's possible responses are shown on the side of the figure. The upper triangle of each box indicates the pay-off for the girl from any combination of girl and boy behaviour; the lower triangle indicates the pay-off for the boy for the same combination of behaviours.

IV. Conclusion

To conclude: the process of making friends or attracting a mate requires a positive effort and a skilled performance: it is not simply the clicking together of pieces that happen to fit. A person who does not make the effort — some types of schizophrenic spring to mind — or whose efforts are misguided so that he or she ends up doing everything wrong, will fail to attract anyone. The review in this chapter should suffice to show that the skill analogy is at least useful as a conceptual framework, while the relative success of behaviour therapy programs (which view attraction and social behaviour in essentially the same terms, namely, practice, feedback, and learning) seems further proof of its value. The model also helps point out those areas—both descriptive and therapeutic—which have received much less research effort than perhaps they deserve. Research on social rules is only beginning to get under way (e.g. Collett, 1971); research on responses, especially non-verbal ones, is flourishing (Argyle, 1975); but research on perception, as the author has argued elsewhere (Cook, 1971) is practically stagnant.

17.

Friendship As An Accomplishment: An Ethogenic Approach To Social Relationships

Subfaculty of Philosophy, Oxford University, England

This paper is a research scenario. The idea, so to speak, is to occupy a territory of research, and to try to develop some fairly clear ideas as to where empirical studies can be done and what they might be.

I want to lay out the territory for a study of friendship and hatred, not as products of predisposing or initial conditions, but rather as mutual achievements. Thus I concentrate, not on the features, cues or stimuli, which initiate attraction or dislike, but on the ritual aspect of maintained friendship and hatred—how we manage these as *social* relations. It is important to emphasize the methodology that is involved. From the start, I want to bring out the idea that the study of any type of structured and maintained pattern of interaction, stable enough to get a name, involves two quite distinct sorts of empirical investigations. The first would be microsociological analysis using familiar liturgical and dramaturgical models (Harré and Secord,

1972) trying to discover exactly what these achieve and how they achieve it. As well as exploring such structure and content one must look at the style which must be maintained by the persons involved to make those rituals authentic, that is one must try to identify the kinds of "personas" which have to be maintained. Then, as the first part of a second stage, on the basis of the microsociology one *attributes* to individuals competent in quarrels and friendship and other related activities, the appropriate range of tacit knowledge. We want to say of these people, they know how to do certain things. I would suppose that for most people this knowledge is not explicit, but it can be made so. That is, these people know how to perform rituals, they know how to understand the ritual gestures of others and they know how to conduct themselves in the course of a friendship or quarrel, or litigation, or whatever form the ritual takes.

This is not enough by itself, because it involves only an *attribution* of tacit knowledge. So in the second phase of the second stage investigators have to get at this knowledge through the analysis of such behaviour as gossip, explanatory speech, produced by people with reference to these activities, and then in analysing accounts (the talk commenting upon friendship, dislike, etc.), we can thus supplement and test the attributions of knowledge which we have made on the basis of the microsociological analysis. Two kinds of studies home in then, on some kind of cognitive or conceptual structure, which individuals must have in order to be socially competent.

Another preliminary matter must be brought up which cannot be emphasized enough. There has been a strong tendency in social psychology to study only nice behaviour (Muscovici, 1972). Thus, in this context investigators concentrate on attraction, friendship, dating, courting or marital choice (see chapters in section 1) but for a fuller understanding of social relationships there must be studies of interpersonal repulsion as well as interpersonal attraction. So I want to bring into this research scenario a study of people being nasty, vicious, unpleasant to each other, going in for backyard litigation, successfully maintaining themselves as enemies, because that is *at least* as important a part of human life. If you doubt that, then I think you ought to reflect on the fact that at least a quarter of marriages finish up in some kind of disruption, the public manifestation of a kind of "enemyship" which has been produced by propinquity and frequency of interaction, amongst other things. So I want to concentrate on both positive and negative mutual attitudes and the associated rituals of feeling.

One interesting semantic point—there is no disliking word in English that corresponds clearly to friendship. There is no word for "enemyship". 'Enmity' in fact will not do since it refers to a feeling or state with respect to somebody. It is not a social *relationship* like friendship. There are lots of words like hatred, enmity and so on, but they do not seem to have quite the sense of the opposite of friendship. I suspect there is a good reason for this, namely that we do not have (currently) a very clear idea of what it is to be somebody's rival, enemy, backyard-litigant etc. The same is not true of other languages. I shall use the words *Bruderschaft* and *Feindschaft* for the expressions of ritual and maintained relations of friendship and enmity respectively. I follow here a suggestion by John Breaux, who also pointed out that a similar opposition can be expressed in Spanish, between *amistad* and *enemistad*, the latter being capable of degrees of comparison. I owe to Michael Argyle the suggestion that relations of enmity could take two forms. One form occurs when one is able to avoid the other person and then there simply ceases to be a social relationship. But if you are, say, in an institution or have rooms in the same college, etc. then of course you cannot avoid each other and you do have a stable, hostile state to maintain. It is strange that there is no word for this second form in English, since it happens in situations like institutional propinquity and is reflected in court cases like those between backyard litigants.

It is important to distinguish the kind of study I am proposing from studies of the initial and predisposing conditions of dislike, enmity or friendship. The initial conditions, for example, for some kind of friendship might be some kind of biological interaction—they might be pheromonic for example: people might become friends because they smell alike, or enemies because they do not like the smell of the other person. There is some empirical evidence for this in the study of inter-racial enmity. Biological phylogenitically based processes like Lionel Tiger's (1971) male-bonding are sometimes made a lot of, but I do not regard those processes as having anything to do with the particular project I am concerned with, that is, they are not explanations of the maintenance of social relations, they are simply the conditions under which these relations and their rituals of affirmation occur. The same is true for predisposing conditions, that is, conditions like similarity of attitudes or opinions and so on, which are often offered as explanations of attraction and friendship (Byrne, 1961a). After it has started one is still faced with having to make the friendship *work*. Indeed, one of the interesting things about opinions—at least it strikes me from my own experience — is their remarkable fluidity and change depending upon the people one is with. One of the techniques of maintaining friendship may be to have a sufficiently fluid range of opinions. There is an empirical study to be made here. It is possible that people who are not really skilled at mutual opinion adjustment tend not to be well liked. People find someone who is particularly and uncompromisingly rigid, a bit tiresome.

I. The microsociological analysis

A. ACTION SEQUENCES

In accordance with the liturgical model, we could look at the action sequences which one might have to carry out to be performing a ritual for the creation or maintenance of a friendship or a state of enmity.

Bruderschaft Ritual

It seems to me that there are two quite separate aspects that can be studied: (i) there are ways of speaking to friends, styles of speech manifestly regardless of content. I notice myself adopting a peculiar half-jocular style of speech with friends. I certainly use such a style for indicating and maintaining friendship. The emergence of this style could be explained by seeing it as a kind of test. If one uses language which if it were taken literally by someone would be insulting, and then make it jocular, this could be a test of the friendship of the other person in that as a friend he does not take offence at being called an "old bastard" or whatever happens to be the local expression. (ii) there are uses of speech and action which are strictly ceremonial in character. Alan Cook has pointed out to me, for example, the reference to fighting as a *Bruderschaft* ritual in D. H. Lawrence, (c.f. *Women in Love* Ch. 20., and the night swim, *The Rainbow,* Ch. 12). I was therefore struck when reading some of the literature on inter-personal attraction to see how it stopped short of the things that we do by way of ritual to *keep* our friends and cement our friendships; for example, friendly eating, friendly drinking, offering people drinks, cigarettes, etc. rides in cars and so on. Some work has already been done on food and drink rituals which opens up a dimension of research in which much study could still be done. I refer to Mary Douglas's recent work (Douglas, 1972). She starts with a formal distinction between the structure of "drinks" and the structure of a meal. She shows that these two forms of entertainment are structurally very different. Drinks are unstructured and thus in contrast to meals which are structured. She gives various examples of the difference in the structuring properties. A meal is structured by the fact that each element in the meal, each course, is different. So there is in fact a very distinct syntax for a meal: you cannot set out the sweet first and the soup last while claiming to be serving a proper meal. There are quite definite rules. Justin Leiber (1973) has worked out a transformational grammar for the Burgundian cuisine, which works pretty well. This does not, of course, show that the meal is the message but rather that meals are highly structured objects. In contrast, there is no particular structure for "a drinks". For example, there is no particular number of drinks at a "drinks", though there are a fixed number of courses in a meal. In some cultures where 'drinks' are ceremonially potent, there *are* a fixed number to be taken. On his first trip to Tibet, Sir Edmund Hilary described how he became quite waterlogged with tea, because every time he and his companions went into a Tibetan house they were offered tea. Thirsty from walking he gulped down the first largish wooden mug of tea mixed with rancid cheese. Then a little lady would come along with a big pot and fill the cup to the brim again and look at him until he drank that one too. Then she would come again and he would be "looked" into drinking the third cup. He eventually discovered that there was a three-toppings-up rule amongst Tibetans, ritually satisfied by taking a sip out of your first cup, top up, another sip, top up, and then, the guest having been honoured and the hospitality of the house certified, one is allowed to drink the rest in peace.

Mary Douglas's theory relates the relative unstructuredness of the entertainment, a tea party for example, to the distance from real intimacy of the social relation it expresses. A Sunday morning "drinks", an even less structured entertainment, can thus serve as a kind of first-opening of social relations with people, reflecting the judgement "the sort of people you have in just for drinks". The empirical investigation of the expressive meaning of an entertainment can be explored with the question: who do you have *only* to drinks? In Britain, for example, workmen are given only cups of tea, never meals.

Douglas's argument, then, is that the relative structuredness of a food and/or drink entertainment is a measure of the degree of intimacy that the entertainment expresses. The hypothesis that meals predominate over drinks on the score of expense cannot be sustained empirically. A champagne and caviare "drinks" is less intimate, though more expensive, than spaghetti and meat balls.

The apparent exception, the business or political lunch or dinner, is intelligible within the same framework since it exploits the *metaphor* of intimacy. In the formal meal we have something which takes on the form of an intimacy ritual but *for that reason* becomes a highly formal interaction. Anthropologists have noted the potency of using in a new context something which has a very definite positive property somewhere else in the culture. By so displacing the usage one emphasizes the negative properties of the thing, as for example, entertaining your boss is not an expression of intimacy just because it makes use of an intimate routine.

Mary Douglas does not see the meal as maintaining given structures like the family, but rather identifies the structural gradation from drinks to the meal as constituting an expressive representation of a sequence through which a person can go towards the ratification of intimacy: and by inversion of meaning when one becomes very intimate with somebody then one can share fish and chips out of a newspaper. I owe to Peter Marsh the observation that *prima facie* the Douglas theory provides a model applying only to a very limited range of "social class". If one looks at "working class" rituals, aside from close relatives there is not much inviting of people to dinner. So at this point the model breaks down, because intimacy is ratified by "going out together". We need another project, complementary to Mary Douglas's to look at how intimacy is "done" amongst cultures other than the British professional classes. Inversion is frequent, I believe, in anomic communities, people who are not very intimate tend to invite each other to a meal. Mary Douglas's hypothesis that passage through more structured objects, more structured rituals, is passing a person through degrees of greater intimacy, needs two further dimensions added, (i) that when a relation goes beyond a certain degree of intimacy, then ratification rituals become less and less structured, and (ii) that when one wishes to express a purely formal relation, though a close one, the rhetoric of friendship may be used, metaphorically and without irony.

There is a way of expressing friendship and similar relations which interests me and which has not been tackled by Mary Douglas. It is the practice of inviting various categories of people to life-cycle events like funerals, christenings, weddings, etc. I suspect that amongst "working-class" people, the decision as to who you invite to funerals is crucial as an expression of who you regard as friends, comparable in formal intimacy with sharing in family rituals. Similarly, the question of who you invite as witnesses to weddings may be important. These questions require a close cross-cultural examination because the funerals of other cultures, e.g. Negro funerals in the United States, involve the principle that the *more* people you invite the better it is, because you show although you were poor when you were alive you are able to get together a vast concourse when it matters. But this reading seems to trade upon a semantics of friendship, since it is surely a concourse of *friends* that is the symbolic object aimed at. That makes their funerals look a bit like our weddings. I think our funerals are rather different, in that despite the decline in formality and public display of funeral rituals there still remains some ritual work to be done. One wonders what it is. For example, Alan Cook has suggested the microsocial study of categories of invitations as such with respect to their social meaning.

Feindschaft Ritual

Correspondingly I think, it would be important, following Muscovici's advice, to look at *Feindschaft* rituals and the form and occasion of humiliation ceremonials. I think there are two aspects here too. (i) There are ways of speaking with people to express your dislike and to actively create bad feelings in another. Here are two examples of speech designed to create anger or a disagreeable response, 'nasty speech'. I call these 'needlings'. English is very rich in syntactical refinements and lends itself to very fine grain needling. Consider the following example reported to be particularly destructive by a participant.

A. Shall we go by the coast road?
B. (wearily) As you like.

The little word "as" does the damage. Compare that exchange in the theatre of the imagination with the more harmless style of:

A. Shall we go by the coast road?
B. (wearily) If you like.

Now what does this little shift from "if" to "as" achieve? Glossing the first style, we get something like this: — "Of course, I wouldn't go by such a stupid route, but if you insist I suppose I'll have to put up with it". B's response in the second dialogue is the harmless "I'm quite indifferent. Either way would be equally boring but we've got to get there somehow". The subtlety of this kind of commonplace syntactical refinement in English allows for a second phase in the needling of A by B. Should A challenge B with the logically soft answer, "O.K., we'll go by the hill", thus refusing the needle, and amplifying the logical implications of B's "as" by making B's preference for the inland route explicit, B can initiate the second phase with, "Did I say to go that way"? This is the same move as Berne (1966) identifies in his life-game "Corner". In the context set by the original use of "as" this is now B's proper response, since B is not really keen to go by the inland route, being intent upon a needling. The proper upshot of this exchange would not be topographical but social, i.e. A's angry silence.

But English syntax contains a nasty little surprise for those who grasp the "as/if" distinction in such cases because there is another dialogue in which "if" itself becomes a needle. For example, a child, "Can I go out now?" "You can, *if* you like". When "if you like" is meant as an addendum to the alternative unqualified "O.K. All right", then the "if" formula is a needle, meaning something like "if you insist", implying an irrationality or perversity in the child's background of wants.

These are kinds of speech which are designed to be irritating and we need to identify a lot more of them. They are not full-scale, formal *Feindschaft* rituals but little ways of talking which are designed to make someone feel angry, injured, nasty and so on; the small change of *Feindschaft,* so to speak.

Needlings do seem to have a general structure, something like this: the technique of needling requires an apparently harmless opening pair of remarks by A and B. But B's remark contains two aspects; it has a literal sense and it has the sense in which it could be used as a needle. If A foiled the initial needle by taking B's needle implication and replying to it, then B has a further move open, namely, "I meant it literally". The detailed structure then emerges. B's remark implies q literally and r as needle. If A takes implication r, then B says, "No, I didn't mean r, I meant q. And what's more you're rat for implying that I'm such a rat as to mean r". Such dialogue seems to me to have a kind of structural property which opens the way for B to trap A into seeming to denigrate the relationship which A and B ought to have. This structure is probably very general.

One must not suppose that these *Feindschaft* ritualized needlings are disruptive, that is: necessarily lead to a break up of the relationship. I think for example in marriage, where people are forced into intimacy, a complex relationship exists which involves some *Bruderschaft* and some *Feindschaft*. The relative quality in the marriage, say, does not depend on whether *Feindschaft* is totally absent but how it is managed and how sustaining it is.

As Berne (1966) seems to imply, some rituals of *Feindschaft* turn out to be highly sustaining to a relationship. I think he has some good examples in the book of games of action-sequences which are if taken literally rather vicious, but since they are played in a ritual way they simply tend to keep the formal relationship going.

(ii) Much less is known about contemporary ritual ways of maintaining a stable, hostile relationship. Social psychologists have tended to look at attraction and altruism rather than their opposites, and even the great Goffman has concentrated more on person supportive rituals such as "face work" than the ritual maintenance of hostility. Ritualized internal family *Feindschaft* has been revealed by Berne in some of his famous "games" and I have myself collected examples of formalized family quarrels and disputes which seem to express the hostile aspect of the usual inter-family ambivalences. A great deal remains to be done, both in the collection of examples and in their analysis and classification and in the investigation of how they work.

In the past there have been much more publicly visible forms of *Feindschaft*-maintaining rituals. I distinguish these into two broad categories, negative rituals where a point of the ritual is a ceremonial and stylistic display of lack of interaction. The obsolete practice of the "cut", the stylized refusal to acknowledge or greet someone, was an example of a negative ritual. Peter Collett has drawn my attention to a good descriptive exposition of this ritual in Wildeblood (1965). Positive rituals, on the other hand, involve hostile but stylized interaction. The hostile actions are strictly controlled by rule. A duel does not fit this pattern since it is not sustaining of the *Feindschaft* relationship, rather it is a formalized way of resolving it. Feuds, on the other hand, are sequences of interaction by which enmity is sustained according to rule. Two avenues of historical research suggest themselves. Feuds seem to have been conducted quite non-violently at times, particularly amongst village women in the past. Historical sources such as the novels of Jane Austen and works of social anthropology such as *Lark Rise to Candleford,* ought to provide material for a study of the forms of such non-violent views. Anthropologists have studied the violent or blood feud and there should be little difficulty in abstracting their material as far as it reveals formal structures into the social psychological study of *Feindschaft*. Finally, a comparative study of the violent and non-violent forms could usefully be undertaken to try to discern any formal parallels in the initiation, maintenance and resolution of the state of enmity.

B. STYLE

So far we have been looking at the action-sequences to see the ritual work being done without looking at what the upshot of that work might be with respect to the expressive *style* of personas. There is a study which ought to be undertaken on the basis of the dramaturgical model, of how an individual sets about appearing as a friend or enemy in a particular culture, *over and above what he does*. What sort of personal style is involved in friendship? In some cultures it is an effusive style. In some it involves an extremely cool kind of expression and effusiveness would be a mark of the friendship not being sincere. There is a sort of cool style amongst very intimate friends with almost no overt interaction response. Goffman (1971) has pointed out how behaviour in public places involves the manifestation of the social groupings of the people in a public space. The social units of street and plaza are not necessarily individual people. He has coined the term "with" for a pair or larger grouping who are manifestly moving through the space and interacting with its other inhabitants as a unit. A "with" is recognized as such by the other people in the space. Goffman argues that the recognition devices form a continuous sequence of formal gestures, postures and so on, which are expressive of the relationship. These he calls "tie signs". A boy holding a girl's arm is a blatant tie sign, whereas differential distancing is a fairly subtle one. I would venture the hypothesis that the tie signs of those at the beginning of a relationship, conscious of the need for public display, are blatant and overt, and as the intimacy and the routine character of the relationship develops become more subtle.

Unfortunately, Goffman has confined his observations to *tie*-signs. But those in a state of enmity, who wish to be seen to be *not* together, are certainly broadcasting their relationship with *un*tie signs. A child in a huff with its parents, studiously avoids their company, publicly, pointedly gazing at different window displays, shrugging off a tentative placating hand with a sharp upward and sideways movement of the shoulder girdle. What are the untie signs by which one broadcasts "I'm not with him"? Perhaps some budding ethogenist can record the means by which a respectable citizen dissociates himself from a "with" thrust upon him by a persistent and importunate drunken beggar. I think it would be interesting to try to see whether the differences in rituals for friendship-work amongst different cultures has some match with the kind of persona that seems to be representative of friend*ship* in that culture. But there is a complication in this. It seems to me (on looking around at people) that the persona style appropriate to the occasion depends on how frequently one sees a friend, rather than on the depth and quality of the friendship. There is an uncharacteristic effusiveness permitted amongst Anglo-Saxons if one has not seen someone for a very long time, or if they have been in hospital etc., whereas to produce the same sort of effusiveness every day, would be an embarrassing solecism.

C. ACTS

The last aspect of ritual I want to deal with is the upshot of performing these action sequences, that is the problem of what acts are performed. It seems to me that obviously the first thing to consider is that the ritual work does actually produce some change in the social world, i.e. does produce friendships or create states of enmity. It might be that the two people might agree to be rivals and there might be a rival-type ritual as amongst schoolchildren near the top of the class. You recognize that you are rivals and you adopt a rivalry-sustaining expressive style.

I think one wants to distinguish sharply at this point between the effect of the friendship creating activities and actions and the creation of feelings whether agreeable or disagreeable. There is a rather complex social psychological problem here because, following the lines developed by Schachter (1964), emotion is to be analyzed as a feeling 'multiplied' by an interpretation. The interpretation of course comes in great part from what social work has been thought to have been done. It *might* be that there is a kind of feeling associated with friendship, namely friendliness or whatever it is—amiability, etc.—which is much more a product of the work, of the meaning-giving operation, than it is of any kind of bonding gut-feeling which relates people together. I suspect that this will turn out to be the case, but it needs looking into as an independent research project.

Secondly, I think it is also the case that people could be quite definite rivals or enemies without a feeling of hatred for one another. I think the feeling of hatred is a rather special feeling and may not go along with being an enemy. Indeed there are times I believe when the feeling of hatred goes along with a predominant social relation of friendship. Sometimes, I suspect, the very demand that friendship puts upon one may lead to occasional flashes of hatred between intimates. Feelings do not, I believe, accurately reflect the social relationships that are dominant in one's life. They rise and fall, pass from the positive to the negative pole, and back again, in ways yet to be fully understood. A spectacular example, alarming to the new parent, is the way one sometimes hates one's beloved child. This is a commonplace phenomena, which does not lead to a crisis amongst people who are well adjusted and fades away when the moment of irritation has gone.

In addition to the formation of a social bond by public ritual acknowledgement, there is something else involved in social rituals, namely the "scenario". The *act* therefore has two aspects, the creating of the bond and the determination of the form of the future. It is rather illuminating, social psychologically, to look at the text of the marriage ceremony. It involves two kinds of propositions. It tells you what you are supposed to do to get married, but it does not stop at that. It also tells you in a general way, about what you are supposed to do after you are married. It gives a kind of scenario of the married state. It mentions things like the help one is to have of the other. Then there are sentences from St. Paul and St. Peter about marriage, such as "Wives, do not rail at your husbands". There is much reference to the future in a rather general, strategic way. So that marriage is represented not just as a matter of forming the social bond between two families, but also a commitment by bride and groom to a generalized scenario of the future. I suspect that in the case of friendship there are also culturally dependent, but in some cultures fairly definite ideas, about what the scenario is that a friend is supposed to act within.

I expect the differences amongst cultures to be quite sharp. I noticed in Pakistan that there was a highly ritualized way of getting to be friends and consequently friendship involved a very structured and hence demanding scenario. If you agreed with someone that you were their Friend, then you had all sorts of commitments. I remember failing very badly on one occasion. Having become Friends with a Pathan, I ran into a friend of his down the town and went with him to the cinema. This led to much anguish and rituals of offended dignity, because it was claimed that if you are a Friend, then you can't go to the cinema with anyone else. Friendship among Pathans is *Bruderschaft* and involves a very highly structured scenario.

The idea that friendship and *Feindschaft* as much as the more formalized social relationships, like marriage and business partnerships, involve scenarios of the general form of the future, implicit to be sure, ought to reveal itself in the many classical studies of the relationship, particularly amongst those cultures where friendship has a specially honoured place in the hierarchy of social relationships. Ancient Greece should provide such a context.

I thought it would be useful to look up Aristotle's discussion of friendship and, as in so much, it turns out that he was there before us. After a little amateur social psychology concerning the conditions for friendship such as similarity of opinions and frequency of meeting, he goes on to give three scenarios for friendship, i.e. expositions of what friends are committed to. He uses, interestingly enough, the idea of having a "motive" once you have committed yourself to being a friend of someone. "They whose motive is utility have no friendship for one another really but only insofar as some good arises to them from one another". A very low form for friendship is characterized by that scenario. A slightly better form involves "That they have friendship for men of easy pleasantry, not because they are of a given character but because they are pleasant to themselves". "Finally for perfect friendship — for those men who wish one another's good in similar ways, insofar as they are good" (that is have plans which are noble in the Aristotelian ideal) "Those are specially friends who wish good to their friends for their sakes." Either party loves his own good and repays his friend equally, both in wishing well and in the pleasurable. Aristotle also notices that there are different principles of justice between different kinds of friends, so if you are friends of equal social status, a distributive ideal of justice is appropriate, but if friends are unequal, then the high status one owes more to the low status one, than the low status one owes to the high status one. This is a rather nice Aristotelian concept in that in rather less civilized societies it is sometimes thought that the low status one owes more to the high status one because the high status one shows great condescension in taking notice of his inferior.

Steve Duck has pointed out to me that the Aristotelian concept of friendship is derived fairly directly from the account given by Socrates in the *Lysis*. In that dialogue there is an exploration both of the psychological conditions for interpersonal attraction and an investigation of the conceptual structure of the idea of a proper or perfect friendship. Plato, like Aristotle, rejects as inferior those human relations which in one way or another involve the exploitation of the partner by the original actor and finds the only proper form of friendship as an ideal relationship among males in the reciprocal effort to enhance the good of the other. There are interesting complexities in the *Lysis* having to do with the differences which existed in Greek society between male/female relationships and male/male relationships. This suggests that the phenomenon of *Bruderschaft* or *Feindschaft* ought not to be considered, at least initially, in a transcultural setting but should be examined in relation to other kinds of interpersonal relationship which exist in the society, such as that between parents and children, husbands and wives, and so on.

There ought, correspondingly, to be scenarios for steady, socially sustained hatred. What is one supposed to do when one hates somebody and wishes to maintain a *proper* flow of hostile acts? Is there anything in our culture which informs one? I think a great deal of empirical work is needed to fill this out, because *officially* we are not supposed to hate anyone. But I am convinced that when people in enmity bear *Feindschaft* to one another, they have to set up a continual state of hostility and a strategic life pattern which is a life of enmity, of which, for example, the "I'm not speaking to you" life-pattern may be one.

But I do think there is one part of our culture where it is clear that the scenarios of what you do with people you dislike are explicit and widely discussed, and that is amongst children. "Why did you do that to so and so?" "Well, you see, she's my enemy". This legitimizes a range of action which is predetermined and formalized. It does not include stabbing or poisoning, but it does include writing nasty notes to somebody else, preparing "traps", and other actions within a certain range of accepted meanings, for if the "enemy" does not read the action as meaning enmity, its *social* steam is lost.

The next stage of this research would involve the examination of intergroup ritualized hostility, the microsociology and social psychology of the feud. I think one would find complementary relationships to those that bind individuals but the matter is more complicated because there would be relationships *between* the people in each group which would be involved in determining what the structure of hostile interaction is to be. In this chapter I am interested only in the cases where two individuals are involved in the attempt to explore their ideas of what it is to be a friend or an enemy or whatever, and their ideas of what ritual is available for sustaining the relationship; that is, in the cognitive resources they must draw upon to maintain the socially defined state. In the case of a feud there is a "political" dimension, illustrated by the discussion around the kitchen table, with the chianti and the spaghetti bolognese, while the family tries to figure out what it would be proper to do back to the Dominici; in short there is a social dimension to the preparation of the action-patterns, taking us away from social psychology, the study of the individual and his preparation and resources for meaningful action.

II. Account analysis

All this is microsociology and in accordance with the principles of ethogenic methodology it needs supplementing with a collection of people's own stories about their friendships, enmities and so on. Analysis of such material would allow one to try to see if the isomorphic cognitive structures appeared in the accounts that had been attributed to competent performers in the microsociological analyses. This, of course, would be partly interactive, since some of the ritual action is carried on through what people are saying about the interaction, and the speech which accompanies also seems to accomplish it, at another level.

The ethogenic scheme depends upon distinguishing the uses of language involved in making what we do and say intelligible, clarifying or sometimes even creating its meaning, and those uses which involve the technique of warranting the action, making it seem proper and socially apt at the moment and in the action sequence it appears. Sometimes this involves commentary upon a particular action, sometimes wholesale reconstrual of the sequence, the fragment of social life into which the action fits. There are a variety of techniques for accounting, the original classification going back to Austin's distinction between excuses and justification (Austin 1961). A much finer grain taxonomy has been recently developed by Backman (1976) in response to his analysis of real justificatory speech. For our purpose account analysis serves the dual function of revealing how people make their actions intelligible and warrantable and of revealing the broad structure of cognitive resources they bring both to accounting and to social action, their definitions of social interactions and their rules for acting in such situations. Further analysis *subsequent to accounting studies* using the methods of G. Kelly, reveals finer structures, and as Mischel (1964) has shown, the constructs elicited by the method are also rules of action. And all this whirl of analytical activity depends upon the material being available for analysis. As a preliminary then, we need

(i) the patient collection of examples of speech relevant to the interpretation and formal clarification of actions *as* friendly or hostile.

(ii) the creation of contexts of justification wherein accounts are elicited which are concerned with demonstrating the propriety of what went on with reference to the fixed points of showing *Bruderschaft* or *Feindschaft*.

(iii) Since we are concerned not just with the synchronic analysis of an existing stable relationship but with the techniques of its creation and maintenance, we need another kind of document, to reveal the diachronic structure of the relationship—a kind of friendship (and enmity) diary in which the stages, both attitudinal and ritual, are recorded. I have assumed on anecdotal grounds alone earlier in this paper, that as friendship ripens ritual eating maintenances of friendship passes through the sequence from unstructured meals to structured meals to casual meals. We need more systematic evidence for such hypotheses.

The formal status of "being a friend" and "being an enemy" is recognized and socially very potent amongst children and casual observation suggests that these categories are maintained by quite definite ritual proceedings, say of exchange of treasures amongst "friends". The fragility of these relationships amongst children and their regular cessation and renewal elsewhere should make them a prime research target. The free commentary method introduced by Secord and Peevers (1974) in their study of children's conceptions of the personhood of others, could easily be extended to elicit commentary upon their friends and enemies and the ritual actions associated with the creation and maintenance of these categories.

Children also seem to have very definite ideas as to what is required of one after the ritual sealing of the relationship, the act-scenario, and it ought to be possible both to elicit such scenarios and to check the match of actual behaviour towards friends and enemies against its descriptions. My own rather scattered observations suggest that much of the treatment of formal enemies is in the realm of fantasy, children devising all kinds of traps and snares for the persons in this category which they make only sporadic attempts to realise. A comparative study of adults' *Feindschaft* fantasies might be very illuminating.

These are some of the ways account analysis could be pursued to complement the microsociological analysis of the routines and rituals we observe and of course our observings are, in part, a product of *our* own cognitive resources for the management and understanding of the rituals of friendship and enmity.

18.

Predictability, Power and Vulnerability in Interpersonal Attraction

PETER KELVIN

University College, London

This essay is *not* about the factors which make one individual attractive to another. It is an attempt to analyse the nature of attraction and, particularly, what happens to the "attracted" individual. It will take us through an examination of more general aspects of social behaviour such as power, conformity, roles and person, and, ultimately into a look at the self-concept, privacy and vulnerability. In the first place, however, it is necessary to provide a broad conceptual framework. For this purpose I shall use the approach which I adopted in *The bases of social behaviour* (Kelvin, 1970): it is an "approach" rather than a "theory".

I. The conceptual framework

The starting point must be a consideration of man as a species. Compared with others, man is unique in his ability to control his environment. He can do so because of his ability to learn: he is able to learn because relatively little of his *behaviour* (as distinct from his anatomy and basic physiological processes) is genetically programmed. If he were thus programmed his scope for learning would be much restricted, because he would have to react to the environment in terms of genetically pre-programmed patterns of response. The paradox, as it were, is that the distinctive genetic programme of man works to the effect that the extent to which he is programmed is relatively limited.

However, any native potential for learning from and manipulating the environment can only be realized if there exist some regularities in that environment—or at least if such regularities are *perceived* to exist. One cannot learn from a constantly changing environment (except that it is constantly changing), nor can one manipulate it: manipulation depends on prediction, and prediction depends on perceived regularities and inferences from them. It therefore follows that we have to stipulate, on purely logical grounds, that man has a need for an at least apparently ordered environment.

Here it is useful to distinguish between the "physical" and the "social" environments. I have set out the argument more fully elsewhere (Kelvin, 1970) and shall confine myself to its gist. Inasmuch as man is regarded as a physical system, to that extent his behaviour is constrained by the properties of that system: a six foot man cannot walk upright through a five foot door. Looked at more closely, however, this system has much that is not programmed, though it is capable of becoming programmed. Hence, when two or more such systems (that is, people) come into relationship with one another, the possible ways in which they might interact may, theoretically, be regarded as innumerable. Yet if the *possible* ways in which men could interact were *actually* innumerable, individuals in direct contact with one another might eventually and laboriously establish systematic relationships; but any wider, more casual, interpersonal relations would be impossible. In practice, of course, a given individual, born into a given society, grows up and operates within its particular structural and functional constraints. The crucial point, however, is that whatever the social "properties" of a particular society, they are not "inherently necessary": as a species, as part of his physical condition, man may have to procreate, but the socially acceptable arrangements for doing so vary from culture to culture; even more significantly, the cues which stimulate this activity (and which on a simplistic biological approach might be assumed as *par excellence* subject to genetic programming) differ not only between cultures but also within them, as a function of fashion.

Since the social environment does not have inherent properties (or at least very few, such as those which may be imposed by, say, geographical conditions), the order which it manifestly does have is made by man himself; and the basic processes of social behaviour (attitudes, norms, roles, power, and so forth) may be regarded as means by which a potentially chaotic and unpredictable environment is shaped into a predictable and manageable one. But of course, there are many things to be ordered, many ways of ordering them. If an order is to be more than aesthetically pleasing, as the cosmology of a schizophrenic may well be, it has to be *valid*. Once again the core issues are the need for predictability and the differences in this respect between the physical and the social environment. The functional criterion of the validity of a system of ordering is its potential for generating predictions which are fulfilled. In the case of objects considered in terms of their physical properties, such orders and predictions are defined by and deduced from these inherent properties. But — however tacit and perhaps accidental — order in the social environment is made by man and can be unmade by him. Miracles apart, a man who jumps from a skyscraper will "conform" to the "laws" of gravity, and hurt himself: in a social setting, anyone can be a non-conformist; as such he may experience anything from severe retribution to complete tolerance; and he may, through his non-conformity initiate change in the very social order itself. Hence, order in the *physical* world flows from its inherent properties, and so does our ordering of it, inasmuch as we can grasp it; order in the *social* world exists inasmuch as its members accept it. Expanding a little on Festinger's (1954) concept of "social reality", an individual's perception of the social order is "valid" to the extent that his perception is similar to that of others, inasmuch as he and they accept the same assumptions concerning it. But assumptions may be rejected — in a way in which the operations of gravity simply cannot be. However great the pressure to comply, an individual can reject the faith of his fathers, the traditions of his people, the norms of his group. Acceptance or rejection of the social order depends on the evaluations of the individuals who compose it; in the final analysis it is therefore an order based on values, not on physical necessity.

From this standpoint, "interpersonal attraction" might be regarded as simply one of the basic processes whereby the individual orders his social environment in terms of his relative preferences for the various people he encounters. Having arrived at such an order (more or less fixed) he can manage his personal relations with them — predict his reactions to them, their reactions to him. The predictions need not be made articulate on every occasion: they may operate as in an acquired skill and become "conscious" only when, as in a skill, something goes awry. But although the notion of attraction as a process of ordering to gain predictability has a certain seductive charm, and although it contains some truth, it is really rather superficial. It says too much, and therefore too little. It would "explain" the attractiveness of similarity of attitudes in terms of the appeal of consensual validation of reality: dissimilar but complementary attitudes it would "explain" in terms of the need of the attracted to find a structure for issues which he has not resolved or cannot resolve for himself. An explanatory principle which can cope so easily with phenomena which are at some level contradictory needs to be treated with caution. I would also resist the tempting inference (it would not be a logical implication) that predictability is itself attractive. Certainly it is hard, even impossible, to form a relationship with someone who is wholly unreliable, unpredictable: yet to be totally predictable is almost equally deadening to relationships, as in the often sad loneliness of the long-distance marriage. It is therefore important not to be simplistic in adopting the concepts of order and predictability: the need for order and predictability may be basic, and the recognition of this may make a fruitful starting-point for enquiry: but the need is also very general.

At this point I should say that I am a new-comer to the field of interpersonal attraction. I have acquainted myself with its literature, but I cannot claim long or exhaustive knowledge of it. As a newcomer I have been struck by a number of features. There has been much concern with problems of methodology (cf. sections 1 and 2). There has been much work on the factors which make for attractiveness, on the antecedents of attraction in reinforcement and learning, on the mutual mediation of rewards between attracted people. But there also seems to be a lack of definition of what is meant by attraction, and therefore of any clear delineation of the phenomenon which is the subject of study. This lack of definition, beyond the assertion that attraction is an attitude to another person, was also pointed out by recent reviewers more competent than I (Marlowe and Gergen, 1969; Huston, 1974). The problem may be that the focus of attention has been partly misplaced. It seems to have been primarily on the *stimulus* side of the phenomenon, on what it is that is *attractive*. The difficulty here is that so many things can be attractive in so many ways: from groin-response to sex-appeal to perceived commonality of ideals. Something may therefore be gained from considering attraction in terms of the kind of response which is evoked, rather than in terms of the stimuli which evoke it. For while the stimuli may be widely diverse, it is, I suggest, the response to them which is the criticial and definitive factor, and common to all phenomena of interpersonal attraction. I shall therefore concentrate on *attraction as a response of the attracted*, and on its implications for him. In relation to the conceptual framework which I have outlined, I shall take it as an axiom that to find someone attractive is to value him within a given context; the more complex, less obvious, issues of attraction considered as a response may then be seen as both directly and indirectly related to predictability.

II. Attraction and power

When attraction is considered as a response it must have some unique and discriminable behavioural characteristics; and although I use the word "behaviour" in its wide sense, to include beliefs and feelings as well as overt actions, the attracted individual must still behave in ways which are distinguishable from those of the indifferent. Now, attraction is a response to another person. This implies that the behaviour of the attracted is somehow affected by the other. This means, in effect, that interpersonal attraction is not only a special case in the study of attitudes but also in the study of *social power*. It is again symptomatic of the stimulus oriented approach to attraction that when power has been discussed (e.g. Heider, 1958; Tedeschi, 1974), it has been considered not as a form of *relationship* but rather as a *property* of the attractive. Yet fundamentally the attractive has no such property — and that fact, and its consequences, is the core of our problem.

Social power refers to a causal relationship between the more and the less powerful; the causal relationship is such that the behaviour of the less powerful is modified by the intervention of the more powerful — the less powerful acts in ways in which he would *not* have acted without that intervention. However, the more powerful is only one factor in the situation, he does not determine the behaviour of the less powerful, he merely alters the relative probabilities of the lesser's possible courses of action (this definition is an amalgam of Emerson, 1962; Simon, 1957; Dahl, 1957; cf. Kelvin, 1970). On this basis interpersonal attraction would be reflected in the modification of the behaviour of the attracted by the attractive — and the degree of attraction may then be gauged by the extent to which the attracted behaves in ways in which he would *not* have done without the "intervention" of the attractive. A "measure" of this might be obtained by a suitable adaptation of scales of "behavioural intention" as developed by Triandis (1964) or Fishbein and Raven (1962). But this still leaves the question of the nature of power in interpersonal relations.

French and Raven (1959), in a classic paper, distinguished five "bases" of social power: reward power (based on incentives), coercive power (based on fear of punishment), legitimate power (as vested in a group leader), expert power (of a doctor, lawyer, plumber), and referent power (as of a pop idol). In doing so they provided a rudimentary taxonomy of species of power, but failed to recognize that these five bases reduce to *two* whose psychological characteristics are utterly different. Reward and coercive power modify behaviour through behaviour control, by means of the positive or negative sanctions available to and distributed by the more powerful. The expert or reference figure has no power in this sense. Legitimate power is a cross-breed to which I shall return. Now behaviour in response to power may be considered as conforming behaviour. The two basic forms of power may then be identified in the language of conformity. Reward and coercive power, rooted in sanctions, lead to *compliance*: the less powerful complies to gain the rewards or to avoid the punishments at the disposal of the more powerful; and his compliance may be no more than public compliance. Expert and referent power are based on *acceptance*: the expert is no expert unless he is accepted as such; the reference figure is selected and accepted as a model by the referring individual. The hybrid "legitimate power", which may cut across the other four, is also a case of acceptance: the less powerful accepts the "right" of the more powerful to influence him.

To the distinction between compliance and acceptance it is necessary to add that between "role" and "person". Through an abuse of analogy and a misplaced application of Occam's Razor, it has become fashionable to look on all human relationships as role relationships. There are times when it is wiser to turn from William of Occam to Thomas à Kempis: "Teach us, oh Lord, to distinguish things that differ". In its strict sense, "role" refers to the functional relations between positions in a social structure — functions which may be, or are expected to be served by whosoever occupies those positions. The concept of a "person" refers to an individual in terms of his unique characteristics, in terms of the idiosyncrasies which he brings to the performance of any role he may hold (Emmerich, 1961). Concepts of roles and of persons are both "constancies" which give stability to the social world, but they do so in very different ways. The concept of a role is a constancy in that it transcends variations between divers individuals in the *same role*; the concept of a person is a constancy in that it transcends variations of behaviour of the *same individual* in divers roles. The widely recognized interplay between roles and person cannot be analyzed and understood unless the two concepts, and the two different constancies to which they refer, are kept distinct; nor would it be feasible to examine and explain role conflict without this distinction (Kelvin, 1970). There may at times be a similar interplay between compliance and acceptance. Compliance may lead to acceptance, perhaps particularly when it is based on reward. Some such process is postulated in Bem's (1972) self-perception theory and in Kelman's (1958) theory of attitude change; and it is implicit in Allport's (1937) earlier concept of the functional autonomy of motives. Conversely, exchange theory implies the possibility of acceptance leading to compliance: the overall acceptance of a relationship, as in a marriage, may lead to reciprocal compliance of the partners according to some of their specific needs and wishes.

Nevertheless, although the distinctions between acceptance and compliance, and between roles and persons may become superficially blurred in daily living, they remain fundamental and essential to the analysis of interpersonal attraction. Attraction is to the person; his "power" is based on acceptance. Compliance is either to brute force, or it may be to the demands of a role—in that the role occupant may in one sense "accept" these demands and yet dissociate himself from them in terms of his concept of himself as a person. It is, of course also possible that a given individual is attractive in a role, solely by virtue of that role—so that any other body in the same role would be equally attractive: there is some evidence for that (Cohen, 1958; Hurwitz, Zander and Hymovitch, 1962). However, in such a case, the attraction would be specific to the role situation. (It would be similarly specific to the situation in any instance of compliance, whether to force or to the demands of a role.) The attraction to a *person* is not thus situation specific, precisely because the concept of a "person" transcends such specificities. For example, even if one initially encounters someone in a role, I suggest that one's liking or dislike of him as an individual relates to the concept one gains of him as a person: if, for instance, one finds him "warm" (cf. Asch, 1946), this is to make a forecast (Altman, 1974) about his likely behaviour in general — because he is (assumed to be) that kind of person, and it is assumed that this will show in all he does. Like McCall (1974), therefore, I believe that we must treat the term "inter*personal* attraction" strictly, so that it refers to the attraction of one *person* for another. But a person *qua* person, that is, the individual outside a defined role (as distinct from in a defined role) does not have the resources of sanctions to modify behaviour, to induce compulsion — except brute force. Consequently, any changes in behaviour as a result of being attracted must have their basis in the *acceptance* by the attracted of the attractive.

The attraction is, of course, a product of evaluation. However, this needs to be examined further. Let us for the moment regard the attractive individual as if he were an object. We would then distinguish between the "properties" inherent in that object and the qualities attributed to it, as it were, between its primary and secondary qualities. In social relations, superior physical strength might be one such property and so, though in more complex ways, might be strictly defined roles and the demands which they make on their occupants. However, the same properties of the same individual may be attractive to some, a matter of indifference to others and repellent to yet a third group. Thus, although there may often be a link between an individual's "properties" and his attractiveness, such a link is neither a necessary nor a sufficient condition for that attractiveness. Attractiveness is not an inherent property of the individual — as magnetism is of iron — but is ultimately always an attribute, attributed by the attracted. It follows that the behavioural consequences of being attracted have their causal origin in the attracted not in the attractive. To find someone attractive is not to surrender to some power which he has but to endow him with that power. Hence, as Tedeschi (1974) has suggested, "one likes to be liked"; in effect one likes to be given power.

This may seem a long argument only to arrive at the conclusion that attraction, like beauty, resides in the eye of the beholder. Furthermore it makes no difference whatever to other aspects of the study of interpersonal attraction. It is wholly compatible with the meta-theoretical position that all behaviour is motivated by reinforcement (Byrne and Lamberth, 1971; Lott and Lott, 1974), and thus with the assumption that the attractive is a source of reinforcement to the attracted. It is fully compatible with the evidence that the attractiveness of different people for the same individual may to some extent vary from context to context (Kerckhoff, 1974). The central point however is this: whatever the type of attraction (physical or ideological) and whatever its level (immediate and superficial or long-lasting and profound), *being attracted,* considered as a *response,* has the same two basic characteristics: first, to be attracted means, and is reflected in the fact, that one's behaviour is affected by others, so that one acts in ways in which one would not have acted without being attracted; and secondly, that this change of behaviour is not imposed by the other but, at its roots, is self-imposed. The attracted is not the passive recipient of an influence process, but is himself actively involved in it, or even in a sense in search of it. If this last assertion seems strange, it may become more acceptable if one imagines a world in which one is never attracted to anyone. In such a world one would either be wholly "free" of all influence (but also very much isolated, not least because one would lack "credible sources" to validate one's perception of social reality); or one would constantly be in a condition of having to comply, precisely because one is not attracted. Some psychopathological states perhaps approximate this condition (e.g. extreme "alienation"). It is a condition in which there is in fact no choice, for neither the wholly isolated nor the wholly compliant can act selectively in his relationships.

I have stressed the active participation of the attracted, which is what makes interpersonal attraction truly interpersonal, because the recognition of this is essential to any attempt to understand what happens in friendship and love. The problem is not so much "What is it that makes the attractive attractive?", which can vary widely from person to person and from context to context; it is rather "What does the attracted do, and what happens to him, when he is attracted?", which, I shall argue, is always much the same.

III. Vulnerability and tolerance of vulnerability

Very simply: in becoming and being attracted, the attracted makes himself vulnerable. There is, of course, an important difference between "*makes* himself vulnerable" and "*is* vulnerable": I *mean* "makes", but the reason for this will become clear only later. The essential first task is to examine vulnerability. However, there is a problem about "vulnerability": the word may be poetically evocative but it is by no means clear what it refers to. Yet, as I hope to show, the concept of vulnerability, and the phenomenon to which it refers, is essential not only to the analysis of interpersonal attraction but also to human relationships in general.

In everyday discourse, albeit perhaps sophisticated discourse, "vulnerable" or "vulnerability" refers to the potential of people to be "hurt". Some such notion of vulnerability has at times been discussed in relation to individuals in psychotherapy. Vulnerability, however, is also implicit in exchange theory (e.g. Thibaut and Kelley, 1959; cf. La Gaipa's chapter in section 1), in the sense that marked discrepancies in resources between bargainers makes the poorer partner vulnerable to exploitation: the exploited then provides "pay-offs" to others at cost to himself but negligible return. Thus there is vulnerability to hurt, there is vulnerability to exploitation; and sometimes the two may be related. In effect, vulnerability is a basic aspect of interpersonal relations.

The bases and nature of vulnerability can be seen most clearly in the analysis of interpersonal attraction, and particularly in tracing the development of friendship and love. Since the issues are often complex it is useful to anchor them at the start in a brief account of some empirical findings. There are the classic studies of the formation of friendship in terms of pre-existing attitudes, and attitude change, when people are thrown together and have to live with one another: studies such as those by Festinger, Schachter and Back (1950), Siegel and Siegel (1958) and Newcomb (1961). This research tradition, through its use of "natural settings", has had the great corrective virtue of showing the importance of ecological factors as well as of personal qualities and attitudes in the formation of friendship. For our immediate purposes, however, a more precise analysis emerges if we approach the problem in terms of the constructs people use in describing others. I am not advocating "personal construct theory" as such (Kelly, 1955), but simply that there is much to be gained from an examination of the cognitions that individuals develop about each other. The nature of these cognitions, or constructs, and the ways in which they change as friendship grows, was recently charted by Duck (1973b), who applied a personal construct theory method in the kind of natural settings used in the earlier studies. His findings are very instructive. As friendship develops through repeated contact, constructs appear to move from a focus on essentially physical features (such a looks) through references to more subtle but still overtly behavioural idiosyncracies (like talkativeness) to "psychological" characteristics (like sociability or generosity). Extrapolating from Duck's findings, further intimacy would probably have elicited such complex notions as sensitivity, confidence, self-consciousness, and so forth. Looked at more closely, these constructs can be grouped into two main classes. There are the constructs which are based on overt features, which are or could be "manifest" to all who cared to notice, for instance appearance and behavioural mannerisms. Secondly, there are the constructs which are "inferred", for example, ambition, generosity, self-consciousness. The difference between these two classes is fundamentally that between "properties" which may be observed by any observer, and "attributes" attributed by a given observer to the observed. Thus there would probably be little argument about whether or not a particular individual is talkative: and, if we saw the list of subscribers, there could be no argument about whether or not he had contributed a thousand pounds to charity. We can, however, always argue about whether he is self-conscious, or about whether he is generous. As soon as we are in the realm of attributes we are in the realm of inferences which go beyond the immediate evidence. With this goes another difference: as we move from constructs about properties to constructs about attributes, we move from descriptive to explanatory constructs: he is talkative *because* he is self-conscious. This move from descriptive to explanatory constructs is the essential fact on which the argument which follows will be based.

I take it as an *axiom* that the normal individual has a concept of himself as a person. In line with the earlier definition of a "person", this means that he perceives some constancy, some consistencies, in his behaviour (including his feelings and beliefs) across the various roles and situations in which he finds himself. The details of the origins of the concept of the self need not concern us here. They can be traced partly to early socialization by parents (Hartley, 1966); they include the reactions of others to the individual, say, as physically attractive or unattractive (Berscheid and Walster, 1974); they grow out of self-descriptive statements (Bem, 1972), and the labelling of one's emotions (Schachter and Singer, 1962). All we need to accept is that the individual is somehow aware of himself as a unit; that he has the capacity to store information about the happenings to, and the activities of that unit; and that he also has the capacity to monitor the behaviour of that unit in terms of the information which he has about it. We know from the effects of amputation and disfigurement (Fisher and Cleveland, 1958; Goffman, 1963), let alone from those of amnesia, that any loss of part of that bodily unit and information about it can be severely disturbing. To this I would add another and, I believe, important point: as with any concept, the concept of the self is defined in part by what it *excludes*, as well as by what it includes. In the context of interpersonal relations, a crucial aspect of the self-concept is the awareness of *lack* of information about others, especially awareness of the inability to perceive another's sensations, pleasures and pains, or to hold another's memories, quite as he does. Thus an integral part of the concept of the self is the recognition of its isolation from certain classes of information which are available only to other selves. Hence, although the way in which we see ourselves may be much influenced by the way in which others see us, we know of our limitations in the way we see them, and, *ipso facto,* we know of their limitations in the way they see us. The limits of information available to others about ourselves, as we perceive these limits, constitute the core of our subjective sense of *privacy.*

I have written about the psychological aspects of privacy elsewhere (Kelvin, 1973). The issues are complex and cannot all be repeated here. However, I did then suggest that areas of privacy are essential to the concept of oneself as a person. This is because an individual perceives himself to have privacy to the extent that, as *he* sees it, he is *not* exposed to the power or influence of others, a power or influence which might lead him to modify his behaviour. He is "himself" to the extent that he perceives himself the agent of his own actions, rather than as complying to, say, the demands of a *particular* role or to the normative pressures of a *particular* social situation. It is therefore only inasmuch as he has a certain sense of independence of specific settings, that he has a sense of continuity across particular roles and situations — the sense of continuity which is the essence of a "person". This sense of independence and continuity is based on a sense of uniqueness, which in turn derives from the areas of privacy that, as it were, he carries with him wherever he goes. Though this argument may commend itself to reason, it is unfortunately hard to substantiate. Perhaps the best though of course indirect evidence is provided by the converse case of people in "total institutions". Total institutions, such as the armed forces, hospitals, prisons, have the individual "in their power", and, for different reasons, seek to have him thus. It is characteristic of such institutions that they systematically set out to reduce the individual's privacy to a minimum (Dornbush, 1955; Goffman, 1961). The less privacy an individual has, the greater the power of others over him, the less he is the agent of his own behaviour, the less he is "himself".

Let us now combine the findings of studies of the growth of friendship with this analysis of the self-concept and its basis in areas of privacy. I shall argue that the growth of friendship depends on, and progresses with disclosures of areas of privacy. The disclosure of areas of privacy reveals the underlying causes and motives of the individual's behaviour: this potentially gives those to whom they are disclosed power over him; and in doing so, disclosures make him vulnerable to exploitation. Related to this, disclosures of areas of privacy may also affect the individual's self-concept and thus, as we shall see, render him vulnerable to hurt.

We have found that when interaction continues over time, the constructs which people form of one another undergo change: from constructs based on initial reactions to appearance and overt behavioural mannerisms ("properties"), there is a move to inferential constructs ("attributes"). As Heider (1958) pointed out, we resort to attributes in our search for causal explanations. In line with the approach set out at the beginning, this search for causal explanations arises from our need to make the world and the people around us predictable. It is now useful to take this a step further and consider the problem more strictly in the language of the philosophy of science. In doing so I am *not* asserting that everyone acts in conformity with the canons of logic. Furthermore it is neither necessary nor justifiable to assume that all "constructs" are verbal or even capable of clear verbalization: the visual arts and perhaps particularly the sculptures, masks, and dances of ritual are also constructs for often highly complex notions about man and his relations to the universe. Such non-verbal constructs do not have the strict, formal logical implications of words or mathematical symbols, but psychologically they may nevertheless function as 'adequate' explanatory concepts. I simply suggest that the process of everyday causal attribution and inference has much in common with the logic of science, and that a brief examination of this may help to clarify what happens in the development of friendship and love.

When in science we seek to understand a phenomenon, we look for some basic regularity, such that the phenomenon can be seen as part of a coherent, orderly system. By identifying the phenomenon as part of a system it becomes predictable in terms of that system. In effect, to "understand" we "explain", and we explain one particular regularity in terms of underlying, more general regularities (Achinstein, 1973). By doing so we can account (rightly or wrongly) not only for the occurrence of a given phenomenon, but also find its connection with other at first sight often contradictory phenomena. Within the present context, for example, we may postulate self-consciousness to account for an otherwise paradoxical mixture of talkativeness and shyness.

Such inferential attributes which label (assumed) underlying regularities of human behaviour are, of course, in part based on manifest actions. However, and this is crucial for interpersonal relations, they are also in part based on what an individual has to say about himself, not least about his beliefs, feelings and motives. We may well see ourselves as others see us, but we usually take great care that they should see us as we see ourselves: and we do so, of course, to counteract the tendency of others to see us according to their lights rather than our own. For example, to say "you do not understand me" is to refer to a discrepancy which the speaker perceives between the concept which he has of himself and the concept of him which he believes is held by his listener; and he attempts to correct the apparent misperception because he regards it as potentially leading to false explanations (and therefore predictions) about him, which in turn might disrupt the relationship. However, as Popper (1963) argued, one of the distinctive features of explanations is that they explain the known in terms of the unknown—at the time the explanation and understanding is sought. In interpersonal relations one of the main "unknowns" (though not the only one) is the information which an individual has about himself: information which is not readily accessible to others, and which may even be inherently inaccessible to them, as when it is about his memories, beliefs and feelings—when it is information about some aspects of his areas of privacy. Consequently if, for example, an individual believes that he is not understood as a person, and wishes to be understood, one way in which he can contribute to such understanding is to make these areas of the unknown known, to open up his areas of privacy.

There are two points of detail which warrant amplification. First, the individual may misperceive himself: one's self-monitoring is not always "objectively" sound; and since one puts constructions on one's own behaviour, seeks explanations for what one observes oneself doing, there is ever the chance that one draws the wrong inferences from one's own actions. Nevertheless, even if misleading in its effects, the "opening up" in such instances is still genuine in its intent; and, as the individual perceives it, it is a disclosure. Second, however, there is the deliberate deception, and that is very significant for the present argument. I would not suggest for one moment that in what I have called the "genuine" case, the disclosing individual always actually verbalizes to himself along the lines: "They don't understand me, they therefore can't explain me, and so they will make the wrong inferences and predictions about me". I do suggest that where there is the intent to deceive, some such plan is quite conscious, in the sense that the whole aim of the deception is to provide a false explanation with implicitly false predictions as a consequence. The function of deception is to mislead prediction, deliberately: the deceiver predicts the consequences for the predictions of others of the false account which he gives of himself. And note: in the 'genuine' case, through making himself better known, the individual gives others the potential power to use that knowledge to influence him; when he deceives he not only blocks their potential power but also in effect exercises power himself, to influence them.

To return to the straightforward situation, the growth of friendship is charted in the move from descriptive to explanatory constructs. It is a move from the manifest to the underlying, from the easily known to the initially unknown and perhaps inaccessible. Inasmuch as the individual opens up his areas of privacy he thereby makes it easier for others to explain and therefore to predict him. To open up one's areas of privacy is thus to risk being exploited. The risk is taken when the risk is shared, when the disclosures are reciprocal—normally at least. If we marry exchange theory with a touch of latent paranoia we could say that reciprocal disclosures reduce risk through being an exchange of potential powers of blackmail. More positively, there is probably an element of knowing exploitation, and willingness to be exploited, in most close relationships; the needs of the participants differ, each of them accepts this, and between them they attempt to provide for those needs. Even more fundamentally but, as far as I can tell, largely ignored, the very same factors which enable one individual to exploit another are also the factors which enable him to protect the other: for in order to protect someone it is necessary to understand him, to be able to explain and predict where he is vulnerable: protection is, after all, forward-looking.

This brings us to the concept of "hurt". The concept of vulnerability implies the complex feelings which we label "hurt". However complicated and confused these feelings may be, and however inadequate the analogy with a gash to the body, the condition of "being hurt" is caused by or attributed to others, and cannot, therefore be ignored in the study of friendship and love. We seem to know little about this — except that among the things we learn as we grow up we learn of our vulnerability. This is part of the breaking down of childish ego-centricity, an ego-centricity which may return in old age (Lickona, 1974; Looft, 1972). The ego-centricity of the very young and the very old and the ease with which they may be hurt provides a clue. At both extremes of age the individual is greatly dependent on others, which reduces the sense of freedom of action which is essential to the concept of the self. The ego-centricity of childhood may be regarded as in part an attempt to define the self, that of old age an attempt to maintain it. In the long years between, however, we can cope with, and therefore accept our vulnerability more easily: we can accept it in *some* areas of our lives precisely because there are many others over which we at least believe we have control, in which we feel that we are being ourselves: we can then handle variations on the theme of our self without fear of the theme becoming lost amongst the variations.

From this standpoint "hurt", in its psychological sense, may be regarded as damage to the integrity of the self-concept. At a superficial but nonetheless important level, a "hurtful" remark may force the individual to recognize a weakness he prefers to ignore (and to recognize that it is recognized), or perhaps to question and even abandon an assumption about himself which is central to his view of himself. A deeper hurt may arise in relation to others on whom he has come to depend. Being dependent on them, committed to them, itself becomes part of his concept of himself. These others come to form a crucial aspect of the world as he perceives it: they help to define that world, its social reality: and his relations with them help to define, locate, his own place in that world. To be criticized, "let down", rejected, thus not only undermines one's assumptions about others, but also the assumptions which one has made about oneself. When the actions of others "hurt", when they negatively affect the concept of oneself, neither the world nor one's self remain as they were: nothing is quite as reliable, as predictable as it was: and so we find the confusion, doubt, anxiety, frustration and anger which so often follow being hurt.

Through opening his areas of privacy the individual doubtless risks being exploited and hurt. Yet it is reasonable to assume that such psychological (as distinct from economic) exploitation and hurt are exceptional. One can, of course, at times recognize near pathological cases of people who seem destined to be "kicked" (Berne, 1966); but these arouse attention precisely because they are exceptional. It is therefore important that the potentially negative aspects of vulnerability, which we may encounter among the psychologically disturbed, do not lead us to ignore its more pervasive positive aspects in 'normal' life. For a self-monitoring species, such as man, a crucial element of reality is the concept which the individual has of himself. Without such a concept the individual cannot locate himself in space and time and, particularly, within the system of relationships he has with others. It is disturbing not to know "who" or "what" one is, "where" one stands: this is part of the distressing disorientation of post-traumatic amnesia; it is part of the problem of many a rapidly growing and changing adolescent; almost everyone experiences it to some extent on moving job or neighbourhood — until he has once more "established" himself. However, it is not sufficient to have just any odd concept of oneself: as with other concepts of reality, it is necessary to perceive that that concept is *valid*. This validation of the self-concept depends largely, even if not wholly, on the reactions and comments of others, on its acceptance by others. Herein lie a number of problems.

Many of the broader categories in terms of which the individual may define his self-concept are based on fairly clear-cut physically and socially determined criteria. There are, for instance, those of sex and kinship, which define ascribed status. There are also mechanisms which define achieved status — in *rites de passage*, such as initiation ceremonies or the award of university degrees. However, and this is critical, such societally defined, stereotypical, aspects of the self-concept relate primarily to the individual in terms of his *roles*, as a man, a father, a doctor: they do not define him, either for others or for himself, as a *person* — as a unique person within the context of his unique personal relationships, over and above, across and even independent of his roles. Furthermore, for certain purposes, role-based self-concepts are not only inadequate, but belong to a quite different realm of discourse. For instance, if "alienation" is a valid concept, it is so because of the discrepancy between the individual's concept of himself as a person and the roles he is constrained to assume.

There are not, there inherently cannot be, *societally* defined categories or mechanisms which can adequately validate the individual's concept of himself as a person. Such validation is provided by the friendships and love which grow out of attraction. Psychologically, I suggest, it is this function of friendship in validating the self-concept which "justifies", or compensates, the vulnerability and the risks attendant on being attracted. Our human condition now presents us with another problem: on the one hand we need a concept of ourselves, we need to perceive it as valid, and we need others to provide the validation; on the other hand, a central aspect of this very self-concept consists of our areas of privacy. Yet precisely because they are areas of privacy, this central aspect of the "self" would seem to be beyond validation by others. The resolution of this paradox may, I think, be one of the essential tasks of love. As friendship grows into love, and is reciprocated, there is an increasing, mutual, opening of areas of privacy: the lovers come to know, to understand, and to accept more and more about each other; as they do so they validate one another's concept of self, even if only in a *folie à deux*. To be unloved, to be unable to love, leaves one "unfulfilled", "incomplete" — not only because of the inability to express the whole range of one's potential emotions, but also because central aspects of the concept of oneself remain forever without adequate validation.

But to be able to love requires the ability to tolerate and accept the vulnerability which follows from disclosures of privacy. This *tolerance of vulnerability*, as I call it, is of course related to the class of phenomena which go under the more familiar label of "tolerance of ambiguity". However, tolerance of vulnerability is not merely yet another member of that class: it is, I suggest, the underlying factor. For if in turn we seek an explanation of the fear of ambiguity, we find it in the nature of the threat which ambiguity poses. An ambiguous situation is threatening because it is unpredictable and therefore uncontrollable: its unpredictability, its uncontrollability imply that one will be shaped by events rather than that one can shape them; and inasmuch as one may be shaped by them, they constitute a threat to the concept of ones self as one has known it. In essence, tolerance of ambiguity involves acceptance of the uncertainties, and therefore of the vulnerability of the self, which ambiguity entails. To disclose areas of privacy, is to put oneself into an uncertain, vulnerable position: the disclosures may extend and therefore enrich the relationship; but they may also lead to exploitation, rejection and hurt. Yet if vulnerability may lead to hurt, so may the attempt to remain invulnerable, albeit at a different psychological level. Granted that the early research into the "authoritarian personality" (Adorno *et al.*, 1950) had profound flaws, the general and recognizable syndrome to which it refers is that of an individual who finds it difficult to tolerate ambiguity, and whose early experience of, and later capacity for, close relationships is often restricted. It is a personality which at a very fundamental level cannot tolerate vulnerability. In effect, the limit of an individual's tolerance of vulnerability is the limit to which he can love; and since this is also the limit to which he can open himself to another, it is also the limit to which he can be loved and, if need be, protected.

We can see this most clearly, even if somewhat paradoxically, in the stereotype of "love" in much of romantic literature: in the love which does not seek, and often deliberately avoids, reciprocation; in the courtly love of mediaeval chivalry (Huizinga, 1924), and in the pure love of Dante for Beatrice. This is indeed metaphysical love: it is never submitted to the empirical test of an actual relationship; it is never exposed to the possibility of falsification. The Dantes of this world are in love with an ideal of their imagination, not with a real person who has flaws, who may laugh and love and scold and spurn. They remain in their private universe, invulnerable to their beloved and, of course, invulnerable to her potential unwillingness to validate their ego-centric self-concepts. Romantic suffering is a self-indulgence: to stay in love when love meets no response is to perpetuate a self-inflicted wound. Love as a *relationship*, however, entails the mutual opening of "private" selves. This may lead to exploitation and to hurt: but it is also the basis of the ability to meet one another's needs, and the source of the power to protect. Dante protected himself, he could not have protected Beatrice.

The conventional connotations of language can be misleading. In the present context it is therefore most important that we do *not* interpret the notions of "self-concept" and of "disclosures of areas of privacy" in an exclusively and narrowly "cognitive" sense — let alone as if they depended on verbal sophistication. The poor in words may love, those rich in them may merely use them as defensive walls. Words may not always be necessary, and they are certainly not always sufficient (Argyle, 1975). There is much communication without words, and some that is beyond them. In particular, it is essential to remember that the body, and its sensations, is one of the most significant areas of privacy, and that to be touched against one's will is, in most cultures, a serious invasion of that privacy. These facts need some consideration. The norms which limit touching may in part have developed from an overt fear of actual bodily harm. In addition, however, there seems to be an inherent immediacy to touch which makes it particularly arousing. This is understandable in terms of evolution: the threat that is seen or heard from a distance (through "distance receptors") is more readily and circumspectly avoided than the threat which is upon us (touch is a "proximal" receptor). Probably because of the "urgency" of responses to touch, these tend to be genetically programmed, that is, to be reflexes. Their reflex nature makes us (at first sight paradoxically) particularly vulnerable to them: for although these responses, being genetically programmed are, at one level, especially predictable, precisely because they are thus programmed "we", at the level of our conscious self-concept, are not fully in command of them. In relation to touch, therefore, we are not only in danger of deliberate harm, but also have a sense of reduced "voluntary" control. Yet it is telling that strangers may embrace on the occasion of some public joy, or to comfort a victim of distress. At such times words are not enough to express happiness or to offer and afford protection. The conceptual has to find expression in the physical. It is allowed to do so for two different reasons with a common source: in happiness we feel safe, the stranger seems no threat, we seem invulnerable; in manifest misfortune our vulnerability is manifest, not least to ourselves, and with it our inability to protect outselves on our own.

Again because of its immediacy a physical relationship is bound to be a powerful relationship, in the strict psychological sense of the term "power": the actions of one partner immediately modify the behaviour of the other. Moreover, since the responses to touch may to a considerable extent be of the nature of reflexes, they may to that extent not be wholly under the control of the touched. This may be fine when we are willingly transported into ecstasy, but it also makes us vulnerable to being "carried away" against our "better" judgement. Physical contact may thus lead to a discrepancy between our actions and the more "rational" concepts which we have of ourselves. It is perhaps significant that the idealized assumption of our culture postulates that love, at the conceptual level, precedes physical, sexual relations — an assumption which implies that we only open our bodies to those to whom we have already safely opened our minds. We tend to ignore, of course, or to be romantically horrified when we realize it, that for most of mankind, for most of its history, marriages were arranged — without undue harm to the species and therefore, presumably, to the majority of its members. On a positive view, then, it is important to recognize that in its full sense the "self-concept" consists not only of the "concepts" which an individual has of himself, but also of his body-image. Given this, the mutual exploration of their bodies may, I think, be regarded as attempts by lovers to gain some understanding, at least empathically, of one another's truly "private" sensations, to gain some insight into each other's body-images. The physical aspects of their relationship, therefore, in the strictest sense adds a crucial dimension to the knowledge which lovers may have of one another. Conversely, just as an adequate or ill-defined self-concept may limit the development of mutual understanding at the conceptual level, so inadequate or distorted body-images may hamper physical relations. Frigidity 's the bodily equivalent of rigidity, and both have their origin in the fear of vulnerability. It is only inasmuch as an individual can accept and tolerate his inevitable vulnerability that he can enter into relationships, conceptual and physical.

All this discussion of vulnerability, its bases and consequences, may seem remote from the mainstream of social psychology—let alone from the hard core of basic psychological processes. It isn't. So far I have in essence only described the phenomenon of vulnerability and its place in interpersonal attraction. Let us now, finally and briefly, analyse the *conditions* under which we make ourselves vulnerable. To do this we have three important facts—or, rather, common observations—to help us. First, friendships take time to develop: that is evident from all the studies on the acquaintance process (e.g. Newcomb, 1961). Second, although the reciprocal validation of self-concepts is a central function of friendship, such validation is by no means an exercise in mutual indulgence: friends criticise, friends correct. Finally, we have the puzzle of the long-term relationship which may have passed through love, only to atrophy thereafter: it is a puzzle because, given that there has been no change in the persons involved (except, of course, that they are no longer lovers) they should still understand each other, be able to predict each other, perhaps even better than when they were in love: thus predictability is a necessary, but not a sufficient condition for lasting relationships.

These three aspects of friendship form a pattern which, I believe, can be accounted for by an elaboration of the concepts of adaptation-level theory (Helson, 1964). I shall limit myself to the conceptual issues because I myself certainly do not have the quantitative data to work out the details, and I rather doubt whether sufficiently precise data could ever be obtained. But the concepts have much to offer. First, repeated contacts between people, for instance as a function of opportunity (e.g. Festinger *et al.*, 1950), creates in each of them an adaptation-level to the others. This adaptation-level is in the form of subjective probabilities concerning patterns of behaviour. For example, when I first meet and greet a colleague in the morning, and he replies, neither of us notes the event: we have adapted to its high probability: I only take note if he does not reply, for his failure to do so has low probability. Herein lies the link between predictability and adaptation-level: adaptation is a product of high probability, and thus provides the basis for predictions that are so reliable that they become "automatic". The function of adaptation, however, is two-fold: it stills sensitivity to the (highly probable) stimuli to which one has become adapted, and thereby sensitises one to changes in these stimuli and to new stimuli. Thus, as first acquaintance progresses into friendship, one quickly adapts to the manifest properties and behavioural trivia of the other; this, as it were, leaves the channels for information processing free to handle the more complex patterns of behaviour, for coding them into "underlying" attributes. (On a point of detail: if interpersonal attraction is regarded as mutual adaptation, the discovery of, for instance, similar attitudes, would facilitate such adaptation.) As contact is maintained over time, one adapts not only to the particular responses of the other but also to the range and variability of these responses. At this point, then, we may introduce two social-psychological concepts, ultimately related to adaptation-level theory: "latitude of acceptance" (Sherif and Hovland, 1961) and "idiosyncracy credit" (Hollander, 1964). The range of another's behaviour to which one has become adapted constitutes the latitude of acceptance within which that behaviour may vary: the occasional "extreme" or "exceptional" response, provided it is not too extreme, can be assimilated without significantly "displacing" the level of adaptation. The established predictability (the "reliability" of the other) based on one's adaptation level to him, allows for his occasional departures from expectations — gives him the "idiosyncracy credit" which, for instance, enables him to criticize without disrupting the relationship. There is some evidence here of a strictly physical kind which is possibly significant. Amputation, which is sudden and traumatic, gives rise to "phantom limbs", the loss of limbs in leprosy does not (Simmel, 1956). The body-image can adapt to slow change, not to trauma; similarly perhaps, damage to the self-concept "hurts" when it is sudden, much less when it is against an adaptation-level which includes some experience and even expectation of criticism. We can take from a friend what might hurt from a stranger.

This leaves the problem of the long-lasting relationship which atrophies. Such atrophy is by no means inevitable, but it does occur, and is of theoretical as well as human significance. Within my limited scope, my approach has been predominantly cognitive, touching on affect only by implication. Here, then, is one of the important links with affective arousal. Adaptation desensitises to the predictable, sensitises to change. Speculatively, therefore, total predictability creates a condition of low arousal, or even none. Hence, in human relations it may be that relationships stay "active", that is aroused, under conditions of "optimal" rather than maximal predictability. This is *not* to advocate the retention of some personal mystery: to prolong a mystery is a bore — creates adaptation to it. The chances are, then, that long-lasting relationships will remain active to the extent that the partners to it jointly develop as individuals, so that there are repeated new inputs which prevent the establishment of a static adaptation-level. But of course, the "new" is always to some extent uncertain; it creates vulnerability and demands tolerance of vulnerability. Hence the kind of persons who can form close relationships are also likely to be the kind of persons who form lasting relationships.

I hope that by tracing the conditions under which an individual can accept his vulnerability productively and can even *make* himself vulnerable I have removed the suspicion that vulnerability is merely a poetic notion, and that by pointing to the connection between vulnerability and adaptation-level phenomena I have shown its links with basic non-emotive non-poetic psychological processes. There finally remains the question of whether the individual *makes* himself vulnerable or whether, somehow, he *is* vulnerable. There is, for instance, the "fatal attraction", the "helpless passion" so dear to romantic literature, and sometimes attributed to those whose loves we cannot understand. It is indeed conceivable that some men are genetically programmed to prefer blondes, and that perhaps all of us are unknowingly in thrall to pheromones exuded by our partners. Attraction of this kind would be to the properties of the attractive, akin to superior physical strength. The response to them would be a form of compliance, not from choice. However, even if there are elements of physiological or, for that matter, of acquired but compulsive psychological factors in being attracted, it simply seems unlikely that they could constitute the *sufficient* conditions for the attraction of one individual to *particular* others. On judgement the world seems fairly generous in providing alternatives: the blondae-tropic appear to be well catered for. Predispositions may define the set, they do not identify the members of it to whom one is attracted. Thus even if we allow the possibility of properties to which the individual *is* attracted, he is attracted to only some of those who have these properties, not to all. The *first* response to another may be to physical features (Berscheid and Walster, 1974b), though even this is likely to be much influenced by social criteria of "attractiveness", rather than by some absolute biological beauty. Beyond the initial meeting, however, beyond the immediate groin-response, the individual *selects* those to whom he is attracted, to whom he is prepared to *make* himself vulnerable. He evaluates them — in terms of his own need, not least his need to validate his self-concept, and in response to their disclosures, their vulnerability, their needs which he may serve. Interpersonal attraction, friendship, love, are processes of mutual evaluation in search of reciprocal confirmation.

19.

Inquiry, Hypothesis and the Quest for Validation: Personal Construct Systems in the Development of Acquaintance[1]

STEVE DUCK

University of Lancaster, England

Although the phenomena of attraction are variously explained (cf. section 1) much actual research in the area over the last 15 years or so has clearly reflected the fact that the area of interpersonal attraction in particular shares several specific emphases of social psychology as a whole. This chapter will identify some of these themes and relate them to a specific theory of personality which, at first sight, has little to say about either social psychology as a whole or interpersonal attraction as a part of it. However, whether one starts with the theory and relates it

1. I am grateful to Don Bannister for his comments on an earlier draft of this chapter, which was written during tenure of grant HR2491/2 from the Social Research Council.

to practice in attraction research or starts with theories of attraction and relates them to the practices suggested by the personality theory then a new approach to attraction and an extension of the theory are jointly produced.

One suggestion with considerable application in social psychology is that put forward by Festinger (1954). His notion of "social comparison" argues that individual have a drive to evaluate themselves; can usually (or, in some cases, can *only*) do this by comparison of themselves with others; and, broadly, select as comparisons those others who facilitate self-evaluation. In the context of attraction this has been taken to imply that individuals seek as acquaintances and friends those who are useful or powerful "comparison others" for salient aspects of self. Whilst this suggestion has been investigated in relation to several facets of the individual (Wheeler, 1974) its most predominant application in this context lies in the sphere of comparison of attitude statements (Byrne, 1961a) although it has also been extended to comparison of personality components (Byrne and Griffit, 1969). In such contexts authors argue that individuals are enabled to assess or evaluate aspects of their cognition or thought processes by comparison with others and can obtain *validational* evidence for such things as beliefs, opinions or hypotheses by finding others who share those beliefs, i.e. who are cognitively similar to themselves. In an extension of this basic position, Byrne and Clore (1967) and Clore and Byrne (1974) have argued that individuals are motivated by a need for effectance (i.e. a need to evaluate their effectiveness in dealing with the world) and so they seek validation for their methods by comparing themselves with other. Through a classical conditioning process, individuals have become conditioned to the reinforcement provided by discovery of useful comparisons (most frequently, but not exclusively, more powerful when others are similar) [cf. Clore, in section 1] and have therefore become conditioned to find such individuals attractive.

A second notion much in evidence in social psychology stems from a different, but not irreconcilable, research tradition: namely, that concerned broadly with the way in which an individual selects and organizes information about others (Bohac and Reboussin, 1967; Warr and Knapper, 1968). Much work has been done to examine the contribution of such research to our understanding of attraction (cf. Ajzen, in section 1). Whilst some recent work has sought to reconcile this approach with the reinforcement tradition (Clore and Byrne, 1974) it is clear that (however it is ultimately explained) the means of selection of the information, the type of information selected, its constructive use, and the creation of models of stimulus others is an agreed (even obvious) component of acquaintance. But these processes of selection and organization of information depend on the personality of the selecting organizer just as much as they relate to the personality of the stimulus. Not only does this follow from work showing that individuals with different personalities react to information differently (Robbins, 1975); it follows from studies of impression formation (Warr and Knapper, 1968) and implicit personality theory (Passini and Norman, 1966) where individual differences in selection and organization of material are clear. Strange, then, that such work in this context has not led to direct consideration of a personality theory based centrally on personal ways of selecting and organizing information (Kelly, 1955). The disadvantage of Personal Construct Theory (Kelly, 1955; 1969; 1970) so far has been that its specific directives for research here are not yet spelt out as are other information processing suggestions (for example, by Ajzen — Section 1). The clear advantage is that it conceives of personality in such a way as to make "personality" as much a testable type of cognition as are attitudes, and it therefore fills a vacuum noted by Lott and Lott (1974).

Such themes of social psychology relate to attraction and to Personal Construct Theory in various ways which will be explored. However, the research on attraction has established its own themes and traditions within the context of social psychology at large. For example, more emphasis is given to mechanisms of selection of acquaintances and less to how acquaintances form and progress (but see Murstein, section 1) and much less attention is paid to how or why relationships are maintained and kept in good repair (cf. Harré, section 3) or to the *functions* of "negative" social relationships. The *development* of relationships will be a main theme in this chapter. Again, the literature on attraction has a dichotomous sub-theme: namely a minor conflict between findings on attitudes (invariably found to be influential upon attraction) and findings on personality (invariably equivocal, ambivalent and hard to interpret). Whilst the place of one is becoming clearer, the only thing to become clear about the other is that it has no clear place! Yet, by adopting a personality theory that deals explicitly with information processing, "attitudes" and "personality" become simply different levels of analysis or different points of cross-section of the same phenomenon, each differently reflecting an organizational level for information. By placing this conceptual step in a context of developing relations, different and developing relationships can be explained in terms of levels of cognitive organization (particularly in terms of the levels or layers of "personality") which are exposed to and compared socially with acquaintances. That is, I shall argue that individuals compare themselves with new acquaintances at one level of cognition and with progressively more intimate acquaintances at progressively more complex levels. Thus the cues relevant to selection, development and maintenance of relationships change as time passes but are changing parts of a single total mechanism. This mechanism (viz. elaboration of the construct system) will also be used as an explanation of the functions and purposes of both positive *and* negative relationships.

Such a view can be both developed and tested within the framework of Personal Construct Theory (PCT). But, in part, the instant neglect previously achieved by this theory in relation to social psychology stems from the discomfort felt by some schools of thought about its ability to handle social psychological concepts, from its apparent lack of empirical viability and in part from its methodology. None of these misgivings need be entertained for long, however, and on closer inspection it is clear that research on attraction is now at a level sophisticated enough to handle the concepts it suggests. Indeed several workers in this volume and elsewhere have drawn on related concepts —even using similar terminology—to those outlined below (e.g. Clore and Byrne, 1974; who argue, as Kelly did, that cognition and affect are not incompatible: Kelly, incidentally was roundly chastized for this suggestion—Bruner, 1956; Ajzen in section 1 talks of "constructive use" of information; Kelvin in section 3 considers layers of privacy of information). This chapter argues that research on attraction would benefit if such similarities were explicated and examined.

I. Some contours of personal construct theory and attraction

It is not the intention of the present chapter to give an exhaustive account of Kelly's (1955, 1969, 1970) Personal Construct Theory (PCT): the purpose here is a conceptual analysis of interpersonal relationship from the standpoint of PCT. In subservience to this aim, only some of its features will be isolated, particularly those that can be brought to bear on the empirical study of attraction and appear to be consonant with the emphases throbbing through the attraction literature. In doing this the formal "postulate and corollary" exposition of PCT will not be reflected in view of its ready availability in other sources (Kelly, 1955; 1970; Bannister and Mair, 1968; Bannister and Fransella, 1971). Some main contours of its general stance will be identified in this subsection: the next will examine what Kelly and later interpreters of PCT have said about social relationships both in the clinic, in the outside world and in the experimental laboratory; in the last subsection I will explore its specific contribution to our conceptualization of the process of developing acquaintance.

The major emphasis of PCT falls on the individual's experience, cognition, action, and what it means *for him* — and this applies no less to social relationships and interpersonal attraction than to other components of an individual's everyday experience. Yet it makes a slight but significant difference to the way in which one approaches attraction: it not only places the focus of attention on the cognitive processes of attracted individuals rather than on the stimulus properties of the attractive individuals (cf. Kelvin, section 3); it also indicates the fruitfulness of looking at the links between the cognitive processes of the *two* individuals in a relationship. Concern over the person in a relationship must mean concern over both persons involved and the theory thus offers a ready consonance with views in the attraction literature that stress cognitive similarity between individuals (see Section 1 of this book). Its peculiar differences from other views will become apparent later.

In taking up these claims, there are 4 emphases of PCT that specifically concern the development of the present argument and derive from attention to the individual's processes. These are: *anticipation* (an individual's predictions about the future); *phenomenalism* (the view that an individual's descriptions of, or beliefs about, reality are more important — especially, more psychologically significant — than the reality as "objectively" observed); *constructive alternativism* (the belief that more than one view of reality is possible, logically defensible and potentially fruitful); and *choice* (the individual's responsibility for choosing his own alternative views and descriptive apparatus, and for deciding its value). These four concepts, central to PCT, are useful starting points for a view of acquaintance that sees individuals embroiled in a quest for order, structure and support in the matter of interpreting the world and dealing with it tolerably effectively (cf. Byrne and Clore, 1967). More important, PCT can form part of a view that sees the development of acquaintance as a successive process of quest for order and structure of different kinds and at different levels as time passes and relationships deepen (Duck, 1973b).

A. ANTICIPATION

Beneath all of Kelly's writings, and sometimes stated explicitly, is the view that Time is the mainspring of all behaviour: people behave because the passage of time takes place willy nilly and individuals cannot *not* behave. The fact of human action—as opposed to inaction —does not need to be explained in psychological terms, Kelly argues, but there is a need to explain the *directions* in which the action tends and why an individual chooses one direction rather than another (this will also apply to why an individual chooses friends rather than enemies or "non-relatedness"). Broadly, Kelly argues that individuals choose order rather than chaos (Adams-Webber, 1970). More specifically, for Kelly (1955, 1969), the direction of an individual's psychological processes is channelized by his anticipation of events. That is, the emphasis of PCT falls not on the future as such, but on Man's feeble attempts to grasp at it, form some expectation of what the future might be like, to construe and understand it. An individual's "constructs" are the ways in which predictions of the future are embodied in his psychological processes and they represent his expectancies of experience. An individual's psychological processes embody his guesses or anticipations about the ways in which past events will repeat themselves and, by induction, he seeks to make his world manageable, predictable and orderly. The problem, of course, is that events never repeat themselves exactly and it is therefore necessary for the individual to pick out those features which seem to him to be most useful and important when it comes to the erection of a model wherewith to understand and be prepared for the future . . . and he erects models of those people he meets just as he does of other events. This is an important step for the argument on acquaintance later on.

Anticipation, Kelly (1969) argues, is a questioning act; behaviour is an individual's way of probing the future, his way not of answering questions but of asking them, a tentative step around a corner. In other words, behaviour is an experiment (Kelly, 1970). This implies a continual process of hypothesis, test, re-evaluation and development as the individual is faced with the predictive success or failure of his anticipations. In the context of research on attraction this has two implications. *First,* it points to a hidden consequence of "reliability" in measures which detect the changes that take place within the individual in his successive attempts to deal with life, and other people, effectively. Many personality tests are constructed in order to meet rigid criteria of reliability, i.e. to show the minimum amount of change in test scores on occasion of re-test. They thus perforce concentrate on those aspects of personality that are more enduring, static and inflexible (or, more accurately, they label aspects of personality with titles which subsume static phenomena). It is argued here that progress in friendship formation depends not only on flexibility within personality characteristics, but also on the ability of the two parties to influence and change each other to be more similar to themselves. This is essentially a matter of faith: one either does or does not believe that the ways in which personality changes are as important as the ways it stays the same, so to speak. For Kelly, change or development is no surprising or unusual thing whether within the individual, in his sociometric preferences or in his relationships. Thus this particular emphasis of PCT would lead one to be as much concerned with the development of relationships as with their original inception and instigation. *Secondly,* this is a first hint of the later stages of an argument that the individual is, in many ways and many respects, faced with problems of validating and testing his construct system. One way in which he can do this is by examining the constructs of other people, to see if these individuals agree with him about ways of looking at the future (Duck and Spencer, 1972).

B. "PHENOMENALISM"

A further step in this latter argument follows from the second emphasis of PCT which stresses that "reality" does not dictate particular descriptions: the individual uses his own descriptions of reality, some of which will be useful and some not. But each is selected by the individual as a reference axis by means of which he helps himself to order and structure the things that he encounters. The things in the world do not leap out, seize him by the throat and thrust a label in his face: he *can* call them what he likes, *can* sort them how he will.

Stated as dogmatically as this, Kelly's position seems untenable: if we all erect our own systems of categorizing and describing the world then how do we have any dealings with others? What are societies if not *shared* assumptions and *similar* beliefs about reality? Yet all the various kinds of social interaction offers at a different level the facility for "checking" various types of construct about various types of event. For example, social structures are a context in which there is agreement about (and test of) appropriate behaviours, linguistic labels, even moral precepts (see Duck, 1973b, p. 10). From social relationships in general the individual can "check" constructs concerning abilities, opinions (Festinger, 1954), emotional responses (Schachter, 1964) and personality structure (Wheeler, 1974). To take the point further, I will argue that particular friends and acquaintances provide opportunities to test the most subjective (and otherwise untestable) constructs: namely, those about other people's personality and the explanation of others' behaviour. Thus at each level of relationship a different level of information can be tested for validity through a different level of social comparison. View this point another way and it has the potential for a developmental theory of acquaintance about the progressive development of closer relationships between given adults in similar terms.

C. CONSTRUCTIVE ALTERNATIVISM

So far attention has been focussed on just the suggestion that individuals erect their own systems of constructs and that they test them through comparison with others' constructs. It has thus been only implicit that this presupposes constructive alternativism, that is, it presupposes that there is more than one way of construing events. This is so in many ways. First and most obvious, PCT presupposes inter-individual differences in the construction of events and people: my way of viewing events and anticipating their replications is different from your way. But, secondly there is the point that each individual himself is conceived of as possessing several ways of describing a given event, several constructs which could apply. He will also have thousands that could not apply: "winsome" is not a description that applies to "windows"; political events are not pizzicato. Occasionally some genius, wit, or headline copywriter may take an accepted and tried way of structuring nature and will show that it can be applied to events that previously lay outside its scope, but in the main a person's constructs each have more limited application ("range of convenience", Kelly, 1955). To the extent that the person construes particular events as lying outside the range of convenience of his construct system as a whole or in specific parts, to that extent, it follows from PCT, he will experience anxiety or simply the inability to deal with those events or people effectively. This has implications for the person's social relationships, since occasionally he may encounter people that he cannot construe usefully in some specific or other. In the last subsection of this chapter this notion of range of convenience will be cast in another guise, for it is relevant to consideration of why some people cannot form relationships at all or *why* people become enemies rather than friends. For example, schizophrenics lack the usual proportions of constructs with a range of convenience that encompasses psychological description of others (McPherson *et al.*, 1971) and it has been suggested that this would predispose them to an inability to form deep or lasting relationships with others (Duck, 1973b). But the social, personal and psychological function of enemies and of dislike can also be derived from this point (see below: "negative social relationships").

However, there is a further aspect to the notion of alternativism that is strongly built into Kelly's approach. In asserting something an individual is also implicitly or explicitly denying something and that which is excluded is often an important psychological part of the message, "as when the disgruntled first mate entered in the ship's log that 'the captain was sober tonight'" (Kelly, 1969, p. 9). In behavioural terms, an action should be seen in the light of what might have happened instead and indeed the individual's actions in everyday life can be evaluated in moral terms only if the individual could have acted otherwise (Aristotle, c. 350 BC) or in the context of what he might have done but did not. To express this notion in construct terms, Kelly argues that all constructs are dichotomous: they not only assert what the individual says something is, they also state what it is not. In many cases the dichotomous nature of a construct helps to clarify the construer's intention: to describe someone as "Fair" is insufficiently clear, but to say he is at the "Fair" end of a "Fair-Dark" dichotomy at least eliminates the ambiguity that he is being described in terms of a "Fair-Unjust" dichotomy.

The suggestion thus has at least two implications in the present context: First, it helps to specify the terms in which one should search for psychological similarity between two individuals; second, it makes an assertion about the psychological importance of friendship *selection*. In the first case, it suggests that psychological similarity is not defined simply by whether two individuals use the same term (X) to describe or evaluate something. It depends crucially on whether they employ the same dimension (X-Y) and for this reason both halves of the dimension must be measured. Kelly sees the dimensions X-Y and X-W as only superficially similar (logically similar, not psychologically similar). In the second case above, it suggests that a claim to have selected a given individual as a friend is implicitly a claim to have rejected something or someone.

D. CHOICE

The notion of alternativism, and particularly the notion of dichotomy, indicates the individual's responsibility for *choice*, another basic theme in Kelly's work. Given the chaos of an otherwise unstructured world and the individual's vast, even excessive, range of means through which to effect description of it and deal with it the individual is faced with several levels of choice. At one level is the simple "ball-park problem" of the kind or range of description that is applicable and here the individual may be encouraged to be lazy by the fact that his social environment has often done some kind of job for him and some sorting of the world can be done by taking in the assumptions and values of his society. Secondly, he is faced with a choice about the nature of the evidence he will accept about the validity of his judgement, description, value, constructs. Thirdly, he is called upon to select the salient features of events and choose from his system a construct which applies; and fourthly, to decide which part of his dichotomous construct is the relevant part. This, clearly, faces him directly with a number of serious evidential and validational problems and in all cases, so an attraction researcher might predict, the individual's choice could be appropriately screened through some form of social comparison, with similarity counting positively, in most circumstances (but only if the Comparison Other was accepted as a learned judge, an upright judge . . .).

Kelly seems, at first sight, to take a different view but it is here that the mutual impact of attraction research and PCT works most excitingly. Faced with all of the decisions above, Kelly predicts that the individual's choices would be directed or influenced by the elaboration of his construct system; that is the individual makes those choices which best assist him (so he judges) to elaborate his construct system. (Note that this elaboration has the effect of making him more and better equipped to anticipate the future and deal with the world and others in it: therefore it satisfied what others — Clore and Byrne, 1974, for example—have termed an effectance motive. Although Kelly's argument deliberately avoids such motivational arguments, the conceptual dimension involved is remarkably comparable.) A system may be elaborated in two ways: either through *extension* or *definition* i.e. through reaching out into new areas or through confirming in greater detail a part of the system that already exists. This is a crucial point in the argument. What determines an individual's preference for one form of elaboration over the other? How does his behaviour in acquaintance relate to elaboration? The full discussion of these points and their relation to attraction research will occupy the rest of this chapter although the main discussion of the implications occurs in the last subsection. As a first step, however, it seems reasonable that once the person has taken the decision to relate to others he is likely to look first for definition of existing structures and second for extention, since growth into new areas could then be based on agreed frameworks of terminology. Consequent upon extension, however, one presumes that the individual would temporize for a while in order to define those parts of his system that concern the new areas so recently broached. This, in any event, is the *logical* way to proceed (be sure of your ground; leap off and land somewhere else; make sure of that ground; leap off . . .). Whether it is a *psychologically* important way is an empirical question. Previous work on attraction, concentrating as it does on similarity (i.e. definition) could have missed an important psychological dimension to developing relationships. However, the nature of elaboration of the system is crucial both to PCT itself and to the extension of PCT into the area of acquaintance in this analysis. Given the personal nature of construing and the meeting of minds which inevitably takes place at some level in social interaction, then elaboration of the system could be hypothesized to be the function for which friendship provides one opportunity. Friends, it will be argued, not only provide *validational* evidence for constructs (and do this at many levels) but also, against this background—and therefore subsequently—offer the individual potential for elaborating his system in areas where it is currently unelaborated. In terms of the previous concepts, friends first provide definition alone (through validation) and then offer means of extension with definition. It is in this context that a function for hostility and enmity will be discussed later. This argument will itself be validated, extended and elaborated in subsequent sections. It does however, represent an extension of PCT from its usual spheres of application, but there is no reason to reject the approach of PCT simply because its *application* has so far had emphases of a different tenor from those apparent in the attraction literature. As can be shown, many of its theoretical stresses are very similar in style to some of the concepts hitherto used in the attraction literature — but such generalities, and the consideration of the main points of the PCT approach, can now be supplemented by specific and particular hypotheses derived from the way in which Kelly spoke of and dealt with social relationships.

II. Personal construct theory and social relationships[2]

It is true, of course, that most work employing, examining and extending Kelly's (1955) Pesonal Construct Theory (PCT) has centred upon clinical psychology although its methodological outgrowth, the Reptest, has been applied vigorously in many other fields — and occasionally in the study of individuals' *social* behaviour. In part the reluctance to employ PCT in social psychology stems from rejection of its theoretical assumptions at a general level; and in part it stems from the false belief that PCT's concern over *individual* cognitive structure and content leaves little to be said about the place of social interaction and its functions.

Some of PCT's applicability stems from the inexorable, but largely pragmatic, association between "clinically oriented" theories of personality and social psychology, for social and clinical psychology are themselves closely related in several ways — both directly and indirectly. Not least of these links is provided by the fact that much experimental social psychology has its "pay-off" in the clinic, where psychotherapy is often directed at restoring normality by excising or altering aberrant or dysfunctional *social* behaviour. Clearly this link is especially relevant in the context of social relationships and friendships, where the malfunction of this particular behaviour causes such fundamental distress. It was in terms of this distress and consequently in the context of psychotherapy that Kelly elaborated what he had to say about personal relationships, thus opening the door for study of friendship and acquaintance from his perspective. But his theory also contains a specific corollary which relates to social behaviour in general and thus encompasses social behaviour within its formal logic.

Social behaviour is explained in PCT to originate from the under-

2. Some of the argument of this section was presented as part of a symposium on "Personal construct theory in action" (F. Fransella, convener) at the British Psychological Society conference, April, 1975.

standing which an individual has of another person's constructs. Kelly (1955) elaborated this view in the formally-stated sociality corollary of his theory which states that: "To the extent that one person construes the construction processes of another he may play a role in a social process involving the other person". The emphasis falls here not on describing, predicting or understanding someone else's *behaviour* but on grasping the way that he thinks, hypothesises, anticipates, construes. It emphasizes the understanding of Other's psychological processes and bases Kelly's view of social relationships and social behaviour upon it. Its applications to several aspects of social psychology have been examined by Bannister and Fransella (1971), but when it comes to social relationships and acquaintance in particular the corollary does not adequately describe the basis for *discriminative* choices of friends or acquaintances. One can grasp the psychological processes of a child, a mental defective or a colleague without any deep personal friendship resulting. So, in the analysis of social relationships more must be added to the fundamental building block provided by the sociality corollary.

Kelly himself added something which amounted to "security" as the extra. Again, given that his analysis of personal relationships is largely in terms of the clinic (Kelly, 1969) what he has to say is this: that in his social behaviour the individual is involved in multiplex, multi-level relationships of dependency and interdependency, and that these necessary and completely normal — even praiseworthy — dependencies are more secure where there exists a framework for understanding each other in terms of construing processes. Already this analysis implies mutuality: one-sided understanding (such as that observable with children or mental defectives) is less valuable in some sense than mutual grasp. Certainly a true social relationship, as normally understood, follows from one rather than the other, whilst the asymmetric (or *vastly* asymmetric) grasp of construing processes implies a differential power structure or a particular function for a relationship. To make this point, that simple understanding of cognitive processes may not be psychologically rewarding for either party, an example of Kelly's own may help. He reports a dialogue between a patient and therapist where the patient complained that there was no-one she could really talk to; that no-one really cared. When pressed, she admitted that the therapist cared — but it was his *job* to care! "What a tragedy it must be", Kelly (1969, p. 195) observes, "to find that your best friend is a psychologist!"

But the situation outside the clinic or in other social behaviour is surely very different, although it is at least conceivable that the two situations may evidence the same function. In going to the clinic an individual often seeks support for his construing processes, or may, in Kelly's terms, be seeking to elaborate his construct system. There are some clear similarities between getting to know a therapist and other people in social encounters (Isaacson and Landfield, 1965). However, the range of constructs exposed to others in social encounters is less restricted and more extensive; less liable to be confined to special areas; less *explicitly* concerned with support. The process of acquaintance is also slower and gets down to certain kinds of brass tacks rather more laboriously. Also, the greater the range of people that are encountered, the greater the chance of finding another person who is in agreement and offers support. The problem for the individual may be the difficulty of recognising the support when it is encountered, simply because in life outside the clinic it is less explicit and less emphatic. However, the probability of such recognition — and indeed the probability of a good grasp of the other person's construct processes — is heightened to the extent that the two individuals are similar to one another. Kelly defines *psychological* similarity in the commonality corollary of his theory: "To the extent that one person employs a construction of experience which is similar to that employed by another, his processes are psychologically similar to those of the other person". The emphasis falls here on similarity of *constructions* of experience (viewed, therefore, from the inside: how people *look* at events) rather than upon similar experiences (viewed from the outside: things that happen to people) or similar behaviours.

If the two corollaries (sociality and commonality) are conjoined and rephrased, then the more similar one's constructs are to those of another person the easier it will be to grasp the other person's psychological processes and play a role in social behaviour with him. Or, to extend this, the greater the probability of understanding one another's constructs the easier two people will find it to communicate and the higher the chance of them preferring one another's company. However, whilst similarity of constructs may lead to attraction in that it provides easier communication, an additional justification is provided by conjoining this outlook with another prevalent in the attraction literature (Byrne, 1961a; Festinger, 1954) and arguing that comparison of one's constructs with those of another person actually provides some measure of validity or support for them (Duck and

Spencer, 1972) which they require because they are a form of scientific hypothesis. Some kinds of constructs (as is true also of attitudes) can be validated through observing the consensus of others or by others' sharing of the constructs with oneself — and PCT is uniquely suited to the notion of hierarchical levels of organization of personality (Hinkle, 1970). Constructs can be classified into many types (Landfield, 1971) and the types can be seen as subordinate and superordinate relatives of one another, just as, for example, "apples" and "oranges" can be seen related to the superordinate category of "fruit" and to the subordinate phenomena "pith" and "pips". In the present, more human context the present approach distinguishes between "attitudes" and "personality" not as *classes* of phenomena but as *levels* of phenomena — levels of organization of hypotheses of particular kinds — and so it implicitly denies any rigid distinction between them as alternative explanations of acquaintance. Thus "attitudes" and "personality" are not alternative but complementary explanations of acquaintance, each with its rightful *and sequential* place in acquaintance.

These are, at least, empirical hypotheses which can be tested experimentally and they bring PCT into the attraction laboratory heavily-laden with suggestions. It offers two broad avenues of study: since both content and organizational structure of content can be examined by PCT it offers simultaneous attack on these two facets of the attraction literature (*content*: cf. Byrne, 1961a, 1971 and many others; *structure*: cf. Tesser, 1971 and others). This section is not the place for an exhaustive summary of work published to date which supports the PCT approach to attraction in various ways.[3] This work has presented evidence to suggest that levels of construing (or levels of information organization) can be experimentally examined and can be shown related to different levels of relationship. Duck and Spencer (1972) found that, although similarity of the whole construct system predicted who would become friends out of a previously unacquainted population, it was similarity of those constructs which related to the psychological description of others that ultimately differentiated established friendship pairs from affectively neutral pairs of subjects.

3. Summaries and discussion of early work can be found in Duck (1973b; in press, b) and particular points or subsequent elaborative hypotheses are examined in Duck (1975a, b; in press, a), Duck and Craig (1975; in press, in prep.) Craig and Duck (in press), McCarthy and Duck (1976, in prep.). One experimental paper is reprinted in section 2 here (Duck, 1973c).

Also, Duck (1975b) found that adolescents' constructs could be classified as Fact (those describing objectively agreed characteristics), Physical, Role (those describing status,etc.), Interaction (those dealing with behavioural characteristics and competence) and Psychological (character descriptions of Others) and that adolescent development could be characterized in terms of predominant construct categories. The different levels of constructs were differently related to, and predictive of, relationships and friendship choices discovered at different ages — suggesting, so it was argued, a functional relationship between personality development and friendship choice.

Such findings help to substantiate the viability of PCT as an experimental approach to interpersonal attraction and validate its particular contribution to our understanding of the basis of acquaintance. In particular they suggest the value of an approach centred around the concept of levels of cognitive organization and levels of social comparison or validation as concomitants of levels of relationship. Given, therefore, that there is support for the general hypothesis outlined earlier, then Kelly was right to concentrate on the clinic in his analysis of relationships, for both his analysis and the present one stress that the person is in some sense in need of help and is deeply involved in dependency in all his social relationships. Of course, Kelly was examining an extreme part of the continuum, but the above discussion indicates that everyone derives support from others through social relationships — support for their construct system. The apparent paradox is that assertion of self as an individual depends on validation of constructs through dependence on others — although the individual does *choose* on whom to depend, and he does this on the basis of similarity. Perhaps this enterprise therefore sounds circular, barren and masturbatory, but it is not. When other people validate his constructs an individual may choose to depend on them for validation and definition: but it is perfectly plausible that he selects people for this purpose because, on the basis of some *obvious* similarity, he guesses, anticipates or assumes that there are other (more significant) similarities to be discovered. By selecting the Other as an acquaintance he gives himself the chance to find out if his anticipation was indeed correct — and he can always withdraw from the acquaintance before it develops if he finds he was wrong in his guess. Thus Duck (1975a) has argued that similarity of attitudes is taken by subjects to imply similarity of personality (i.e. similarity of one level of cognitive organization indicates the possibility of similarity at other levels). The possibility of similarities that lie at different depths in personality (public ones, less superficial or more notably subjective ones — see above) is one which not only suggests the possibility that relationships develop in terms of the particular depths that have been probed or remain to be inspected (see Duck, 1973b for detailed discussion of these layers); it also prompts an explanation of why formed or forming relationships collapse or founder as the parties discover that the suspected depth of similarity does not exist as hitherto anticipated. It also mediates that view that "attitudes" and "personality" are not different phenomena but different levels of analysis for the same basic phenomenon: organization of information.

But it is not implicit in this view that friends are totally similar and simply "stroke" one another's personality in various ways. It is true that, if personality is seen in terms of constructs (that is, in terms of similarity of dichotomies), then similarity confirms not only a person's prediction of what *would* happen, but also that his anticipation has been placed in a "correct" context of what might have happened instead (i.e. it defines the construct system). However, the ability to grasp another's psychological processes (whilst increased by similarity) does not imply total identity, merely the improved ability to wear another person's cognitive spectacles. After it is clear that the spectacles do not continually fall off the nose, rub the ears or make the eyes water, then it may be useful to examine the view visible through them. In the previous terms, after defining the system it may be useful to extend it. Friends can offer new perspectives, new possible outcomes without necessarily invalidating all of a previous view. Alternatives offered against a background of similarity are, after all, easier to adopt into one's own system. McCarthy and Duck (1976) have shown that where a background of similarity exists, then, in certain circumstances, dissimilarity becomes more attractive than do further examples of similarity. But the background of similarity is a pre-requisite for such a phenomenon since it would be hard to accept the confrontation offered by a new philosophy without benefit of any prior "softening" procedure. At a different level, and in a different context, this point is precisely that urged by Clore and Byrne (1974) that a paradigm (. . .view of the world . . .) is best developed by workers (. . . individuals . . .) with slightly different perspectives working towards the same final goal by building on agreements, polishing, building again, refining and extending methodology and conceptual structure (. . . construct systems . . .). Subtly, also, the comparison between scientific paradigms and thought processes in developing human relationships also helps to support Kelly's well-known and oft-cited view that Man is a Scientist! Certainly, whilst consistent with his view, it also sows the seeds for the growth of a theory of development, change and *mutual* growth in a relationship: which can explain *how* others become more similar even if they started similar in some specific respects. The important question is *not* "Do friends start similar or become similar?" but "Are the types of similarity at the start and finish of relationship's development similarities of the *same* kinds or levels?"

As an extension of this point it is clear that the psychological study of interpersonal attraction often suffers from an unnecessarily blinkered view that there are not two persons in an interaction but one person and one stimulus other. Whilst one person radiates stimuli and cues, the other gathers this information avidly. The present extension of PCT looks at the individual not from the outside but from inside the cognitive maze through which he operates with others and with the world and the understanding that he has of the Other's "maze". There is an intensely important *psychological* difference for the individual between *what* he knows about the Other, what he *does* with it and, most important, how and why he gets it (Duck, in press, b). Everything known about some new acquaintance was once uncertain and complexly mysterious but has now been built into a system and constitutes a view of the Other. The process and purpose of building it is as important as the bricks themselves — but also in this case the blueprints may be changed as new bricks are added . . . and this has several implications.

III. The double-sided nature and function of social relationships

So far the discussion has centred upon the way in which an individual processes information about others and how he selects associates. Although under the guise of discussing longitudinal progression of relationships the argument has seemed to examine development, it has really done so only superficially since it has construed this development in terms of filtering, i.e. successive *selection* against different criteria. Although these criteria are ordered and sequential, they are still criteria for *selection* of acquaintances rather than maintenance or development of relationships although it can be seen that there is a suggestion in this analysis that selection and maintenance merge into one another gradually. Discussion now focusses more on "relationships" rather than on selective "sociometric choices" and particularly on both positive and negative manifestations of them.

Levinger (1974) and Levinger and Snoek (1972) have argued for a model of attraction based on different degrees of pair-relatedness and Levinger, Senn and Jorgensen (1970) have claimed that there are two components to a developing relationship: (1) development of the relationship itself in terms of mutual interdependence; (2) disclosure and discovery of co-orientation. Whilst major work on attraction has concentrated on the latter (itself a concept of considerable complexity, Duck, in press, a), there are aspects of the former notion which are useful adjuncts to any study of acquaintance. All too often research on attraction concentrates on either person A as a perceiver or person B as a stimulus (see Introduction) without taking account of the implications *for each person* himself of the relationship between them (although another naive version of this point has occasionally surfaced as a complaint that work on attraction is superficial or artificial). These points have been considered in more detail in the Introductory chapter to this book.

A. THE FRAMEWORK OF SOCIAL RELATIONSHIPS

Reconsider some points emphasized earlier. It is now clear that several of the emphases of PCT are implicitly or explicitly shared by the attraction literature, even though many workers have not expressed these emphases directly in PCT terminology. It is also plain that the PCT approach to attraction can be explicated and proves fruitful. Some emphases, however, offer a somewhat different perspective on attraction and evince reconsideration of some of the approaches to it. The most emphatic stress of PCT on development and change has the substantive implication that work in attraction should examine the development of relationships with equal vigour to that expended in examining selection of interactions. For example, whilst personality may be relevant to selection it also influences development of relationships. Personality influences selective interaction in two distinct ways (Duck, in press, a): it affects an individual's willingness to enter interactions of certain types (e.g. anxious people are less willing to interact, more prone to seek similarity, Goldstein and Rosenfeld, 1969 and see below); it affects an individual's satisfaction with individual others as a function of their particular properties (Wright, 1968). However, normal progress in friendship formation depends not only on a certain flexibility within personality characteristics (e.g. openness to change, non-rigidity) but also on the ability of the two persons to influence and change each other to become more similar to themselves. Since the concept of change and development of personality is a theme in PCT, it follows that change and development in *similarity* of personality is also implicit and this notion can be used to explain the development of relationships both in terms of formation and maintenance, both negative ones and positive.

The previous argument has stressed the relationship between similarity, attraction, constructs and development or elaboration of the construct system. It has also placed great weight on the contention that comparison of several levels and types of cognitive element is accomplished during friendship formation and that these components can be structured in a sequence that has "attitudes" preceding "personality" as levels of cognitive organization (Duck, 1975a). When ultimately comparison of personality comes to the fore directly, individuals compare their location on the "large" categories within this broad cognitive classification (e.g. Introversion level; Dominance level; Sociability level . . .) and proceed by various steps and levels to compare themselves on dimensions of Psychological constructs (Duck, in press, a; b).

However, although this type of comparison begins principally at the points where interaction and selection takes place, it would be an error to see it as occurring only when interaction occurs. The evidence from studies of impression formation and person perception indicates that individuals form impressions, assumptions or models of personality on the basis of most superficial cues (Warr and Knapper, 1968) and whilst this has most usually been investigated in terms of its occurrence in first encounters, there is no reason to assume that the process of assumption occurs only there. The relationship between impression formation and initial attraction is clear (Bohac and Reboussin, 1967) but is not logically limited in scope to early points of acquaintance. At many points of acquaintance individuals can use the evidence available *as it becomes available*, or as they could reasonably make assumptions about it, in order to erect models of the other's personality. This is necessary for two reasons: *first* (trivially) certain types of information only are available at certain points of a developing acquaintance. One does not find out deep information about another at the first encounter: it takes time and involves processes of assimilation of evidence and self-disclosure (Cozby, 1973). Note, however, that the point here is not that self disclosure (in the sense of openness) must occur, nor that it must do so in noticeable amounts: the point concerns the types and statuses of the information that is progressively revealed. *Second*, and more important, in forming relationships with others the individual seeks confirmation for the hypotheses embodied in his personality structure, or in the terminology of Byrne and Clore (1967), is satisfying an effectance motive. Since several levels of personality similarity exist (Duck, 1975b), a full satisfaction of an effectance motive involves testing of capacity at these several levels. The long term function of 'impression formation' or 'model erection' as this account has it, is to fill the void otherwise observable: i.e. to make guesses about features of the other that have currently *not* been observed and to do this on the basis of the cues that *have* been observed. In some cases a short cut is rapidly taken and similarity is assumed rather than tested (Newcomb, 1961). But the processes occur throughout acquaintance, even though the *changes* induced in an individual's model of his acquaintance presumably become successively less drastic as he gains more knowledge about him. Having erected a model however, individuals can then compare their own personality with their model of the Other's personality and can thus scrutinize it for expected similarities in appropriate ways (Duck and Craig, 1975). The erection of models thus involves not only an element of affective evaluation (of the cues actually presented) but also an element of expectancy and future evaluation (of the characteristics and similarities *presumed* to exist). As the relationship proceeds, the individual is able to evaluate the extent to which his model of the Other fits the reality. He can then erect a new model if necessary or modify the old one and again assess the potential levels of similarity that he now perceives to exist when these new criteria are employed. He can also extend his construct system in ways indicated or argued for by the Other. At every stage an entirely new judgement of the viability of the relationship is involved, based upon the new *presumed* similarity levels — thus even relatively long-established relationships can eventually break down as an individual's expectancy model of his acquaintance's personality is suddenly found to need such revision that it becomes not only discrepant with previous experience, but also (if the difference is important and unresolved) affects the *perception* of similarity and shows it to be *actually* erroneous.

This speculation leads to others. It seems plausible that if this model is correct, then some kind of filtering does take place (Kerckhoff and

Davis, 1962; Duck, 1973b) with individuals either being rejected as they fail to satisfy one of the progressively-established criteria or succeeding in passing through to the next level. This "permission to continue" may look to the outsider (and even to the participants themselves) as if friendship exists. In a strict sense, however, it does not but has simply been increased in probability. The early points of friendship are thus more concerned with establishing the credibility of the witness; that is with establishing the value of the Other as a person against whom to compare oneself. Individuals ask themselves "Would I value similarity or support from this person, if there is any?" *before* they go on to ask themselves "Does any similarity exist at the right level?". Clearly, however, the Other could make himself *appear* similar on certain crucial issues for a variety of reasons, only some of which are disinterested or relationship-oriented, e.g. he could be a liar or an ingratiator. In any case the individual may prefer to encounter the spice of honest argument from time to time rather than to find himself reflected in every respect. To find the occasional disagreement would enhance the belief that the Other is a discriminating judge (Mettee and Aronson, 1974). Indeed, McCarthy and Duck (1976) found that at about 4-6 months of relationship, individuals reacted more positively to dissimilarity of attitudes than they did to similarity. The authors argued that at such a stage of relationship, the value of continued comparison at different levels could be established. But the ultimate function of relationships can still be seen to be validation of the construct system at its various levels through definition.

This speculative model suggests several phases in the development of a relationship: the original decision to engage, the assessment of Other as a suitable comparison other, the inferential processes from observable cues to inner structure, the assessment of the inferred structure for similarity, given that the function of all social interactions is support for the construct system. At all of these points (and note that no claim is made that each stage is equally long or equally complex) some judgement relative to the validity of the construct system can be made. At whatever point an individual fails to discover required support, definition or extension (whether through the "fault" of the stimulus person or the perceiver himself) he may withdraw. In broad terms, therefore, failures in relationship are due to the individual's failure to discern the relevant cues in those to whom he relates: that is, relationships fail to form at any of the levels or phases outlined above because the individual supposes that personality similarity at the appropriate level is not available. But such similarity is ultimately a catalytic means of serving the aim of validating the construct system, or, in previous terminology, of elaborating the system through definition of areas currently within it. What if such definition is not available due to the peculiarity of the system? Then, it is argued below, the individual initiates *negative* social relationships. Where definition and validation are available at one level, positive relationships (i.e. attraction) begin as the search for other levels of definition is initiated. Once an acceptable level of definition is reached the individual seeks to elaborate his construct system through extension into the new areas indicated by his acquaintance, as suggested earlier. Positive feelings toward someone thus instigate both definition and extension of the construct system — but both are psychologically important and personally significant.

By concentrating on this notion of elaboration I have hoped to do no violence either to Kelly or to work on attraction. The two views are consonant and mutually instructive. But by involving this concept it is also possible to cast both negative and positive social relationships in the same explanatory terms with a unifying conceptual and teleological dimension working through and providing the weft to the warp and pattern of all the other themes identified in this analysis of acquaintance. To do this (which is a new departure for the attraction literature) is to invoke a consideration of Kelly's conceptualization of anxiety, threat and hostility and to explore their ties — coming as they do from a *clinical* provenance — with social relationships and friendship formation (which is a new departure for PCT).

B. NEGATIVE SOCIAL RELATIONSHIPS

One remarkable concentration of the attraction literature (also noted in the chapter by Harré here) is on the positive side of things, and while this commendable Panglossery redounds pleasantly upon the nature of Psychologists, the negative side of relationships is equally important. In the present context of analysis, what can be said about this negative side of human relationships? First, that few people have studied it directly. Second that a parallel analysis is possible between positive and negative relationships: that is, the place of each with respect to selection and maintenance can be seen in the same terms. Third, that there are several kinds and levels of negativity in social relationships just as there are kinds and levels of positive relationships. If one counts indifference as negative then Kelly may argue that others

treated indifferently lie outside the range of convenience of the
construct system. On the other hand, those more actively disdained
could be conceived of as supporting the construct system by embodying
the negative ends of the dichotomies inherent in the constructs (i.e.,
instead of supporting construct A-B by being A and approved, they
support by being B and disapproved). However, these are feelings
about people rather than actual relationships occasioned by feeling.
Just as Harré (section 3) discussed maintenance of negative relationships, so I want to look at states or acts or social relationships of a
negative sort and I therefore hope to examine the way that they arise
and probe what their psychological importance and *function* might
be. Yet *explanations* of failure to make friends, to start relationships or
to court successfully are rare and failures are usually simply a control
group for relationships that start (i.e. experimental workers make
comparisons between subjects who form relations and those who do
not form them, without examining a *function* for negative relationships: rather they tend to see them as coincidental negative correlates).
For Kelly, the individual's choices reflect not only what he accepts but
what he rejects: therefore, insofar as an individual is intentionally
involved in a negative relationship (enmity, hostility, threat, aggression . . .) the negative pole of the dichotomy/choice is informative. Of
course not everyone does set out to enter negative relationships: they
happen to us all, although some people experience this more frequently
than others. They thus have two sides: the intentional side (examined
here) and the unintentional, fault or failure side (examined below). I
will speculate about each, in the spirit of the intention of this section.

Kelly defined hostility in a characteristic way. He was less interested
in hostility in the everyday sense of aggressiveness, anger and strained
faces: he was more interested in what such behaviour meant for the
individual, what it told us about the subject's internal strategic
states — and his definition reflects this. Hostility, Kelly (1969) says, is
the continued effort to extort, beat, drag or kick validational evidence
out of events in favour of a type of social prediction which has already
been recognized as a failure (for example, a screaming child who is
attempting "to prove to the neighbours that his parents have made a
horrible mistake", Kelly, 1969, p. 276). Hostility can thus be a means
whereby to *support* the construct system through "definition" — since,
when validational evidence is not available from others by consensus,
the individual extracts it from them or events by distorted perception.
In this case therefore a similar purpose (validation) can be discovered

in friendship and hostility. Hostility is thus a reactive state: a reaction to something perceived in the environment, a failure of the environment and the people within it to provide validation. It is choice to behave in a particular way. The important empirical question here is (again a Kellian point): "If the individual construes his dimensions of elaborative development as either *definition plus extension* through positive relationship (friendship) or *definition alone* through negative relationship (hostility), then what makes him choose one rather than the other?"

In all the previous discussion I have argued that elaboration of the construct system through definition precedes elaboration through extension. Let us apply this to social relationships by means of Kelly's notions of anxiety and threat. For Kelly, anxiety implies that the individual feels that certain events lie outside the range of convenience of his system, i.e. he cannot presently handle them. An anxious person might prefer to have his system defined (i.e. to satisfy himself at all costs that, whatever he had thought, his system really *can* without violent change, handle the relevant events). If the definition is not forthcoming from others through confirming similarity then the individual needs must supply it for himself by himself by becoming hostile. For an anxious person with no recourse to validation through consensus, therefore, hostility is predicted here to be the next best thing — and likewise defines his system through elaboration. Similar arguments apply to the function of negative social relations invoked by threat. For Kelly, threat is the awareness of an imminent *comprehensive* change in a person's core (self maintenance) constructs. It is clear that similar desires for definition apply to the threatened person as apply to the anxious person and both suggest that hostility in Kelly's sense serves as a means of supporting the construct system. A further supportive dimension is added to this argument by Johnson's (1975) view that anxiety is a state where individuals attribute too much significance to events in the environment and lose the ability to distinguish the relevant from the irrelevant. In terms of the present discussion this behavioural manifestation of anxiety could indicate an increased search for validation, but employing a greatly loosened evidential framework. Within, this analysis, then, negative social relationships are as important means to the end of construct system elaboration as are positive social relationships. PCT could thus employ a single dimension to explain both, and can offer a functional explanation for negativity.

However, not all negative relationships are intentionally entered or purposefully maintained—some arise through failure of one sort or another. These are theoretically equally interesting but practically more significant for one major reason. The above filtering hypothesis suggests that different levels of information form the basis for the *development* of acquaintance. Therefore, in order to develop relationships an individual must both release to others and gather from others information at the appropriate level at the appropriate time. Development of acquaintance is thus a skilled performance. In other contexts where the concept of "social skill" is employed (Argyle, 1969, 1975) there is stress on the parallel processes of "encoding" (putting one's internal states into their appropriate behavioural form) and "decoding" (understanding Others' behavioural activity in terms of the internal states which produced it). Failure to form relationships could be due to failure of either of these processes through unawareness of the appropriate levels of information to seek or release at appropriate times (Duck, 1973b). This speculation is not entirely devoid of theoretical interest (Are there such *cognitive* skills?, Does friendship formation fall into the category of social skill, both behavioural—i.e. operating correct "friendly" or maintenance behaviours—and cognitive—i.e. gathering and releasing information correctly?). However, its main thrust lies in the veiled implication that (once the correct levels of information are more thoroughly identified) friendship formation could be *trained*. Those individuals who suffer clinical symptoms through relational failures may thus be assisted by the researches of social psychology.

These latter considerations once more iterate the close ties between normal and clinical states which, because of his experiential antecedents, Kelly tended to emphasize. They also expose gaps in the present conceptualization of social relationships which PCT helps to illuminate and about which it can generate hypotheses and predictions. Although its relation to the acquaintance literature is oblique and complex, PCT offers promising lines of enquiry coupled with a methodology capable of matching the complexities devised by the very subjects that we study.

References

Abrahamsson, B. (1970). Homans on exchange: Hedonism revisited. *Am J. Sociol.*, **76**, 273-285.

Achinstein, P. (1971). *Law and Explanation: An Essay in the Philosophy of Science.* Oxford University Press, Oxford.

Adams, J. S. (1965). Inequity in social exchange, *In* L. Berkowitz (Ed.), *Advances in Experimental Social Psychology.* (Vol. II), pp. 267-299. Academic Press, New York and London.

Adams-Webber, J. (1970). Actual structure and potential chaos: relational aspects of progressive variations within a personal construct system, *In* D. Bannister (Ed.) *Perspectives in Personal Construct Theory.* Academic Press, London and New York.

Adorno, T. W., Frenkel-Brunswick, E., Levinson, D. J. and Sandford, R. N. (1950). *The Authoritarian Personality.* Harper, New York.

Ajzen, I. (1974). Effects of information on interpersonal attraction: similarity versus affective value. *J. Pers. Soc. Psychol.* **29**, 374-380.

Allport, G. W. (1937). *Personality: A Psychological Interpretation.* Houghton Mifflin, Boston.

Altman, I. (1973). Reciprocity of interpersonal exchange. *J. Theory. Soc. Beh.* **3**, 249-261.

Altman, I. (1974). The communication of interpersonal attitudes: an ecological approach, *In* T. L. Huston (Ed.) *Foundations of Interpersonal Attraction.* pp. 31-59. Academic Press, New York and London.

Altman, I. and Taylor D. A. (1973). *Social Penetration.* Holt, Rinehart and Winston, New York.

Anderson, L. R. and Fishbein, M. (1965). Prediction of attitude from the number, strength, and evaluative aspect of beliefs about the attitude object: A comparison of summation and congruity theories. *J. Pers. Soc. Psychol.* **2**, 437-443.

Anderson, N. H. (1962). Application of an additive model to impression formation. *Science* **138**, 817-818.

Anderson, N. H. (1965). Averaging versus adding as a stimulus-combination rule in impression formation. *J. Exp. Psychol.* **70**, 394-400.

Anderson, N. H. (1967). Averaging model analysis of set size effect in impression formation. *J. Exp. Psychol.* **75**, 158-165.

Anderson, N. H. (1968). Likableness ratings of 555 personality-trait words. *J. Pers. Soc. Psychol.* **9**, 272-279.

Anderson, N. H. (1970). Functional measurement and psycho-physical judgement. *Psychol. Rev.* **77**, 153-170.

Anderson, N. H. (1971). Integration theory and attitude change. *Psychol. Rev.* **78**, 171-206.

Anderson, N. H. and Barrios, A. A. (1961). Primacy effects in personality impression formation. *J. Abn. Soc. Psychol.* **63**, 346-350.

Anderson, N. H. and Jacobson, A. (1965). Effect of stimulus inconsistency and discounting instructions in personality impression formation. *J. Pers. Soc. Psychol.* **2**, 531-539.

Argyle, M. (1967, 2nd edn. 1972). *The Psychology of Interpersonal Behaviour.* Penguin, Harmondsworth.

Argyle, M. (1969). *Social Interaction.* Social Science Paperbacks, London.

Argyle, M. (1975). *Bodily Communication.* Methuen, London.

Argyle, M., Alkema, F. and Gilmour, R. (1972). The communication of friendly and hostile attitudes by verbal and non-verbal signals. *Eur. J. Soc. Psychol.* **1**, 385-402.

Argyle, M. and Cook, M. (1976). *Gaze and Mutual Gaze in Social Interaction.* Cambridge University Press, London.

Argyle, M. and Dean, J. (1965). Eye contact, distance and affiliation. *Sociometry*, **28**, 289-304.

Argyle, M., Lefebrvre, L. and Cook, M. (1974). The meaning of five patterns of gaze. *Eur. J. soc. Psychol.* **4**, 125-136.

Argyle, M. and Kendon, A. (1967). The experimental analysis of social performance, *In* Berkowitz, L. (Ed.) *Advances in Experimental Social Psychology* (Vol. 3). Academic Press, New York and London.

Argyle, M. and Little, B. R. (1972). Do personality traits apply to social behavior? *J. Theory Soc. Beh.* **2**, 1-35.

Argyle, M. and McHenry, R. (1971). Do spectacles really affect judgements of intelligence? *Brit. J. Soc. Clin. Psychol.* **10**, 27-29.

Argyle, M., Trower, P. and Bryant, B. (1974). Explorations in the treatment of personality disorders and neuroses by social skill training. *Brit. J. Med. Psychol.* **47**, 63-72.

Aristotle, (c. 350 BC). *Nichomachean Ethics* **8**, 1156a.

Aronson, E. (1969). The theory of cognitive dissonance: A current perspective, *In* L. Berkowitz (Ed.), *Advances in Experimental Social Psychology.* (Vol. 4). Academic Press, New York and London.

Aronson, E. (1973). *The Social Animal.* Freeman: New York.

Aronson, E. and Carlsmith, J. M. (1968). Experimentation in social psychology, *In* G. Lindzey and E. Aronson (Eds.), *The Handbook of Social Psychology,* (Vol. 2, 2nd edn.) pp. 1-79. Addison-Wesley, Reading, Mass.

Aronson, E. and Linder, D. (1965). Gain and loss of esteem as determinants of interpersonal attractiveness. *J. Exp. Soc. Psychol.* **1**, 156-171.

Aronson, E., Willerman, B. and Floyd, J. (1966). The effect of a pratfall on increasing interpersonal attractiveness. *Psychon. Sci.* **4**, 227-228.

Aronson, E. and Worchel, P. (1966). Similarity versus liking as determinants of interpersonal attractiveness. *Psychon. Sci.* **5**, 157-158.

Asch, S. E. (1946). Forming impressions of personality. *J. Abn. Soc. Psychol.* **41**, 258-290.

Austin, J. L. (1961). A Plea for Excuses, *Philosophical Papers,* Clarendon Press, Oxford.

Averill, J. R. (1974). An analysis of psychophysiological symbolism and its influence on theories of emotion. *J. Theory Soc. Beh.* **4,** 147-190.

Averill, J. R. (1976). Emotion and anxiety: Sociocultural, biological, and psychological determinants, *In* M. Zuckerman and C. D. Spielberger (Eds), *Emotions and anxiety: New concepts, methods and applications.* LEA—Wiley, New York.

Back, K. W. and Bogdonoff, M. D. (1964). Plasma lipid responses to leadership, conformity and deviation, *In* P. H. Leiderman and D. Shapiro (Eds). *Psychobiological Approaches to Social Behavior,* pp. 24-42. Stanford University Press, Stanford.

Backman, C. (1976). Psychoethics, *In* Harré, R. (Ed.) *Life Sentences,* pp. 98-108. Wiley, London.

Bannister, D. and Fransella, F. (1971). *Inquiring Man.* Penguin, Harmondsworth.

Bannister, D. and Mair, J. M. M. (1968). *The Evaluation of Personal Constructs.* Academic Press, London and New York.

Banta, T. J. and Hetherington, M. (1963). Relations between needs of friends and fiances. *J. Abn. Soc. Psychol.* **66,** 401-404.

Becker, G. (1964). The complementary need hypothesis: Authoritarianism, dominance and other Edwards Personal Preference Schedule scores. *J. Personal.* **32,** 45-56.

Beier, E. G., Rossi, A. M. and Garfield, R. L. (1961). Similarity Plus Dissimilarity of Personality: Basis for Friendship? *Psych. Rep.* **8,** 3-8.

Bem, D. J. (1972). Self-perception theory, *In* L. Berkowitz (Ed.), *Advances in Experimental Social Psychology,* (Vol. 6) pp. 1-62. Academic Press, New York and London.

Berkowitz, L. (1972). Social norms, feelings and other factors affecting helping and altruism, *In* L. Berkowitz (Ed.), *Advances in Experimental Social Psychology,* (Vol. 7) pp. 63-108. Academic Press, New York and London.

Berne, E. (1966). *Games People Play: The Psychology of Human Relationships.* Deutsch, London.

Berscheid, E., Dion, K. K., Walster, E. and Walster, G. W. (1971). Physical attractiveness and dating choice: A test of the matching hypotheses. *J. Exp. Soc. Psychol.* **7,** 173-189.

Berscheid, E. and Walster, G. W. (1968). Liking reciprocity as a function of perceived basis of preferred liking. Unpublished manuscript. Department of Psychology, University of Minnesota.

Berscheid, E. and Walster, E. H. (1969). *Interpersonal Attraction.* Addison Wesley, Reading, Mass.

Berscheid, E. and Walster, E. (1972). Beauty and the best. *Psychology Today* March, **5,** 424.

Berscheid, E. and Walster, E. (1974a). Physical Attractiveness, *In* L. Berkovitz (Ed.), *Advances in Experimental Social Psychology,* (Vol. 7) pp. 158-216. Academic Press, New York and London.

Berscheid, E. and Walster, E. (1974b). A little bit about love, *In* T. L. Huston (Ed.), *Foundations of Interpersonal Attraction,* pp. 355-402. Academic Press, New York and London.

Birnbaum, M. H. (1974). The non-additivity of personality impressions. *J. Exp. Psychol. Monographs,* **102,** 543-561.

Blau, P. M. (1964). *Exchange and Power in Social Life.* John Wiley, New York.

Bleda, P. R. (1974). Toward a clarification of the role of cognitive and affective processes in the similarity-attraction relationship. *J. Pers. Soc. Psychol.* **29**, 368-373.

Bogartz, R. S. and Wackwitz, J. H. (1970). Transforming response measures to remove interactions or other sources of variance. *Psychon. Sci.* **19**, 87-89.

Bohac, N. C. and Reboussin, R. (1967). Effects of varying ratios of favourable to unfavourable adjectives on the primacy effect in forming impressions of personality. Paper to Annual Convention of Midwestern Psychological Association, Chicago.

Bowerman, C. E. and Day, B. R. (1956). A test of the Theory of Complementary Needs as Applied to Couples During Courtship. *Amer. Sociol. Rev.* **21**, 602-605.

Bruner, J. S. (1956). You are your constructs. *Contemp. Psychol.* **1**, 355-357.

Bruner, J. S. and Postman, L. (1948). Symbolic value as an organizing factor in perception. *J. Soc. Psychol.* **27**, 203-208.

Burdick, J. A. (1972). Cardiac activity and attitude. *J. Pers. Soc. Psychol.* **22**, 80-86.

Burdick, J. A. and Burns, A. J. (1958). A test of "strain toward symmetry" theories. *J. Pers. Soc. Psychol.* **57**, 367-370.

Burgess, E. W. (1961). *Aging in Western Societies.* University of Chicago Press, Chicago.

Byrne, D. (1961a). Interpersonal attraction and attitude similarity. *J. Abn. Soc. Psychol.* **62**, 713-714.

Byrne, D. (1961b). Interpersonal attraction as a function of affiliation need and attitude similarity. *Hum. Rels.* **3**, 283-289.

Byrne, D. (1962). Response to attitude similarity-dissimilarity as a function of affiliation need. *J. Personal.* **30**, 164-177.

Byrne, D. (1966). *An Introduction to Personality: A Research Approach.* Prentice-Hall, Englewood Cliffs, N.J.

Byrne, D. (1969). Attitudes and attraction, *In* L. Berkowitz (Ed.), *Advances in Experimental Social Psychology,* (Vol. 4) pp. 36-90. Academic Press, New York and London.

Byrne, D. (1971). *The Attraction Paradigm.* Academic Press, New York and London.

Byrne, D., Baskett, G. D. and Hodges, L. (1969). Behavioral indicators of interpersonal attraction. Paper presented at meeting of the Psychonomic Society, St. Louis, November.

Byrne, D. and Blaylock, B. (1963). Similarity and assumed similarity of attitudes between husbands and wives. *J. Abn. Soc. Psychol.* **67**, 636-640.

Byrne, D., Bond, M. H. and Diamond, M. J. (1969). Response to political candidates as a function of attitude similarity-dissimilarity. *Hum. Rels.* **22**, 251-262.

Byrne, D. and Clore, G. L. (1966). Predicting interpersonal attraction toward strangers presented in three different stimulus modes. *Psychon. Sci.* **4**, 239-240.

Byrne, D. and Clore, G. L. (1967). Effectance arousal and attraction. *J. Pers. Soc. Psychol.* Monograph (6: Whole No. 638).

Byrne, D., Clore, G. L., Griffit, W., Lamberth, J. and Mitchell, H. E. (1973). When research paradigms converge: Confrontation or integration? *J. Pers. Soc. Psychol.* **28**, 313-320.

Byrne, D., Clore, G. L. and Worchel, P. (1966). Effect of economic similarity-dissimilarity on interpersonal attraction. *J. Pers. Soc. Psychol.* **4**, 220-224.

Byrne, D. and Ervin, C. R. (1969). Attraction toward a Negro stranger as a function of prejudice, attitude similarity, and the stranger's evaluation of the subject. *Hum. Rels.* **22**, 397-404.

Byrne, D., Ervin, C. R. and Lamberth, J. (1970). Continuity between the experimental study of attraction and real-life computer dating. *J. Pers. Soc. Psychol.* **16**, 157-165.

Byrne, D., Gouax, C., Griffit, W., Lamberth, J., Murakawa, N., Prasad, M. B. and Ramirez, M. (1971). The ubiquitous relationship: attitude similarity and attraction. A cross cultural study. *Hum. Rels.* **24**, 201-207.

Byrne, D. and Griffit, W. (1966). Similarity versus liking: A clarification. *Psychom. Sci.* **6**, 295-296.

Byrne, D. and Griffitt, W. (1969). Similarity and awareness of similarity of personality characteristics as determinants of attraction. *J. Exp. Res. in Pers.* **3**, 179-186.

Byrne, D., Griffitt, W. and Stefaniak, D. (1967). Attraction and similarity of personality characteristics. *J. Pers. Soc. Psychol.* **5**, 82-90.

Byrne, D. and Lamberth, J. (1971). Cognitive and reinforcement theories as complementary approaches to the study of attraction, *In* B. I. Murstein (Ed.), *Theories of Attraction and Love*, pp. 59-84. Springer, New York.

Byrne, D., London, O. and Reeves, K. (1968). The effects of physical attractiveness, sex and attitude similarity on interpersonal attraction. *J. Personal.* **36**, 259-271.

Byrne, D. and McGraw, C. (1964). Interpersonal attraction toward Negroes. *Hum. Rels.* **17**, 201-213.

Byrne, D. and Nelson, D. (1965a). Attraction as a linear function of proportion of positive reinforcements. *J. Pers. Soc. Psychol.* **1**, 659-663.

Byrne, D. and Nelson, D. (1965b). The effect of topic importance and attitude similarity-dissimilarity on attraction in a multi-stranger design. *Psychon. Sci.* **3**, 449-450.

Byrne, D., Rasche, L. and Kelley, K. (1974). When "I Like You" indicates disagreement: An experimental differentiation of information and affect. *J. Res. in Pers.* **8**, 207-217.

Byrne, D. and Rhamey, R. (1965). Magnitude of positive and negative reinforcements as a determinant of attraction. *J. Pers. Soc. Psychol.* **2**, 884-889.

Byrne, D. and Wong, T. J. (1962). Racial prejudice, interpersonal attraction and assumed dissimilarity of attitudes. *J. Abn. Soc. Psychol.* **65**, 246-253.

Campbell, D. T. and Fiske, D. W. (1959). Convergent and discriminant validation by the multitrait-multimethod matrix. *Psych. Bull.* **56**, 81-105.

Canfield, F. E. and La Gaipa (1970a). Friendship expectations at different levels in the development of friendship. Paper read at Southeastern Psychological Association Meeting, Louisville, April, 1970.

Canfield, F. E. and La Gaipa, J. J. (1970b). A multidimensional approach to friendship. Paper read at the meeting of the Canadian Psychological Association, Winnipeg.

Cartwright, D. (1968). The Nature of Group Cohesiveness, *In* D. Cartwright and A. Zander (Eds) *Group Dynamics: Research and Theory*, 3rd Edn., pp. 434-464. Harper and Row, New York.

Cartwright, D. and Zander, A. (1968). *Group Dynamics: Research and Theory*, 3rd Edn. Harper and Row, New York.

Cattell, R. B. and Nesselroade, J. R. (1967). Likeness and Completeness Theories Examined by 16 Personality Factor Measures on Stably and Unstably Married Couples. *J. Pers. Soc. Psychol.* **7**, 351-361.

Centers, R. (1972). The Completion Hypothesis and Compensatory Dynamic in Intersexual Attraction and Love. *J. Psychol.* **82**, 111-126.

Chaikin, A. L. and Derlega, V. J. (1974). *Self Disclosure.* General Learning Press, Morristown, N.J.

Clements, W. H. (1967). Marital interaction and marital stability; a point of view and a descriptive comparison of stable and unstable marriages. *J. marr. Fam.* **29**, 697-702.

Cline, V. B. (1964). Interpersonal perception. *In* Maher, B. A. (Ed.) *Progress in Experimental Personality Research* (Vol. 1). Academic Press, New York and London.

Cline, V. B. and Richards, J. M. (1960). Accuracy of interpersonal perception — a general trait. *J. Abn. Soc. Psychol.* **60**, 1-7.

Clore, G. L. (1975). *Interpersonal Attraction: An Overview.* General Learning Press, Morristown, N.J.

Clore, G. L. and Baldridge, B. (1970). The behavior of item weights in attitude-attraction research. *J. Exp. Soc. Psychol.* **6**, 177-186.

Clore, G. L. and Byrne, D. (1974). A reinforcement-affect model of attraction, *In* T. L. Huston (Ed.), *Perspectives on Interpersonal Attraction.* Academic Press, New York and London.

Clore, G. L. and Byrne, D. (In press). The process of personality interaction, *In* R. B. Cattell and R. M. Dreger (Eds), *Handbook of Modern Personality Theory.*

Clore, G. L. and Gormly, J. B. (1974). Knowing, feeling, and liking: A psychophysiological study of attraction. *J. Res. in Pers.* **8**, 218-230.

Clore, G. L. and Kerber, K. (1975). Sources of likeability. Unpublished research, University of Illinois at Urbana-Champaign.

Clore, G. and McGuire, H. (1974). Attraction and conversational style. Paper presented at the Society of Experimental Social Psychology, Urbana, Illinois.

Clore, G. L., Wiggins, N. H. and Itkin, S. (1975a). Gain and loss in attraction: Attribution from nonverbal behavior. *J. Pers. Soc. Psychol.* **31**, 706-712.

Clore, G. L., Wiggins, N. H. and Itkin, S. (1975b). Judging attraction from nonverbal behavior: The gain phenomenon. *J. Consult. Clin. Psychol.* **43**, 491-497.

Cohen, A. R. (1958). Upward communication in experimentally created hierarchies. *Hum. Rels.* **11**, 41-53.

Cohen, E. (1971). Arab boys and tourist girls in a mixed Jewish-Arab community. *Int. J. Comp. Sociol.* **12**, 217-233.

Coles, M. G. H. (1972). Cardiac and respiratory activity during visual search. *J. Exp. Psychol.* **96**, 371-379.

Collett, P. (1971). On training Englishmen in the non-verbal behaviour of Arabs. *Int. J. Psychol.* **6**, 209-215.

Comfort, A. (1971). Likelihood of human pheromones. *Nature,* **432-433**, 479.

Cook, M. (1971). *Interpersonal Perception.* Penguin, Harmondsworth.

Cook, M. and McHenry, R. (1976). *The Psychology of Sexual Attraction.* Simon and Schuster, New York.

Cook, M. and Smith, J. M. C. (1975). The role of gaze in impression formation. *Brit. J. Soc. Clin. Psychol.* 14, 19-25.

Coopersmith, S. (1967). *The Antecedents of Self-Esteem.* Freeman, San Francisco.

Corah, N., Feldman, M. J., Cohen, I. S., Gruen, W., Meadow, A. and Ringwall, E. A. (1958). Social desirability as a variable in the Edwards Personal Preference Schedule. *J. Consult. Psychol.* 22, 70-72.

Cozby, P. C. (1972). Self-disclosure, reciprocity, and liking. *Sociometry* 35, 151-160.

Cozby, P. C. (1973). Self-disclosure: a literature review. *Psychol. Bull.* 79, 73-91.

Craig, R. G. and Duck, S. W. (in press). Similarity, interpersonal attitudes and attraction: the evaluative descriptive distinction. *Brit. J. Soc. Clin. Psychol.*

Crow, W. J. and Hammond, K. R. (1957). The generality of accuracy and response sets in interpersonal perception. *J. Abn. Soc. Psychol.* 54, 384-390.

Crowne, D. P. and Marlowe, D. (1960). A new scale of social desirability independent of psychopathology. *J. Consult Psychol.* 24, 349-354.

Crowne, D. P. and Marlowe, D. (1964). *The Approval Motive.* Wiley, New York.

Dahl, R. A. (1957). The concept of power. *Behav. Sci.* 2, 201-215.

Dailey, C. A. (1971). *Assessment of Lives.* Jossey-Bass.

Dalto, C. A., Ajzen, I. and Kaplan, K. J. (1975). Self disclosure and attraction: Effects of intimacy and desirability of information about another person. Unpublished manuscript, University of Massachusetts, Amherst.

Darlington, R. B. (1968). Multiple regression in psychological research and practice. *Psychol. Bull.* 69, 161-182.

Davis, J. D. and Skinner, A. E. G. (1974). Reciprocity of Self Disclosure in interviews: modelling or social exchange? *J. Pers. Soc. Psychol.* 29, 779-784.

Davis, M. S. (1973). *Intimate Relations.* The Free Press, New York.

Derlega, V. J., Chaikin, A. L., Easterling, R. and Furman, G. (1973). Potential consequences and self-disclosure reciprocity. Unpublished manuscript, Old Dominion University.

Derlega, V. J., Harris, M. S. and Chaikin, A. L. (1973). Self-disclosure reciprocity, liking, and the deviant. *J. Exp. Soc. Psychol.* 9, 277-284.

Derlega, V. J., Walmer, J. and Furman, G. (1973). Mutual disclosure in social interactions. *J. Soc. Psychol.* 90, 159-160.

Dermer, M. (1973). When beauty fails. Unpublished doctoral dissertation, University of Minnesota, Minneapolis.

Deutsch, M. and Solomon, L. (1959). Reactions to evaluations of others as influenced by self-evaluations. *Sociometry* 22, 93-112.

Dickson, H. and McGinnes, E. (1966). Affectivity in the arousal of attitudes as measured by GSR. *Am. J. Psychol.* 79, 584-587.

Dimascio, A., Boyd, R. W. and Greenblatt, M. (1957). Physiological correlates of tension and antagonism during psychotherapy. *Psychosom. Med.* 19, 99-104.

Dion, K., Berscheid, E. and Walster, E. (1972). What is beautiful is good. *J. Pers. Soc. Psychol.* 24, 285-290.

Dittes, J. E. (1959). Attractiveness of group as a function of self-esteem and acceptance by group. *J. Abn. Soc. Psychol.* 59, 77-82.

Doering, E. and Seipel, K. H. (1975). Attribution und Selbstwertgefuhl. Unpublished term paper. Fachbereich Psychologie, Universitat Marburg.

Dornbusch, S. M. (1955). The military academy as an assimilating institution. *Social Forces* 33, 316-321.

Douglas, M. (1972). Deciphering a Meal, *Daedalus,* Winter.

Duck, S. W. (1972). Friendship, Similarity and the Reptest. *Psychol. Rep.* 31, 231-234.

Duck, S. W. (1973a). Similarity and perceived similarity of personal constructs as influences on friendship choice. *Brit. J. Soc. Clin. Psychol.* 12, 1-6.

Duck, S. W. (1973b). *Personal relationships and personal constructs: a study of friendship formation.* Wiley, London.

Duck, S. W. (1973c). Personality similarity and friendship formation: similarity of what, when? *J. Personal* 41, 543-558.

Duck, S. W. (1975a). Attitude similarity and interpersonal attraction: right answers and wrong reasons. *Brit. J. Soc. Clin. Psychol.* 14, 311-312.

Duck, S. W. (1975b). Personality similarity and friendship choices by adolescents. *Eur. J. Soc. Psychol.* 5, 70-83.

Duck, S. W. (in press, a). Personality similarity in friendship formation, *In* Stroebe, W. and Mikula, G. (Eds), *Freundschaft und Liebe.* Huber, Bern.

Duck, S. W. (in press, b). Interpersonal communications in developing acquaintance, *In* G. Miller (Ed.), *Explorations in Interpersonal Communication.* Sage,

Duck, S. W. (in press). *The Study of Acquaintance.* Teakfield, London.

Duck, S. W. and Craig, R. G. (1975). Effects of type of information upon interpersonal attraction. *Soc. Beh. and Personal.* 3, 000-000.

Duck, S. W. and Craig, R. G. (in prep.). Personality similarity and the longitudinal development of friendship: an experimental study.

Duck, S. W. and Craig, R. G. (in press). The relative attractiveness of different types of information about another person. *Brit. J. Soc. Clin. Psychol.*

Duck, S. W. and Spencer, C. P. (1972). Personal constructs and friendships formation. *J. Pers. Soc. Psychol.* 23, 40-45.

Duke, M. P. and Nowicki, S. (1972). A new measure and social learning model for interpersonal distance. *J. Exp. Res. in Pers.* 6, 119-132.

Dutton, D. G. (1972). Effect of feedback parameters on congruency versus positivity effects in reactions to personal evaluations. *J. Pers. Soc. Psychol.* 24, 366-371.

Dymond, R. (1954). Interpersonal perception and marital happiness. *Can. J. Psychol.* 8, 164-171.

Edwards, A. L. (1959). *Edwards Personal Preference Schedule Manual.* Psychological Corp, New York.

Edwards, W. (1954). The theory of decision making. *Psychol. Bull.* 51, 380-417.

Efran, M. G. (1969). Visual interaction and interpersonal attraction. Unpublished doctoral dissertation. University of Texas.

Ehrlich, H. J. and Graeven, D. B. (1971). Reciprocal self-disclosure in a dyad. *J. Exp. Soc. Psychol.* 7, 389-400.

Eibl-Eibesfeldt, I. (1975). *Ethology: the Biology of Behavior.* (2nd edn.). Holt,

Eiser, J. R. and Smith, A. J. (1972). Preference for accuracy and positivity in the description of oneself by other. *Eur. J. Soc. Psychol.* 2, 199-201.

Ekman, P. and Friesen, W. V. (1969). Nonverbal leakage and clues to deception. *Psychiatry,* 32, 88-106.

Elliott, R. (1969). Tonic heart rate: Experiments on the effects of collative variables lead to a hypothesis about its motivational significance. *J. Pers. Soc. Psychol.* **12**, 211-228.

Ellison, C. W. and Firestone, I. J. (1974). Development of interpersonal trust as a function of self-esteem, target status and target style. *J. Pers. Soc. Psychol.* **29**, 655-663.

Ellsworth, P. C. and Carlsmith, J. M. (1968). Effects of eye contact and verbal content on affective response to dyadic interaction. *J. Pers. Soc. Psychol.* **10**, 15-20.

Emerson, R. M. (1962). Power-dependence relations. *Amer. Sociol. Rev.* **27**, 31-41.

Emmerich, W. (1961). Family role concepts of children ages six to ten. *Child. Dev.* **32**, 609-624.

Engelhart, R. S., Lockhart, L. M. and La Gaipa, J. J. (1975). Friendship expectations of psychiatric patients. Paper read at the meeting of Southeastern Psychological Association, Atlanta.

English, H. B. and English, A. C. (1958). *A Comprehensive Dictionary of Psychological and Psychoanalytical Terms.* David McKay, New York.

Epstein, S. (1973). The self-concept revisited. *Amer. Psychol.* **28**, 404-416.

Esser, J. K. and Komorita, S. S. (1975). Reciprocity and concession making in bargaining. *J. Pers. Soc. Psychol.* **31**, 864-872.

Exline, R. V. and Winters, L. C. (1965). Affective relations and mutual glances in dyads. *In* S. S. Tomkins and C. Izzard (Eds) *Affect, Cognition and Personality.* Springer: New York.

Feather, N. T. (1959). Subjective probability and decision under uncertainty. *Psychol. Rev.* **66**, 150-164.

Festinger, L. (1950). Informal social communication. *Psychol. Rev.* **57**, 271-282.

Festinger, L. (1954). A theory of social comparison processes. *Hum. Rels.* **7**, 117-140.

Festinger, L., Schachter, S. and Back, K. (1950) *Social Pressures in Informal Groups.* Harper, New York.

Fishbein, M. (1963). An investigation of the relationships between beliefs about an object and the attitude toward that object. *Hum. Rels.* **16**, 233-240.

Fishbein, M. (1967a). A consideration of beliefs and their role in attitude measurement, *In* M. Fishbein (Ed.), *Readings in Attitude Theory and Measurement*, pp. 257-266. Wiley, New York.

Fishbein, M. (1967b). A behavior theory approach to the relations between beliefs about an object and the attitude toward the object, *In* M. Fishbein (Ed.), *Readings in Attitude Theory and Measurement*, pp. 389-400. Wiley, New York.

Fishbein, M. and Ajzen, I. (1972). Attitudes and opinions. *Ann. Rev. Psychol.* **23**, 487-544.

Fishbein, M. and Ajzen, I. (1975). *Belief, Attitude, Intention, and Behavior: An Introduction to Theory and Research.* Addison-Wesley, Reading, Massachusetts.

Fishbein, M. and Coombs, F. S. (1974). Basis for decision: An attitudinal analysis of voting behavior. *J. Appl. Soc. Psychol.* **4**, 95-124.

Fishbein, M. and Hunter, R. (1964). Summation versus balance in attitude organization and change. *J. Abn. Soc. Psychol.* **69**, 505-510.

Fishbein, M. and Raven, B. H. (1962). The AB scales: an operational definition of belief and attitude. *Hum. Rels.* **15**, 35-44.

Fisher, J. D. and Nadler, A. (1974). The effect of similarity between donor and recipient on recipient's reactions to aid. *J. Appl. Soc. Psychol.* **4**, 230-243.

Fitts, P. M. and Posner, M. I. (1967). *Human Performance.* Brooks Co.

Foa, U. G. and Donnenwerth, G. V. (1971). Love poverty in modern culture and sensitivity training. *Sociol. Inquiry.* **41**, 149-159.

Foa, U. G. and Foa, E. B. (1971). Resource exchange: Toward a structural theory of Interpersonal relations, *In* A. W. Siegman and B. Pope (Eds), *Studies in Dyadic Communication.* Pergamon Press, New York.

Ford, C. S. and Beach, F. A. (1952). *Patterns of Sexual Behaviour.* Methuen, London.

French, J. P. R. and Raven, B. (1959). The bases of social power, *In* D. Cartwright (Ed.). *Studies in Social Power.* University of Michigan Press, Ann Arbor.

Garfinkel, H. (1962). Common sense knowledge of social structures: The documentary method of interpretation in lay and professional fact finding, *In* J. M. Scher (Eds), *Theories of the Mind,* pp. 689-712. Free Press, New York.

Gergen, K. J. (1962). Interaction goals and personalistic feedback as factors affecting the presentation of self. Unpublished Doctoral Dissertation, Duke University.

Gergen, K. J. (1969). *The Psychology of Behavior Exchange.* Addison-Wesley, Reading, Mass.

Gergen, K. J., Bode, K. A. and Morse, S. J. (1974). Overpaid or overworked? Cognitive and behavioral reactions to inequitable rewards. *J. Appl. Soc. Psychol.* **4**, 259-274.

Gergen, K. J., Ellsworth, P., Maslach, C. and Seipel, M. (1975). Obligation, donor resources, and reactions to aid in three cultures. *J. Pers. Soc. Psychol.* **31**, 390-400.

Gergen, J. J. and Marlowe, D. (Eds), (1970). *Personality and Social Behavior.* Addison-Wesley: Reading, Massachusetts.

Gibbins, K. (1969). Communication aspects of women's clothes and their relation to fashionability. *Brit. J. Soc. Clin. Psychol.* **8**, 301-312.

Goffman, E. (1956). *The Presentation of Self in Everyday Life.* Edinburgh University Press.

Goffman, E. (1961). *Asylums: Essays on the social situation of mental patients and other inmates.* Doubleday, Garden City.

Goffman, E. (1963). *Stigma: notes on the management of spoiled identity.* Prentice Hall, Englewood Cliffs.

Goffman, E. (1971). *Relations in Public.* Allen Lane, The Penguin Press, London.

Goldstein, J. W. and Rosenfeld, H. M. (1969). Insecurity and preference for persons similar to oneself. *J. Personal.* **37**, 253-268.

Gollob, H. F. (1974a). Some tests of a social inference model. *J. Pers. Soc. Psychol.* **29**, 157-172.

Gollob, H. F. (1974b). The subject-verb-object approach to social cognition. *Psychol. Rev.* **81**, 286-321.

Gormly, J. (1971). Sociobehavioral and physiological responses to interpersonal disagreement. *J. Exp. Res. in Pers.* **5**, 216-222.

Gouaux, C. (1971). Induced affective states and interpersonal attraction. *J. Pers. Soc. Psychol.* **20**, 37-43.

Gouaux, C., Lamberth, J. and Friedrich, G. (1972). Affect and interpersonal attraction: A comparison of trait and state measures. *J. Pers. Soc. Psychol.* **24**, 53-58.

Gough, H. G. (1964). *Manual, California Psychological Inventory,* (2nd edn.). Consulting Psychologists Press, Palo Alto.

Gouldner, A. W. (1960). The norm of reciprocity: A preliminary statement. *Amer. Sociol. Rev.* **25,** 16-179.

Goyette, M. (1975). Unpublished master's thesis, Connecticut College.

Grabitz-Gniech, G. (1971). Bericht über eine Analyse von sieben Persönlichkeitsfragebogen. Bericht aus dem Sonderforschungsbereich 24 der Universitaet Mannheim, Mannheim.

Greenberg, M. S. and Shapiro, S. P. (1971). Indebtedness: An adverse aspect of asking for and receiving help. *Sociometry* **34,** 290-301.

Griffitt, W. B. (1966). Interpersonal similarity as a function of self-concept and personality similarity-dissimilarity. *J. Pers. Soc. Psychol.* **4,** 581-584.

Griffitt, W. B. (1969). Personality similarity and self-concept as determinants of interpersonal attraction. *J. Soc. Psychol.* **78,** 137-146.

Griffitt, W. B. (1970). Environmental effects of interpersonal affective behavior: Ambient effective temperature and attraction. *J. Pers. Soc. Psychol.* **15,** 240-244.

Griffitt, W. (1974). Attitude similarity and attraction, *In* T. L. Huston (Ed.), *Foundations of Interpersonal Attraction.* pp. 285-308. Academic Press, New York and London.

Griffitt, W. and Veitch, R. (1971). Hot and crowded: influences of population density and temperature on interpersonal behaviour. *J. Pers. Soc. Psychol.* **17,** 92-98.

Griffitt, W. and Veitch, R. (1974). Preacquaintance attitude similarity and attraction revisited: Ten days in a fall-out shelter. *Sociometry* **37,** 163-173.

Gross, A. E. and Latane, J. G. (1974). Receiving help, reciprocation, and interpersonal attraction. *J. Appl. Soc. Psychol.* **4,** 210-223.

Grush, J., Clore, G. L. and Costin, F. (1975). Dissimilarity and attraction: When difference makes a difference. *J. Pers. Soc. Psychol.* **32,** 783-789.

Haggard, F. A. and Isaacs, K. S. (1966). Micromomentary facial expressions as indicators of ego-mechanisms in psychotherapy, *In* L. A. Gottschalk and A. H. Auerbach (Eds), *Methods of Research in Psychotherapy.* Appleton Century Crofts, New York.

Hall, C. S. and Lindzey, G. (1957). *Theories of Personality.* Wiley, New York.

Hansvick, C. L. and La Gaipa, J. J. (1974). Self disclosure, friendship and interpersonal distance. Unpub. MS., University of Windsor.

Harré, R. and Secord, P. F. (1972). *The Explanation of Social Behaviour,* Blackwell, London.

Hartley, R. E. (1966). A developmental view of female sex-role identification. *In* Biddle, B. J. and Thomas, E. J. (Eds). *Role Therapy: Concepts and Research,* pp. 354-360. Wiley, New York.

Heath, A. (1968). Economic theory and sociology: A critique of P. M. Blau's "Exchange and power in social life". *Sociology,* **2,** 273-292.

Heider, F. (1958). *The Psychology of Interpersonal Relations.* Wiley, New York.

Heilbronn, M. (1975). A longitudinal study of the development and dissolution of friendship. Unpublished doctoral dissertation, University of Windsor.

Helmreich, R., Aronson, E. and Lefan, J. (1970). To err is humanizing — sometimes: Effects of self-esteem, competence, and a pratfall on interpersonal attraction. *J. Pers. Soc. Psychol.* **16,** 259-264.

Helson, H. (1964). *Adaptation-level Theory.* Harper and Row, New York.

Hendrick, C. and Brown, S. (1971). Introversion, extroversion, and interpersonal attraction. *J. Pers. Soc. Psychol.* **20,** 31-36.

Hendrick, C. and Page, H. (1970). Self-esteem, attitude similarity and attraction. *J. Pers.* **38,** 588-601.

Herzberger, S. (1975). Determinants of self-other discrepancy in attribution: situational factors and individual differences. Unpublished Doctoral Dissertation. University of Illinois at Urbana-Champaign.

Hess, E. H. (1965). Attitude and pupil size. *Sci. Amer.* **212,** 46-54.

Hewitt, J. and Goldman, M. (1974). Self-esteem, need for approval and reactions to personal evaluations. *J. Exp. Soc. Psychol.* **10,** 201-210.

Hinkle, D. (1970). The game of personal constructs, *In* D. Bannister (Ed.), *Perspectives in Personal Construct Theory.* Academic Press, London and New York.

Hirschman, R. and Katkin, E. S. (1971). Relationships among attention, GSR activity, and perceived similarity of self and others. *J. Pers.* **39,** 277-288.

Hogan, R. and Mankin, D. (1970). Determinants of interpersonal attraction: a clarification. *Psych. Rep.* **26,** 235-238.

Hoffman, L. R. and Maier, N. (1966). An experimental re-examination of the similarity-attraction hypothesis. *J. Pers. Soc. Psychol.* **3,** 145-152.

Hollander, E. P. (1964). *Leaders, Groups and Influence.* Oxford University Press, New York.

Homans, G. C. (1974). *Social Behavior: Its Elementary Forms.* (revised edition.) Harcourt, Brace. Jovanovich, New York.

Homans, G. C. (1971). Commentary, In H. Turk and R. L. Simpson (Eds) *Institutions and Social Exchange: The Sociologies of Talcott Parsons and George C. Homans,* pp. 363-377. Bobbs-Merrill, Indianapolis.

Horst, P. and Wright, C. E. (1959). The comparative reliability of two techniques of personality appraisal. *J. Clin. Psychol.* **15,** 388-391.

Howitt, R. (1975). A self-other attributional model of friendship formation. Unpub. Doc. diss., University of Windsor.

Howitt, R. and La Gaipa, J. J. (1975a). The role of individual differences in an attributional model of friendship formation. Paper read at meeting of the Canadian Psychological Association, Quebec City, Quebec.

Howitt, R. and La Gaipa, J. J. (1975b). A longitudinal study of an attributional model of friendship formation. Unpublished manuscript, University of Windsor.

Huesmann, L. R. and Levinger, G. (1976). Incremental exchange theory: A formal model for progression in dyadic social interaction, *In* L. Berkowitz and E. Walster (Eds), *Advances in Experimental Social Psychology,* (Vol. 9). Academic Press, New York and London.

Huffman, D. M. (1969). Interpersonal attraction as a function of behavioral similarity. Unpublished doctoral dissertation, University of Texas.

Huizinga, J. (1924). *The Waning of the Middle Ages.* (1955 printing). Penguin Books, London.

Humphrey, R. A. L. (1970). *Tea-room Trade: Impersonal Sex in Public Places.* Aldine, Chicago.

Hurwitz, J. I., Zander, A. and Hymovitch, B. (1960). Some effects of power on the relations among group members, *In* D. Cartwright and A. Zander (Eds), *Group Dynamics: Research and Theory*, (2nd edn.). Harper and Row, New York.

Huston, T. L. (1973). Ambiguity of acceptance, social desirability, and dating choice. *J. Exp. Soc. Psychol.* **9**, 32-42.

Huston, T. L. (1974). A perspective on interpersonal attraction, *In* T. L. Huston (Ed.), *Foundations of Interpersonal Attraction*. Academic Press, New York and London.

Inbau, F. E. (1942). *Lie Detection and Criminal Interrogation*. Williams and Wilkins, Baltimore.

Insko, C. A., Thompson, V. D., Stroebe, W., Shaud, K. F., Pinner, B. E. and Layton, B. D. (1973). Implied evaluation and the similarity-attraction effect. *J. Pers. Soc. Psychol.* **25**, 297-308.

Isaacson, G. S. and Landfield, A. W. (1965). Meaningfulness of personal versus common constructs. *J. Indiv. Psychol.* **21**, 160-166.

Izard, C. E. (1960a). Personality similarity and friendship. *J. Abn. Soc. Psychol.* **61**, 47-51.

Izard, C. E. (1960b). Personality similarity, positive affect and interpersonal attraction. *J. Abn. Soc. Psychol.* **61**, 484-485.

Izard, C. E. (1963). Personality Similarity and Friendship: A Follow-up Study. *J. Abn. Soc. Psychol.* **66**, 598-600.

Jaccard, J. J. and Fishbein, M. (1975). Inferential beliefs and order effects in personality impressions formation. *J. Pers. Soc. Psychol.* **31**, 1031-1040.

Jacobs, L., Berscheid, E. and Walster, E. (1971). Self-esteem and attraction. *J. Pers. Soc. Psychol.* **17**, 84-91.

Jahoda, G. (1963). Refractive errors, intelligence and social mobility. *Brit. J. Soc. Clin. Psychol.* **1**, 96-106.

Janis, I. L. and Field, P. B. (1959). The Janis and Field Personality Questionnaire. *In* C. I. Hovland and I. L. Janis (Eds), *Personality and Persuasibility*. pp. 300-305. Yale University Press, New Haven.

Johnson, F. N. (1975). Depression: Some proposals for future research. *Dis. Nerv. Syst.* **36**, 228-232.

Jones, E. E. (1964). *Ingratiation*. Appleton Century Crofts, New York.

Jones, E. E., Bell, L. and Aronson, E. (1972). The reciprocation of attraction from similar and dissimilar others, *In* C. C. McClintock (Ed.), *Experimental Social Psychology*. Holt, New York.

Jones, E. E. and Davis, K. E. (1965). From acts to dispositions: the attribution process in person perception, *In* L. Berkowitz (Ed.), *Advances in Experimental Social Psychology*, (Vol. 2) pp. 219-266. Academic Press, New York and London.

Jones, E. E., Davis, K. E. and Gergen, K. J. (1961). Role playing variations and their informational value for person perception. *J. Abn. Soc. Psychol.* **63**, 302-310.

Jones, E. E. and Gerard, H. B. (1967) *Foundations of Social Psychology*. Wiley, New York.

Jones, E. E. and Gordon, E. M. (1972). Timing of self-disclosure and its effects on personal attraction. *J. Pers. Soc. Psychol.* **24**, 358-365.

Jones, E. E. and Harris, V. A. (1967). The attribution of attitudes. *J. Exp. Soc. Psychol.* **3**, 1-24.

Jones, E. E. and Nisbett, R. R. (1971). *The Actor and the Observer: Divergent Perceptions of the Causes of Behavior.* General Learning Press, New York.

Jones, E. E., Worchel, S., Goethals, G. R. and Grumeit, J. F. (1971). Prior expectancy and behavioral extremity as determinants of attitude attribution. *J. Exp. Soc. Psychol.* **7**, 59-80.

Jones, S. C. (1966). Some determinants of interpersonal evaluating behavior. *J. Pers. Soc. Psychol.* **3**, 397-403.

Jones, S. C. (1973). Self and interpersonal evaluations: Esteem theories versus consistency theories. *Psych. Bull.* **79**, 185-199.

Jourard, S. M. (1971). *Self-disclosure: An Experimental Analysis of the Transparent Self.* Wiley, New York.

Jourard, S. M. and Friedman, R. (1970). Experimenter-subject "distance" and self-disclosure. *J. Pers. Soc. Psychol.* **25**, 278-282.

Kahn, A. and Tice, T. E. (1973). Returning a favor and retaliating harm: The effects of stated intentions and actual behavior. *J. Exp. Soc. Psychol.* **9**, 43-56.

Kanin, E. J. (1969). Selected dyadic aspects of male sex aggression. *J. Sex. Res.* **5**, 12-28.

Kaplan, K. J. and Fishbein, M. (1969). The source of beliefs, their saliency, and prediction of attitude. *J. Soc. Psychol.* **78**, 63-74.

Kaplan, M. F. and Anderson, N. H. (1973). Information integration theory and reinforcement theory as approaches to interpersonal attraction. *J. Pers. Soc. Psychol.* **28**, 301-312.

Katz, D. and Braly, K. W. (1935). Racial prejudice and racial stereotypy. *J. Abnorm. Soc. Psychol.* **30**, 175-193.

Katz, H., Cadoret, R., Hughes, K. and Abbey, D. (1965). Physiological correlates of acceptable and unacceptable attitude statements. *Psych. Rep.* **17**, 78.

Katz, I., Glucksberg, S. and Krauss, R. (1960). Need satisfaction and Edwards Personal Preference Scores in married couples. *J. Consult. Psychol.* **24**, 205-208.

Kelley, H. H. (1967). Attribution theory in social psychology, *In* D. Levine (Ed.), *Nebraska Symposium on Motivation.* University of Nebraska Press, Lincoln.

Kelley, H. H. (1971). *Attribution in Social Interaction.* General Learning Press, Morristown, N.J.

Kelly, E. L. (1941). Marital compatibility as related to personality traits of husbands and wives as rated by self and spouse. *J. Soc. Psychol.* **13**, 193-198.

Kelly, G. A. (1955). *The Psychology of Personal Constructs.* Norton, New York.

Kelly, G. A. (1969). *Clinical Psychology and Personality,* (Ed. B. Maher). Wiley, New York.

Kelly, G. A. (1970). A brief introduction to personal construct theory, *In* D. Bannister (Ed.), *Perspectives in Personal Construct Theory.* Academic Press, London and New York.

Kelvin, P. (1970). *The Bases of Social Behaviour: an approach in terms of order and value.* Holt, Rinehart and Winston, London.

Kelvin, P. (1973). A social-psychological examination of privacy. *Brit. J. Soc. Clin. Psychol.* **12**, 248-261.

Kendon, A. (1967). Some functions of gaze direction in social interactions. *Acta. Psych.* **26**, 1-47.

Kendon, A. & Farber, A. (1973). A description of some human greetings, *In* R. P. Michael and J. H. Crook (Eds), *Comparative Ecology of Behaviour.* Academic Press, London and New York.

Kerckhoff, A. C. (1972). Status-related value patterns among married couples. *J. Marr. Fam.* **34,** 105-110.

Kerckhoff, A. C. (1974). The social context of interpersonal attraction, *In* Huston, T. L. (Ed.), *Foundations of Interpersonal Attraction,* pp. 61-78. Academic Press, New York and London.

Kerckhoff, A. C. and Davis, K. E. (1962). Value consensus and need complementarity in mate selection. *Amer. Sociol. Rev.* **27,** 295-303.

Kiesler, S. B. and Baral, R. L. (1970). The search for a romantic partner: The effect of self-esteem and physical attractiveness on romantic behavior, *In* K. J. Gergen and Marlowe, D. (Eds), *Personality and Social Behavior.* pp. 155-165. Addison-Wesley, Reading, Massachusetts.

Kiesler, C. A. and Goldberg, G. N. (1968). Multi-dimensional approach to the experimental study of interpersonal attraction: Effect of a blunder on the attractiveness of a competent other. *Psych. Rep.* **22,** 693-705.

Kinsey, A. C. *et al.* (1948). *Sexual Behavior in the Human Male.* Saunders, Philadelphia.

Kinsey, A. C. *et al.* (1953). *Sexual Behaviour in the Human Female.* Saunders, Philadelphia.

Kirkendall, L. A. (1961). *Premarital Intercourse and Interpersonal Relationships.* Julian Press, New York.

Kissel, S. (1965). Stress reducing properties of social stimuli. *J. Pers. Soc. Psychol.* **2,** 378-384.

Kleck, R. E. and Rubenstein, C. (1975). Physical attractiveness, perceived attitude similarity, and interpersonal attraction in an opposite-sex encounter. *J. Pers. Soc. Psychol.* **31,** 107-114.

Kleinke, C. L. (1972). Interpersonal attraction as it relates to gaze and distance between people. *Rep. Res. in Soc. Psychol.* **3,** 105-120.

Kleinke, C. L., Staneski, R. A. and Berger, D. E. (1975). Evaluation of an interviewer as a function of interviewer gaze, reinforcement of subject gaze, and interviewer attractiveness. *J. Pers. Soc. Psychol.* **31,** 115-122.

Knupfer, G., Clark, W. and Room, R. (1966). The mental health of the unmarried. *Amer. J. Psychiat.* **122,** 841-851.

Kohen, A. S. (1972). Self disclosing behavior in cross sex dyads. Unpublished doctoral dissertation, University of Iowa.

Krantz, D. H. and Tversky, A. (1971). Letters to the editor. *Psychol. Rev.* **78,** 457-458.

Ktsanes, T. (1955). Mate Selection on the Basis of Personality Type: A Study Utilizing an Empirical Typology. *Amer. Sociol. Rev.* **20,** 547-551.

Kubie, L. S. (1956). Psychoanalysis and marriage: Practical and theoretical issues, *In* V. E. Eistenstein (Ed.), *Neurotic Interaction in Marriage.* Basic Books, New York.

Lacey, J. I. (1967). Somatic response patterning and stress: Some revisions of activation theory, *In* M. H. Appley and R. Trumbell (Eds), *Psychological Stress: Issues in Research.* Appleton Century Crofts, New York.

La Gaipa, J. J. (1969). A factor analysis of friendship items. Unpublished manuscript, University of Windsor.

La Gaipa, J. J. (1972a). The perception of friendship rewards and affiliation arousal. *Psychon. Sci.* **28,** 69-71.

La Gaipa, J. J. (1972b). Personality factors in friendship. Paper read at Canadian Psychological Association, Montreal, June, 1972.

La Gaipa, J. J. and Bigelow, B. J. (1972). The development of friendship expectations. Paper read at the meeting of the Canadian Psychological Association, Montreal.

La Gaipa, J. J. and Werner, R. E. (1971). Effects of topic relevancy and attitude similarity on two measures of affiliation. *Psychon. Sci.* **24,** 67-68.

Landfield, A. W. (1971). *Personal Construct Systems in Psychotherapy.* Rand McNally, Chicago.

Larsen, K. S. (1971). An investigation of sexual behavior among Norwegian college students: a motivational study. *J. Marr. Fam.* **33,** 219-227.

Lazarus, R. S. (1968). Emotions and adaptation: Conceptual and empirical relations, *In* W. J. Arnold (Ed.) *Nebraska Symposium on Motivation,* (Vol. 16) pp. 175-266. University of Nebraska Press, Lincoln.

Leiber, J. (1973). A Generative Grammar for Menus, unpublished paper read at Linacre College, Oxford.

Lerner, M. J. (1974a). Social psychology of justice and interpersonal attraction, *In* T. Huston (Ed.), *Perspectives on Interpersonal Attraction,* pp. 331-351. Academic Press, New York and London.

Lerner, M. J. (1974b). The justice motive: "Equity" and "parity" among children. *J. Pers. Soc. Psychol.* **29,** 539-550.

Lerner, M. J., Miller, D. T. and Holmes, J. G. (1976). Deserving versus justice: A contemporary dilemma, *In* L. Berkowitz and E. Walster (Eds), *Advances in Experimental Social Psychology,* (Vol. 9). Academic Press, New York and London.

Levinger, G. (1964). Note on need complementarity in marriage. *Psych. Bull.* **61,** 153-157.

Levinger, G. (1974). A three-level approach to attraction: Toward an understanding of pair relatedness, *In* T. Huston (Ed.), *Foundations of Interpersonal Attraction,* pp. 99-120. Academic Press, New York and London.

Levinger, G. and Senn, D. J. (1967). Disclosure of feelings in marriage. *Merrill-Palmer Quarterly* **13,** 237-249.

Levinger, G., Senn, D. J. and Jorgensen, B. W. (1970). Progress towards permanence in courtship: a test of the Kerckhoff-Davis hypotheses. *Sociometry* **33,** 427-443.

Levinger, G. and Snoek, J. D. (1972). *Attraction in Relationship: A New Look at Interpersonal Attraction.* General Learning Press, Morristown, N.J.

Liberman, P. (1965). On the acoustic basis of the perception of intonation by linguists. *Word* **21,** 40-54.

Lickona, T. (1974). A cognitive-developmental approach to interpersonal attraction, *In* T. L. Huston (Ed.) *Foundations of Interpersonal Attraction,* pp. 31-59. Academic Press, New York and London.

Lindzey, G. and Byrne, D. (1968). Measurement of social choice and interpersonal attractiveness, *In* G. Lindzey and E. Aronson (Eds), *The Handbook of Social Psychology* (2nd edn. Vol. 2, pp. 452-525). Addison-Wesley, Reading, Mass.

Lischeron, J. A. and La Gaipa, J. J. (1970). Expectancy-confirmation and friendship. A paper read at the meeting of Canadian Psychological Association, Winnipeg, Manitoba, May.

Lischeron, J. A. and La Gaipa, J. J. (1971). The friendship expectancy inventory: prediction of the growth of friendship. Paper to Can. Psycho. Assoc., St. John's, Newfoundland, June, 1971.

Lombardo, J. P., Weiss, R. F. and Buchanan, W. (1972). Reinforcing and attracting functions of yielding. *J. Pers. Soc. Psychol.* **21**, 359-368.

Longabaugh, R. (1963). A category system for coding interpersonal behavior as social exchange. *Sociometry,* **26**, 319-344.

Looft, W. R. (1972). Ego-centrism and social interaction across the life span. *Psych. Bull.* **78**, 73-92.

Lott, B. and Lott, A. J. (1960). The Formation of Positive Attitudes Toward Group Members. *J. Abn. Soc. Psychol.* **61**, 297-300.

Lott, A. J. and Lott, B. E. (1974). The role of reward in the formation of positive interpersonal attitudes, *In* T. L. Huston (Ed.), *Foundations of Interpersonal Attraction,* pp. 171-192. Academic Press, New York and London.

Lykken, D. T. (1959). Properties of electrodes used in electrodermal measurement. *J. Comp. Physiol. Psychol.* **52**, 629-634.

Lykken, D. T., Rose, R., Luther, B. and Maley, M. (1966). Correcting psychophysiological measures for individual differences in range. *Psych. Bull.* **66**, 481-484.

McCall, G. J. (1974). A symbolic interactionist approach to attraction, *In* T. L. Huston (Ed.), *Foundations of Interpersonal Attraction,* pp. 217-231. Academic Press, New York and London.

McCarthy, M. F. and Duck, S. W. (1976). Friendship duration and responses to attitudinal agreement-disagreement. *Brit. J. Soc. Clin. Psychol.* **15**, 377-386.

McCarthy, M. F. and Duck, S. W. (in prep.). When "I disagree" means "I will like you": attribution of causality in acquaintance.

McGuire, W. J. (1960). Cognitive consistency and attitude change. *J. Abn. Soc. Psychol.* **60**, 345-353.

McGuire, W. J. (1969). The nature of attitudes and attitude change, *In* G. Lindzey and E. Aronson (Eds), *The Handbook of Social Psychology,* (2nd edn. Vol. 3, pp. 136-314). Addison-Wesley, Reading, Mass.

McHenry, R. (1971). New methods of assessing the accuracy of interpersonal perception. *J. Theory Soc. Beh.* **1**, 109-119.

McKeachie, W. J. (1952). Lipstick as a determiner of first impressions. *J. Soc. Psych.* **36**, 241-244

McLaughlin, B. (1970). Similarity, recall, and appraisal of others. *J. Personal.* **38**, 106-116.

McLaughlin, B. (1971). Effects of similarity and likableness on attraction and recall. *J. Pers. Soc. Psychol.* **20**, 65-69.

McNulty, J. A. and Walters, R. H. (1962). Emotional arousal, conflict and susceptibility to social influence. *Can. J. Psychol.* **16**.

McPherson, F. M., Buckley, F. and Draffan, J. (1971). "Psychological" constructs, thought process disorder and flattening of affect. *Brit. J. Soc. Clin. Psychol.* **10**, 267-270.

McWhirter, R. M., Jr. (1969). Interpersonal attraction in a dyad as a function of the physical attractiveness of its members. Unpublished doctoral dissertation, Texas Tech. University.

Malmo, R. B., Boag, T. J. and Smith, A. A. (1957). Physiological study of personal interaction. *Psychosomatic Medicine.*, **19**, 105-119.

Marlowe, D. and Gergen, K. (1969). Personality and social interaction, *In* G. Lindzey and E. Aronson (Eds), *The Handbook of Social Psychology*, (2nd edn. Vol. 3, pp. 590-665). Addison-Wesley, Reading, Mass.

Maslow, A. H. (1953). Love in healthy people, *In* A. Montagu (Ed.), *The Meaning of Love.* The Julian Press, New York.

Megargee, E. I. (1956). A study of the subjective aspects of group membership at Amherst. Unpublished manuscript, Amherst College.

Mehlman, B. (1962). Similarity in Friendship. *J. Soc. Psychol.* **57**, 195-202.

Mehrabian, A. (1969). Significance of posture and position in the communication of attitude and status relationships. *Psych. Bull.* **71**, 359-372.

Melbin, M. (1972). *Alone and With Others.* Harper and Row, New York.

Mettee, D. R. (1971). Changes in liking as a function of the magnitude and affect of sequential evaluations. *J. Exp. Soc. Psychol.* **7**, 157-172.

Mettee, D. R. and Aronson, E. (1974). Affective reactions to appraisal from others, *In* T. Huston (Ed.), *Foundations of Interpersonal Attraction.* Academic Press, New York and London.

Mettee, D. R. and Riskind, J. (1974). Size of defeat and liking for superior and similar ability competitor. *J. Exp. Soc. Psychol.* **10**, 333-351.

Mettee, D. R. and Wilkins, P. C. (1972). When similarity "hurts": The effects of perceived ability and a humorous blunder upon interpersonal attractiveness. *J. Pers. Soc. Psychol.* **22**, 246-258.

Miller, N., Campbell, D. T., Twedt, H. and O'Connell, E. J. (1966). Similarity, contrast and complementarity in friendship choice. *J. Pers. Soc. Psychol.* **3**, 3-12.

Mischel, T. (1964). Personal Constructs, Rules, and the Logic at clinical Activity. *Psych. Rev.* **71**, 180-192.

Mittelman, B. (1944). Complementary neurotic reactions in intimate relations. *Psychoanalytic Quarterly*, **13**, 479-491.

Moreno, J. L. (1934). *Who Shall Survive?* Nervous and Mental Diseases Monograph, No. 58. Washington, D.C.

Moss, M. K. (1969). Social desirability, physical attractiveness, and social choice. Unpublished doctoral dissertation, Kansas State University.

Mulkay, M. J. (1971). *Functionalism, Exchange and Theoretical Strategy.* Schocker Books, New York.

Murray, H. A. (1938). *Exporations in Personality*, Science Editions, New York.

Murray, H. A. (1962). Toward a Classification of Interaction, *In* T. Parsons and E. A. Shils (Eds), *Toward a General Theory of Action.* Harvard University Press, Cambridge, Mass.

Murray, H. A. (1963). Studies of stressful interpersonal disputations. *Amer. Psychol.* **18**, 28-36.

Murstein, B. I. (1966). Psychological determinants of marital choice. (Progress Report 1965-1966, NIHM Grant 08405-2). Connecticut College, New London.

Murstein, B. I. (1967a). The relationship of mental health to marital choice and courtship progress. *J. Marr. Fam.* **29,** 447-451.

Murstein, B. I. (1967b). Empirical Tests of Role, Complementary Needs, and Homogamy Theories of Marital Choice. *J. Marr. Fam.* **29,** 689-696.

Murstein, B. I. (1970). Stimulus-value-role: A theory of marital choice. *J. Marr. Fam.* **32,** 465-481.

Murstein, B. I. (1971). A theory of marital choice and its applicability to marriage adjustment and friendship. *In* Murstein, B. I. (Ed.), *Theories of Attraction and Love.* Springer, New York.

Murstein, B. I. (1972). Physical attractiveness and marital choice. *J. Pers. Soc. Psych.* **22,** 8-12.

Murstein, B. I. (1974). *Love, Sex and Marriage Through the Ages.* Springer, New York.

Murstein, B. I. (1976). *Who Will Marry Whom? Theories and Research in Marital Choice.* Springer, New York.

Murstein, B. I., Goyette, M. and Cerreto, M. (1975). A theory of the effect of exchange-orientation on marriage and friendship. Unpublished paper, Connecticut College.

Muscovici, S. (1972). Society and theory in social psychology, *In* Israel, J. and Tajfel, H. (Eds), *Social Psychology in Context,* pp. 17-68. Academic Press, London and New York.

Nadler, A., Fisher, J. D. Streufert, S. (1974). The donor's dilemma: Recipients' reactions to aid from friend or foe. *J. Appl. Soc. Psychol.* **4,** 275-285.

Nemeth, C. (1970). Effects of free versus constrained behavior on attraction between people. *J. Pers. Soc. Psychol.* **15,** 302-311.

Newcomb, T. M. (1953). An approach to the study of communicative acts. *Psych. Rev.* **60,** 393-404.

Newcomb, T. M. (1961). *The Acquaintance Process.* Holt, Rinehart and Winston, New York.

Newcomb, T. M. (1971). Dyadic Balance as a Source of about interpersonal attraction, *In* B. I. Murstein (Ed.), *Theories of Attraction and Love.* Springer, New York.

Nisbet, R. A. (1970). *The Social Bond: An Introduction to the Study of Society.* Knopf, New York.

Novak, D. W. and Lerner, M. J. (1968). Rejection as a consequence of perceived similarity. *J. Pers. Soc. Psychol.* **9,** 147-152.

Osgood, C. E. (1969). On the whys and wherefores of E, P, and A. *J. Pers. Soc. Psychol.* **12,** 194-199.

Palmer, J. and Byrne, D. (1970). Attraction toward dominant and submissive strangers: Similarity versus complementarity. *J. Exp. Res. in Pers.* **4,** 108-115.

Parsons, R. and Shils, E. A. (1962). *Toward a General Theory of Action.* Harvard University Press, Cambridge, Mass.

Passini, F. T. and Norman, W. T. (1966). A universal conception of personality structure? *J. Pers. Soc. Psychol.* **4,** 44-49.

Perrin, F. A. C. (1921). Physical attractiveness and repulsiveness. *J. Exp. Psychol.* **4,** 203-217.

Picher, O. L. (1966). Attraction toward Negroes as a function of prejudice, emotional arousal, and the sex of the Negro. Unpublished doctoral dissertation, University of Texas.

Pierce, R. A. (1970). Need Similarity and Complementarity as Determinants of Friendship Choice. *J. Psychol.* **76,** 231-238.

Plato, *Lysis, Symposium, Gorgias* (translated and edited by W. R. M. Lamb). Heinemann, London, 1925.

Popper, K. (1963). *Conjectures and Refutations: The Growth of Scientific Knowledge.* Routledge and Kegan Paul, London.

Reiss, I. L. (1960). Toward a sociology of the heterosexual love relationship. *Marr. Fam. Living* **22,** 139-145.

Robbins, G. E. (1975). Dogmatism and information gathering in personality impression formation. *J. Res. in Pers.* **9,** 74-84.

Rogers, C. R. (1959). A Theory of Therapy, personality and interpersonal relationships, as developed in the client centered framework, *In* S. Koch (Ed.) *Psychology: A Study of a Science,* pp. 184-256. McGraw-Hill, New York.

Rokeach, M. (1972). Rokeach's value survey. Halgren tests. Sunnyvale, California.

Rose, R. J. (1966). Anxiety and arousal: A study of two-flash fusion and skin conductance. *Psychon. Sci.* **6,** 81-82.

Rosenberg, M. J. (1956). Cognitive structure and attitudinal affect. *J. Abn. Soc. Psychol.* **53,** 367-372.

Rosenberg, M. and Abelson, R. (1960). An analysis of cognitive balancing, *In* C. Hovland and M. Rosenberg (Eds), *Attitude Organization and Change,* pp. 112-163. Yale University Press, New Haven, Connecticut.

Rosenberg, S. (1968). Mathematical models of social behavior, *In* G. Lindzey and E. Aronson (Eds), *The Handbook of Social Psychology,* pp. 179-244. Addison-Wesley, Reading, Mass.

Rosenblatt, P. C. (1971). Communication in the practice of love magic. *Soc. Forces* **49,** 482-487.

Rosenblatt, P. C. (1974). Cross-cultural perspective on attraction, *In* E. L. Huston (Ed.), *Foundations of Interpersonal Attraction.* Academic Press, New York.

Rubin, Z. (1970). Measurement of romantic love. *J. Pers. Soc. Psych.* **16,** 265-273.

Rubin, Z. (1973). *Liking and Loving: An Invitation to Social Psychology.* Holt, New York.

Rubin, Z. (1975). Disclosing oneself to a stranger: Reciprocity and its limits. *J. Exp. Soc. Psychol.* **11,** 233-260.

Rychlak, J. F. (1965). The similarity, compatibility, or incompatibility of needs in interpersonal selection. *J. Pers. Soc. Psychol.* **2,** 334-340.

Schachter, S. (1959). *The Psychology of Affiliation.* Stanford University Press, Stanford.

Schachter, S. (1964). The interaction of cognitive and physiological determinants of emotional state, *In* L. Berkowitz (Ed.), *Advances in Experimental Social Psychology,* pp. 49-80. Academic Press, New York and London.

Schachter, S. and Singer, J. E. (1962). Cognitive, social and physiological determinants of emotional state. *Psych. Rev.* **69,** 379-399.

Scheflen, A. (1965). Quasi-courtship behaviour in psychotherapy. *Psychiatry* **28,** 245-257.

Scherwitz, L. and Helmreich, R. (1973). Interactive effects of eye contact and verbal content on interpersonal attraction in dyads. *J. Pers. Soc. Psychol.* **25**, 6-14.

Schneider, D. J. (1973). Implicit personality theory: A review. *Psych. Bull.* **79**, 294-309.

Schopler, J. and Thompson, V. D. (1968). Role of attribution processes in mediating amount of reciprocity for a favor. *J. Pers. Soc. Psychol.* **10**, 243-250.

Schulman, M. L. (1971). Idealisation in engaged couples. *J. Marr. Fam.*

Schutz, W. C. (1960). *FIRO: A Three-dimensional Theory of Interpersonal Behaviour.* Holt, New York.

Secord, P. F. (1958). The role of facial features in interpersonal perception. *In* R. Tagiuri and L. Petrullo (Eds), *Person Perception and Interpersonal Behaviour.* Stanford University Press, Stanford.

Secord, P. F. and Backman, C. W. (1964a). *Social Psychology.* McGraw-Hill, New York.

Secord, P. F. and Backman, C. W. (1964b). Interpersonal congruency, perceived similarity, and friendship. *Sociometry* **27**, 115-127.

Secord, P. F. and Backman, C. W. (1965). An interpersonal approach to personality, *In* B. Maher (Ed.), *Progress in Experimental Personality Research,* pp. 91-125. Academic Press, New York and London.

Secord, P. F. and Peevers, B. H. (1974). The development and attribution of person concepts, *In* Mischel, T. (Ed.), *On Understanding Persons,* pp. 117-142. Blackwells, Oxford.

Senn, D. J. (1971). Attraction as a function of similarity-dissimilarity in task-performance. *J. Pers. Soc. Psychol.* **18**, 120-123.

Seyfried, B. A. and Hendrick, C. (1973a). Need similarity and complementarity in interpersonal attraction. *Sociometry* **36**, 207-220.

Seyfried, B. A. and Hendrick, C. (1973b). When do opposites attract? When they are opposite in sex and sex-role attitudes. *J. Pers. Soc. Psychol.* **25**, 15-20.

Seymour, W. D. (1966). *Industrial Skills.* Pitman, London.

Shapiro, D. and Leiderman, P. H. (1967). Arousal correlates of task role and group setting. *J. Pers. Soc. Psychol.* **5**, 103-107.

Shapiro, D. and Schwartz, G. E. (1970). Psychophysiological contributions of social psychology, *In* P. H. Mussen and M. R. Rosenzweig (Eds), *Annual Review of Psychology,* Vol. 21, pp. 37-107. Annual Reviews, Palo Alto.

Sheffield, J. and Byrne, D. (1967). Attitude similarity-dissimilarity, authoritarianism, and interpersonal attraction. *J. Soc. Psychol.* **71**, 117-123.

Sherif, M. and Hovland, C. I. (1961). *Social Judgment.* Yale University Press, New Haven.

Siegel, A. E. and Siegel, S. (1957). Reference groups, membership groups and attitude change. *J. Abnorm. Soc. Psychol.* **55**, 360-364.

Sigall, H. & Aronson, E. (1967). Opinion change and the gain-loss model of inter-personal attraction. *J. Exp. Soc. Psychol.* **3**, 178-188.

Silverman, I. (1971). Physical attractiveness and courtship. *Sexual Behaviour,* (Sept.), pp. 22-25.

Simmel, G. (1950). *The Sociology of Georg Simmel* (trans. by K. H. Wolff). The Free Press of Glencoe, New York.

Simmel, M. L. (1956). On phantom limbs. *Arch. Neurol. Psychiat.* **75**, 637-664.

Simon, H. A. (1957). *Administrative Behavior*. (2nd edn.). MacMillan, New York.

Simpson, R. L. (1972). *Theories of Social Exchange*. General Learning Press, Morristown, N. J.

Skipper, J. K. and Nass, G. (1966). Dating behaviour: a framework for analysis and an illustration. *J. Marr. Fam.* **28**, 412-420.

Skolnick, P. (1971). Reactions to personal evaluations: a failure to replicate. *J. Pers. Soc. Psychol.* **18**, 62-67.

Smith, C. E. (1936). The autonomic excitation resulting from the interaction of individual and group opinion. *J. Abnorm. Soc. Psychol.* **31**, 138-1964.

Snoek, J. D. and Dobbs, M. F. (1967). Galvanic skin responses to agreement and disagreement in relation to Dogmatism. *Psych. Rep.* **20**, 195-198.

Stalling, R. S. (1970). Personality similarity and evaluative meaning as conditioners of attraction. *J. Pers. Soc. Psychol.* **14**, 77-82.

Stapert, J. C. and Clore, G. L. (1969). Attraction and disagreement-produced arousal. *J. Pers. Soc. Psychol.* **13**, 64-69.

Staub, E. (1974). Helping a distressed person: Social, personality and situation determinants, *In* Berkowitz (Ed.), *Advances in Experimental Social Psychology*, pp. 294-341. Academic Press, New York and London.

Steiner, I. D. (1970). Strategies for controlling stress in interpersonal situations, *In* J. E. McGrath (Ed.), *Social and Psychological Factors in Stress*. Holt, Rinehart and Winston, New York.

Stephan, W., Berscheid, E. and Walster, E. (1971). Sexual arousal and heterosexual perception. *J. Pers. Soc. Psych.* **20**, 93-101.

Storms, M. D. (1973). Videotape and the attribution process: Reversing actors' and observers' points of view. *J. Pers. Soc. Psychol.* **27**, 165-175.

Stroebe, W., Eagly, A. H. and Stroebe, M. S. (in press). Friendly or just polite? The effect of self-esteem on attributions. *Eur. J. Soc. Psychol.*

Stroebe, W., Insko, C. A., Thompson, V. D. and Layton, B. D. (1971). The effects of physical attractiveness, attitude similarity and sex on various aspects of interpersonal attraction. *J. Pers. Soc. Psychol.* **18**, 79-91.

Stroebe, W., Thompson, V. D., Insko, C. A. and Reisman, S. R. (1970). Balance and differentiation in the evaluation of linked attitude objects. *J. Pers. Soc. Psychol.* **16**, 38-47.

Sullivan, H. S. (1953). *The Interpersonal Theory of Psychiatry*. Norton, New York.

Tagiuri, R. (1958). Social preference and its perception, *In* R. Tagiuri and L. Petrullo (Eds.), *Person Perception and Interpersonal Behaviour*, Stanford University Press, Stanford.

Taylor, D. A. (1968). The development of interpersonal relationships: Social penetration processes. *J. Soc. Psychol.* **75**, 79-90.

Taylor, H. F. (1970). *Balance in Small Groups*. Von Nostrand, Rheinhold, New York.

Taylor, H. F. (1972). Linear models of consistency: some extensions of Blalock's strategy. *A. J. Sociol.* **78**, 1192-1215.

Taylor, M. J. (1956). Some objective criteria of social class membership. Unpublished manuscript, Amherst College.

Tedeschi, J. T. (1974). Attributions, liking and power, *In* E. L. Huston (Ed.), *Foundations of Interpersonal Attraction*, pp. 193-215. Academic Press, New York and London.

Teichman, M. (1971). Satisfaction from interpersonal relationship following resource exchange. Unpublished doctoral dissertation: University of Missouri at Columbia.

Tesser, A. (1969). Trait similarity and trait evaluation as correlates of attraction. *Psychon. Sci.* **15**, 319-320.

Tesser, A. (1971). Evaluative and structural similarity of attitudes as determinants of interpersonal attraction. *J. Pers. Soc. Psychol.* **18**, 92-96.

Tesser, A., Gatewood, R. and Driver, M. (1968). Some determinants of gratitude. *J. Pers. Soc. Psychol.* **9**, 233-236.

Tharp, R. G. (1963). Psychological patterning in marriage. *Psych. Bull.* **60**, 97-117.

Thibaut, J. W. and Kelley, H. H. (1959). *The Social Psychology of Groups*. Wiley, New York.

Thompson, W. R. and Nishimura, R. (1952). Some determinants of friendship. *J. Personal.* **20**, 305-313.

Thornton, G. R. (1944). The effect of wearing glasses upon judgements of personality traits of persons seen briefly. *J. Appl. Psychol.* **28**, 203-207.

Tiger, L. and Fox, R. (1972). *The Imperial Animal*. Secker and Warburg, London.

Todd, J., Mackie, J. R. M. and Dewhurst, K. (1971). Real or imaginary hypophallism: a cause of inferiority feeling and morbid sexual jealousy. *Brit. J. Psychiat.* **119**, 315-318.

Tognoli, J. and Keisner, R. (1972). Gain and loss of esteem as determinants of interpersonal attraction. *J. Pers. Soc. Psychol.* **23**, 201-204.

Triandis, H. (1964). Exploratory factor analysis of the behavioral component of social attitudes. *J. Abnorm. Soc. Psychol.* **68**, 420-430.

Turner, J. H. (1974). *The Structure of Sociological Theory*. Dorsey Press, Homewood, Illinois.

Turner, J. L., Foa, E. B. and Foa, U. G. (1971). Interpersonal reinforcers: classification, interrelationship and some differential properties. *J. Pers. Soc. Psychol.* **19**, 168-180.

Upshaw, H. S. (1969). The personal reference scale: an approach to social judgement, *In* L. Berkowitz (Ed.) *Advances in Experimental Social Psychology*, Vol. 4, pp. 315-371. Academic Press, New York and London.

Van Dyne, E. V. (1940). Personality traits and friendship formation in adolescent girls. *J. Soc. Psychol.* **12**, 291-303.

Vital Statistics of the United States (1972). Vol. 3, *Marriage and Divorce*. DHEW Publication No. (HSM 73-1103), Rockville, Maryland.

Wagner, R. V. (1975). Complementary needs, role expectations, interpersonal attraction and the stability of working relationships. *J. Pers. Soc. Psychol.* **32**, 116-124.

Waller, W. (1938). *The Family: A Dynamic Interpretation*. Cordon, New York.

Walster, E. (1965). The effect of self esteem on romantic liking. *J. Exp. Soc. Psychol.* **1**, 184-197.

Walster, E., Aronson, V., Abrahams, D. and Rottmann, L. (1966). Importance of physical attractiveness in dating behavior. *J. Pers. Soc. Psychol.* **4**, 508-516.

Walster, E. and Berscheid, E. (1971). Adrenaline makes the heart grow fonder. *Psychology today*, **5**, 47-62.

Walster, E., Berscheid, E. and Walster, G. W. (1973). New directions in equity research. *J. Pers. Soc. Psychol.* **25**, 151-176.

Walster, E., Walster, G. W., Piliavin, J. and Schmidt, L. (1973). Playing hard to get: understanding an elusive phenomenon. *J. Pers. Soc. Psychol.* **26**, 113-121.

Warr, P. B. (1965). Proximity as a determinant of positive and negative sociometric choice. *Brit. J. Soc. Clin. Psychol.* **4**, 104-109.

Warr, P. B. and Knapper, C. (1968). *Perception of People and Events.* Wiley, London.

Weiner, B. (1972). *Theories of Motivation from Mechanism to Cognition.* Markham Pub. Co., Chicago.

Weiner, D. J. (1969). Effectance arousal and interpersonal attraction relating to a perceptual task: effects of certainty, consensual validation and availability of verification. Unpub. doc. diss., University of Texas.

Wengreniuk, K. (1971). Friendship expectations in small groups. Unpub. MS., Univ. of Windsor.

Werner, C. and Latané, B. (1974). Interaction motivates attraction. *J. Pers. Soc. Psychol.* **29**, 328-334.

Werts, C. E. and Linn, R. L. (1970). A general linear model for studying growth. *Psych. Bull.* **73**, 17-22.

Wheeler, L. (1974). Social comparison and selective affiliation, *In* E. L. Huston (Ed.) *Foundations of Interpersonal Attraction.* Academic Press, New York and London.

Wiggins, J. S. (1973). *Personality and Prediction: Principles of Personality Assessment.* Addison Wesley, Reading, Mass.

Wildeblood, P. (1956). *A Way of Life.* Weidenfeld, London.

Wildeblood, J. (1965). *The Polite World.* Oxford University Press, London.

Winch, R. F. (1955a). The theory of complementary needs in mate selection: a test of one kind of complementariness. *Amer. Sociol. Rev.* **20**, 52-56.

Winch, R. F. (1955b). The theory of complementary needs in mate selection: final results on the test of the general hypothesis. *Amer. Sociol. Rev.* **20**, 552-555.

Winch, R. F. (1958). *Mate Selection: A Study in Complementary Needs.* Harper and Row, New York.

Winch, R. F. (1963). *The Modern Family.* Holt, Rinehart and Winston, New York.

Winch, R. F. (1967). Another look at the theory of complementary needs in mate selection. *J. Marr. Fam.* **29**, 756-762.

Winch, R. F., Ktsanes, T. and Ktsanes, V. (1954). The theory of complementary needs in mate selection: an analytic and descriptive study. *Amer. Sociol. Rev.* **19**, 241-249.

Winch, R. F., Ktsanes, T. and Ktsanes, V. (1955). Empirical elaboration of the theory of complementary needs in mate selection. *J. Abn. Soc. Psychol.* **51**, 509-513.

Worthy, M., Gary, A. L. and Kahn, G. M. (1969). Self-disclosure as an exchange process. *J. Pers. Soc. Psychol.* **13**, 59-63.

Wright, P. H. (1965). Personality and interpersonal attraction: Basic assumptions. *J. Indiv. Psychol.* **27**, 127-136.

Wright, P. H. (1968). Need similarity, need complementarity and the place of personality in interpersonal attraction. *J. Exp. Res. in Pers.* **3**, 126-135.

Wright, P. H. (1969). A model and technique for studies of friendship. *J. Exp. Soc. Psychol.* **5**, 295-309.

Wright, P. H. (1974). The delineation and measurement of some variables in the study of friendship. *Rep. Res. in Soc. Psychol.* **5**, 93-96.

Wyer, R. S., Jr. (1974). *Cognitive Organization and Change: An Information Processing Approach.* Erlbaum, Potomac, Maryland.

Wyer, R. S., Jr. (1975). Some informational determinants of one's own liking for a person and beliefs that the others will like this person. *J. Pers. Soc. Psychol.* **31**, 1041-1053.

Zetterberg, H. L. (1966). The secret ranking. *J. Marr. Fam.* **28**, 134-142.

Author Index

(Only first authors of published work are classified in this index)

Subject Index

438

HM
132
T47

Theory and Practice in
Interpersonal Attraction